PRAISE FOR
ROME: A HISTORY IN SEVEN SACKINGS

"This magnificent love letter to Rome comes in the form of a vivid chronicle of the great city's repeated catastrophes and recoveries. Sharp-eyed, richly informed, tirelessly curious, and often wryly amusing, Kneale is the perfect Virgil to accompany any pilgrim who wishes to trace the vast spiral that leads from the ancient past to the bittersweet present."

—Stephen Greenblatt, author of *The Swerve:*
How the World Became Modern

"Evokes [Rome] with casual brilliance. . . . The most exciting passages relate the sacks themselves, from motley barbarian armies appearing below the walls (several times in fact) to the horror of Allied bombing raids. . . . This is not a tale of decline and fall so much as a slow roller-coaster ride through the fortunes of a place deeply entangled in its past."

—Greg Woolf, *The Wall Street Journal*

"The brilliance of [Kneale's] own raid on Rome lies in the principle of selectivity he has brought to it—what is done to Rome matters as much as what Rome does to the world—and the depth of his research. . . . Kneale [is] one step ahead of most other Roman chroniclers."

—Aaron Retica, *The New York Times Book Review*

"*Rome: A History in Seven Sackings* is that rarest of treats: an erudite history that reads like a page-turner. With a novelist's eye for the revealing detail, and the genial grace of your favorite tour guide, Matthew Kneale plunges us into the fascinating palimpsest they call the Eternal City. Magnificently entertaining all around!"

—Maria Semple, author of *Today Will Be Different* and
Where'd You Go, Bernadette

"What's not to love about a historical book that reads like a novel? Long-time resident (and novelist) Matthew Kneale tells the story of Rome through the lens of seven key battles. . . . You'll come away with a new understanding of one of the world's most well-preserved cities, its famed ruins, and the tenacity and pride of its people."

—*Afar*

"Like most very old and very storied cities, Rome has as many scars as trophies. This hard reality is the guiding genius of Matthew Kneale's absorbing new book. . . . [Rome's] long, uneven, colorful history feels new when it's examined this way, through its defeats instead of its victories."

—Steve Donoghue, *The Christian Science Monitor*

"Panoramic and deeply researched. . . . Kneale's love for the city in all its incarnations, past and present, is clear."

—*Publishers Weekly*

"With an eye for detail and an ear for language, Kneale guides a journey through seven bloody events spanning more than two millennia in the history of the place he knows well, the world's most fascinating city, Rome. It's an unforgettable trip."

—Barry Strauss, Cornell University, author of *Ten Caesars: Roman Emperors from Augustus to Constantine*

"A sprawling city with an ancient history, Rome defies a neat narrative of its past. Novelist and historian Kneale takes a fresh historical approach by focusing on groups of invaders that indelibly shaped the contemporary city. . . . A lively perspective on Rome's rich history."

—*Kirkus Reviews*

"Matthew Kneale shapes the span of Roman history into one compelling narrative, focusing on seven historical moments that defined the metropolis that stands today. Whether you're unfamiliar with one of the world's greatest cities or want to see it in an entirely new light, you'll want to take this journey with Kneale as your intrepid guide."

—JP Morgan Summer Reading List

"Kneale's account is a masterpiece of pacing and suspense. Characters from the city's history spring to life in his hands."

—Peter Thonemann, *The Sunday Times* (London)

"A richly textured chronicle, teasing meaning out of intense turbulence."

—*Booklist* (starred review)

MATTHEW KNEALE

ROME

A HISTORY IN SEVEN SACKINGS

SIMON & SCHUSTER PAPERBACKS

NEW YORK   LONDON   TORONTO   SYDNEY   NEW DELHI

For Alexander and Tatiana –
our two young Romans

Simon & Schuster Paperbacks
An Imprint of Simon & Schuster, Inc.
1230 Avenue of the Americas
New York, NY 10020

First Simon & Schuster trade paperback edition May 2019

SIMON & SCHUSTER PAPERBACKS and colophon
are registered trademarks of Simon & Schuster, Inc.

For information about special discounts for bulk purchases,
please contact Simon & Schuster Special Sales
at 1-866-506-1949 or business@simonandschuster.com.

The Simon & Schuster Speakers Bureau can bring authors
to your live event. For more information or to book an event, contact
the Simon & Schuster Speakers Bureau at 1-866-248-3049
or visit our website at www.simonspeakers.com.

Manufactured in the United States of America

1   3   5   7   9   10   8   6   4   2

The Library of Congress has cataloged the hardcover edition as follows:

Names: Kneale, Matthew, author.
Title: Rome : a history in seven sackings / by Matthew Kneale.
Description: New York : Simon & Schuster, 2018. |
Includes bibliographical references and index.
Identifiers: LCCN 2017045287 | ISBN 9781501191091 | ISBN 1501191098
Subjects: LCSH: Rome—History. | Rome—History, Military. |
Rome (Italy)—History. | Rome (Italy)—History, Military.
Classification: LCC DG209 .K57 2018 | DDC 945.6/32—dc23
LC record available at https://lccn.loc.gov/2017045287

ISBN 978-1-5011-9109-1
ISBN 978-1-5011-9111-4 (pbk)
ISBN 978-1-5011-9110-7 (ebook)

CONTENTS

ILLUSTRATIONS
AND MAPS

Black and white illustrations

Colour section

Aurelian Walls (*Photo by author*)

Fabricius Bridge (*Photo by author*)

Ivory diptych of Stilicho, *c.* AD 395 (*Archiv Gerstenberg/Ullstein Bild/ Getty Images*)

Depiction of classical Rome (*Photo by author*)

Colosseum (*Photo by author*)

Interior of the Pantheon (*Photo by author*)

Trajan's market (*Photo by author*)

Porta Salaria (*Photo by author*)

Mosaic depicting Emperor Justinian and his retinue, Basilica of San Vitale, Ravenna (*Christine Webb/Alamy Stock Photo*)

Santo Stefano Rotondo (*Photo by author*)

Asinaria Gate (*Photo by author*)

Robert Guiscard invested by Pope Nicholas II, detail from a miniature (*Granger Historical Picture Archive/Alamy Stock Photo*)

Leonine Wall (*Photo by author*)

Porta Latina (*Photo by author*)

San Giovanni a Porta Latina (*Photo by author*)

Santa Maria in Trastevere (*Photo by author*)

View of Rome from 'De Civitate Dei' by St Augustine of Hippo (354– 430), 1459 (*Bibliotheque Sainte-Genevieve, Paris, France/Bridgeman Images*)

View of Rome from the Nuremberg Chronicle by Hartmann Schedel, 1493 (*Private Collection/The Stapleton Collection/Bridgeman Images*)

Pope Julius II ordering work on the Vatican and St Peter's Basilica. Painting by Emile Jean Horace Vernet (1789–1863), Louvre Museum, Paris (*Leemage/Corbis/Getty Images*)

Pasquino statue (*Photo by author*)

Castle of San Angelo, painting by J.M.W. Turner (1775–1851) (*Victoria & Albert Museum, London, UK/Bridgeman Images*)

The sack of Rome, 1527, painting attributed to Pieter Brueghel the Elder, sixteenth century (*Granger Historical Picture Archive/ Alamy Stock Photography*)

Porta Santo Spirito (*Photo by author*)

Medieval tower (*Photo by author*)

View of the Piazza Navona, painting by Canaletto (1697–1768) (*Hospital Tavera, Toledo, Spain/Bridgeman Images*)

Festivals of *moccoletti* (tapers) (Carnival in Rome), painting by Ippolito Caffi (1809–1866), 1852 (*Galleria Nazionale d'Arte Moderna, Rome, Italy/De Agostini Picture Library/A. Dagli Orti/Bridgeman Images*)

St Peter's Dome at dusk (*Photo by author*)

Fountain of the Four Rivers, Piazza Navona (*Photo by author*)

Bernini's arcade columns at St Peter's (*Photo by author*)

Street corner religious image (*Photo by author*)

Garibaldi statue (*Photo by author*)

View from St Peter's dome (*Photo by author*)

The Square Colosseum (*Photo by author*)

Obelisk at the Foro Mussolini (*Photo by author*)

Fascist mural depicting Mussolini (*Photo by author*)

American officers lined up for a lowering of the flag ceremony in the Piazza Venezia, 4 July 1944 (*Carl Mydans/The LIFE Picture Collection/Getty Images*)

Italian civilians shortly after the liberation of Rome (*Hulton-Deutsch Collection/Corbis/Getty Images*)

MAPS

NOTE ON NAMES

For the sake of clarity and continuity I have referred to Rome's hills and churches by their modern, Italian names, even when looking at early centuries when Latin would have been used. I have made one exception: St Peter's is so well known by its English title that it seemed wrong to refer to it as San Pietro.

INTRODUCTION

THERE IS NO CITY LIKE ROME. No other great metropolis has preserved its past so well. In Rome you can cross bridges that were crossed by Cicero and Julius Caesar, you can stand in a temple nineteen centuries old or walk into a church where a hundred popes have celebrated mass. As well as the city's famous sights – the fountains, the Pantheon, the Colosseum, St Peter's, the Sistine Chapel – you can also see Mussolini's Fascist propaganda, much of it still intact. The Romans have even kept the city's Gestapo headquarters from the Nazi occupation. That so much has survived is all the more remarkable considering what Rome has endured over the centuries: dozens of catastrophic floods, fires, earthquakes, plagues and, most of all, attacks by enemy armies.

When I first came to Rome at the age of eight I had never seen a city that had so much of its past on show. My fascination grew and as I became older I returned many times. For the last fifteen years I have lived in Rome, studying it and getting to know every stone of the city. I realized I wanted to write about Rome's past and show how it has become the city it is today: to tell the city's whole story from three thousand years ago to present times.

There was a problem. Rome's past is a vast subject. The city has changed so greatly that there have been many Romes, each of which would be largely unrecognizable to Romans of other times. Books that try to recount the city's entire history tend to suffer from being too long, and yet also too hurried, as they struggle to race through events. Much of my writing has been fiction, and novels, among many other things, require a strong, clear structure. I began wondering what structure could be used to frame Rome's history while avoiding an endless stream of *and thens*. An idea came to me: focusing on a handful of moments throughout the city's existence – moments that changed the city and set it on a new direction. Sackings were the obvious choice. As Romans ruefully observe, Rome has had no shortage of them.

Seven seemed a good number. Seven hills, seven sackings. I found the ones that were most important to Rome's history, and which also fell at moments when the city had a character wholly distinct from other eras. I began to envisage how each chapter could be told, like a story. First, we would see the enemy advancing on the city and we would learn who they were and what had brought them. Next, we would pause and look at what the city had been like before the crisis had begun, when it still enjoyed a sense of normality. We would be presented with a kind of vast postcard from Rome describing what it looked like, felt like and smelt like; what Romans – rich and poor – owned; what united and divided them; what their homes were like; what they ate; what they believed; how clean they were; how cosmopolitan; how they amused themselves; what they thought about sex; how their men and women treated one another; and how long they could expect to live. Along the way we would see how Rome had changed since the last postcard and so – like joining the dots in a puzzle – we would glimpse the city's whole history. Finally, we would return to the drama of the sacking, discovering how the enemy broke into the city, what they did there and how Rome was changed by what took place.

I have been researching this book for fifteen years. It has been a pleasure to write as it has allowed me better to understand a city which, for all its flaws, I greatly love, and which I find no less fascinating now than I did when I first came here as a child. In these strange days when our world can seem fragile I have also found something rather reassuring in Rome's past. Romans repeatedly shrugged off catastrophes and made their city anew, adding a new generation of great monuments. Both peace and war have played their part in making Rome the extraordinary place it is today.

Rome, 2017

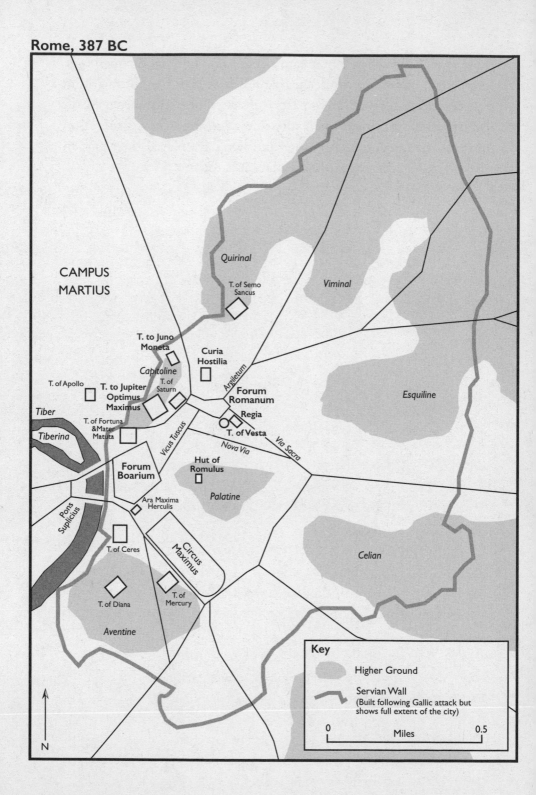

Rome, 387 BC

CAMPUS MARTIUS

Quirinal

Viminal

T. of Semo Sancus

T. to Juno Moneta

Curia Hostilia

Capitoline

T. of Apollo

T. of Saturn

T. to Jupiter Optimus Maximus

Argiletum

Forum Romanum

Regia

T. of Fortuna &Mater Matuta

T. of Vesta

Tiber

Tiberina

Vicus Tuscus

Nova Via

Via Sacra

Esquiline

Forum Boarium

Hut of Romulus

Palatine

Pons Suplicius

Ara Maxima Herculis

T. of Ceres

Circus Maximus

Celian

T. of Diana

T. of Mercury

Aventine

N

Key

Higher Ground

Servian Wall
(Built following Gallic attack but
shows full extent of the city)

0   Miles   0.5

CHAPTER ONE

GAULS

I

FOURTEEN KILOMETRES NORTH of Rome where the river Tiber winds and turns through a small plain, it is joined by a tiny tributary – no more than a brook – called the Allia. These days it is a hard spot to notice. Beyond the Tiber trucks roar down the A1 motorway and high-speed trains hurry north to Florence and Milan. A dose of imagination – and probably a set of earplugs, too – is required to see this for what it once was: a battlefield. Here, in the year 387 BC on the 18th of July, a day the Romans would long consider unlucky, the full army of the Roman Republic, of between six and a half and nine thousand men, drew up to fight. Before them advanced an army of Gauls.

The Romans would have looked more impressive. Their soldiers were in formation and equipped with metal helmets, armour, long spears and large round shields. They used tactics invented by the Greeks, in which shields and spears formed a formidable barrier. As the enemy struggled to break through, the Romans would strike low with their spears, jabbing at legs, stomachs and groins, and then stab from up high, at necks and faces. Warfare two and a half thousand years ago was brutally up close.

By comparison, the Gauls were an undisciplined horde. Few, if any, women and children would have held back to watch the battle. This was not a tribe on the move but a war band looking for trouble, glory and treasure. Like any wandering army of this time its warriors would have stunk and been infested with lice. Though little can be said with absolute certainty about this early period, we can surmise a good deal about them. Some would have been on foot, some on horseback and others would have ridden two-man chariots that could whisk them to a key part of the battlefield. They would have been armed with small rectangular shields, swords and spears, and worn finely crafted helmets. They would have had long hair, moustaches and worn torques around their necks. Yet more noticeable was what they were *not* wearing. While some would have been clothed, others probably wore nothing but a belt or cloak. Later sources confirm that Gauls sometimes fought naked as they believed that this would make them more terrifying to the enemy.

Finally, they would have been confident. At this moment Celtic-speaking Gauls dominated Europe. To get an idea of the extent of their territories one has only to look to regions named Galicia, meaning *land of the Gauls*. One Galicia can be found in north-western Spain, a second in the Ukraine and a third in Turkey. And, of course, there is Wales, whose French name is the same again: *Pays des Galles*. During the two centuries before the battle on the Allia, Gallic peoples had seized northern Italy's Po valley from the Etruscans. Around 391 BC one of these peoples, the Senones, who had settled along Italy's Adriatic coast close to the modern seaside resort of Rimini – less than 200 kilometres from Rome – crossed the Apennines and raided the Etruscan city of Clusium. Four years later they were back. It was Rome's turn.

The Gauls' successes owed much to two skills in which they excelled. As the smiths of Europe, they were famous for their ironworking, and produced beautiful ornaments with complex geometrical patterns, often intertwined with animals. They were also renowned for their wheeled vehicles and the few Celtic words that managed to infiltrate Latin were mostly terms for these, from handcarts to carriages. War chariots and finely crafted weapons had carried the Celts across Europe.

When it comes to everyday life among the Senones, we rely on written sources that date from several centuries after the battle on the Allia, yet these offer some intriguing clues. Later Celtic peoples were far less male-dominated than the Romans. Female rulers were relatively common and there were even female druids. The Celts also had a certain amount in common with their distant cousins in India. They had a caste system which, like that of early Hinduism, included separate classes of priests, warriors, artisans and poor farmers. Celtic druids, who were not magician healers but priest judges and royal advisors, enjoyed the same high status as Indian Brahmins. Celts also believed in reincarnation. Julius Caesar – who became something of an expert during his years conquering them – tells us so, while early Irish legends have stories of butterflies and mayflies that are reborn as humans.

It is doubtful that any of this would have impressed the Romans. Once again our knowledge of what the Romans thought of Gauls comes from later centuries, but there is no particular reason to believe that their prejudices did not already exist in 387 BC. Later Romans saw the Celts as eloquent speakers but as primitive, woefully lacking in self-control, obsessed with war, feckless, drunken and greedy for gold. Scathing though these views were, some had an element of truth. The Gauls enjoyed a drink and their graves in northern Italy were filled with sophisticated wine-serving vessels. They had a strong liking for both fighting and gold and when possible they combined the two. They were probably doing precisely this when they marched on Rome. Just a few months after the battle on the Allia, a group of Gauls appeared in Sicily, where they fought as mercenaries for the Greek ruler of Syracuse, Dionysius, and it seems highly likely that this was the same war band who charged at the Romans on 18 July. Rome was not the Gauls' intended destination, it seems, but it offered a chance to break a long journey with a little profitable violence.

Although later Romans may have felt superior to the Gauls they had rather more in common with them than they knew. The early Gallic and Latin languages were extremely similar, so much so that it is thought that they had a common origin around sixty generations earlier. In other words, only 1,500 years before they met by the Allia the Celts and Romans had been a single people.

But now they were strangers and enemies, embroiled in a furious battle. One would have expected the Romans to do well. Their army was at its best on flat, open ground where they could keep formation: exactly the kind of place where they now found themselves. Their tactics were far more sophisticated than those of the Gauls, who relied on the shock of a sudden charge. Yet everything went wrong for the Romans that day. The fullest account comes from the Roman historian Livy. Livy was not a dispassionate narrator. He wrote three and a half centuries after the battle, by which time Rome ruled the whole Mediterranean world, yet he felt that much had been lost during the city's extraordinary rise. He looked back with nostalgia to an era when, as he believed, Romans had been tougher, plainer, more frugal, moral and selfless. He sought to inspire contemporary Romans with stirring tales of their ancestors' courage.

Unfortunately, the battle of the Allia offered little in the way of inspiration. Livy did the best of a bad job and tried to find some excuses. He wrote that the Romans were greatly outnumbered, though, as we have seen, the Roman army was far from small. He may have been closer to the mark when he suggested the Romans were shocked by the strangeness of the Gauls. The two appear never to have met in battle before. The Romans may have been shaken by the speed and mobility of the Gauls hurtling towards them on horses and in chariots with their long, razor-sharp swords. And there was their nakedness. One could hardly blame the Romans for feeling intimidated by the sight of a horde of huge, mustachioed, barely clothed warriors, yelling and gesticulating and filling the air with the strange sound of their war horns.

The Romans may also have been let down by their strategy. Fighting a battle in front of a deep river was unwise. Livy wrote that their commander was worried that his army would be outflanked and so decided to split his forces in two, placing a force of reserves to their right where the ground was a little higher. The Gallic leader, Brennus – probably not his actual name, as it is very similar to the Gallic word for king – sent his full force tearing into the Roman reserves. The soldiers of the main Roman army watched as their comrades were cut down. As Livy relates, they did not wait to see if they would fare any better:

> The main body of the army, at the first sound of the Gallic war-cry on their flank and in their rear, hardly waited even to see their strange enemy from the ends of the earth; they made no attempt at resistance; they had not courage even to answer his shouted challenge, but fled before they had lost a single man. None fell fighting; they were cut down from behind as they struggled to force a way to safety through the heaving mass of their fellow fugitives. Near the bank of the river there was a dreadful slaughter; the whole left wing of the army had gone that way and had flung away their arms in the desperate hope of getting over. Many could not swim and many others in their exhausted state were dragged under water by the weight of their equipment and drowned.[1]

Later that same day the Gauls reached Rome. The city was at their mercy. The stage was set for some of the most famous stories of antiquity, which would be told and retold over the centuries, shaping the Romans' views of themselves, and others' views of the Romans.

II

Before coming to these stories, and trying to piece together what really happened that summer, we should pause for a moment and see what kind of Rome the Gauls had reached. To modern eyes it hardly seems like a city that would grow into a great power. In the 380s BC it was still a small town with a population of probably no more than 25,000, and it may have been a good deal smaller. It was also primitive. At this time the Athenians had already built the Parthenon, a huge stone building with dazzlingly sophisticated friezes. By contrast, Rome, like other central Italian cities, was a city of bricks, timber and simple terracotta statues. Some parts were very simple indeed: archaeological excavations have revealed that only a century before the battle of the Allia, Rome had numerous daub and wattle, African-style huts with thatched roofs. Nearby cities had huts of this type around 387 BC and it is highly likely that Rome still had them, too. We know that at least one stood at this time: on the Palatine a hut was carefully maintained by priests as 'The hut of Romulus'.

It was in huts of this kind that the very first Romans had lived. We can set aside the legends of Romulus and Remus, the royal princes turned shepherd bandits who were suckled by a she-wolf. Stories of newborn heirs to kingdoms cast adrift were fairly common in the archaic world, as were founder stories involving ferocious animals. Equally spurious is the later tradition that Rome was founded on 21 April 753 BC. Rome's origins were both earlier and more gradual. People were already living on the site by 1500 BC, probably as itinerant pastoralists who stayed only for some seasons of the year. By 1000 BC they were more settled, and buried their dead in the marshy valley between the hills. They lived in two villages of huts on the Palatine and Esquiline hills. Far from being romantic shepherd bandits the first Romans were farmers who grew crops and kept pigs.

Whether they knew it or not, they could hardly have picked a better spot. Their villages looked down on one of Italy's key trade routes, which led up the Tiber valley, and along which salt was carried from the coast to people in the hills. They also overlooked a place where the Tiber was both navigable and relatively easy to cross, by the Tiber Island. The high ground on which the villages were built – which later became known as the seven hills, though in reality some were more like ridges – offered protection from marauding enemies. And it was less prone than the lowlands to malaria, which, though it probably was not present in 387 BC, soon would be.

If the stories of Romulus and Remus are myths, one detail holds some truth. Rome's first king Romulus is said to have shared power for several years with Titus Tatius, the king of the Sabines. Romulus and his Latins lived on the Palatine Hill and Titus Tatius' Sabines lived on the Esquiline: two peoples, diverse yet united. Intriguingly, archaeological discoveries and early traditions support the idea that Rome was originally inhabited by two separate peoples. The hut village on Palatine Hill was populated by Latin speakers from the area south-east of Rome around the Alban Hills, while the Esquiline Hill was peopled by Sabines from hills to the north. In other words, from its very beginnings Rome was a cosmopolitan place formed of two nations.

Or rather, three. Early Rome was a frontier city. Just across the river Tiber on the Gianicolo Hill – where, on a hot summer night, today's Romans go for an ice cream and to enjoy the view – lived Etruscans. The Etruscans could hardly have been more different from the Romans. Their language, which is still little understood, was not Indo-European and so was as distant from Latin or Sabine as modern English is from Mandarin Chinese. It is thought that the Etruscans may, like the Basques, have been an ancient aboriginal people who inhabited Europe long before Indo-Europeans arrived. They would have a huge influence on early Rome, contributing kings, noble families and numerous cultural traditions, from the bundles of rods (*fasces*) that symbolized a state officer's power, to purple-bordered togas for high officials, to gladiator fights.

If life were not already complex enough, two other peoples can also be added to the mix. Soon after the first villages grew up on

the Palatine and Esquiline hills, Phoenicians from today's Lebanon
appeared on the Italian coast and they almost certainly traded with
the Romans. Next came Greeks, who from 800 BC established cities
in southern Italy and Sicily, and sold high-quality banqueting items
across the peninsula. Pottery finds reveal that a small Greek colony
may have existed below the Palatine Hill as early as the eighth century
BC, when the Romans were still living in huts. Some of Rome's earliest
temples were to Greek gods.

It was almost certainly the Greeks who inspired the Romans to
move on from village life and build a city. This did not happen through
gradual evolution but seems to have been the result of an epic, planned
effort. In the mid-seventh century BC the swampy valley between
Rome's first villages was cleared of huts, drained, filled with earth by
the ton and paved over. The Roman Forum was born. At the time of
the battle on the Allia, some 250 years later, many of the city's first
monuments – though some had burned down and been rebuilt – still
existed. These included the Senate, a hall where Rome's parliament
of aristocrats met, the temple of Vesta – the goddess of the hearth
and the family, whose staff of virgins were responsible for tending a
perpetual fire to help keep Rome safe – and a complex of buildings
that appears to have been a royal palace.

Yet the complex had no royal occupant at the time of the battle
by the Allia. In the 380s BC Rome had been a republic for over a
century. The fact that they had freed themselves from royal rule was
a source of great pride to early Romans, much as it is to modern
Americans. Livy, who wrote this first part of his great history in
the early 20s BC, when Romans were slipping back into autocratic
rule – now under emperors – did his best to glorify the moment
when the city's kings were thrown out. He depicted Rome's last
king, Tarquin, as a kind of Macbeth figure, brave but murderous and
with an evil, scheming queen. When King Tarquin's son raped the
beautiful wife of a nobleman, Tarquin's nephew, Brutus, led angry
Romans in rebellion in 509 BC. Desperate to regain power, Tarquin
treacherously allied with an enemy of Rome, the Etruscan warlord

Lars Porsena, and fought against his own people, only to meet a well-deserved defeat.

The truth, as far as it can be reassembled, seems to have been rather less romantic. Rome's kings were probably thrown out not by American-style popular patriotism but by the city's rich, quite possibly in alliance with the same Lars Porsena with whom King Tarquin was supposed to have sided. Aristocratic takeovers were common in Italian and Greek city states in the late sixth century BC. The ranks of their heavy infantry armies were filled by the rich, as only they could afford the expensive equipment required. Knowing they were the power behind the state, aristocrats sought to flex their political muscles.

But that was probably not the only reason for the fall of Rome's kings. Another could be seen from any part of Rome in 387 BC. Perched on the Capitoline Hill, it dominated the city's skyline, as the Parthenon did Athens. The temple to Rome's most celebrated god, Jupiter Best and Greatest, was built not from stone but from timber and brick, and was crude compared to Greek temples of the time – whose overall design it copied – but it made up for this in size. When first constructed it was one of the largest temples, if not the largest, in the central Mediterranean. It was built by King Tarquin, and, according to Livy, the Romans resented being forced to work on the building. No doubt they also resented paying for it. Livy describes how the temple was almost complete when Tarquin fell from power in 509 BC. He would not be the last ruler to fall victim to extravagant architectural ambitions.

Tarquin would have built the temple to give him and his city prestige, yet, like Rome's other temples, it also had a practical role: it was expected to give the Romans insider knowledge of the future and help them avoid nasty surprises. Like other early societies, Romans did not believe in paradise. Their religion was concerned firmly with the here and now. They hoped their gods would give them information to help them make good decisions, whether in their personal lives, their politics, their farming or their military campaigns. Roman priests looked for signs from the gods, which might be found by looking into the sky and watching in which direction birds flew, or by sacrificing animals on temple altars and then carefully studying their intestines.

Like those of other early religions, Roman beliefs had a distinctly anxious side. Bad omens were constantly watched for and could be found in anything from the birth of a deformed lamb to a fox straying into the city. Rituals to placate the gods and ward off threatened disaster were complex and if a single mistake was made then all had to be redone. Romans also feared one another. They feared their neighbours might chant an evil charm that would harm them, or make someone close to them fall in love, or that would steal the fertility of their land. The classical era is often seen as a time of rationalism, at least compared to the medieval period that followed, and so it was for some of the educated elite, but for many sorcery was – and would continue to be – a cause of profound unease.

Early Rome's priests were responsible for trying to ease people's fears. The city's first kings may have evolved from priest kings and in the early 380s BC their successors came from the Roman nobility, some of whom would have lived in the city's most desirable area, on the Palatine Hill. One home of this era has been excavated and it was palatial: a spacious villa with a garden, a reception room and a vast hall with an opening in the roof so rainwater landed in a pool, from which it was stored in a cistern below. The design became a classic in Italy and wealthy Pompeiians were still living in homes like it six centuries later, when Vesuvius erupted. In 387 BC, Rome was already a city of the very rich and the very poor: a pattern which was distinctly Italian. Excavations of another fourth-century city, Olynthos in Greece, have revealed an arrangement that is, to modern eyes, rather suburban: long rows of houses identical in shape and size. The free inhabitants of Olynthos – and many were not free – lived in relative equality. Not so the Romans. Little is known of the homes of Rome's poor but they would have been modest. As we have seen, some were almost certainly daub and wattle huts.

Strange though it may seem, the wide gap between rich and poor was probably widened by Rome's revolutionary ejection of its kings.

The city's kings were not members of the wealthy patrician class and so would have felt a certain kinship with the poor, who were their natural allies against powerful nobles. After the kings, Rome entered economic hard times and many of those who were outside the noble elite – the plebeians – struggled badly. Crippled by debts and barred from many political offices, they fought back as best they could, using a tactic that seems distinctly modern: strike action. They abandoned Rome en masse and camped out on a hill outside the city. They also formed themselves into a kind of state within the state, with their own organization and even their own temples where they kept their records.

Among the concessions that the plebeians managed to squeeze from reluctant patricians, one in particular offers a fascinating glimpse of Roman life in these early times. This was Rome's first written law code: the Twelve Tables. Compiled around 450 BC, or sixty years before the battle on the Allia, it was written in an archaic Latin that was hard even for classical Romans to understand, but it is comprehensible enough to reveal what seems, to our eyes, a rather brutal society.

Roman life was intensely male-controlled and the eldest male in every family – the paterfamilias – ruled over his relatives like a king ruling over slaves. He owned all the family's property and made all key decisions. He could lawfully sell members of his family or kill them, if he chose. On the birth of a new child he decided whether it would live or die and if the child was deformed he was expected to select death. For all the efforts of the plebeians, the Rome of the Twelve Tables was still very much a rich man's world. Any debtors who could not pay their debts became bonded labourers of their creditor, who could take them abroad – just across the Tiber – and sell them into slavery. Rome would have had its own slave market where foreigners could be bought and sold, though it was still a long way from the fully-fledged slave society it would become in later centuries. The great majority of the city's inhabitants were still free.

Yet most Romans were not from the city at all. In the 380s BC most were farmers who lived in the nearby countryside. Rome was a

country town and its main market, the Forum Boarium, beside the
river just below the Palatine Hill, sold every kind of animal – from
horses to ride, to oxen to pull one's plough and sheep to sacrifice. Most
Romans would have purchased animals as investments not food, as
their daily diet was plain and largely vegetarian. They ate cereal raw
or cooked into polenta gruel or unleavened bread, along with herbs,
hazelnuts, chestnuts, figs, olives and grapes. If the rich enjoyed meat
at banquets, for most Romans it was a rare treat that was eaten only
after a sacrifice, and even then it would have been tough, as it was the
meat of working animals.

Another rare treat could be found just round the corner from the
Forum Boarium, in the valley between the Palatine and the Aventine
hills. Here, on simple wooden stands, Romans watched chariot races
in the Circus Maximus, perhaps making a bet or two. In the early
380s BC races were rare events, held to celebrate a military victory,
but within a few decades they would be held regularly, for several
days each September. The games were closely tied to religion. The
Circus Maximus was lined with temples and shrines, while in later
centuries – and probably already in 387 BC – races were preceded by a
procession of floats carrying images of gods, which set out from the
great temples on the Capitoline Hill and wended its way down Via
Sacra to the chariot course.

Among the gods closest to Roman hearts was Victory, which takes
us to an aspect of early Rome that would eclipse all others in later
memory. It was a city that was extremely interested in war, and as
early as the 380s BC it had an impressive record in this area. In some
ways Rome's successes were not so very surprising. Though it would
have seemed a small, primitive town to modern eyes, it was already
the largest city in central Italy and had long dominated other Latin-
speaking city states to the south. In 396 BC, only nine years before the
disaster at the Allia, Rome had achieved what was easily its greatest
military triumph to date, when it defeated the Etruscan city of Veii.

It is worth pausing for a moment to take a look at the Veiian war,
as it says much about what kind of people the Romans were. The

Veiians, like other Etruscan peoples, were skilled in the arts – never the Romans' strong point – and were responsible for some of Rome's finest landmarks. The terracotta god in Rome's great temple to Jupiter Capitolinus was made by a Veiian sculptor, Vulca, as were the statues that decorated the temple's roof. For the most part, though, the two cities regarded one another as enemies. They had far too much in common. Veii lay just fifteen kilometres north of Rome – not far from the Allia battlefield – and both cities sought control of the same trans-Italian trade route along the Tiber: Rome controlled the left bank and Veii controlled most or all of the right. Veii was in Rome's way, blocking her so effectively that the city's expansion had been pushed in the other direction: south towards the Latins. Veii was much more of a force to be reckoned with than Rome's smaller Latin neighbours. Its location, on a rocky plateau surrounded on almost all sides by sheer cliffs, was defensively far superior to that of Rome. Rome, though, was larger and stronger. At the beginning of the fourth century BC, when the two cities began their third and final war, Rome had close to twice the land territory of Veii.

Today Veii, or what is left of it, is preserved in a small national park surrounded by outer Rome commuter settlements. It is a rather haunting spot, reached by a bridge over a small waterfall that plunges into a deep chasm. Walking into the site one soon comes across a clue as to how Veii met its end: a tunnel cut into the cliff. The volcanic rock that Veii was built upon is soft and easily mined. The Etruscans were masters at digging water channels and one of these, over half a kilometre long, passed directly under the place where the Romans probably set up their camp. Livy describes how, frustrated by a long siege, the Romans dug a tunnel into the city. When it was ready they launched an attack on Veii's walls, and while the city's defenders were distracted, Rome's soldiers poured out from their tunnel:

A fearful din arose: yells of triumph, shrieks of terror, wailing of women, and the pitiful crying of children; in an instant of time the defenders were flung from the walls and the town gates opened; Roman troops came pouring through, or climbed over the defenceless walls; everything was overrun, in every street the battle raged. After a terrible slaughter, resistance began to slacken.[2]

Rome's aggression against Veii was not unusual. In this era Mediterranean city states routinely fought wars with their neighbours. Yet in their war with Veii the Romans exhibited a noticeable thoroughness. When other Mediterranean cities suffered defeat they usually continued to exist, but after Veii fell to Rome it all but vanished from history. According to Livy, the very next morning after the city was captured, the Roman commander sold all its surviving inhabitants into slavery. It was the first instance of mass enslavement in Roman history.

III

The Veiians, unlike most of Rome's later enemies, were at least able to enjoy a little *Schadenfreude*. Just nine years after their city fell, the Gauls crushed the Roman army at the battle by the Allia and advanced on their city. Livy describes how the Romans watched as they approached. 'All too soon cries like the howling of wolves and barbaric songs could be heard, as the Gallic squadrons rode hither and thither close outside the walls. All the time between then and the following dawn was filled with unbearable suspense. When would the assault come?'[3]

Livy claims that the Gauls caught the city so much by surprise that they found the gates open, but the truth is probably simpler. There were no gates. At this time Rome seems to have had little in the way of walls. Its weak points were defended by ditches and earth ramparts, and though its citadel, the Capitoline Hill, may have had some walling, other hills probably relied on their steepness. Rome was virtually an open city.

So we come to Livy's famous stories of Roman heroism, many of which are still familiar today. One tells of a plebeian, Lucius Albinius, who was fleeing the city in a cart with his family when he saw the Vestal Virgins walking beside the road carrying the sacred objects of their temple. Albinius did not hesitate. Knowing his duty, he ejected his family from the cart and carried the Vestals to the safety of Rome's chief ally of the time, the Etruscan city of Caere.

There is the story of the venerable senators. As the Gauls approached the city the Romans retreated to their citadel on the Capitoline but realized their supplies would soon be exhausted if everyone took refuge there. The city's elders who had served Rome all their lives volunteered to remain below, even though they knew this meant certain death. They dressed in all the finery of their rank and then waited in the courtyards of their great houses. When the Gauls found them and saw their 'grave, calm eyes, like the majesty of gods', they became entranced. Finally, a Gaul tugged the beard of one of the senators, who struck him on the head with his ivory staff. The Gaul, 'flamed into anger and killed him, and the others were butchered where they sat'.[4]

There is the tale of Gaius Fabius Dorsuo, whose family had a solemn religious obligation to make a sacrifice on the Quirinal Hill on a fixed day each year. The Quirinal was now held by the Gauls, yet when the day came Dorsuo did not hesitate. He carefully dressed himself for the ritual and then strode towards the Gauls, who were so amazed at his audacity that they let him pass.

The story that is best known today, of course, is that of the geese. After a frontal attack on the Capitoline was foiled by the bravery of the Romans, the Gauls resorted to stealth. In the dead of night they climbed the steep cliff of the hill, so quietly that not even the Romans' dogs raised the alarm. But the sacred geese of Juno's temple heard: 'The cackling of the birds and the clapping of their wings awoke Marcus Manlius – a distinguished officer who had been consul three years before – and he, seizing his sword and giving the alarm, hurried, without waiting for the support of his bewildered comrades, straight to the point of danger.'⁵ One Gaul was already clambering on to the hilltop but Manlius hurled him back with a blow from his shield and he fell, dislodging those who were climbing up behind him.

Finally, Livy tells the story of how the Romans, at the very last moment, managed to save their city's honour. Besieged on the Capitoline they learned that a rescuer was on his way. Camillus, their heroic commander at Veii, who had been driven into exile by false accusations of corruption, was raising an army. Yet time was running out. After their night attack failed, the Gauls determined to starve the Romans into surrender. When the Romans became so weakened that they could hardly hold their weapons they knew they had no choice but to sue for peace. Their leader, Quintus Sulpicius, negotiated with the Gallic leader Brennus, who agreed to end the siege in exchange for a payment of 1,000 pounds of gold. The Gauls then added insult to injury by using over-heavy weights: '… and when the Roman commander objected the insolent barbarian flung his sword onto the scale, saying, "Woe to the vanquished!" – words intolerable to Roman ears.'⁶

Yet help was at hand. At that very moment Camillus appeared with his army and the Gauls were forced to fight a second battle. This time their barbarian impetuosity let them down: '… they attacked, but with more fire than judgement. Luck hard turned at last; human skill, aided by the powers of heaven, was fighting on the side of Rome, and the invaders were scattered at the first encounter with as little effort as had gone into their victory on the Allia.'⁷

If these stories seem like patriotic propaganda, that is exactly what they were. The question is, can any truth be found in them? Other accounts, fragments and archaeological discoveries all offer fascinating clues. Especially useful are later references to the temple to Juno Moneta where the geese were kept. Though nothing of the building survives today we know that it was dedicated by the Roman military hero Camillus, and that inscriptions on its walls listed a couple of names that will now be familiar. One of these was Manlius Capitolinus who, in the temple inscription, was described as Camillus' cavalry

Brennus puts his sword to the weighing pan in this nineteenth-century illustration.

commander. Also mentioned was Fabius Dorsuo, who is named as one of the city's two consuls: republican Rome's power-sharing rulers.

Something strange seems to be going on. The last two names are both heroes in Livy's stories but the details are all wrong. Livy's Manlius Capitolinus – the officer who drove back the Gauls' night attack single-handed – was not a cavalry commander. Likewise Livy's Fabius Dorsuo – who braved the Gallic lines to perform his family's religious duties – was not mentioned as being consul. This was an impossible omission, the equivalent of failing to mention that a man named Barack Obama was president of the United States.

Yet there is an altogether greater problem. It is known that the temple of Juno Moneta was first dedicated in 345 BC. In other words, it did not exist until forty years after Rome's struggle with the Gauls. According to Livy, Camillus, to whom the temple was dedicated, commanded the Roman army at Veii, nine years before the Gallic attack. If he had been thirty at this time – young for a Roman commander – he would have been over eighty when the temple of Juno Moneta showed he was still commanding Rome's forces.

Camillus is real enough. Early records confirm that he led Rome's military with great success in the era after the Gallic attack. But there is nothing to show he did so at the time of the disaster, let alone during the war with Veii. Livy evidently pushed his career further back into the past. It is easy enough to imagine why: he gave Rome an excuse for her defeat. By making Camillus the hero of Veii and then having him unfairly forced into exile, he presented him as blameless for the Allia disaster. He suggests that the Romans would have won had their hero commander not been absent.

In fairness, Livy simply embroidered stories that would already have existed long before his time. An intriguing explanation has been proposed as to how these first came to life. Romans strolled up to the temple of Juno Moneta and began wondering at its name and at the inscriptions on its walls. They looked at writings they no longer understood and made up stories. The temple's name, Moneta, had two meanings. It meant *advisor*, which was probably the relevant meaning, and would have referred to temple priests looking for signs in the skies. But it also meant *warner*. Romans assumed, wrongly, that it been built as thank-offering for the saving (warning) of the Capitoline citadel. This error led them to believe the temple was forty years older than it actually was, and that the people whose names were inscribed on its walls had been living at the time of the Gallic sack. The story of the geese that quacked and the dogs that failed to bark would also have come into existence thanks to poorly understood antiquities. One of Rome's earliest public contracts was for the feeding of Juno's sacred geese, while there was a tradition – probably far more ancient than Rome's struggle with the Gauls – that a dog be sacrificed on the Capitoline.

As Rome's early history was not written down until two centuries after 387 BC there was ample room for patriotic misconceptions. These probably crystallized in the late third century – 180 years after the actual events – by which time the Romans had defeated numerous enemies, from Pyrrhus' Greeks to Hannibal's Carthaginians, leading them to view themselves as a super-nation, divinely destined to rule the world. By then the Capitoline Hill had acquired a special religious significance in their eyes and so would have been a natural focus of heroic invention.

Yet not all of Livy's account seems to have been fiction. A couple of elements held some truth. One was the gold. Chance mentions in a couple of other sources are revealing. The Greek historian Diodorus Siculus, who wrote at the same time as Livy, recounts how, after their attack on Rome, the Gauls returned from the south and were attacked by forces of Rome's ally, Caere, which retrieved gold that Romans had given as ransom. A second story comes from five centuries after the battle on the Allia, in the writer Suetonius' life of the emperor Tiberius. Suetonius mentions that Tiberius' family, the Drusii, had an old traditional explanation as to how they got their name. During Rome's wars with the Gauls in northern Italy – centuries before Suetonius' time, and centuries after the sack of Rome – one of their ancestors fought and killed a Gallic chief named Drausus in single combat. Afterwards the ancestor was said to have recovered the gold that Rome had paid Brennus.

The meaning of the two stories is clear. The Romans paid up. What's more, they may have done so without ever defending the Capitoline Hill. A series of references have been found which indicate that the Gauls captured *all* of Rome. As the city's defences were negligible it would not be surprising. This version of events also fits with archaeological discoveries. Excavations in the Forum in the later nineteenth century uncovered an extensive burned layer and at first it was assumed that this dated from the Gallic sack. Later, though, when dating methods improved, the layer was found to be much older, dating from the unstable times of the late sixth century, when Romans threw out their last king and formed a republic. No burned layer has been found anywhere from the 380s BC. It seems the city was hardly damaged. So a new narrative offers itself that is altogether less romantic than Livy's. The Gauls crushed the Romans at the Allia, swept into the city and were paid to go away. Paid promptly, too, judging by the lack of damage.

Even then, it must have been a brutal moment. Though no details have been preserved one could expect nothing else when a large, well-armed horde of young, poorly disciplined males found themselves in a position of unrestrained power. The Gauls would have raided farms around the city to feed themselves. Unless the Romans paid up very promptly indeed, there would have been outrages in the city, too: robbery, violence and sexual attacks.

Another story of Livy's also seems to hold some truth, though the evidence for this comes by a most convoluted route. The Greek philosopher, Aristotle, who was born shortly after the Gauls' attack on Rome, mentioned the sacking in one of his writings. Unfortunately, the writing is lost, but it was briefly referred to by the later Greek historian, Plutarch. According to Plutarch, Aristotle wrote that Rome was saved by a certain Lucius. This is almost certainly the Lucius Albinius who chucked his own family from his cart to give a lift to the Vestal Virgins.

Albinius, it seems, was the true of hero of the hour. Before the myths of heroic Capitoline holdouts emerged, Albinius' story was probably the one that Romans told to one another to put their humiliating defeat in a better light, much as the British did after their catastrophe in France in 1940 with the story of their valiant escape at Dunkirk. If Rome had been lost, at least her religious treasures were saved. The city's spirit and the favour of her gods had been preserved. Albinius may have done a great deal more for his city that has been forgotten. There are clues as to why his role became diminished with time. Livy mentions that he was of humble, plebeian origins, a detail that would have reduced his appeal to later history commentators who preferred to ascribe heroism – fake heroism, as it turns out – to members of their own aristocratic class. Another likely victim of downgrading was Rome's Etruscan ally, the city of Caere, where the Vestals and their treasure were taken. Caere, too, probably had a greater role than is remembered, but it ceased to interest Romans after Caere city turned from ally to enemy, and then to a conquered enemy.

Yet, however much the Romans prettified and fictionalized the events of 387 BC they did not forget what had happened. The Gauls left a permanent mark on the Romans' worldview, giving them a new sense of fear. Romans had an enduring and increasingly irrational conviction that the Gauls would return one day and finish the job by destroying their city. When Gallic raiders returned to Latium – which they did at least twice – the Romans responded by declaring a state of emergency, a '*tumultus Gallicus*', under which all exemptions from military service were suspended and officials could recruit soldiers without restraint.

Roman fears also drove them to something decidedly un-Roman: human sacrifice. In later times when Rome suffered alarming defeats involving Gauls, the Romans took two Greeks and two Gauls – one male and one female of each – and buried them alive in the Forum Boarium animal market. This grisly ritual took place on at least three occasions: during wars with the Gauls in 228 BC, in 216 BC after the Romans' defeat at Cannae by Hannibal – half of whose army were Gauls – and again in 114 BC, when Gallic forces defeated the Romans in Macedonia. As late as AD 21, by which time Rome ruled the Mediterranean and had conquered all of Europe's Celts except in Britain and Ireland, a minor revolt by two Gallic tribes in France caused panic in Rome.

Yet Rome's fears also led her citizens to more rational responses, which played a key role in their city's remarkable rise. After the Gallic attack of 387 BC the Romans belatedly gave their city some proper defences. In a huge undertaking that may have taken as long as twenty-five years to complete, they built a city wall 11 kilometres long, stretches of which can still be seen today. The new wall, now known as the Servian Wall, proved invaluable on several occasions during Rome's numerous later wars. The Romans also reorganized their army to make it less vulnerable against a mobile, fast-moving enemy like that of Brennus. Infantry were protected by javelin throwers and stone slingers and troops were divided into independent units, so if one part of the line collapsed other sections might hold and rally. With these changes the Roman army became a formidable fighting machine.

So Rome's shock drubbing by the Gauls made her stronger, as she rose, phoenix-like, from disaster. Bribing barbarians to go away may have seemed shameful to later Romans, and an episode that was best rewritten, but it had been the right decision. The Romans and their state survived. As we have seen, the city's main monuments, such as the vast temple to Jupiter Best and Greatest, were preserved. Not for the last time, Rome escaped lightly from catastrophe.

The city was soon back on her expansionist path. Though the Latin cities that Rome had dominated rebelled, Rome quickly reasserted control and within a few decades of the Allia defeat Roman armies were campaigning further afield than ever before. In long, gruelling wars against the Samnites of southern Italy, the Etruscans, King Pyrrhus' Greeks and Hannibal's Carthaginians, the Romans repeatedly shrugged off disastrous setbacks – and they had quite a few – to rally and fight again. In doing so they acquired the very qualities of courage and no-nonsense gritty determination that Livy prematurely ascribed to them during the Gallic attack. King Pyrrhus spoke for many of Rome's enemies when he observed that if he won one more victory over the Romans he would be utterly lost.

The Romans' victories allowed them to enjoy some revenge. The Gauls seem to have seen what was coming and in every one of Rome's early wars they took the side of Rome's enemies, yet it did them no good. In 232 BC the Roman commander P. Nasica led his forces into the lands of the people who had sacked their city a century and a half earlier, the Senones, and by the end of his campaign Nasica boasted that he had left only boys and old men alive. The Romans took care to ensure their victory was permanent. The area's best farming land was seized and given to Roman citizens and their Latin allies. Senone territory was crossed by Roman roads and a military city, Sena Gallica, was built on the coast, dominating the region.

By the early second century BC all of Gallic northern Italy was subdued, and subdued with a thoroughness that was unusual even for the Romans. Large parts of the population were killed, dispersed or enslaved. Afterwards Italy's Gauls continued to be treated with distrust and they were the very last people in Italy to be granted Roman citizenship.

Eventually, though, the Gauls and the Romans came to terms with one another. The Romans accepted Gauls as participants in their imperial project and, once accepted, the Gauls began to take up the ways of their conquerors. They studied Latin, which, as it was closely related to their own language, they found pleasingly easy to learn. They watched Roman entertainments, gave their children a Roman education, worshipped Roman gods and lived in cities whose temples and amphitheatres were modelled on those of Rome. They were even stirred by Livy's stories of Rome's gritty early heroes. Until, eventually, they came to think of themselves as Romans. Rome's victory could hardly have been more complete.

By then Gauls and Romans were united against a common enemy. The Romans were not the only ones who had defeated the Gauls and taken their territory. As Julius Caesar conquered Gallic France another people was seizing Celtic heartlands in Central Europe. These were the new barbarians on the block.

The Germans were coming.

Rome, 410 AD

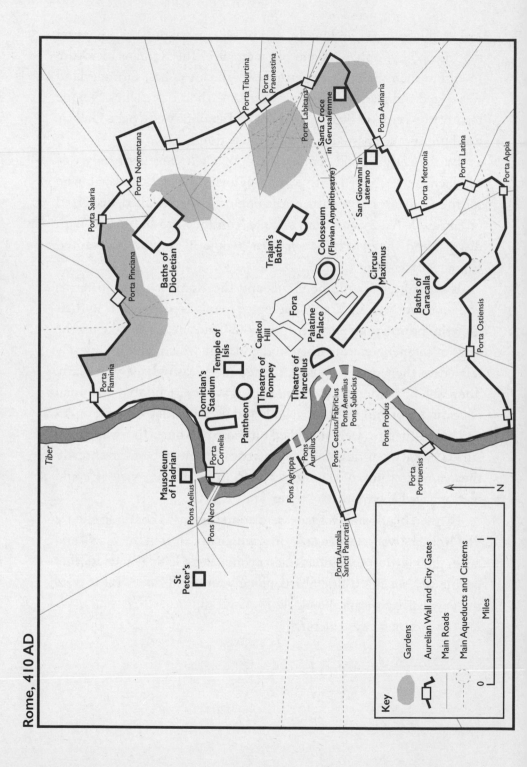

Tiber

St Peter's

Mausoleum of Hadrian

Pons Aelius

Pons Nero

Porta Cornelia

Domitian's Stadium

Pantheon

Temple of Isis

Theatre of Pompey

Capitol Hill

Theatre of Marcellus

Pons Agrippa

Pons Aurelius

Pons Cestius/Fabricius

Pons Aemilius

Pons Sublicius

Pons Probus

Porta Aurelia Sancti Pancratii

Porta Portuensis

Porta Flaminia

Porta Pinciana

Baths of Diocletian

Porta Salaria

Porta Nomentana

Porta Tiburtina

Porta Praenestina

Trajan's Baths

Fora

Palatine Palace

Colosseum (Flavian Amphitheatre)

Porta Labicana

Santa Croce in Gerusalemme

San Giovanni in Laterano

Porta Asinaria

Porta Latina

Porta Metronia

Porta Appia

Circus Maximus

Baths of Caracalla

Porta Ostiensis

N

Key

Gardens

Aurelian Wall and City Gates

Main Roads

Main Aqueducts and Cisterns

0   Miles

CHAPTER TWO

GOTHS

I

COSENZA, JUST ABOVE ITALY'S TOE in Calabria, is not too used to visitors. It is a place where people may stop and ask if you are a local, rather hoping you're not as it makes a change. Though there are no important sights to see, it is a welcoming, likeable city. The old town which sits on a hillside beneath a castle and above the confluence of two rivers, the Crati and the Busento, contains a maze of steep, winding streets and stairways. Calabria may be one of Italy's poorest regions but Cosenza is working hard to improve itself. The main square of the new town has just been remade, with elaborate skateboard slopes and a long pedestrianized street is filled with modern artworks for Cosenzans to admire as they take their evening *passeggiata*.

It was a smaller and sleepier city when, at dawn on 19 November 1937, a group of people gathered by the riverside, at the point where the Busento and Crati rivers meet. They included all of Cosenza's high officials, led by the prefect. As well as being bleary and a little resentful at having been forced to get up at such an early hour, they were also

nervous. They had assembled at the request of a visitor who had arrived
with his wife and interpreter the evening before. The three had had a
long and trying drive. They had begun by ascending Vesuvius only to
find it was cold, windy and lost in cloud. After a further 350 kilometres
and several breakdowns they finally reached Cosenza after midnight.
The visitor was the commander of the German SS, Heinrich Himmler.

Himmler's interpreter, Eugene Dollmann, later wrote an account
of what happened that morning. Himmler surveyed the river, which
was low almost to the point of dryness, and cautiously tested the
muddy waters. He then began to lecture the Cosenzan officials on
ways in which the river might be diverted from its course so its bed
could be drained. At this point, a second group appeared beside the
river, made up of French archaeologists led by a young and attractive
female diviner:

> As the dawn light grew stronger Sweet France became ever
> more appealing to the Italian delegation … The enraptured
> eyes of the sons of the south followed each movement of her
> diviners' rods that rose and fell with her ample breasts. The
> willowy sticks acted like Circe's magic wand and the sombre
> city representatives slowly edged further from Himmler and
> closer to the French, and especially to their diviner. Impassive,
> cold, undeviating, only the melancholy prefect and the police
> chief stayed beside their German ally, to whom nothing
> remained except to promise speedily to send an archaeological
> expedition from Germany.[1]

Himmler and the French water diviner had both been drawn
to Cosenza by a narrative written fourteen centuries earlier by the
chronicler Jordanes. In his *History of the Goths*, Jordanes recounted
how in AD 410 Visigothic warriors had halted at the very spot where
Himmler and the French archaeologists now gathered. The warriors
had their slaves divert the Busento from its stream and then dig a deep
grave. In it they placed a corpse, together with numerous other items,

before filling in the grave and returning the river to its old path, so the burying place was concealed by its waters. The warriors then killed all the slaves to ensure the grave's precise location would remain forever secret. In it lay Alaric, the Visigoths' king, and the objects buried with him, Jordanes wrote, were all the golden treasures of Rome, which Alaric and his followers had looted only a few weeks earlier.

The Visigoths' road to Rome was a long and convoluted one. It had begun more than two centuries before Alaric's death on the southern shores of the Baltic. Here the Visigoths' ancestors had followed the glint of Roman gold, raiding and conquering their way south along trade routes to the Black Sea, where they established kingdoms that stretched from the Danube to the Crimea. Their move south made them neighbours of the Roman Empire and an intense and frequently violent relationship began, which would have a profound effect on the destiny of both.

The first aggression was by the Goths. From the late 230s AD they and other barbarian peoples launched waves of raids into the southern Balkans, Asia Minor and Greece, sacking some of the Empire's greatest cities, from Ephesus and Corinth to Athens. The Goths played their part in what is known as the Third Century Crisis: a dire fifty years for the Roman Empire, during which it struggled to cope with barbarian attacks, invasions by the Persian Empire, runaway inflation and endless civil wars between would-be emperors. At times it seemed questionable whether the Roman state would survive.

A century later the Romans got their revenge. By the fourth century AD the Goths were doing well in their Black Sea kingdoms, modernizing their farming and developing simple industries. In AD 327 Emperor Constantine crossed the Danube and led his forces into Gothic territory to show who was boss. The Goths fell back to the Carpathian mountains but it was not far enough. Constantine starved them into surrender and forced them to accept a humiliating treaty that made them vassals of the Empire.

Worse was to come. Half a century later, in AD 376, several Gothic peoples camped by the Danube frontier and begged the Romans to

give them sanctuary inside their empire. They had been forced into
this humiliating position because of attacks by a Central Asian people,
the Huns, whose tactics even the warlike Goths found impossible to
cope with. Hun cavalry archers would shower them with arrows from
a safe distance and then move in for the kill. Some Goths fled to the
fringes of the Roman Empire in Central Europe. The rest, camped
by the Danube seeking pity from their old enemies, would gradually
become fused into a new people, who called themselves the *Valiant
Goths*, or Visigoths.

Valens, the Eastern Roman Emperor – by now the Empire was
so unwieldy that it was split in two – let them in, probably because
they were too numerous to keep out. He may also have hoped to
use them to bolster his armies. Whatever his thinking, it proved a
bad mistake. Roman officials profited from the Visigoths' hunger
by selling them overpriced food and then made a botched attempt
to kidnap their leaders at a banquet. The Visigoths responded
with a rampage of plundering. Two years later, at the battle of
Adrianople, they inflicted the Romans' worst defeat for five hundred
years, massacring two-thirds of the Eastern Empire's field army and
killing Emperor Valens. It was a sea change moment. Thereafter
the Romans, who ever since their recovery after the battle on the
Allia had been confident of defeating barbarian enemies, fought
them with caution, as equals.

For the next three decades the Visigoths were unwelcome tenants
of the Empire, with which they were sometimes at war and sometimes
at peace. Driven by fear of the Romans and the need to extort pay-
offs from them, their tribes united. The Visigoths also picked up some
Roman habits. They abandoned their old pagan gods and took up
Christianity. To some extent this was forced upon them, as Emperor
Valens had insisted their leaders convert before they could be admitted
into the Empire. The Visigoths took up a creed favoured by Valens
– Homoean Christianity – which would bring them all kinds of
difficulties in the future. After Valens' death the Eastern Empire
adopted the creed that would become mainstream Christianity,

A seventeenth-century view of Alaric's forces in battle, from Alaric or the Conquest of Rome *by Georges de Scudery, 1654.*

leaving the Goths stranded as heretics. Yet it was an arrangement that probably suited them, as it meant their religion was safely outside Roman control.

It was also during these limbo years that the Visigoths chose Alaric as their leader. The sources tell us almost nothing about his character or even his appearance, describing only what he did, yet one can understand a good deal from his actions. He rose to power on a surge of Visigothic resentment at the way the Romans treated them. At the battle of Frigidus in AD 394 the Visigoths were required by treaty obligations to fight for the Eastern Emperor against a western usurper. Placed on the front line the Visigoths suffered huge casualties, leading them to suspect – correctly – that the Romans were deliberately seeking to weaken them. Alaric led them in a second revolt against the Empire, embarking on raids into Greece that were among the most destructive the region had ever seen. Athens was sacked and huge numbers of people were taken as slaves. Five years later Alaric did much the same in northern Italy. One begins to envisage him as a kind of action film villain, spoiling for a fight and revelling in his own cruelty.

Yet the truth was very different. Sources of the time do not portray Gothic leaders bellowing orders but rather ruling through persuasion. Alaric may have enjoyed raiding but it was also something he needed to do, as if he did not reward his warriors with regular loot they would turn against him. To stay at the top of the greasy pole of Visigothic politics, which Alaric did with great success, he must have had a talent to convince, even charm. Also revealing is his military record. In his years as leader he fought surprisingly few battles, while those he did fight were rarely if ever decisive. Alaric played for the draw rather than the win. One can understand his caution. A single major defeat and his people would have been destroyed: enslaved or drafted into the Roman army. He himself would have been publicly garrotted at an imperial triumph.

What led cautious, charming Alaric from the Balkans to the walls of Rome? The answer lies with another skilled political survivor of this era, Flavius Stilicho. Half Roman and half Vandal German, Stilicho was the military chief of the Western Empire at this time and the power behind its young emperor, Honorius. Having fought Alaric twice, beating back his earlier raids in Greece and then northern Italy, in AD 406 Stilicho proposed they ally against the Eastern Empire. To this day it is not entirely clear why, though conflicts between the two halves of the Empire were common. Alaric, whose Visigoths were lost in limbo in the Balkans, in a world that was growing ever more dangerous – the Huns had now set up camp in Central Europe – needed a powerful patron and he accepted.

But the alliance never happened. Alaric fulfilled his part of the deal, moving his people into today's Albania to link up with Stilicho's forces, but Stilicho did not turn up. He had a good excuse. Within weeks of the alliance being agreed several Germanic peoples, pushed by Hun aggression, swept into what is now France. It was the beginning of the attacks that would eventually destroy the Western Empire. Alaric waited in Albania for a year and then lost patience. His followers would have been growing impatient for loot. He marched them to the Alps where he could hover threateningly above the Western Imperial Court in nearby Ravenna, and then demanded 4,000 pounds of gold for his trouble.

Stilicho, who had more than enough worries already, agreed to pay up, but it cost him dearly. A Roman senator named Lampadius complained that paying off Alaric was not peace but servitude. His outburst was the beginning of the end for Stilicho. As the gold was raised and paid, his enemies at the Ravenna court poisoned Emperor Honorius against him, claiming that Stilicho, whose Germanic origins made him suspect in Roman eyes, had secret dynastic ambitions for his young son. Late Roman regime change was anything but pretty. In August 408 AD Stilicho was beheaded in a Ravenna church and all his close associates, including his son, were killed. Worse, his death provoked a wave of anti-barbarian feeling across Italy, as Roman troops massacred the families of Germanic soldiers whom Stilicho had recruited.

Alaric's patron had been killed and his fellow Goths slaughtered. One might have expected him to seek revenge. The force he commanded was stronger than ever, as he had recently been joined by another tribe of Visigoths, led by his brother-in-law Ataulf, as well as numerous warriors fleeing from the pogroms in Italy. As ever, though, Alaric was cautious. He needed to make a new deal with emperor Honorius, yet his demands were modest: all he asked for was a home for his people in a part of the Empire that was barely under Roman control any more, in today's Hungary and Croatia. The Ravenna government, which was still locked into anti-barbarian intransigence, still refused. Frustrated, Alaric finally struck out, but even now his thinking was tactical. He needed a bargaining chip that would force the Emperor to make a deal: a place that had not yet been destroyed, and which the Romans valued so highly that they would make any concession to ensure it was not harmed.

The Visigoths packed up their possessions and began heading south in a forced march. Though little can be said about them with absolute certainty, they were not a war band, like Brennus' Gauls but were a whole people on the move: warriors, their wives and their children. There were also many non-Goths. Alaric's followers were no simple horde but had a complex and clearly defined hierarchy. At the top was a small political elite. Below them was a large group of free warriors, who formed fewer than half the total and may have accounted for as little as one-fifth. Beneath these was a subservient population who outnumbered the warriors and who were also divided, some of them slaves and others free, and who were probably prohibited from intermarrying with their superiors. Only the minority of free warriors truly thought of themselves as Goths and it is doubtful how willingly the rest followed them. Though they would not have seemed so at the time, Gothic tribes were fragile entities. If the free minority became too reduced in numbers the whole tribe would collapse.

The Visigoths, though, were in no danger of collapse now. Their total numbers have been estimated as some 150,000 people, or enough to populate a good-sized city of the Roman Empire, of whom as many as 30,000 were fighting men. By the standards of the time, when imperial armies were growing ever smaller, it was a huge horde: an exodus of people, some on horseback, others on foot and yet others crowded into carts. Long-haired – the German fashion of the time – the elite would have had finely ornamented weapons and metal armour, while the rest made do with leather tunics or scavenged Roman breastplates and helmets. They would have carried an array of weapons from shields and lances to swords and even wooden clubs. And, like Brennus' followers, they must have stunk and been infested with lice. This was the multitude that, on a November day in AD 408, appeared as if from nowhere outside the walls of Rome.

II

What kind of city awaited Alaric and his Visigoths? Mostly they would have found themselves looking up at a high wall. Though Alaric would not have known, it was something for which he himself was partly responsible. This was not the Servian Wall that had been built after the Gallic sack, most of which had long ago succumbed to demolition and city construction. This wall – the Aurelian – was twice as long as the Servian had been, and it showed precisely how the city had shifted over eight centuries. The lozenge-shaped Servian Wall had enclosed only the seven hills, while the Aurelian formed a square that reached down to the river and beyond, to the Trans Tiberina district on the far bank. It had been built towards the end of the Third Century Crisis, when, for the first time in many generations, Rome again seemed vulnerable, and it was built in a hurry, slicing through buildings and gardens. Constructed too low, it was raised a few decades later, and when Alaric's Visigoths raided northern Italy in 401–3, Stilicho raised it again to 20 metres. He also built a new section that encircled Trans Tiberina on the far side of the river, which had previously been left undefended. The city Alaric looked upon in the autumn of AD 408 had never been so well protected.

And inside the walls? If someone had been transported across the centuries from the Rome of the Gallic sack to the Rome of AD 408 they would have hardly known where to look. The small town they had known had grown forty times over. Though its greatest days had been three centuries earlier, and many of its buildings would have been a little run down, it was still the largest metropolis on earth, whose architectural treasures made the Roman Empire's other leading cities, from Trier to Carthage and Constantinople, seem drab and provincial. Rome in 387 BC had been a city of timber and brick. Now it gleamed white and red: white walls and red terracotta roof tiles. Its great temples and palaces were faced with every kind of marble: white marble from Tuscany, Greece and the Sea of Marmara; black-red and purple marble from Asia Minor; green marble from Euboea; pink-grey marble from Chios; red marble from the southern Peloponnese and yellow marble from North Africa.

Itineraries of the city from just a few decades prior to Alaric's arrival tell us that Rome had 2 main markets, 2 colossal statues, 2 circuses, 2 amphitheatres, 3 theatres, 4 gladiator schools, 5 artificial lakes for mock sea battles, 6 obelisks, 8 bridges, 10 basilicas, 11 forums, 11 public baths, 19 aqueducts, 22 equestrian statues, 28 libraries, 29 avenues, 36 marble arches, 37 gates, 46 brothels, 74 ivory statues of gods, 80 gold statues of gods, 144 public latrines, 254 bakeries, 290 warehouses, 423 neighbourhoods, each with its own temple, 856 private bath houses, 1,790 houses, 2,300 oil sellers, and 46,602 blocks of flats.

Was there anything that an early republican from the time of the Gallic attack would have recognized? Not much. The Forum Boarium animal market was still held in the same spot, between the river and the Palatine Hill, though its shrines would have been rebuilt many times. The Circus Maximus chariot-racing circuit was still in the valley between the Aventine and Palatine hills, though by AD 408 its simple wooden stands had long ago been replaced by a vast structure, with two stone tiers of seats and more above of wood, that could hold a quarter of a million Romans. Races that had been rare celebrations of military victories were now commonplace events, held throughout the year. Even the parade that opened the games had changed. Though floats still made their way down from the Capitoline Hill they no longer contained images of Rome's gods. They almost certainly displayed images of the Emperor.

Here at least was something that had not changed. Looking up, an early republican would see the familiar profile of the temple to Jupiter Best and Greatest, dominating the city's skyline just as it had done eight hundred years earlier. But it was not the same temple. The original one had burned down and been rebuilt three times since the Gallic sack. Compared to the wood and brick original the present version was gaudy: covered with marble and with golden roof tiles. And our early republican would be shocked when he came closer. Rome's most famous temple was closed. It had not been used for more than a decade.

But there was one tiny building that they would find wholly familiar. To reach it one had only to cross the main Forum and climb up to the Palatine Hill, which had changed completely over the centuries, even in its shape, as huge platforms had been built out from it, artificially extending its summit. The grand aristocratic houses that overlooked the Forum in 387 BC were long gone and the crown of the hill was now occupied by a vast single dwelling: the Imperial Palace. For the past four centuries the Roman state had been an autocracy ruled by emperors.

Emperors? The word conjures up an image of a romantic, courtly world but the truth was rather different. In some ways, the Roman imperial state seems eerily familiar in our own times when dictatorships try to pass themselves off as democracies. After Rome's first new autocrat Julius Caesar was assassinated for seeming too like a king, his successors kept up a pretence that the old Republic still existed.

Emperors had spin doctors and propagandists, and leading poets extolled their rulers' virtues. Free speech had been among the Empire's earliest victims; even under the more benign emperors, writers who dared to criticize their ruler or mock him – and few did – could find themselves accused of treason and exiled, or worse. In AD 408, republican officials were still appointed though their titles were purely ornamental, rather like a modern British knighthood. Real power lay with imperial officials, including their secret police, the much-feared *frumentarii*. Occasionally, Romans found the courage to express resentment through sheer force of numbers, and unpopular emperors might be jeered by the crowd in one of the city's large arenas. Yet even mass protest could be dangerous, and more visible complainers could find themselves dragged away by imperial agents.

In 387 BC, Roman politics had been a public business, argued over in the Senate, the Forum and the city's streets. Now it was private, secret and also curiously domestic. An ambitious politician needed to be able to flatter, bribe or scare those who mattered. Most of all he (in this age no females held high office) had to be able to swallow his pride. To win the era's greatest political prize – a few moments alone to whisper in the emperor's ear – he needed to charm those who were closest to him, whether this was his wife, his mistress, his steward, his food taster or his slave dresser.

But no bribing or crawling was going on in the Imperial Palace when Alaric arrived outside the city walls in November AD 408. It was empty. The last time it had been used was a few months earlier, when the young Western Emperor Honorius paid a visit with his court: the occasion when the Senate met to agree to pay Alaric's gold and when Senator Lampadius sealed Stilicho's fate by denouncing the decision as servitude. Imperial visits were now rare and decades could pass without one, while no emperor had lived permanently on the Palatine for more than a century. Rome was no longer capital of her own empire. These days the emperors made their homes close to the frontier and to the soldiers who could make or destroy them: in Milan, in Trier on the Rhine, or in the new Rome of the east, Constantinople. As we saw, Emperor Honorius' court was currently in Ravenna, where it was kept safe from roving barbarians by encircling marshes. The balcony of the Palatine Palace, from which emperors had once greeted crowds of morning visitors, would have looked forlorn these days, as would the vast throne room behind, the courtyard with its ornamental fountain and the great banqueting hall.

Beyond these, in a small open space by the Temple to the Great Mother, was the building our republican Roman would have found familiar. After eight centuries the Hut of Romulus

is documented as standing just a decade or two bef
Visigoths appeared beneath the walls of Rome a
certainly still to be found in AD 408. Several centurie
of Halicarnassus described how it was carefully prese
'add nothing to it to render it more stately, but if any part of it is injured
either by storms or the lapse of time they restore the hut as nearly as
possible to its former condition'.[2] In AD 408 there had been no priests to
look after it for at least ten years so it would have been in a poor state,
and the thatched roof may have fallen in. Romans had not forgotten
their ancient origins and they still loomed large in their thinking.

But our early republican would be shaking his head. How had
autocrats, whom the Romans had been so proud of having thrown
out, crept back? For an answer one has only to step down the grand
entrance ramp from the Palatine Palace and walk towards the river.
Here, facing each other just a few hundred yards apart, were two vast
structures, created to impress and awe the Roman population. The
Theatre of Pompey was built by its namesake, one of the greatest
generals and politicians of the last decades of the Republic. The
Theatre of Marcellus was begun by the rival who defeated him:
Julius Caesar. Pompey and Caesar were two of a number of military
politicians who grew so wealthy and powerful that they could no
longer be contained by the Republic's constitutional rules. In many
ways Rome's aristocrats, whose ancestors created the Republic, were
responsible for its fall. Eager to outdo one another they destroyed the
class of small farmers that had been the pillar of the early Roman state,
evicting them from their land to create highly profitable slave estates.
The Republic was also a victim of its own success. Its victories led its
armies ever further away, till soldiers lost their sense of loyalty to Rome
and instead followed the general who led and fed them. Eventually
they were willing to fight for him against other Romans, and to march
against Rome itself, as Julius Caesar had them do.

Caesar not only killed off the Republic, he and Pompey also
inadvertently murdered Roman drama, which was long dead by AD

58. In their determination to impress Romans the theatres they built were absurdly large. The Theatre of Marcellus held over 20,000 people, most of whom could barely see the actors on the stage, let alone hear them. Plays were adapted, becoming simplified to key quotes that were recited by a chorus, while actors, whose masks and clothes made them easily recognizable, performed a kind of miming dance. Themes, too, became increasingly crude: a mother mourning her massacred children or incest between a father and daughter. Highly popular was the story of a wicked brigand named Laureolus, who was eventually caught and executed. Roman drama reached its lowest point in the late first century AD when the actor playing Laureolus would be switched shortly before the end of a production and replaced by a condemned criminal who was then killed live on stage.

It is not hard to see where this idea had come from. Across the main Forum lay another of Rome's great landmarks: the Colosseum, which in AD 408 was still known as the Flavian Amphitheatre. Its later name would come from a colossal golden statue 35 metres high that stood just beside it. The statue had been commissioned by Emperor Nero, whom it depicted, quite naked, until his successor Vespasian had the head removed and replaced by that of the sun god Helios. The towering Flavian Amphitheatre was by far the largest of its kind in the Empire: a dazzling feat of engineering that could be emptied of its 50,000 spectators in minutes and which had water fountains at every level. It was a source of immense pride to Romans, though it was less solidly designed than one might think. The highest seating levels were poorly supported and became strained when the huge awning over the stadium – which was suspended by a complex arrangement of masts and ropes – was buffeted by high winds. The awning was also susceptible to lightning strikes and in the early third century the whole north-east section of the building burned to the ground.

In AD 408, though, the Colosseum was in full working order. Its subterranean tunnels would have been filled with men and wild animals, ready to be raised through trapdoors into the arena. Killing as public entertainment was a phenomenon that was beginning to decline at this time, and thanks to Christian pressure gladiator fights had been banned just four years earlier. They were originally an Etruscan invention – a form of human sacrifice in which a pair of gladiators fought to the death at the funeral of an important figure – and appeared in Rome two centuries after the Gallic sack in 387 BC. They soon became hugely popular, so much so that attempts were made to rein in extravagant games financed by ambitious individuals. It was no use. Though sensitive Romans found killings in the arena abhorrent, most were hooked. For the best part of six hundred years they watched gladiators fighting and killing gladiators, gladiators fighting wild animals, wild animals fighting each other, and animals mauling condemned criminals to death. Though gladiatorial combat may have been abolished, fights between men and wild animals would continue in Rome's arena for another century and more.

To our eyes killing as entertainment seems only abhorrent. If any explanation for such a thing can be found, it is that this was a far more violent age than our own, not only in Rome but worldwide, and that a certain amount of brutality was part of everyday life. The Romans developed their own justifications, claiming that a visit to the games was their patriotic duty, and that having their children – and especially their sons – watch the gore of gladiator fights toughened them up, as befitted future defenders of the Empire.

A first visit to the amphitheatre was an important rite of passage. It was also a day out and families would bring elaborate picnics. Finally, Romans went to the Colosseum in the hope of making a penny or two. They were addicted to gambling, whether on chariot races, dice or gladiators, and the crowd's exultant shouts of, 'Well washed!' when one gladiator managed a lethal stab against another and blood gushed, was all the louder because they had just won some money. The Colosseum was often almost deserted during public executions because no bets could be made.

The main reason Romans went to the amphitheatre, though, was neither patriotism nor to bet, but for thrills. A single visit could be enough to leave even the most reluctant visitor addicted. To this day the Colosseum remains the world's most concentrated killing ground, and it is estimated that between a quarter and half a million people had their lives abruptly ended in its arena, along with several million animals large and small, common and rare. Species became extinct in its service. Perhaps its most disturbing legacy, though, is what it says about human nature. Humans, if they are reassured that their behaviour is socially acceptable, are quite capable of enjoying the sight of others enduring a gruesome death in front of them, and of enjoying it again and again.

If Romans were proud of their amphitheatre, visitors to the city tended to be more impressed by the city's public squares, the fora. At the time of the Gallic sack there had only been one, which was the city's political heart, where crowds gathered, speeches were made and the Senate met. By AD 408 political power had long ago migrated and the main Forum was more like a modern Italian piazza: a place where you ran into friends, settled a few business matters and perhaps did a little shopping. In appearance it has been compared with the Piazza San Marco in Venice: faintly triangular in shape, lined with porticoes and shops, and with a series of tall flagpoles along one side. However, Rome's main Forum would have been far more cluttered than the Piazza San Marco, with statues, shrines and monuments to past and present emperors. The cluttering may have been a deliberate ploy to extinguish ghosts of public politics and to crowd out popular gatherings.

By AD 408 the only political activity that still went on in the main Forum took place inside the Senate House: a relatively new building, which, like everything else in the Forum, had been rebuilt following a bad fire in AD 283. Imposingly tall and square though it was, little of importance occurred inside at this time. Once the Senate had ruled the whole Mediterranean but after the fall of the Republic its power had steadily seeped away. Emperor Constantine tripled its membership to 2,000, making it bloated and ineffective. Three generations later, Emperor Valentian I, who, like many emperors

GOTHS   45

before him had a strong fear of magic spells, made its powerlessness brutally apparent. In a McCarthy-like witch hunt, senators and their wives were tried for adultery, incest and, most of all, sorcery, and some of Rome's leading citizens were tortured; something that would have been unimaginable in earlier times. In AD 408 the Senate was little more than a town council notable for its sycophancy. Senator Lampadius' outburst against Stilicho was highly unusual and probably reflected higher political stirrings rather than his own independence of mind. When a new emperor rose to power Rome's senators would chant their approval in unison.

As the Senate lost its significance, so did the Forum. Fora, like theatres, offered emperors a chance to leave their mark and by AD 408 the original Forum was one of eleven. Of these, visitors to the city were particularly impressed by that of Emperor Trajan, which was part of a vast complex whose construction had required the removal of an entire hillside. It included a huge equestrian statue of Trajan; Trajan's famous column that depicted his epic campaign to conquer Dacia, modern Romania (most of which had long ago been abandoned as imperial territory by AD 408) – as well as a huge basilica hall, two libraries, one for Latin texts and one for Greek, and also a kind of ancient Roman mall that contained shops on three elegant, curving levels. Like other great monuments of the Empire, the complex had been built using a substance that had not been dreamed of at the time of the Gallic sack: concrete. Made from lime and volcanic sand, it was poured into temporary wooden moulds till it set, and then faced with brick and stone. With concrete, Roman emperors could build gargantuan structures that perfectly reflected their own power and offered their subjects a suitable sense of their own insignificance.

But Romans' skill with concrete could also produce great beauty. The Pantheon temple, built by Emperor Hadrian three centuries before Alaric's Visigoths marched on Rome, used the substance masterfully. Its dome, with a huge circular hole at its centre, was ingeniously constructed from different mixes of concrete that grew lighter as the dome became higher and thinner. The Pantheon showed how far the

Romans had come in developing their own architectural style and if the city's early temples were Greek imitations the Pantheon was purely Roman. In place of Greek straight lines, the Pantheon – aside from the portico fixed awkwardly to its front – was all curves, inside and out. It was an exquisite building, whose interior was proportioned precisely to contain a vast sphere. The floor sloped imperceptibly towards tiny holes in the paving, through which rainwater from the hole in the ceiling drained away. Yet something appears to have gone badly wrong with its portico. The decoration on the main part of the building does not align with its roof, and is far higher. Likewise, the supports beside the doorway do not match the portico's columns and are much wider. It seems something went awry with the granite columns, which came from Egypt. They may have arrived too small or the right ones may have sunk to the bottom of the Mediterranean and had to be replaced in a hurry.

The Pantheon was not Rome's only place of wonder. Although classical Rome did not yet have the beauty it would one day achieve – it was a chaotic, crowded, functional city – it did have oases of beauty. There were delightful parks, both private and public, such as the Portico of Octavia, which contained a whole posse of equestrian statues looted from Greece that depicted Alexander the Great and his generals charging into battle. Alongside the vast buildings one could also find others that were small and delicate. At the northern end of the Campus Martius was an instance of Roman art at its best: Augustus' Temple to Peace, whose exquisite reliefs included a portrait of Augustus, his family and the Roman elite attending a sacrifice.

Then Rome in AD 408 was crammed with art. There were numerous famous Greek statues, some looted from Greece and others that were Roman copies of Greek originals. To our eyes these would seem rather gaudy as they were not plain marble – as their survivors have now become – but had every detail, from their faces to their clothes, brightly painted. Alongside Greek masterpieces Rome's open spaces were crowded with drearier statues that depicted emperors, city prefects and other high officials who had achieved the great Roman dream and been immortalized in stone. Though many had been immortalized less than they hoped, and a good few had already had their heads changed.

Yet this was not the only odd thing one might notice about them. To modern eyes, a careful look at Rome's statues could give the impression that time had somehow gone into reverse. The older ones were delicate and realistic in a way we associate with the classical world. By comparison the newer ones seemed more primitive: heavier in style with emotionless faces and large staring eyes. The same was true of the inscriptions on the plinths. Those carved two centuries ago or more had perfectly squared letters, while the new ones were rounder, less upright and more crowded together. This artistic change occurred during the Third Century Crisis when the Roman Empire struggled to stay afloat. It may have resulted simply from a lack of skilled craftsmen, or, in an era of high inflation and low tax revenues, from a lack of money to pay them. Or the new style may have reflected a deeper change. As their empire wobbled and life became increasingly a matter of survival, people ceased to be so interested in perfection.

Another great change had been going on in the decades before AD 408 and for signs of it one needed only to look down almost any street. Rome was a city crowded with religious buildings. Alongside temples to the traditional Greek and Roman gods were temples to gods that our early republican would have found entirely unfamiliar. The cults of most of these reached Rome during the late Republic and early Empire and though at first they had been regarded with some suspicion, they eventually became accepted as fully Roman. They also tolerated one another. Some cults permitted images of rival gods to be kept in their temples, though naturally their own gods always held pride of place.

In the Campus Martius stood a huge temple belonging to the Greek–Egyptian cult of Isis and Osiris, who offered worshippers hopes of paradise. Rome also had temples to Syrian gods and Algerian gods, as well as those dedicated to a whole series of deified emperors, from Julius Caesar onwards. There were temples to the ancient cult of Mater Magna – the Great Mother – which had developed a bizarre ritual whereby devotees became reborn to eternity by standing beneath a grate and being spattered with blood from a lamb or bull that had its throat cut above them. The cult of Mithras offered its male-only worshippers old-fashioned morality and dinner gatherings, and had three dozen cave-like meeting places across the city.

Among the best known of these temples was that of Asclepius on the Tiber Island, which was not only a temple but was, in its strange way, the nearest the city had to a hospital. In its heyday, it was crowded with Romans suffering from every kind of medical complaint, and who hoped that the god Asclepius would guide them to a cure. In Asclepius' great temples in the eastern Mediterranean – and the one on the Tiber Island was probably no different – patients slept in underground chambers filled with incense, hoping that the god would visit them in their dreams and give them instructions for a cure. If their dreams were unclear – as they frequently were – priests (who fortunately had medical experience) would help with interpretation. Even then, prescriptions could be very odd. Asclepius instructed one patient with a stomach abscess to carry the heaviest stone he could find into the temple. A pleurisy sufferer was told to add wine to ashes from the temple's altar and place the mixture by his side. If Asclepius' dream advice did not work there was always the hope that one of the temple's sacred snakes might bring a cure by licking one's wound.

Yet in AD 408 every pagan temple in Rome, from that of Asclepius to the temple of Jupiter Best and Greatest that dominated the city, had been closed for more than a decade. It was the latest stage in a slow squeeze that had begun almost a century earlier, when Emperor Constantine won the battle of the Milvian Bridge, just north of Rome, captured the city and declared himself a supporter of Christianity. During most of the fourth century the old pagan religions, in spite of Church pressure to ban them, had largely been left in peace. That this tolerance ended was, in some ways, the Visigoths' fault. The last religiously easy-going emperor was the Valens they killed at the battle of Adrianople. His successors took a harsher line. In AD 383 Emperor Gratian confiscated temples' estates, and priests – including the Vestal

Virgins – lost their tax breaks. Eight years later Emperor Theodosius went further and closed all Rome's pagan temples altogether.

In AD 408 only two kinds of religious institution were still permitted to function. Rome had a number of Jewish synagogues, which remained open despite blood-curdling anti-Semitic rhetoric by some emperors, and two recent arson attacks, both inspired by churchmen. Most of all, though, Rome had churches, which were its newest great monuments. By AD 408 there were at least seven churches within the city. Most were built over the remains of apartment blocks or grand aristocratic houses, where Christians may have met in earlier times, when Christianity was illegal and its followers had to keep a low profile. The building of Rome's first officially sanctioned church, the Lateran basilica, was ordered by Emperor Constantine himself. Pointedly, he had it constructed on the demolished headquarters of the city's cavalry regiment, which he had disbanded together with the Praetorian Guard, as punishment for their both having fought against him. These new Christian temples would have looked very familiar to Romans as they were modelled on that most Roman of buildings, the basilica: an all-purpose hall with aisles and a higher central section with windows, which was used for everything from court trials to army drill.

Rome's greatest churches, though, were not in the city but outside its walls. The Romans were fortunate that the Visigoths had converted to Christianity and so treated these churches with respect. These were cemetery churches, built directly above the tombs of Christian martyrs: San Sebastiano, San Lorenzo, Sant'Agnese, San Paolo fuori le Mure and, dwarfing all the rest in size, St Peter's on the Vatican Hill. Plain on the outside, they were lavish within. St Peter's, whose construction had involved the removal of part of a hillside, had a grand colonnade, a gleaming atrium with a fountain, columns made from stone of five different colours, a ceiling adorned with gold leaf, huge chandeliers and a large gold cross that had been presented by Constantine and Empress Helena.

By the late fourth century St Peter's had its own great ceremonies, and on 29 June – the feast day of Peter and Paul – it became filled with huge crowds for whom quantities of food were made ready on tables. It was already much more than just a church, and by AD 408, like several other martyr churches, it formed the nucleus of a religious township, whose devout inhabitants wanted to live as close as they could to the saint's tomb. Most Romans, whether pagan or Christian, would still have found such a choice distasteful. Romans had long seen corpses as unclean things that should be kept well away from the living and buried outside the city. But times were beginning to change.

By AD 408 St Peter's was drawing in visitors from far away. Rome was already becoming a great pilgrimage site and its martyr churches had stolen the temple of Asclepius' role as a healing centre, attracting crowds of the sick, the blind and the disabled. They also drew those who believed they were possessed, who might be seen outside their doors, howling and barking like animals, writhing and twisting as they screamed the names of pagan gods – the demons they believed were within them – in the hope that the saint would drive them out. Most of all, though, pilgrims came in the hope that they might be forgiven their sins and improve their chances of reaching paradise. Saint Peter, as prince of the apostles, was believed to hold the keys to heaven. Feeling they were in the actual presence of a saint, pilgrims became highly excited and the city's great churches were carefully designed to keep them at a distance from martyrs' body parts. Visitors to the church of San Lorenzo could see his grave but were prevented from touching it by a heavy silver grille. Saint Peter was better protected still. Visitors unlocked a little gate to reach a kind of well into which they could lower a piece of cloth to the tomb below and then pull it up, supposedly heavier as it was now steeped with blessings.

This was the dawn of a new age of martyrs. On the wane were guardian angels, Christianity's first personal protectors, who were believed to shepherd individuals through life. By AD 408 Christians were looking increasingly to martyrs who, like pagan gods, offered specialist help, carrying one through every kind of dangerous situation, from a sea journey to childbirth. Martyrs, who were believed to have a

living presence in the churches that held their remains, were important
to their local towns, bringing them pilgrims and putting them on
the map. Competition was intense. In the Christian world Rome
was second only to Jerusalem as a pilgrimage centre, yet this had not
happened by accident and a good deal of work had been required.
When Christianity became the official religion of the Empire under
Constantine it was the cities of the Eastern Empire and North Africa
that were best provided with martyrs, as it was here that persecution
– which had been far less extensive than the Church liked to claim –
had been most thorough. By contrast Rome was poorly provided with
martyrs.

In the 370s and '80s AD an energetic bishop of Rome, Damasus,
remedied the situation by actively seeking out new martyrs. Some, like
San Agnese and San Lorenzo, he plucked from obscurity by giving
them a church in their name. Others, such as Saint Sebastian, were
foreign saints who had died in Rome and who – much to the annoyance
of the inhabitants of their home towns – Damasus now claimed for
the city. Even then Damasus needed more. He retrieved bones from
abandoned catacombs and came up with a new crowd of saints, some
of whom were barely remembered, and others who had never even
existed. Under Damasus' guardianship they were each provided with
a name, a feast day and an account in verse of their grisly death. Their
ends were memorably varied, from Saint Lawrence, who was grilled
to death on a large gridiron, to Saint Sebastian, who was shot full of
arrows and, when this failed to kill him, cudgelled to death. By the
end of Damasus' reign every road into Rome had a martyr's shrine or
catacombs for pilgrims to descend into, and the city was completely
encircled by dead Christian heroes, fictional or otherwise.

Yet the most important work to place Rome firmly at the top
of Christianity's hierarchy – at least after Jerusalem – had already
been done long before. At some unremembered moment during
Christianity's early, wilderness years, Rome's bishops claimed a unique
authority for themselves. They traced their office directly back to Jesus
himself, through the city's first bishop, Saint Peter, whom Jesus was

said to have anointed. It was no wonder that St Peter's was Rome's greatest church.

Yet there is some doubt as to whether the claim by Roman bishops was actually true. None of the early scriptures mention that Peter ever came to Rome. He fades from the record soon after Jesus' death. Rome's Christians claimed he came to the city with Saint Paul, but this seems a little unlikely. There are hints in the scriptures that Paul, who never met Jesus and who led the religion away from Jesus' brand of Judaism so that it could appeal to non-Jews, had strained relations with Jesus' disciples in Jerusalem. During the Second World War Pope Pius XII decided to do some investigating and had a German churchman, Ludwig Kaas, excavate the ancient cemetery beneath St Peter's. Sure enough, directly beneath the cathedral's altar Kaas found a plain tomb monument, yet his discovery brought more questions than answers. Among graffiti scratched into the walls Peter's name was written only once (by contrast, in the cemetery beneath San Lorenzo, Lawrence's name was scratched numerous times). Worse, the bones in the grave, which belong to a man in his sixties, appeared to date from the time not of Emperor Nero, when Peter was said to have died, but of Emperor Vespasian. Neither Pius nor Kaas were happy with the finds and the bones went missing for a while. It seems the claim on Saint Peter by Rome's early Christians may have been a case of sleight of hand.

If so, it was a dazzlingly successful one, which would be the making of Rome, keeping the city afloat during the long, difficult centuries that lay ahead. By AD 408 it did not matter who really lay in the simple grave far below the altar of St Peter's, as everyone believed it was Peter. He and Paul were fast stealing the role of Rome's protectors from that other alliterative pair, Romulus and Remus, and the great and the good sought to be buried in the city of Christianity's famous martyrs. Emperor Constantine built a complex for his family on the Via Nomentum, which included an exquisite circular church tomb for his daughter – Santa Costanza – filled with mosaics that were barely Christian, depicting birds, people treading grapes to make wine, and strange, staring blue faces. In AD 408 the Western Emperor Honorius had just completed a tomb complex for himself and his family beside St Peter's.

The direct link back to Jesus was also useful when it came to religious politics. At this time, Rome's bishops held sway all across the fracturing Western Empire and their supremacy was accepted by bishops from as far afield as Gaul, Spain and Britain. Though they were still not yet quite popes, they were on their way. They also lived very comfortably, at least according to the pagan historian Ammianus Marcellinus, who, in the late fourth century, reported that they rode in carriages, enjoyed splendid gifts from wealthy women, dressed in finery and outdid kings in the lavishness of their meals.

A post of this kind was clearly worth having and competition for it could be intense, even violent. In the late 360s AD, both Damasus and a rival, Ursinus, were proclaimed bishop of Rome in different parts of the city, and for two years the supporters of each launched raids against their opponents' churches. In one skirmish more than a hundred people were killed. The dispute seems not to have been theological but was instead a turf war between Christians on either side of the Tiber. The imperial authorities responded by prohibiting factional Christian meetings within twenty miles of the city, but it would take a lot more than a legal ban to prevent such disputes, which continued to dog Catholicism for the next thousand years.

Of course Rome in AD 408 was not only a city of government and religion. In many ways the functional side of the city – the machinery required to keep Romans fed, watered and clean – was every bit as impressive as its monuments. Rome's eleven aqueducts provided the city with the equivalent of a million bathtubs of water every day. As well as supplying numerous street fountains and – for a lucky few – fountains in private homes, the aqueducts also supplied Rome's eight hundred baths, large and small. Here was another opportunity for emperors to outdo their predecessors. In AD 408 the city had eleven great public baths. The greatest were those of Diocletian, built barely a century earlier, whose vast complex had required the demolition of an entire district of the city. Diocletian's baths were the size of a dozen football pitches and could accommodate 9,000 bathers in the open-air swimming pool, the cold hall, tepid hall and the spacious hot hall.

As well as bathing, Romans had to be fed. Between May and September AD 408 when the seas were calm, convoys of ships sailed across the Mediterranean, as they had done every summer for centuries, to Rome's main port. Here grain, olive oil, wine, fish sauce and every luxury the city could demand, from Chinese silks to spices from Sri Lanka and eastern Indonesia – lands so distant that the Romans knew of them only from hearsay – were unloaded into river barges, which were then hauled by slaves along 35 kilometres of winding Tiber river to Rome's river docks. Above these, on the left bank of the Tiber, stood a remarkable testament to the extent of Romans' appetite. It was a good-sized hill though it was like no other hill on earth. It was formed entirely from the remains of imported clay jars that were used to transport olive oil from Spain and the province of Africa. The jars could not be reused and so, after their contents were poured into barrels, they were broken in two and chucked on to the constantly growing heap.

At the docks, Rome's food supplies were transferred to handcarts, wheelbarrows or on to the backs of donkeys or slaves, but not into horse-drawn carts, not in daytime, anyway. Since the days of Julius Caesar such carts had been banned from Rome's streets except at night, to prevent the city becoming gridlocked. Earlier Roman writers complain that thanks to the carts' endlessly rattling through the hours of darkness, among many other disturbances, it was almost impossible for Romans to sleep, and though evidence concerning life in early fifth-century Rome is harder to come by, as sources are rarer, there is nothing to suggest that matters had changed. Considering the Romans' skills in organization and engineering, their city was surprisingly poorly designed. Most streets were very narrow, aside from a handful of main streets, and none of them were wide. Back lanes were crammed with rubbish. Fire was a constant danger and despite nightly patrols by firemen, blazes occurred with distressing regularity. The central area that contained most of the city's great monuments was not exempt and, even though they were protected by a huge firewall, in AD 283 the main Forum was burned to the ground. Rome's labyrinthine topography also made it a mugger's paradise and most Romans avoided going out at night without a bodyguard to see them safely home.

It was an option few Romans could afford. Here is something else that would have shocked our early republican. If Rome had been a place of social extremes in the 380s BC then it was far more so now. The city had never been so unequal, a situation that helped its barbarian attackers, as it diminished poorer Romans' sense of loyalty to their state. At the top end of the social scale were a small number of immensely wealthy Romans who formed a closely knit class of educated, interrelated families. Grouped around the Senate, theirs was a world not unlike that of Jane Austen's novels, in which parents sought good marriages for their daughters and a promising post in the army or in the imperial administration for their sons. Launching a son's career was an expensive business. A first rung on the ladder to power was one of the old republican offices – the quaestorship and praetorship – whose chief role was largely confined to staging lavishly expensive games. Fortunately, there were many who could pay the bills for such events, as Rome's great families were astonishingly wealthy. They owned landed estates that stretched across the Western Empire. They lived in huge town houses, of which some owned a dozen or more. The home of one wealthy family beneath Palazzo Valentini, which has been carefully excavated, was a vast pile, more than 1,800 square metres in area, that contained garden courtyards, stables, storerooms and even a private bath complex.

One of the pleasures of Rome's nobility was to hold dinner parties. Romans could dine out, as the city had hotels with dining rooms that catered to their needs, but overwhelmingly they entertained at home. Most of what is known about Roman banquets comes from two or three centuries earlier, but they still took place at the beginning of the fifth century and there is no reason to imagine they had greatly changed. They mixed formality with pure pleasure, and by all accounts they could be hugely enjoyable. Hosts and guests reclined on large couches – usually there were nine, sometimes eighteen and occasionally twenty-seven – and guests' proximity to their host's couch was decided by their status. Wives sat up next to their reclining husbands. Guests were welcomed with a glass of spiced wine or mead and wore wreaths (a tradition which was opposed by Christians and may have been dying out by AD 408). The air would have been thick with the smell of incense and perfume that was used by guests both female and male. Guests ate mostly with their fingers and might wipe their hands on a napkin that they had brought, or on the tablecloth, or in the hair of one of the serving boys, who were encouraged to grow it long for this purpose. Each dish was announced and all the while slaves would sing, dance, act, recite poetry, juggle and even fence to keep everyone entertained.

As to the dishes themselves, these were divided, rather as they still are in Rome, between a first course, a second course and a pudding, and classical Romans may have eaten an early form of pasta (Greek texts refer to something called *lasagnon*). Otherwise, though, imperial Roman and modern Italian cuisine have little in common. To our taste classical Roman dishes would be more Thai than Mediterranean. They would have been quite alien to a visitor from early republican Rome used to a simple diet of vegetables and an occasional binge on sacrificial meat, not least because they included something completely unknown to early republicans: sea fish. They were also highly flavoured. A popular ingredient, which seems to have been a Carthaginian invention, was a fermented fish sauce, garum, that probably tasted much like today's Thai and Vietnamese fish sauces. Roman cooking also used coriander and plentiful quantities of black pepper, giving it a spicy flavour. Many recipes would have been simpler than we might expect: cucumber salad, cauliflower with cumin, eggs with anchovies. Though at a grand feast one might be offered highly exotic items, such as dolphin balls, sausages of lobster and other fish, sow's womb and nipples, flamingo or ostrich ragout.

Eventually guests' hands were given a good wash and dishes were cleared away for some after-dinner enjoyment. This might be a session of drinking and conversation. One of the diners would be appointed to decide how much watered wine everyone could have without them becoming maudlin, aggressive or simply drunk. Also carefully controlled were the subjects discussed, and conversation would be halted if it grew too argumentative. Guests could recline and settle into some storytelling, or they could play a game, from backgammon, draughts and dice to something sillier, like trying to sink a little boat floating in a bucket by hurling wine at it.

The delights of a grand dinner, needless to say, were known to few Romans in AD 408. For most, life was very different. Ordinary Romans lived in apartment blocks that were not too different in structure and appearance from central Rome's apartment blocks today, though in terms of comfort they were far more basic. Beneath the main stairway was a shared latrine and residents regularly trudged up the stairs, carrying water, and down, carrying chamber pots. Five, six and even seven floors high, a single block contained a rainbow of social layers. The wealthiest residents – who might own the building – lived on the ground floor, where the haulage of fluids was fairly painless and where they probably had their meals prepared in a small, slave-run kitchen. The higher up the stairway one climbed, the worse everything became. A second-floor apartment had balconies and perhaps a simple portable stove or two on which to cook. Higher again and cooking became all but impossible, so people relied on the hot food bars that lined every street and which offered simple dishes similar to those consumed by early republicans eight centuries earlier: porridge, bread, bean stew and vegetables. The top floor was a slum crowded with inhabitants who endured leaking roofs and flimsy wooden walls that left them baking in summer and frozen in winter. And, of course, there was the constant fear of fire. The higher you lived, the less chance you had of saving yourself.

Another constant cause of fear was disease. Here, the Romans had some reasons to be thankful. The city's streets were kept fairly clean, its aqueducts left Romans relatively safe from waterborne diseases, and its baths would have reduced infestation by parasites. Still, the picture was far from good. Rome stank. As we have seen, apartment blocks were built above cesspits, and poorer Romans' homes were filthy. The city's six main sewers, filled with the discharges of baths, latrines, food stalls and every kind of workshop, flowed directly into the Tiber, which was so polluted that fish caught at sea within miles of its estuary were all but inedible. At dawn the air was fresh but it soon became filled with odours, dust and, most of all, with smoke that poured from the city's hot-food shops, from stoves and from its 800 bathhouses, large and small.

Mostly, Rome was unhealthy because it was large, crowded and cramped. Its huge population meant that measles, mumps, tuberculosis and smallpox were endemic. The city's greatest scourge, though, was malaria. A poem by the first-century AD satirist Juvenal reveals that Romans commonly became infected with three forms of malaria simultaneously. When, after months of dangerous fevers, they came down with quartan fever – the least dangerous, which until then had been masked by the other two – they knew they were finally on the mend. Judging by better documented times the city would have been struck by an intense malaria epidemic every half-dozen years, usually after heavy summer rainstorms. The disease was worst near the river, where mosquitoes thrived and which, naturally, was where the poorest Romans lived. Children were particularly at risk, as were visitors from the north, who lacked immunity.

All in all, Rome was not a healthy place. Figures from the early modern era reveal it was a population sieve, that needed constant replenishing with immigrants to keep up its numbers, and this was almost certainly true also at the start of the fifth century. Studies have estimated that classical Romans lived on average to around the age of 25 but it is probably more useful to distinguish two quite separate life expectancies. Most poor Romans would have lived considerably less long while the rich – many of whom lived far away from the malarial lowlands, on one of the seven hills, and who could leave the city for their country homes when the disease was at its worst in August and September – would have lived longer.

If sick, Romans who could afford it would visit a doctor. In AD 408 there were large numbers of these, from well-informed professionals to quacks. The better ones had studied the medical writings of Hippocrates and Galen, who, though they had some misleading notions, and claimed that bad health stemmed from an imbalance of the four humours, each of which could be too hot or too cold and too wet or too dry, also offered some good advice based on careful observation. Some doctors had studios in their homes, others had a shop on a street. Others again visited patients in their homes, carrying bronze boxes with sliding lids that were filled with remedies (of which some four-fifths have been calculated as having no medical value). Or one could bypass the medical profession entirely. The temple to Asclepius might be closed but one could turn to his successors and pray to a saint in his church.

Despite their city's unhealthiness, there were plenty of Romans. It is generally thought that at its height in the second century, Rome probably had a little over a million inhabitants, and possibly as many as a million and a half. The population is thought to have declined after AD 150, as the city was struck first by a plague (possibly smallpox) and then by political chaos and inflation during the Third Century Crisis, but then it appears to have recovered. Studies of records of food dole rations indicate that in the late fourth century the city still had a vast population, of at least 800,000, making it the largest city on earth.

Our early republican would be mystified by talk of dole rations. Rome had become a city of handouts. Food distribution centres across the town offered grain, oil, wine and pork. To modern eyes the logic of who was included in the lists of recipients seems odd, if not bizarre. Food was given out not to feed the desperate but rather to honour ordinary Romans for being Romans. The very poorest Romans were not on the lists and for them life would have been a grim round of begging, hunger and sleeping rough. Though change was beginning to come. During the last decades of the fourth century a new patron had begun to help them out: the Church.

But what, our early republican might ask, of the plebeians? What of their impressive political organization, their state within a state, that had had its own temples, archives, and strategy of strike action? All of this vanished during the later Republic and ordinary Romans had become politically neutered centuries before AD 408. Only when their food dole was cut, because of bad weather at sea or perhaps a usurping general in Africa, did they come to life, rioting, or burning down the house of the city prefect.

The root cause of their political powerlessness walked beside them: slaves. In the early Republic slaves were still relatively scarce – except after the capture of Veii – but at the height of the Empire they abounded. They came from across the Roman state and from far beyond its borders. Together with the city's free immigrants they made Rome as cosmopolitan as today's London or New York: a city where one might hear a dozen languages on a single street, from German to Syrian to Scythian. Slaves were found everywhere and did everything: they worked as house servants and house builders, as water haulers, prostitutes, shopkeepers, cooks, concierges, decorators, entertainers, jewellery makers and just about anything else one could think of. In the country, armies of slaves manned huge farming estates. Free Romans found their role undermined in all activities except warfare, and with it their political power.

In AD 406, just two years before Alaric appeared outside Rome, the city's slave markets would have been crowded. A large group of Goths, whose leader Radagaisus was less cautious than Alaric, raided Tuscany only to be trapped, starved and captured en masse by Stilicho. Though some had ended up in Stilicho's armies and, after his death, fled the anti-German pogroms to join Alaric, others remained captives inside the walls. This slave glut, though, was exceptional. In this era, as the Empire struggled to win battles and take prisoners, Rome's slave economy was firmly in decline. If very rich Romans had no difficulty procuring slaves, their poorer compatriots struggled to afford them. Romans were forced to look after themselves as they had been in republican times, six centuries earlier.

Another area where time seemed to be moving backwards was the family. A stroll through the city during its heyday in the first and second centuries AD would have given the impression that, in terms of the power balance between men and women, Romans' views had not changed much since the days of the harsh laws of the Twelve Tables in the fifth century BC. Few women would have been visible on the streets, while affluent Roman women rarely worked, and spent most of their time at home or visiting the homes of friends. Men, or their slaves, even did the shopping at the market and those women who did venture out often wore a veil, so Rome would have felt a little like some Middle Eastern cities today. Yet this impression would be misleading, as in many respects Roman society in its prime was quite modern. Rome's laws had changed greatly since its early days and women – or at least well-off women – frequently controlled their own inheritance, and kept it if they divorced. Many had no husbands to tell them what to do, as it was common for women to marry at around fifteen years of age, to men who were a decade or so older, so widowhood was common. Children, too, were much better off than they had been in early times. Affluent children were treated kindly by their parents, if not downright spoiled.

Yet by AD 408, as with the city's statues and inscriptions, family life was regressing. From the Third Century Crisis onwards a new traditionalism became fashionable. Women were again expected to behave modestly and with subservience towards men. One might ascribe this change to the rise of Christianity, whose values were intensely conservative but, curiously enough, it began several decades before Christianity's triumph. In fact, Christianity may have appealed in part because it matched a deeper cultural shift. As Rome was assailed by enemies, confidence became fragile and fears grew, and so people of the Empire turned to the past.

A similar transformation also occurred in sexual attitudes. At the height of the Empire, three centuries before Alaric's Visigoths appeared, Romans' views on sex seem to modern eyes both refreshingly open and lamentably brutal. Romans viewed sex positively, as a pleasure given to them by the gods that should be enjoyed. The enjoying of it was even thought to produce healthier children. Nor were Romans much troubled by what kind of sex it was, whether between males and females or males and males (though they were uneasy when it came to females and females). Compared to society today, Romans were uninterested in sexual categorization. If a man slept with a woman or a man that did not mean he was expected to keep doing the same thing. He could seek out pleasure wherever he saw it.

Yet Romans did have sexual taboos and, like so much else in classical Rome, these were all about class. For a rich Roman to sleep with another aristocrat's wife was adultery, but he was free to sleep with a social inferior. That was so long as the aristocrat was the active partner and the inferior an object of exploitation. Nobody greatly cared if a master, or mistress, made sexual use of their slaves, as they were his or her property. There were instances – regarded at the time as rather humorous – of Romans who saved on trips to the slave market by fathering their whole slave household. Likewise, Romans were not much bothered by the thought of men sexually abusing children so long as they were not the children of aristocrats.

This last attitude, which we find entirely unacceptable, probably did not exist at the time of the Gauls' sack of Rome in 387 BC. It appears to have been imported a couple of centuries later from the Greek east. Yet its acceptability was already waning by AD 408, as Christianity brought Near Eastern morality westwards. As exploitation of children became taboo, though, so did sexual openness. Saint Paul's Christianity regarded all but the plainest and most functional sexual activity as abhorrent, and *all* sex – let alone its enjoyment – was seen as highly doubtful. Devout early Christians idealized virginity, chastity and sexless marriages. The change could hardly have been more extreme.

Not that everybody thought in this way. Rome's rulers had been Christians for almost a century and, as we have seen, it was now a city of great churches, whose temples were shut for more than a decade, yet closed temples did not mean that pagan belief was dead. In all the Empire, Rome was the city where the old religions still survived most strongly. They held sway particularly among aristocrats who saw Rome's greatness and their own prestige as inseparable from her ancient beliefs.

As it happened, Alaric and his Visigoths arrived outside Rome at a fascinating moment. Though public pagan worship had been banned for more than a decade, both paganism and Christianity still had strong adherents among the city's elite. And in wealthy families, Christians and non-Christians dined side by side. There must have been tensions, especially when a family member changed loyalties, as the thinking of the two groups could hardly have been more different. While pagans looked to logic and philosophical argument, Christians looked to faith and their own intense emotion. Each side had good reason to view the other with a certain amount of disgust. To Christians, pagans were worshippers of demons who possessed and ruled them. To pagans, Christians defiled themselves with their love of cadavers. As the short-lived last pagan emperor, Julian, complained, 'You keep adding many corpses newly dead to the corpse of long ago. You have filled the whole world with tombs and sepulchres.'3

Yet struggles between the pagans and Christians in Rome seem to have been relatively civil (it was very different elsewhere). Battles were fought, most of all, over that favourite deity of early Rome, Victory. The Senate had an ancient tradition that before beginning the day's business they had to offer a sacrifice on an altar to Victory. Emperor Constantius II, Constantine's son and successor, had the statue of Victory removed, but when he visited Rome in AD 357 he was so impressed by the city's monuments that he ordered the statue to be brought back. A generation later, in AD 382, the emperor Gratian had Victory removed again. A leading pagan of the time, Symmachus, begged Gratian to change his mind, and became embroiled in a debate with the bishop of Milan, but he got nowhere. Victory did not return.

Some Roman Christians probably viewed Symmachus' efforts with sympathy. If both churchmen and devout pagans saw no room for compromise, many Romans strove to find a kind of religious middle ground, in which Christianity was seen as compatible, if not with pagan beliefs, then with a patriotic nostalgia for old pagan ways. Though the Empire had been ruled by Christians for a century – with a brief interlude under pagan Julian – in AD 408 paganism was still widely present in Romans' lives. To the disgust of zealous Bishop Ambrose in Milan, crowds of Romans, including Christians, continued to enjoy taking part in the city's old pagan festivals. Especially popular was Lupercalia, during which groups of young men ran round the city, honouring the she-wolf by striking young women with thongs, which was believed to make them fertile. Also hugely popular was the old midwinter pagan festival of Saturnalia, when Romans gave one another gifts, and servants and masters briefly exchanged roles. Likewise, most Romans saw nothing wrong with living surrounded by images of pagan gods, which still decorated the city's great monuments and stood in its closed temples. Schoolchildren continued to learn by heart the patriotic prophecy of the pagan god Jupiter, from Virgil's *Aeneid*, which foretold that Rome would endure without end. Even the emperors who acted against paganism had a contradictory attitude. Theodosius, who ordered Rome's old temples closed, also issued decrees ordering them to be protected. Churchmen might see these buildings as the devil's work but to Theodosius they were an important part of the Empire's heritage and his own prestige.

The greatest tensions, at least within Rome's aristocracy, were often not between pagans and Christians, but between both of them and a small group of intensely devout Christians. These were Christian ascetics: a circle, mostly female, that formed in the early 380s AD around an anti-materialist priest, Jerome, whose views even some Roman churchmen found extreme. Jerome (later Saint Jerome) was disgusted by the way Rome's wealthy Christians paid lip service to their beliefs while taking care to look after their dynastic needs. If they gave one daughter to Christ as a virgin they would keep another firmly in the world and, if need arose, they felt no qualms at taking Christ's virgin back and putting her on the market for a good marriage. Similarly, they saw nothing wrong in holding lavish dinner parties, using a handsome set of antique plates decorated with pagan symbols. And while they were delighted to give money to the poor – preferably in public view, outside St Peter's – they made sure to preserve their real wealth to pass on to the next generation.

Under Jerome's encouragement, women in his circle spurned such compromises. When widowed, they refused to remarry, even if this meant they left no heir, and they sought to give away their fortunes to the Church and the poor. Naturally this behaviour went down badly with their families, who saw it as a threat to all they held most dear: the continuance of their dynastic power. The first of Rome's ascetics, Marcella, was disinherited by her own mother in the 380s AD, to prevent her from disposing of the family's fortune. When Jerome's patron and protector, Bishop Damasus, died, Jerome was all but hounded out of the city.

Yet Rome's Christian ascetic movement continued without him. Just before the end of the fourth century a young couple brought it back to life: Valerius Pinianus and his wife Melania, whose grandmother – Melania the Elder – had been one of Jerome's circle. Melania the Younger, after nearly dying in childbirth, became determined to give up all her worldly goods. A glance at what she and her husband sought to be rid of reveals how astonishingly unequal late Roman society had become. At a time when most Romans lived on handouts and many lacked even these, Melania's husband alone had an annual income of at least 2,000 pounds of gold. This was half the amount that Alaric sought for all his Visigoths from the Western Roman Empire. Pinianus owned a house on the Caelian Hill in Rome that was so valuable it was beyond the means even of the Western Emperor Honorius' niece. Between them Melania and Pinianus possessed estates that extended across the Western Roman Empire, in southern Italy, Sicily, Spain, Tunisia, Algeria, Morocco and Britain.

Melania and Pinianus' desire to give it all away played a part in bringing Alaric to Rome. Their efforts were blocked in the courts, which were run by their fellow aristocrats, which decided that Melania, though twenty years old, was still too young to make such a rash decision. Frustrated, Melania and Pinianus decided to pull a few strings. In late 407 or early 408 AD, when the imperial court paid its rare visit to Rome, they asked Stilicho's wife Serena to appeal to Emperor Honorius on their behalf. Serena was sympathetic and managed to win Honorius round. It was at the very same meeting of the Senate, where Stilicho gained the senators' agreement to pay off Alaric – with their own gold – which elicited Lampadius' famous outburst that it was not peace but servitude, that the Senate also found itself approving Melania and Pinianus' act of class betrayal. By making high-ranking enemies Serena's intervention may well have contributed to her husband Stilicho's downfall, which in turn left Alaric a patronless loose cannon.

Melania and Pinianus did not linger. Having tried and failed to sell Pinianus' sumptuous town house to the emperor Honorius' niece, they set in motion the sale of their Italian, Gallic, Spanish and British estates and then sailed away to Africa. By this point they were probably far from welcome in Rome. As events turned out, their timing could not have been better. Just a few months after they left, Alaric and his Visigoths had sealed off the city and cut all traffic on the Tiber.

III

The Romans were baffled by the vast horde that appeared below the city walls. The Visigoths had moved so rapidly that they arrived without warning, and at first the Romans wondered if they were a force of Roman auxiliaries that one of Stilicho's generals was leading against the Empire. Even when they realized the truth, the Romans were optimistic. It was true that, thanks to Emperor Constantine having spitefully disbanded the city's cavalry regiment and the Praetorian Guard a century previously, they had no garrison, yet they were confident that the Empire would come to their rescue. How could it not when it had itself been created by Rome? It seemed unimaginable that the city would be left to its fate. There was also the matter of who was in Rome. Alaric's arrival had been so sudden that nobody had had a chance to escape. As well as some of the wealthiest landowners in the Empire, there were several celebrities of the era, including Stilicho's widow, Serena, the widow of the emperor Gratian, and also Galla Placidia, emperor Honorius' sister.

But nobody came to Rome's rescue. Emperor Honorius did not dare intervene. A new usurper, Constantine III from Britain, had recently set up camp in Arles, just over the Alps, ready to pounce into Italy, and Honorius feared – probably rightly – that if he sent troops to Rome he would give Constantine his chance. With 800,000 or more Romans in the besieged city, conditions quickly began to deteriorate. The city prefect cut the bread ration to half and then to a third. People went hungry. After eight centuries of ladling out punishment to enemies near and far, the Romans, who had thought themselves immune from disaster, now found they were at the sharp end of things. The shock must have been tremendous. Romans' first instinct was to find a scapegoat. Stilicho's widow Serena, who was doubtless still resented by wealthy Romans for having helped Melania and Pinianus with their great inheritance giveaway, was accused, groundlessly, of having drawn the enemy to Rome and, in the hope that Alaric might lose interest once she was gone, she was strangled to death. But, of course, Alaric had not come for Serena: he had come for treasure and to win a settlement for his people. The siege went on. Emperor Gratian's widow and her mother distinguished themselves by distributing food but, with hundreds of thousands of mouths to feed, charity could not do much. Hunger turned to famine and then, as people grew weaker, disease struck. As ancient laws forbade burials within the city, bodies were left in the open and a terrible stench filled the air.

By now word of what was happening had spread. The Empire had suffered its fair share of catastrophes during previous decades, but still the news caused profound shock. The Christian thinker Augustine of Hippo at first refused to believe the rumours. By contrast, ascetic Jerome in the Holy Land was happy to enjoy a little *Schadenfreude* towards the Romans who had flung him out, and decided that their hunger was a just punishment for having lived so extravagantly. They were certainly suffering. The pagan historian Zozimus wrote, '… the distress was now arrived in such an extremity that they were now in danger of being eaten by one another. They tried all methods of support which are abominable in the eyes of mankind.'[4] No rat or cat was safe. Eventually the city's desperate authorities decided to send an embassy to Alaric. The Romans took an aggressive line, claiming that the city's inhabitants had been training for war and were ready to sally forth and attack. The encounter inspired an account that offers a rare, brief glimpse of Alaric's personality, though whether it holds much truth is doubtful, as it seems a cliché of barbarian arrogance that could have been ascribed to Brennus, eight centuries earlier:

> When Alaric heard … that the people had been training to fight and were ready for war, he remarked, 'The thickest grass is more to easy to cut than the thinnest.' He then laughed immoderately at the ambassadors … He declared that he would raise the siege only if he was given all the gold and silver in the city, all the household goods, and all the Barbarian slaves. When one of the ambassadors observed, 'If you take all these, what will you leave for the citizens?' Alaric replied, 'Their Souls.'[5]

It was at this moment that the Roman authorities did something rather interesting. They looked to their past. As Zozimus wrote,

> Pompeianus, the prefect of the city met by chance with some people who had come to Rome from Tuscany, and who explained how their town, Neveia had saved itself from great danger. The Barbarians were driven back from it by storms of thunder and lightning, which had come because of the inhabitants' devotion to the ancient gods. Having talked with these men, he performed all that was in his power according to the books of the chief priests.[6]

Pompeianus then got cold feet. Realizing that he could find himself in a good deal of trouble for what he had done, he consulted the bishop of Rome, Innocentius. Rather surprisingly, Innocentius gave the nod to making an appeal to the devil's agents. Things must have been very bad. The sources differ as to what took place next, each picking a narrative that showed their religion was not to blame for what happened afterwards. According to pagan Zozimus, when senators realized that tradition required them to make public sacrifices on the Capitoline Hill and in markets of the city, they lost heart. By contrast the Christian writer Sozomen claimed the sacrifices were made but were useless.

Reluctantly the Roman authorities sent a second delegation to Alaric. They returned with the news that, like Brennus before him, Alaric was willing to be paid off, though his price made Brennus' demand seem a bargain. Alaric wanted 5,000 pounds of gold, 30,000 pounds of silver, 4,000 silk robes, 3,000 scarlet fleeces and 3,000 pounds of pepper. He also wanted all slaves of barbarian origin in the city, who would have included Radagaisus' captured Goths. Additionally, he wanted the sons of a number of high imperial figures as hostages. There was nothing for the Romans to do but pay. The only ones who could come up with such a ransom were the city's wealthy and an emergency tax was calculated on their estates, but Rome's rich obfuscated, hiding their fortunes. Desperate, Pompeianus resorted to an act that appalled Zozimus:

> The evil genius who presided over the human race at that time then incited the persons employed in the transaction to the highest pitch of wickedness. They resolved to supply the deficiency from the ornaments that were about the statues of the gods ... they not only robbed the statues of their ornament, but also melted down those that were made of gold and silver. Among these was that of Valour or Fortitude, which the Romans call Virtus. This having been destroyed, all that remained of the Roman valour and intrepidity was wholly extinguished.[7]

Yet the melted statues did the trick. Alaric was paid and Rome was
saved. The crisis, though, was far from over. During the next year it
went through a number of complex evolutions in which the city was
always the loser. Alaric took his loot, and his forces, swelled by freed
Gothic slaves, withdrew to Tuscany, only to find that the imperial
court at Ravenna was still locked in belligerence: Emperor Honorius
refused to make a peace deal and would not even hand over hostages.
In the autumn of AD 409 Alaric marched south and besieged Rome
for the second time in a year, but this time he tried a new tack and
appealed to the Romans to take his side against their emperor. The
Romans, faced with another dose of famine, agreed. So the Senate
chose their own usurper emperor, an ambitious aristocrat from the
east named Attalus.

For a short time, Rome was not the besieged but the besieger, as
Attalus, Alaric and the Visigoths surrounded Honorius in Ravenna.
Honorius was on the point of fleeing when he received reinforcements
from the Eastern Empire. Safe now behind his swamp, he began to
squeeze his attackers, ordering the governor of Africa to stop food
convoys sailing to Rome. So, for the second or third time in just over a
year, Romans starved, now thanks to the efforts of their own emperor.
Merchants hoarded grain to force prices even higher and so add to
their profits, and as Zozimus recounts, 'By these means the city was
reduced to such extremities that some persons, as if they wished that
human flesh might be eaten, cried out in the Hippodrome, "Fix a
price on human flesh."'[8]

Alaric was as far as he ever was from gaining the peace deal he
wanted. In July 410 AD he sacked his puppet emperor, Attalus, and
travelled north to negotiate directly with Honorius, but instead of
gaining a deal he was ambushed. As he waited outside Ravenna
to begin negotiations he was attacked by a fellow Visigoth named
Sarus, who was probably an old rival for the Visigothic throne.
Whether Honorius had sent Sarus against him is unknown but
Alaric, who emerged unscathed, clearly thought so. In August he
once again marched on Rome. This time, finally, he got inside. As

to how the Visigoths overcame Rome's high new walls, the church historian Sozomen tells us that, 'Impelled by rage and terror at this incident, Alaric retraced his steps, returned to Rome and took it by treachery.'[9] The Visigoths did not need to break down walls or dig tunnels or climb scaling ladders. Somebody opened the gates and let them in.

As to who it was, the only narrator who offers an answer is Procopius of Caesarea, an Eastern Roman historian who wrote a century and a half after the events, though he offers too many answers. According to Procopius, Alaric, finding himself thwarted outside Rome once again, came up with an ingenious plan. He gathered together 300 Visigothic beardless youths who were chosen both for their courage and their good birth. Ambassadors were then sent to the Roman Senate to explain that Alaric was so impressed by the senators' bravery that he had decided to raise the siege and give them each some beardless youth slaves as a gift. The senators, suspecting nothing, accepted their presents and watched as the Visigoths outside the walls began to pack up to leave:

> But when the appointed day had come, Alaric armed his whole force for the attack and held them in readiness close by the Salarian Gate where they had been encamped from the beginning of the siege. At the time agreed upon, the youths came to the gate and, taking the guards by surprise, killed them all. They then opened the gates and received Alaric and the army into the city at their leisure.[10]

Perhaps realizing that this story might seem a little far-fetched, Procopius then offered an alternative:

> But some say that Rome was not captured in this way by Alaric, but that Proba, a woman of unusual eminence in wealth and fame among the Roman senatorial class, felt pity for the Romans who were being destroyed by hunger and other

suffering. For already they were tasting each other's flesh. And seeing that every good hope had left them, since both the river and the harbour were held by the enemy, she commanded her domestics, they say, to open the gates by night.[11]

This second version may seem far more plausible than the first, yet it, too, is open to doubt. It could have been fabricated by Proba's enemies, of whom she would have had many. Anicia Faltonia Proba, to give her full name, was a member of one of Rome's wealthiest families, the Anicii, who had opposed the selection of Attalus as emperor. She was also a Christian ascetic and kept a small colony of virgins in her home; some suspected she was intending to follow Melania's example and give away her fortune. Yet even if Proba was innocent, Procopius' second account may offer some truth as to what happened. Whoever opened the gate may have done so because they could not endure the prospect of yet another siege.

So, in the heat of a summer's night, on AD 24 August 410, Alaric's stinking, lice-ridden Visigoths poured through the Salarian Gate and into the city. As to what happened next, the sources who describe the actual sack – all of whom were Christian – agree that the occupation was brief, lasting only three days. That, though, is about the only thing they agree on. Their accounts are so much at odds, in fact, that one could be excused for wondering if they are describing the same event.

The church historian Socrates of Constantinople, writing three decades after the sack, reports that numerous senators were killed and that most of the city's monuments were burned. Likewise, Procopius, writing a century later again, states that the Visigoths destroyed most of the Romans. It is ascetical Jerome, though, writing in his home in the Holy Land just two years after the sack, who offers the most apocalyptic version of what took place. He states that by the time Alaric's Visigoths entered the city most of the inhabitants had already died of famine:

A nineteenth-century imagining of Alaric's entrance into Rome.

In their frenzy the starving people had recourse to hideous food and tore each other limb from limb that they might have flesh to eat. Even the mother did not spare the babe at her breast. In the night was Moab taken, in the night did her wall fall down. Oh God, the heathen have come into your inheritance. Your holy temple they have defiled. They have made Jerusalem an orchard. The dead bodies of your servants are meat for the fowls of the heavens, the flesh of your saints is taken by the beasts of the earth. Their blood they have shed like water round about Jerusalem, and there were none to bury them. Who can tell of the carnage of that night? What tears are equal to its agony? A sovereign city of ancient date has fallen, and lifeless in its streets and houses lie numberless bodies of its citizens.[12]

Another source, Orosius, who wrote eight years after the sack, probably in Spain, painted a very different picture, reporting that the sack involved little if any loss of life, and was instead a remarkable example of Christian charity. Orosius claims that Alaric went to great lengths to protect the Romans, especially Christian Romans, from danger:

> [Alaric] gave orders that all those who had taken refuge in sacred places, especially in the basilicas of the holy Apostles Peter and Paul, should be permitted to remain inviolate and unmolested; he allowed his men to devote themselves to plunder as much as they wished, but he gave orders that they should refrain from bloodshed.[13]

Orosius then tells a story of a Visigoth who found an elderly Christian virgin taking refuge in a church and demanded she give him her gold and silver. The elderly virgin brought out great quantities of both but then warned the Visigoth that they were the sacred plate of Saint Peter, and that if he took it, he would be punished by God. The Visigoth then

> ordered that all the vessels, just as they were, should be brought back immediately to the basilica of the Apostle, and that the virgin also, together with all Christians who might join the procession, should be conducted thither under escort. The building, it is said, was at a considerable distance from the sacred places, with half the city lying between. Consequently the gold and silver vessels were distributed, each to a different person; they were carried high above the head in plain sight, to the wonder of all beholders. The pious procession was guarded by a double line of drawn swords; Romans and barbarians.[14]

The church historian Sozomen, writing a little after Orosius, offered another story of a Visigoth with a good heart. Having drawn his sword to rape a beautiful Christian woman, he was taken aback when she offered him her neck:

> For she preferred to die in her chastity than to survive, after having consorted lawfully with a husband, and then to be

attempted by another man. When the barbarian repeated his purpose, and followed it with more fearful threats, he accomplished nothing further; struck with wonder at her chastity, he conducted her to the church of Peter the apostle, and gave six pieces of gold for her support to the officers who were guarding the church, and commanded them to keep her for her husband.[15]

As to how such different accounts could be written, all by Christians, the explanation is that they represented two wholly different responses to what had happened. The advocates of a brutal sack, including Jerome – who was doubtless still smarting at the wealthy Romans who had driven him out of their city – saw the disaster as divine punishment of the Romans for their luxury and paganism. In Jerome's eyes the sack must have been terrible because that was what the Romans deserved. By contrast, those who supported the gentle sack looked to a bigger political picture. They wanted to counter pagan accusations that the sack had taken place because the Romans had closed the temples to their old gods and melted down their images. This second group wanted to show that Peter and Paul had done a good job protecting the city and that, thanks to their lobbying, God had softened the hearts of the Visigoths.

So much for propaganda. What actually happened? Archaeology has no religious affiliations and so should provide some more reliable answers. In a living city like Rome excavations are necessarily patchy, but they have nevertheless yielded some interesting discoveries. A good number of hurried human burials from this time have been discovered around the Colosseum. As most Romans felt repugnance towards allowing the living and the dead to mix, and burying corpses inside cities was prohibited, these give a glimpse of the horror of the city's sieges.

And the sack? Buildings in the monumental centre that are known to have been damaged around this time include the huge Basilica Aemilia in the main Forum, which was largely burned out, along with the nearby secretariat of the Senate House and the Forum of Peace, both of which are mentioned by the sources as being targets of Visigothic violence. Several of the city's great mansions were also badly affected. A house on the Caelian Hill that belonged to the Valerii family was damaged and abandoned afterwards. The Domus Gaudentius, also on the Caelian, was transformed into stables, workshops and poor-quality housing. Finally, Procopius, writing 150 years later, tells us that the home of the early imperial historian, Sallust, which was just inside the Salarian Gate, was partially burned down and was still unrepaired when he visited Rome.

It is not a very long list. So far, Orosius and the friendly sacking group seem to be closer to the truth. One can almost picture the scene. Before they entered the city, Alaric commanded his Visigoths to behave themselves. Such an approach would fit with his cautious nature. If he destroyed Rome the city would lose all value as a bargaining counter and he would have little chance of striking a deal with the Western Empire. In spite of his orders, when the Visigoths poured in through the Salarian Gate some of them grew over-excited at having finally entered the city after repeated frustrating sieges, and they burned down a few houses close to the gate, including that of Sallust.

They then made their way into the city centre and enjoyed a little further catharsis. The secretariat of the Senate would have suffered because of its connection with the city's rulers, who, having changed sides twice – supporting Honorius, Attalus and then Honorius again – would not have impressed the Visigoths. The Basilica Aemilia was close by and might have caught fire by accident. As to the Forum of Peace, there is no mystery as to why this was attacked. For three centuries it had housed the great menorah and other valuables that had been looted by the Roman commander Titus from the Great Temple of Jerusalem in AD 70. We know that the Visigoths made off with these objects after the sack. Finally, the Visigoths looted a few of the city's great houses, lighting a fire or two as they went.

All in all, Rome had a lucky escape in AD 410. Compared to the fate of other cities that were sacked at this time, which saw extensive arson and their inhabitants enslaved, Rome got off very lightly indeed. Yet we should not underestimate what happened. Orosius' and Sozomen's stories of soft-hearted Visigoths are probably far from the mark. Archaeological work has uncovered a good number of inscriptions recording rebuilding work that dates from just after the Visigothic attack. Rome was still capable of restoring itself, and some destruction may have escaped notice because it was repaired.

Passages in some sources hint at the brutality of the event. The papal history, *Liber Ponficalis*, reports that the barbarians carried away a 2,000-pound silver tabernacle, which was not the act of good Christian Samaritans. Augustine of Hippo, who responded to the sack from North Africa in a series of sermons, from which grew his famous work, *City of God*, mentions that Roman refugees were present in his congregation. They would hardly have fled their city if the sack had been a non-event. In a passage that now seems decidedly sinister, Augustine also addresses Roman virgins who had been raped during the sack, insisting that God had not misjudged them or let them down, and insinuating that they may have brought rape upon themselves for having been excessively proud of their virginity.

Telling details have also survived relating to a number of individual Romans – all of them wealthy ascetic Christians – who were caught up in the sack. The palatial house of Melania's husband Pinianus, on the Caelian Hill, was left so badly damaged by the Visigoths that it was all but worthless. Anicia Faltonia Proba, too, saw her splendid home partially ruined, while the Visigoths also made off with all her virgins. If she had let them into the city, as Procopius claimed, they were very ungrateful. Finally, there is the story of the very first of Rome's ascetics, Marcella, who in AD 410 was an old woman. Her tale was recounted by Jerome, in a letter to Marcella's friend Principia, but which was clearly intended for general circulation. It was in this same letter that Jerome made melodramatic claims that starving Romans had torn one another limb from limb, yet the passage concerning Marcella is calmer and has a strong ring of truth. He tells of how a group of Visigoths broke into Marcella's house demanding gold:

She pointed to her coarse dress to show them that she had no buried treasure. However they would not believe in her self-chosen poverty, but scourged her and beat her with cudgels. She is said to have felt no pain but to have thrown herself at their feet and to have pleaded with tears for you [Principia] that you might not be taken from her, or owing to your youth have to endure what she as an old woman had no occasion to fear.[16]

Marcella died just a few days later. Her badly damaged home was never repaired. Perhaps the most telling account of the sack is by one of the few writers who was actually there. This was an austere British monk named Pelagius, whose ideas would develop into a heresy that Augustine of Hippo became much involved in stamping out. In a letter to a Roman woman he described how it had felt: 'Everyone was mingled together and shaken with fear: every household had its grief and an all-pervading terror gripped us. Slave and noble were one. The same spectre of death stalked before us all.'[17]

And then after three days, to the great relief of the Romans, the Visigoths left the city and marched south. Alaric hoped to travel to Sicily and then go on to Africa but he was unable to cross the Straits of Messina. Two months later he died in Cosenza, probably of malaria contracted in Rome. The city had had its revenge. His tomb has yet to be discovered, though attempts continue to be made. If it ever is found, it is very doubtful that it will contain more than a few trinkets. Among Germanic tribes plunder bought loyalty and power, and was far too important to bury in the ground.

For a time the Visigoths' light burned brightly. Alaric's brother-in-law and successor, Ataulf, led them out of Italy to Gaul where, in Narbonne, he made a brief and unsuccessful attempt to found his own imperial dynasty, marrying part of the loot taken from Rome: Emperor Honorius' sister, Gallia Placidia. Her wedding gifts were said to include the treasures of the temple of Jerusalem that the Visigoths had seized in Rome – further evidence that Himmler was wasting his time. In AD 418 the Visigoths finally succeeded where Alaric had failed and made a treaty with Rome that gave them a permanent homeland within the Empire, in Aquitaine. For several decades they were the Romans' firmest allies and they fought side by side at the Western Empire's last great battle in AD 452, at the Catalaunian Fields, close to Troyes, where they drove back Attila and his Huns. Several decades later, as the Western Empire went down for the third time, the Visigoths created an empire of their own, which included most of Iberia. Here they merged with the local aristocracy and finally abandoned their heretical Christianity for orthodox Christianity. But they lost all in AD 711, when Muslim Arabs invaded. They are last heard of in the mountains of the Asturias in the far north of Spain, where they formed part of a small local resistance group, from which would eventually grow the Spanish Reconquista.

As to Rome, though the city had not been destroyed, it had still endured quite a mauling. Many Romans had died in the famines, while others had fled and had no wish to go back. The city's pork supply lists indicate that in AD 419 the population was still little more than half what it had been before the sack. No less serious was the damage done to the city's reputation. After AD 410 the prophecy of Jupiter from Virgil's *Aeneid*, that every Roman schoolboy learned by heart, and which boasted that Rome would endure without end, seemed very hollow. The most devastating blow to Rome's self-image as the civilizer of the world came from North Africa. The shock disaster of the sack inspired Augustine of Hippo to attack the whole moral basis of Roman power. Citing examples of Rome's early history – from the same Livy who described Brennus' sack – Augustine argued that the Roman Empire was no different or better than other empires that had preceded it, and he claimed that, rather than being founded to bring civilization to the world, it had been built from a simple lust for domination. The Veiians would have agreed with him. If Christians wanted an eternal city, Augustine urged, they should look to the Heavenly City of Jerusalem that awaited them in the sky. No earthly city, including Rome, would endure for ever.

Still, Romans could count themselves lucky that things had not been worse. In many ways the city recovered surprisingly quickly from its disaster. A year after the sack the would-be imperial usurper across the Alps, Constantine III, was dead and the emperor Honorius was finally able to leave Ravenna. He visited Rome to celebrate games and to encourage people who had fled to return, which many did. In AD 414 the urban prefect, Albinus, wrote to Honorius requesting that grain supplies be increased, as they were no longer enough to feed the city. Rome's population might have halved but it was still the largest and greatest city in Western Europe, if not in all of Europe. Most of its great monuments had survived unscathed and in AD 418 Orosius complained that from the way Romans talked and acted one would think that nothing had happened.

It was a pretence that would not be possible for long.

CHAPTER THREE

MORE GOTHS

I

Tʜᴇsᴇ ᴅᴀʏs ᴛʜᴇ ᴛɪɴʏ ɪsʟᴀɴᴅ of Martana in Lake Bolsena, 120 kilometres north of Rome, cannot be visited. Crescent-shaped, like an upturned new moon, it is privately owned and its only inhabitant is the custodian who watches over the island's few buildings and cares for the gardens. If you are curious and have money to burn, a boat can be hired from the nearby port of Marta that will tour you around the island so you can see its rocky, wooded shore.

By all accounts almost nothing remains from the one time Martana achieved notoriety, in ᴀᴅ 535. There are a few steps on the shore that the Ostrogothic princess Amalasuntha might have walked on when she was brought to the island at the end of April that year. Remnants of walls could be the ruins of the building where she was held prisoner. We have no idea if, a few weeks after she arrived, she saw the boat that set out from the shore of the lake. Having ruled all of Italy, Sicily and a good part of the western Balkans for eight years, she would have had a shrewd understanding of the politics of her age and, if she did see it, she probably guessed

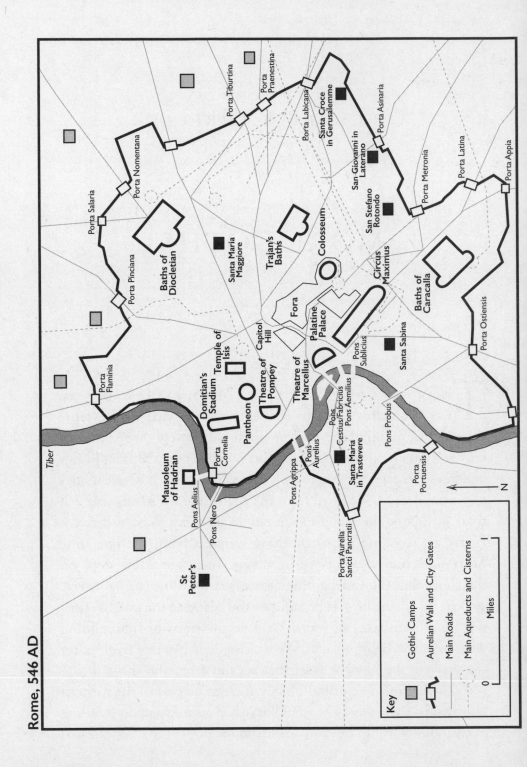

Rome, 546 AD

Tiber

Mausoleum
of Hadrian

St
Peter's

Pons Aelius
Pons Nero

Porta
Cornelia

Pons Agrippa
Pons
Aurelius

Pons
Cestius/Fabricius
Pons Aemilius

Santa Maria
in Trastevere

Pons Probus

Porta Aurelia
Sancti Pancratii

Porta
Portuensis

Domitian's
Stadium

Pantheon

Temple of
Isis

Theatre of
Pompey

Theatre of
Marcellus

Capitol
Hill

Pons
Sublicius

Santa Sabina

Porta
Flaminia

Porta Salaria

Porta Pinciana

Baths of
Diocletian

Porta Nomentana

Porta Tiburtina

Porta
Praenestina

Santa Maria
Maggiore

Trajan's
Baths

Fora

Palatine
Palace

Colosseum

Circus
Maximus

Porta Labicana

Santa Croce
in Gerusalemme

San Giovanni in
Laterano

San Stefano
Rotondo

Porta Asinaria

Porta Latina

Porta Metronia

Porta Appia

Baths of
Caracalla

Porta Ostiensis

N

Key

Gothic Camps

Aurelian Wall and City Gates

Main Roads

Main Aqueducts and Cisterns

0   Miles

its significance. Sure enough, those on board, who were Ostrogoths like herself, were coming to kill her. What she could not have guessed were the consequences that would follow from her murder. It would be used to justify an invasion of her former kingdom, and would lead to one of the most destructive wars in Italy's violent history. At its centre would be Rome. In March 537, less than two years after Amalasuntha died, a huge army of Amalasuntha's Gothic compatriots appeared outside the city, determined to retake what they saw as rightfully theirs.

Like their cousins the Visigoths, the Ostrogoths' journey to Italy had been a long one. We have already glimpsed them once, if briefly, 150 years before Amalasuntha met her death. When the Visigoths' ancestors were camped by the Danube, begging the Roman Empire to give them sanctuary from the Huns, the ancestors of the Ostrogoths were taking their chances outside the imperial borders, in Central Europe. Things did not go easily for them. While Alaric's followers were enjoying their time in the sun, raiding their way round the Mediterranean, their Gothic cousins were subjugated by the Huns, who occupied the Hungarian Plain. For two generations they were Hun vassals, required to grow their crops and fight their wars.

When the Huns' empire finally collapsed in the 450s, their servants broke free. Living on the fringes of the Eastern Roman Empire, in today's Bulgaria and former Yugoslavia, they underwent the same process of amalgamation that the Visigoths had gone through, as different tribes fused together to form a force large enough to stand up to the Eastern Romans, and to threaten them into handing over food and gold. In the 480s they became united under a single leader, Theodoric. Their name, Ostrogoths, which meant Eastern Goths, was not their own choice but was given to them by the Roman authorities, to distinguish them from the Visigoths. The Eastern Roman Emperor of the time, Zeno, was understandably nervous of this new power bloc on his doorstep and his anxiousness in turn made Theodoric uneasy. Theodoric knew how skilled the Eastern Empire could be at setting Goths at one another's throats. Zeno might prise their fragile new federation apart. Most of all Theodoric feared that Zeno might connive in having him assassinated.

In 488, Zeno and Theodoric agreed on a solution that suited both sides. Theodoric should lead his Ostrogoths to Italy. As far as Zeno was concerned, it was up for grabs. A decade earlier, in 476, Odovacar, the Germanic leader of the remnants of the imperial army in Italy – an army that was now almost entirely made up of barbarians – decided that the Western Roman Empire, which was largely a dead letter, should finally be laid to rest. With Zeno's tacit approval, Odovacar deposed the last Western Roman Emperor, Romulus Augustulus, and sent him into retirement near Naples. Zeno now proposed that Theodoric oust Odovacar and rule what he could seize of the Western Empire as his, Zeno's, viceroy. As Alaric had done eighty years earlier, Theodoric organized his people in a vast convoy of wagons, and they trekked across the Balkans, fighting another barbarian people, the Gepids, who blocked their path, to reach the Julian Alps and then the Po valley. Getting rid of Odovacar did not prove easy, but after besieging him in Ravenna for three years Theodoric eventually settled matters by negotiating a truce and then, at a celebratory banquet, personally slicing him in two. For the next thirty-three years Theodoric ruled Italy and an expanding list of territories, which he did more efficiently than any Roman emperor had done for centuries, as king of the Ostrogoths and viceroy of the Eastern Empire.

Theodoric, though, had a problem. He had two daughters but no sons. Germanic peoples were more open to the idea of female rulers than the Romans, but only just. Theodoric did what he could. He made sure his daughters were well educated – Amalasuntha became fluent in Gothic, Latin and Greek – and well married. Amalasuntha's husband was a high-ranking Ostrogothic warrior, Eutharic, by whom she had soon had a son, Athalaric. Unfortunately, Eutharic, who might have acted as a stand-in leader till their son came of age, then died. In 526, so did Amalasuntha's father, King Theodoric. Amalasuntha was evidently an able politician. For eight years she ruled as regent on behalf of her young son, countering the plots of disgruntled Ostrogothic nobles, and also of her cousin, Theodohad, who had political ambitions of his own. Then in 534 disaster struck. Amalasuntha's son Athalaric, who was now fourteen years old, died. Her position as the kingdom's ruler was gravely undermined.

The blow could hardly have come at a worse moment. Having come close to collapse the previous century, the Eastern Roman or Byzantine Empire was finally experiencing better times and was stronger than it had been for generations. Its emperor, Justinian, decided it was time to rebuild the old empire, at least in part, by reconquering its lost, western lands. In 533 he sent his ablest general, Belisarius, against the Germanic Vandals in modern Tunisia, whom Belisarius overcame with surprising ease. Encouraged, Justinian turned his eyes to Ostrogothic Italy.

For all that happened next we rely heavily on one account: *A History of the Wars*, by Procopius of Caesarea; so much so that we should know a little about the man. He is the same Procopius who told us that Alaric entered Rome by means of a commando unit of beardless youths. Fortunately, he is far more plausible when it comes to great events of his own time, many of which he witnessed at first hand. Having worked as a lawyer and rhetorician in Constantinople, he then accompanied Belisarius as his private secretary during his campaigns in Africa and Italy. Later, Procopius returned to Constantinople, where he wrote a highly sycophantic account of the emperor Justinian's building campaign in the city, *Buildings*. The sycophancy proved effective and he was raised to the high rank of *Illustris*. Procopius, though, was living dangerously. He had written a third book, which, wisely, he kept secret. In the *Anecdota*, better known as *The Secret History*, he vented his frustrations with the elite of the Eastern Empire, and especially the emperor and empress.

In Procopius' clandestine account Justinian is depicted as 'insincere, crafty, hypocritical, dissembling his anger, double-dealing, clever, a perfect artist in acting out an opinion which he pretended to hold' and, 'a fickle friend, a truceless enemy, an ardent devotee of assassination and of robbery'. Yet Justinian gets off relatively lightly compared to his empress, Theodora. According to Procopius she first came to Justinian's notice as one of Constantinople's most notorious prostitutes:

> The girl had not a particle of modesty, nor did any man ever see her embarrassed, but she undertook shameless services without the least hesitation, and she was the sort of a person who, for instance, when being flogged or beaten over the head, would crack a joke over it and burst into a loud laugh; and she would undress and exhibit to any who chanced along both her front and her rear naked.[2]

Even Belisarius, whom Procopius praises in *History of the Wars*, comes in for criticism, notably for being in thrall to his unfaithful, devious, sorceress wife, Antonina, who was a close friend of empress Theodora. Overall, though, the impression left by the *History of the Wars* and *The Secret History* together is that Belisarius was resourceful, brave and, when compared to other imperial commanders of the time, ungrasping.

Procopius tells us how, after her son died, Amalasuntha tried to shore up her political position. She invited her ambitious cousin, Theodohad, who had a power base in Tuscany, and a bad reputation for illegally seizing people's lands, to become her co-ruler. One can guess at her thinking. By ruling alongside Theodohad she would counter Ostrogothic unease at having a female ruler, and she would ease the resentments of her greatest political rival. It proved to be a bad miscalculation. Procopius claims Amalasuntha had Theodohad swear a secret oath that she would remain the real power in the land but if she did, the oath had little effect. Theodohad used his new position to move against her. Within months his followers seized her, took her from Ravenna to the island of Martana where, some weeks later, Theodohad had her killed.

According to Procopius, Amalasuntha had been a friend and ally of the Eastern Emperor, Justinian, and, when he heard of her killing, he was so angry that he ordered Belisarius to prepare for an invasion of Theodohad's kingdom. Justinian's real thinking probably involved less emotion and more devious calculation. His wife, Theodora, had kept up a secret correspondence with king Theodohad's wife, Gudelina, and Procopius claims that – promising Byzantium would turn a blind eye – Theodora had Gudelina persuade her husband to execute Amalasuntha. The claim is made in Procopius' poisonous *Secret History*, and he gives empress Theodora a suitably malevolent motive, writing that she wanted the regent dead because she feared that Amalasuntha – who was known for her beauty and intelligence – might steal away Justinian. It is an unlikely story, and yet it may contain an element of truth. Emperor Justinian may have encouraged Amalasuntha's murder, as it would give him an excuse to attack the Ostrogothic kingdom. He needed an excuse as, in theory, he was attacking his own territory, which was ruled by his viceroy. He may also have felt that Theodohad would prove a less dangerous opponent than Amalasuntha.

If this was his thinking, he was soon proved right. In many ways Theodohad made an unlikely Ostrogothic king. Germanic people in this era were suspicious of learning, especially in their leaders, as they felt it undermined their warlike instincts. Theodohad was not only literate but highly educated in Plato and Latin literature, and he considered himself a philosopher. In his case, Germanic prejudices were proved correct. In 535 Belisarius seized Sicily. The following year he landed in mainland Italy and captured Naples, which he did by sneaking soldiers into the city through an aqueduct, and where his troops went on a spree of killing and plunder. Theodohad did nothing, remaining in Rome, frozen with indecision. It seemed that Italy would fall even more easily than Africa. But then the Ostrogoths, disgusted at their philosopher king, cut his throat and acclaimed a new and more warlike leader: Witigis.

As with Alaric and Brennus before him, we know disappointingly little about Witigis. He was born into the Ostrogothic elite, served in King Theodoric's bodyguard and led Ostrogothic forces with success in the western Balkans. He was not a skilled tactician, yet his first decisions as king were shrewd enough. As well as Belisarius' army in the south, he faced war bands of Franks, who Justinian had encouraged to raid from across the Alps. Witigis decided to deal with the Franks first. He marched north, leaving a garrison of several thousand Ostrogoths in Rome in the hope that the Romans would prove loyal. The Romans, though, had no risk of suffering the sort of killings and plundering that the Neapolitans had just endured at the hands of Belisarius' soldiers. They sent a delegation to Belisarius inviting him into the city. Cannily, they also managed to persuade the Ostrogothic garrison to leave. So, on 9 December 536, as the Ostrogoths filed out through the city's northern Flaminian Gate, Belisarius' troops marched in through the Asinarian Gate to the south. The Romans could hardly have arranged matters more tidily. They had switched sides without so much as a scuffle. It seemed their war was over.

A late nineteenth-century depiction of Belisarius entering Rome, from Cassell's Illustrated Universal History *by Edward Ollier, 1890.*

But it would not be quite so easy as that. King Witigis quickly made peace with the Franks. Hearing that Belisarius' army was far smaller than he had thought, he determined to crush this puny invasion and turned his forces southwards. Unlike Alaric's horde more than a century earlier, this was not a whole tribe on the move – the warriors' wives and children remained in the north and central Italy, where they had settled – but an army. In other respects, though, it resembled Alaric's forces. Some Ostrogoths would have been on foot, others on horseback or riding in the back of wagons. They would have carried a variety of weapons, though, like the Visgoths, an aristocratic minority would have been noticeably better equipped than their underclass helpers. As ever, they all would have stunk and been infected with lice. And they were many. Procopius claims Witigis' army totalled 150,000 men and though his figure is almost certainly much exaggerated there is no doubt that it was a huge force. In March 537, only three months after the Romans had believed they had saved themselves, the Ostrogoths came in sight of Rome's walls.

II

As to what kind of Rome awaited them, if a Roman had been transported there from the previous century, just before before Alaric's sack, he or she would have been shocked at the state of the city. Most of all they would have found it eerily empty. It has been estimated that by 530 the city's population was in the tens of thousands, or a tenth or twentieth of what it had been in 408. Streets once teeming with people would have felt almost deserted. Blocks of flats that had been packed with Romans had become desolate, with families camped out on ground floors, as upper levels were now a chaos of rotting timbers, fallen stairways, leaking roofs and birds' nests. Many buildings would have been wholly abandoned.

Rome was also more parochial. Long gone were the days when one could hear a dozen languages in a single street. In 537 most Romans would have spoken one language only: a crude Latin that was already tending towards an early form of Italian. A few would have spoken a little Gothic German, but the bilingualism of the grand days of Empire was long gone and only the most highly educated Romans would have had a good knowledge of Greek. Though, as Belisarius' army marched into the city, some Romans were doubtless brushing up on their Greek grammar as fast as they could. They would have needed it. More than a century earlier Latin had ceased to be the official language of the Eastern Empire, and now few high officials spoke anything but Greek.

Something had gone very badly wrong for Rome. When last seen, it was in good shape, recovered from Alaric's sack-lite to the extent that its inhabitants were behaving as if nothing had happened. The answer lay on the Capitoline Hill. The temple to Jupiter Best and Greatest that had dominated the city's skyline for a thousand years was now in ruins, its roof stripped of its bronze tiles. More clues could be found in the main Forum, which had been crowded with statues but was now filled with empty marble plinths. In June 455, four decades after Alaric's attack, the city was sacked again, and far more brutally, by a war band of Vandals from Africa led by Genseric. The Vandals stayed in the city for two weeks, during which time, among other destructive acts, they made off with the temple of Jupiter's roof tiles and heaved away statues by the cartload. The city suffered again seventeen years later when it became a battleground in one of the Western Empire's last civil wars, in which the military chief Ricimer hunted down Emperor Anthemius, whom he had beheaded in one of Rome's churches. It was no wonder that most Romans had voted with their feet and abandoned their city.

Rome was not only damaged by war. Sources of the time describe how it suffered also at the hands of its own inhabitants. In 458 Emperor Majorian, who was the latest in a long line of emperors to issue ineffective decrees intended to halt Rome's decay, complained that the city's ancient buildings were being torn down and their fabric used for minor repairs elsewhere. Rome's antiquities were often desecrated with the connivance of the city authorities, and even Majorian accepted that some were now so far gone that they might as well be scavenged. In the decades before Witigis' arrival the bronze elephants on the Via Sacra were decrepit. Aqueducts were being misused – their water was probably being siphoned off – and decorative bronze and lead were regularly stolen from public buildings. The old granaries used to distribute food to the Romans were in a bad way, as was an elegant curved portico in the old Forum, which was only saved by being turned into private housing.

Archaeology confirms the bleak picture. After Alaric's sack, the area around the Crypt of Balbus, between the theatres of Pompey and Marcellus, became a waste ground of collapsed porticoes, fallen columns and robbed paving. For a time it seems to have been used as a depot for looted marble. As well as being pillaged by Romans, the area was also damaged by earthquakes, of which there were a number at this time, and which would have had a doubly destructive effect on buildings that had been robbed of stone, and also of the metal clamps that held their stonework together. As the fifth century wore on, houses and apartment blocks became filled with rubbish. Parks and squares turned to empty wilderness. Belisarius found there was enough grassland within the city walls to graze all of his cavalry's horses. From this collapse emerged one of Rome's few growth industries of the era. In the Forum and elsewhere lime kilns were built, where marble columns, plinths, statues and parts of buildings were baked and destroyed to be sold as plaster.

Yet however wrecked Rome was, it was still in a better state than most other Italian cities. It still had functioning aqueducts and baths and it could still amaze and impress visitors. Cassiodorus, who served as chief minister under Ostrogothic rulers, wrote that, 'It can be truly said that the whole of Rome is a marvel,' and described it as 'a wonderful forest of buildings' with, 'baths built as large as provinces, the huge Colosseum whose top is almost beyond human vision; the Pantheon with its lofty and beautiful dome as large as a whole region of the city'.[3] It was probably also a little less unhealthy than it had been. Malaria will have been as prevalent as ever but with the city's population reduced and the streets far less crowded, diseases such as measles would no longer have been endemic.

And the city still had admirers who sought to preserve its wonders. The most determined of these, a little surprisingly, was the barbarian leader who had led the Ostrogoths into Italy and who sliced his rival in two over dinner: Theodoric. During Theodoric's three-decade rule he came to Rome at least once, probably twice, staying in the old palace on the Palatine for six months, which was longer than any imperial visit for two centuries. It seems it was not a comfortable visit and he afterwards set aside 200 pounds of gold to have the palace repaired. He also had 25,000 tiles made to repair other buildings in the city, including the Baths of Caracalla, the remnants of the burned-out Basilica Aemelia in the main Forum, Emperor Domitian's old athletic stadium in the Campus Martius, and even the Temple to Vesta, which had been empty of virgins for more than a hundred years. He ordered that the city's sewers should be cleaned and repaired, the aqueducts too, and gave Rome an architect to supervise the upkeep of the city's old buildings.

Theodoric was not only interested in the architecture. He also sought to preserve the city's ancient traditions. He revived the corn dole and ordered a million litres of wheat to be distributed to the inhabitants along with rations of pork. Though he had no liking for the games, which he considered morally repugnant, he nevertheless revived them to bring the Romans a little pleasure, and hired acrobats, who offered a new and economical form of entertainment: rather than killing wild animals they would taunt them and leap out of their way, in an early form of bullfighting. Finally, Theodoric honoured the Roman Senate in a way that had not been seen for a long time. On coins and official inscriptions he used the old abbreviation SC, meaning *Senatus Consulto*, or 'by decree of the Senate', and *Res Publica*, keeping alive the five-hundred-year-old fiction that Rome was still a Republic. He even referred to *Invicta Roma*, or 'Unconquered Rome': a rather optimistic claim, seeing as by this time it had already endured two sackings.

It is doubtful Theodoric's good intentions had much effect. Twenty-five thousand tiles would have made little difference to the city's decaying monuments while reviving ancient titles could not make Rome what it had been. As ever, the city's traditions were kept alive by its aristocratic class and this was in a poor way by the sixth century. A wealthy Christian noble from 408 would have found their cosy social world had all but vanished. The Senate, which in their time had included 2,000 members, was now reduced to between 50 and 80, many of whom probably struggled to meet the required property qualifications. Most of the city's great families had fled to Sicily or Constantinople after the Vandals' sack, and their town houses were closed up or ruined. The city was now dominated by a single family, the Anicii – the family of Proba, who was blamed for opening the city's gates to Alaric's Visigoths – which now formed an international clan, with highly placed cousins from Gaul to Constantinople.

Rome's traditions declined with her aristocrats. The last time that we hear of a senator spending lavishly on games is in 424, a decade after Alaric's attack. After the Vandal sack expensive games were beyond anyone's budget. Besides, with the Vandals occupying North Africa it was hard to procure exotic animals. By the end of the fifth century even cheap games were so rare that senators no longer bothered to have their names carved on their seats in the Colosseum. The ancient republican positions that included responsibility for holding games likewise vanished. We know of no consular games after 523 and no consuls after 534.

Yet even in these difficult days, when much of Rome was decaying, there was also new growth. Several of Rome's finest churches were created at this time. The vast Santa Maria Maggiore was built in the 430s, the elegant church of Santa Sabina on the Aventine Hill was completed about the same time and the circular Santo Stefano Rotondo on the Caelian Hill was built later in the same century. The satellite settlements around the great martyrs' churches to Peter, Paul and Lawrence expanded, with new monasteries and hostels for pilgrims, who were plentiful during the four decades of Ostrogothic peace. Around the year 500, a large public latrine was set up in front of San Pietro for their needs.

This brings us to another great change in the city. Our Christian aristocrat from 408 would have found Rome in 537 almost free of paganism. Christianity was on the verge of achieving absolute triumph. Sadly this did not mean the city was religiously unified, and in many ways it was more divided than before, though tensions were now among Christians. From 498 to 506, the Church in Rome experienced one of its worst schisms between rival papal candidates, which was all the more divisive because it had both class and international dimensions. At this time the stability of the Byzantine Empire was threatened by the passionate struggle of two rival Christian movements, the Monophysites and Dyophysites, who disagreed as to the human and divine natures of Jesus. The Byzantine emperor Anastasius tried to heal the split by imposing a compromise dogma, *Henotoikon*, and backed a papal candidate, Laurentius, who would cooperate. Ordinary Romans resented Anastasius' interference, which they saw as a challenge to their pope's primacy above Constantinople. Class warfare broke out, as the city's aristocrats and high clergy supported Laurentius and low clergy and the poor supported his rival, Symmachus. Even the city's chariot teams became involved, with fans of the populist Green team backing Symmachus and the aristocratic Blues, Laurentius. The greatest violence came from the city's aristocrats who had their slaves attack Symmachus' followers and drive them from the city centre. Street battles were fought, priests were murdered and nuns were flung from their convents, stripped and beaten. The dispute was so protracted that it affected Rome's buildings. As Symmachus was barred from central Rome he embarked on construction in the suburbs, where new churches sprang up, such as San Pancrazio on the Gianicolo Hill. St Peter's, which was also outside the city at this time, gained a grand new stairway, a new fountain and its new public latrine.

The only figure who remained scrupulously neutral throughout the dispute was King Theodoric, yet even he was eventually drawn into religious conflict. Like Alaric's Visigoths, he and most of the Ostrogoths followed Homoean Christianity – now usually referred to as Arianism – which held yet another view of the nature of the human and divine natures of Jesus, and was regarded as heretical by Monophysites and Dyophysites alike. Theodoric had a rather modern, relaxed attitude towards religion and never sought supremacy for his form of Christianity, yet he did expect it to be tolerated. Towards the end of Theodoric's reign, Emperor Justinian's uncle and predecessor, Justin, began a campaign of persecution in the Byzantine Empire against Arian Christians and also Jews. To make matters worse, intolerance then spread west. In 523 the pope in Rome, John, tried to rededicate Rome's several Arian churches, and mobs burned synagogues in Ravenna, Verona and Rome. In reprisal Theodoric had those responsible lashed and a church in Verona burned. The dispute soured the last years of what had been an otherwise highly successful period of rule, causing an ugly rift between Theodoric and many Romans.

When Belisarius marched into Rome a decade later more religious trouble beckoned. Like Anastasius before him, Justinian supported a new, compromise doctrine, Theopaschism, which he hoped would heal his empire's divisions. He needed a solution also for personal reasons. While, like the population of the Empire's capital, Constantinople, Justinian was Dyophysite, his wife Theodora was pro-Monophysite. On Justinian's orders, one of Belisarius' first actions in Rome was to depose the pope, Silverius, who was a Gothic appointee and so was unlikely to cooperate with Justinian's plans. Silverius was dispatched to the island of Palmaria where he promptly and conveniently died. He was replaced by Justinian's candidate, a former papal legate to Constantinople, Vigilius, who could be relied upon to support Justinian's Theopaschism. Whether Vigilius would last any longer than Silverius was soon doubtful, though. He had barely been installed when Witigis and his vast army of Ostrogoths appeared outside the city.

III

The Romans' first loss was their comforts. Witigis invested the city, building seven large fortified camps around its northern side and cutting its aqueducts. Belisarius – who knew all about the dangers posed by aqueducts after his attack on Naples – then made matters more permanent by blocking the sections inside the city with tons of masonry. The city's baths ceased to function and the Romans, who had enjoyed public bathing for more than six centuries, were forced to clean themselves and drink from the city's springs and wells or from the Tiber. They were short of food and sleep, too, as Belisarius required them to do night guard duty on the walls.

Yet comfort was not the Romans' greatest concern. Like Witigis, they had been struck by how tiny Belisarius' army was. Its numbers had been modest when it first landed in Sicily and it had been depleted since then by Belisarius' need to leave garrisons in the cities he captured. His forces in Rome totalled fewer than 5,000 men. As we saw, Procopius claims that Witigis' Ostrogoths totalled 150,000, and though 25,000 to 30,000 is probably closer to the mark, his army still dwarfed that of Belisarius. The Romans began to regret inviting him into the city, complaining that they had never asked him to invade Italy. When Witigis heard of their grumbling he sent an envoy to demoralize them further. Having denounced them for their treachery he then reproached them for having, as Procopius tells us, 'exchanged the power of the Goths for Greeks, who were not able to defend them, although they had never before seen an army of the Greek race come to Italy except actors of tragedy or mime and thieving sailors'.[4]

Interestingly, some Romans responded to their fears in the same way as their ancestors had done during Alaric's first siege. They looked to the past. Long before, when Rome went to war, the doors to the Temple of Janus were opened. The temple, which was beside the Senate House in the main Forum, was still in a good state and Procopius, who saw it himself, describes it as a square, bronze building just large enough to contain a statue of Janus. As Witigis' siege dragged on, some of the city's inhabitants secretly visited the temple and tried to open its doors. They failed, as the hinges must have been too rusted, but it was evident the attempt had been made as the doors were no longer closed true. As Procopius tells us, 'those who had attempted to do this escaped detection; and no investigation of the act was made, as was natural in a time of great confusion, since it did not become known to the commanders, nor did it reach the ears of the multitude, except of a very few'.⁵ Times had changed since Alaric's day. Then some of the most powerful men in the city had flirted with paganism. Now it was only an unknown few, who were lucky to escape punishment.

Yet the Romans, like the Witigis, had underestimated Belisarius. If the Ostrogoths' tactics and weapons had changed little since Alaric's time, this was not true of the Eastern Roman Empire. In these cash-strapped days the Byzantines could not field the vast armies of earlier times but they had become adept at making the most of the little they had. Belisarius' army had almost nothing in common with the heavy infantry legions of the old Roman Empire, and in many ways it was closer to a war band of Huns. For that matter, it contained Huns, along with Slavs, Germanic Heruli, Gepids and Lombards, and also the Isaurians, a tough people from the mountainous south of Asia Minor. All of these disparate elements had one thing in common: they were expert archers. So was Belisarius himself. In one of the first skirmishes of the siege he aimed an arrow at an ox that was pulling an Ostrogothic siege tower and killed it with one shot.

Belisarius took on the besiegers Hun-style, sending out small parties of mounted bowmen, who lured the Ostrogoths from their camps, showered them with arrows, inflicting high casualties, and then sped away having hardly lost a man. He also employed an array of ingenious machines. Ballistae fired large metal bolts with great force for long distances, and one impaled a gigantic Goth against a tree. Wild-asses – a form of catapult – hurled boulders. Wolves, which were portcullis-like frames with jagged points, were suspended above the battlements, and when enemies tried to scale the walls on ladders they were swung down, stabbing into attackers' backs. The defenders also used anything that came to hand. When a force of Ostrogoths managed to reach the strongpoint of Hadrian's Tomb unseen, by sneaking beneath the long portico built to keep pilgrims dry on their way to St Peter's, the defenders beat them back by breaking up the huge statues on the tomb's summit and hurling pieces on to their heads.

Belisarius was also helped by Witigis' strategic errors. Most of all he failed to fully encircle the city, as his seven encampments contained Rome only from the north. He established just one fortress to the south, which was created by blocking up the arches of two intertwined aqueducts, and which reduced supplies to the city, but he failed to take Rome's seaport, Portus. For a time the Romans were reduced to eating wild herbs, but then supplies were sneaked into the city several times, along with money and soldiers from the east. The Romans were even able to grind flour for their bread. When mills driven by the aqueducts ceased to function, Belisarius ingeniously built floating mills on the Tiber that were powered by the river's current. As Witigis' army slowly became depleted by hunger, disease, and skirmishes with archer cavalry, Belisarius' force was strengthened by reinforcements. Eventually he was able to spare some troops, who slipped out of Rome and made their way to the Adriatic coast, where many of the Ostrogoths' families lived, unprotected. Witigis panicked and in March 538, after a siege that had lasted almost exactly a year, his Ostrogoths burned their camps and marched away. Two years later, Witigis, deserted by his followers, surrendered to Belisarius in Ravenna. Only the Ostrogoths north of the river Po still held out. The war appeared to be all but over.

Yet celebrations proved premature. Having won, the Byzantines then threw away all their gains. The Empire's other war, with Persia, went badly wrong and Belisarius was recalled to the east. The commanders he left behind in Italy proved fractious, sluggish and most of all grasping. Emperor Justinian, who was determined that Italians should pay for their liberation, sent an imperial fiscal agent or *logothete* named Alexander, who was nicknamed 'Clippings' from his habit of shaving off the edges of coins that passed through his hands. As well as squeezing all he could from Italy's struggling population and seizing their property, Alexander drastically cut payments to the imperial army in Italy, which in turn encouraged soldiers and commanders – who needed no lessons in rapaciousness – to join in his extortion. Procopius writes that the Italians soon longed for barbarians.

Then, when Italians already had more than enough troubles, they were struck by an even greater catastrophe. Italy suffered an outbreak of the same bubonic plague that would rage across Europe eight centuries later as the Black Death. Procopius had left Italy with Belisarius by this time, so we have no descriptions of how Rome was affected, but he gives a vivid account of what happened in Constantinople, which, unlike Rome, was still a thriving, heavily populated city:

> …at first the deaths were a little more than the normal, then the mortality rose still higher, and afterwards the tally of dead reached five thousand each day, and again it even came to ten thousand and still more than that. Now in the beginning each man attended to the burial of the dead of his own house, and these they threw even into the tombs of others, either escaping detection or using violence; but afterwards confusion and disorder everywhere became complete. For slaves remained destitute of masters, and men who in former times were very prosperous were deprived of the service of their domestics who were either sick or dead, and many houses became completely destitute of human inhabitants.[6]

If it was as lethal as the Black Death – which is highly likely, as it was the same disease – then between a third and half of the Italians would have succumbed.

With wars being lost on two fronts and his citizens dying by the tens of thousands, Emperor Justinian knew just what to do.

He embarked on further religious interference. His last attempt to find a compromise between the Monophysites and Dyophysites having got nowhere, he now tried another, which involved the official condemnation of three Christian texts known as *The Three Chapters*. Unfortunately Pope Vigilius in Rome, though he had been installed by Justinian, refused to follow the new doctrine. On 22 November 545, Vigilius was in the midst of celebrating mass in the church of Santa Cecilia in Trans Tiberina when he was seized by a squad of imperial troops and marched to a ship waiting on the Tiber. Vigilius had a poor reputation in Rome at this time, as he was widely believed to have murdered both his secretary and his niece's husband, and he was followed by a crowd of bemused Romans who, as the ship cast off – Vigilius still reciting the final blessings of his interrupted mass – threw stones and shouted that the plague should take him.

It was not Justinian's religious interference, nor his rapacious tax-gathering, nor the plague that finally undid Byzantium's hold on Italy. The Ostrogoths north of the river Po, who Belisarius' lacklustre successors had never got round to subduing, chose a new leader who proved far more formidable than Witigis: Totila. For once we have a description, if brief, of his character: Procopius writes that he was 'a man gifted with remarkable discretion, energetic in the extreme and held in high esteem by the Goths'.[7] Discreet, energetic Totila discovered an answer to his Ostrogoths' tactical inferiority. He used surprise, catching out his enemies with ambushes that allowed his warriors to get past the showers of arrows and inflict damage close up. The Byzantines, struggling in their war against the Persians to their east, were unable to reinforce their Italian forces.

Totila was also politically shrewd and far more skilful at winning Italian hearts and minds than his opponents. After inflicting several crushing defeats on Belisarius' successors in the north, he bypassed Rome and besieged Naples, and when the city surrendered, Totila treated its famished inhabitants with scrupulous concern. They were so weak that had they fled the city in panic, many would have died. Totila locked them inside the city and brought in supplies of food until they were strong enough to venture out. When one of his bodyguards raped a Neapolitan woman Totila insisted on having him executed, even though the man was very popular in the Ostrogothic army. He also left Italian farmers in peace, urging them to till their fields but to pay taxes to him rather than to the grasping imperial officials. Most were probably happy to do so.

Having taken Naples, Totila then turned his eyes on Rome, but he was careful not to repeat Witigis' mistakes. First he captured a series of cities to the north, including nearby Tibur (Tivoli). Next he created an Ostrogothic navy of small, fast ships, which he based in Naples and the Aeolian Islands, ready to intercept convoys sent from the east. This blockade from a distance proved far more effective than Witigis' incomplete siege. At the end of 545, seven years after Witigis had departed, Totila was finally ready to move on Rome itself. The Byzantine commander in the city, a Goth named Bessas, tried to replicate Belisarius' tactics and sent out a force of mounted archers to harry the besiegers, only to be lured into one of Totila's ambushes and suffer high casualties. It was the last time Bessas risked an attack.

As the siege began to bite and Romans grew hungry, help was sent from an unexpected source. Pope Vigilius, who we last saw sailing down the Tiber as a Roman mob hurled stones and abuse, was being held in Sicily to reconsider his religious scruples over condemning *The Three Chapters*. As chance would have it, Sicily was one of the few places in the region at this time that was peaceful enough to enjoy a relative abundance of food. Vigilius sent several grain ships to help out his Roman parishioners. The Romans, though, were out of luck. As the ships approached Portus they were spotted by some Ostrogoths, who slipped inside the harbour and hid. Imperial troops on the battlements tried to warn the vessels away by waving their cloaks but the crews misunderstood, thinking they were excited to see them, and sailed on. All were captured. If Totila could be kindly to ordinary Italians, he had no tolerance of

An eighteenth-century engraving of Pope Vigilius, elected 536.

those who opposed him. He had the ships' crews killed and when a bishop was found aboard the convoy, Totila enquired about the man, concluded that he was an out and out liar and cut off both his hands.

Even if Vigilius' food had reached Rome, it is doubtful whether it would have reached many of the Romans. As Procopius tells us, the city's commander, Bessas, saw the siege as a chance to make his fortune and he and his commanders:

> … stored away a vast supply of grain for their own use within the walls of the city of Rome … they as well as the soldiers were constantly taking from the portion assigned for their own needs and selling it at a great price to such Romans as were rich, for the price of a bushel had reached seven gold pieces.[8]

When desperate Romans sent a deputation to Bessas complaining that he should either feed them, kill them or let them leave, Bessas and his officers replied that to feed them was impossible, to kill them would be unholy, and that to release them would be too dangerous. Poor Romans ate boiled nettles and the rich spent their gold on Bessas' extortionate grain. When they ran out of gold they offered their valuables. Eventually, even the garrison ran out of food and everybody – aside from Bessas himself – was reduced to nettles.

> But this food was insufficient for them, for it was utterly impossible to satisfy themselves with it, and consequently their flesh withered away almost entirely, while their colour, gradually turning to a livid hue, gave them a most ghostly appearance. And it happened to many that, even as they walked along chewing the nettles with their teeth, death came suddenly upon them and they fell to the ground. And now they were even beginning to eat each other's dung. There were many, too, who because of the pressure of the famine, destroyed themselves with their own hands; for they could no longer find either dogs or mice or any dead animal of any kind on which to feed.[9]

After a father of five leapt to his death from one of the city's bridges in front of his children, Bessas finally relented and allowed the Romans to leave the city, which a good number did, but by then they were so weakened that many died fleeing, while others were caught and killed by the besiegers.

Then, just when all seemed lost, there was new cause for hope. Belisarius landed with a new army at Portus. Justinian, parsimonious and mistrustful of his general, had given him only a meagre force but Belisarius was determined to do the best he could, and he devised an ingenious plan to relieve the city. Knowing that Totila had blocked the Tiber between Portus and Rome with a chain and two high wooden towers, Belisarius built a convoy of fortified riverboats, one of which had a wooden tower higher than those of the Goths, on top of which he placed a small rowing boat filled with pitch, sulphur, resin and other combustible materials. Leaving his wife – whom he brought with him on his campaigns – in Portus, and instructing the commander Isaac that he was not, under any circumstances, to risk venturing outside the city walls, Belisarius set out with his convoy.

He soon succeeded in raising the chain blocking the river, and in burning down one of the Goths' towers with the incendiary rowing boat. Then, though, Isaac, hearing of Belisarius' successes and determined to share in his glory, sallied out from Portus and attacked the Gothic camp outside, only to fall into an ambush and be captured. When a garbled account of what had happened reached Belisarius, he was 'thunderstruck at what he heard and without investigating in what manner he could have been captured, but thinking that both Portus and his wife were lost... he fell into a state of speechlessness, an experience which he had never had before'.[10]

Belisarius hurried back to Portus. When he realized his mistake and saw the opportunity that he had thrown away, he fell sick – probably from either plague or malaria – and almost died. Rome's last chance had passed.

In Rome, Bessas, intent on his self-enrichment schemes, had neglected to make sure that the city was properly guarded. Officers failed to do night rounds of the walls and guards – of whom there were few now, as most Romans had died or left – dozed. Four Isaurians who were in charge of the Asinarian Gate next to San Giovanni in Laterano, saw a money-making opportunity of their own. They lowered ropes outside the wall, climbed down, made their way to Totila's camp and offered to let him into the city. Totila agreed to reward them generously and a few nights later, on 17 December 546, as his army gathered nearby, the Isaurians led four Goths up the ropes on to the wall. Using axes, the Goths smashed the huge wooden bars that held the doors shut and the ironwork of the lock, and the gates swung open. After a year-long siege, Rome had again fallen not to assault or famine but through treachery:

... tumult and confusion, as was natural, fell upon the city, and most of the Roman soldiers were fleeing with their commanders through another gate, each one taking whatever course he found easy to follow, while only a few with the rest of the Romans were taking refuge in the sanctuaries. Among the patricians Decius and Basilius, in company with a few others (for horses happened to be at hand for them) succeeded in escaping with Bessas … Among the common people, however, it so fell out that only 500 men had been left in the whole city, and these with difficulty found refuge in the sanctuaries.[11]

The Ostrogoths, intoxicated by their having got into the city after eight years of trying, killed any Romans they found, till a churchman, Pelagius, convinced Totila to make them stop, and they turned to plunder instead: 'Now he [Totila] found much of value in the houses of the patricians, but most of all in the house where Bessas had lodged. For that ill-starred wretch had been collecting for Totila the outrageous sums which, as set forth above, he had charged for the grain.'[12]

In 1,500 years and three sackings the Romans had never reached the depths they did now: 'They found themselves reduced to such straits that they clothed themselves in the garments of slaves and rustics, and lived by begging bread or any other food from their enemies.' Totila protected the women of the city from his soldiers, so that 'not one of them had the ill fortune to suffer personal insult, whether married, unwed, or widow', but he felt no pity for the city itself. Fires broke out and the whole district of Trans Tiberina, on the far bank of the river, went up in flames. Totila prepared to destroy the remainder. After rebuking the few senators he had caught for their ingratitude to the Goths, he 'tore down the fortifications in many places so that about one third of the defences were destroyed. And he was on the point of burning the finest and most noteworthy of the buildings and making Rome a sheep-pasture.'[13]

That he changed his mind, so Procopius tells us, was thanks to Belisarius. Having learned of Totila's intentions he sent him a letter, which Procopius quotes in full. This is almost certainly the work not of Belisarius but Procopius; however, it is a remarkable text. Procopius, as we have seen, had spent time in Rome during the first siege and it had clearly made a great impression on him. His words are far truer of the city today than when they were written, fifteen centuries ago:

> Now among all the cities under the sun, Rome is agreed to be the greatest and most noteworthy. For it has not been created by the ability of one man, nor has it attained such greatness and beauty by a power of short duration, but a multitude of monarchs, many companies of the best men, a great lapse of time, and an extraordinary abundance of wealth have availed to bring together in that city all other things that are in the world, and skilled workers besides. Thus, little by little, have they built the city, such as you behold it, thereby leaving to future generations memorials of the ability of them all, so that insult to these monuments would properly be considered a great crime against the men of all time.[14]

After reading the letter several times, so Procopius tells us, Totila relented and agreed not to burn the city after all. Rome had been saved. Still it was a nadir moment:

> As for the Romans, however, he kept all the members of the Senate with him while all the others, together with their wives and children he sent into Campania, refusing to allow a single soul into Rome, but leaving it entirely deserted.[15]

For the first time in its existence, Rome, which a century and a half earlier had been the largest and greatest city on earth, with close to a million inhabitants, was empty.

The sources report that it remained so for forty days. Even then its traumas were not over and during the next five years it changed hands no fewer than three times. Totila, having spent years capturing the city, then abandoned it, marching away to campaign in the south. Seeing his chance Belisarius hurried up from Portus, enticed a few inhabitants back with offers of food and had his troops pile stones back into the walls' breaches. Totila, realizing his mistake, thundered back but Belisarius managed to hold off his Ostrogoths, despite the fact that the city's gates had no doors, by packing them with soldiers and scattering four-pronged caltrops to thwart the Gothic cavalry. It was a short-lived victory. Two years later, in 549, Totila again besieged the city for a year and again he broke in thanks to treachery, when some more Isaurians, impressed by how rich their compatriots had become from their betrayal, decided to follow their example.

This time at least, Totila had no thoughts of destroying Rome. Instead he made it his capital. Eager to impress a Frankish princess whom he hoped to marry, he gave orders that all damage was to be repaired without delay, though it seems hard to believe much was accomplished in a city that was barely inhabited. Totila summoned all members of the Senate he could find and had them meet. He even organized horse races in the Circus Maximus.

At this moment of triumph, the Ostrogoths would never have guessed that their days were almost over. The Byzantine Empire's eastern war with the Persians finally went better, and in 551 Justinian sent out a new and comparatively large army to Italy under the command of an ageing eunuch named Narses. After two decades of fighting the Ostrogoths had become so reduced in number that, for once, they were outnumbered by imperial forces. Worse, Totila had forgotten how to ambush. In early 552 at Taginae in Umbria, his cavalry tried and failed to catch Narses' army by surprise. Narses' mounted archers overwhelmed them and Totila himself was killed. After several further struggles the elite, free Ostrogoths became too few to sustain their tribe and in 561 their nation imploded, ceasing to exist as a political force. Over the next centuries Gothic names occasionally appear in the Italian records, but ever less frequently. After a few generations they vanish altogether.

Rome had survived, yet it was profoundly changed by the Gothic War, and far more so than it had been by the sackings by Alaric's Visigoths or the Vandals. As far as is known, Totila's horse races were the last ever held in the Circus Maximus and within decades it had become a grassy wasteland. Justinian, who had intended to bring the city gloriously back within the folds of the Empire, had instead accelerated its decline. During and after the wars the last of the city's old ways died away. Justinian, in his Pragmatic Sanction, which outlined his plans for the new imperial province of Italy, announced that he would repair the main Forum, the city's river embankments, its port and its aqueducts, but little if anything was done.

One casualty of the wars was cleanliness. The final mention we have of functioning public baths, of which Rome had once possessed more than eight hundred, is from just a few decades later. This change was not only the result of a lack of resources. Public bathing was becoming ideologically unfashionable. In Christian eyes water was for drinking, not bathing, while it was certainly not for pleasure bathing, which smacked of licentiousness. Two centuries after the Gothic War a couple of aqueducts were restored and their waters were diverted to simple baths outside St Peter's and San Lorenzo, for use by clergy and also recently arrived pilgrims – who would have needed a thorough wash – but soap was rarely provided. Dirt was the new clean. As to private baths, only a single one remained in working order after the Gothic War. Alone and unique, it continued to function for centuries. It was in the Lateran Palace, home of the popes.

As public baths disappeared so did the state food dole. In the decades after the Gothic War what remained of the old system was replaced by Church distributions to the poor. In some cases Church handouts were organized in the old state granaries. It was a sign of the times: Church was replacing state. Despite its defeat of the Ostrogoths, the Byzantine Empire's hold on Italy proved fleeting. In 568, only seven years after the last Ostrogoth holdouts had been defeated, a new Germanic people swept into the country. These were the Lombards, who had first been introduced to Italy when serving in the Byzantine Empire's armies. Imperial rule became reduced to a handful of areas close to the sea. As Byzantine control faded, power shifted to the Church. Popes had no interest in preserving the imperial, pagan past and, free of political authority, they actively erased it. At the end of the sixth century Pope Gregory embarked on a thorough purge of the city's pagan statues. Shaken by earthquakes and with no King Theodoric or Emperor Majorian to keep an eye on them, Rome's great pagan monuments suffered from decay and pilfering. In the lower parts of the city they were also damaged by floods. As the Tiber embankments rotted, the city suffered devastating inundations two or three times each century. One of the worst occurred in 589 and was described two centuries after the event by Paul the Deacon, whose account reveals yet another casualty of this era, reliable reporting:

> In this outpouring of the flood the river Tiber at the city of Rome rose so much that its waters flowed in over the walls of the city and filled great regions of it. Then through the bed of the same stream a great multitude of serpents and a dragon of astonishing size passed by the city and descended to the sea.[16]

Yet some of Rome's monuments were actually preserved thanks to the tough times. The century and a half that followed the Gothic War saw, unusually, almost no new churches built in Rome, at least of any size, as the popes struggled to maintain those already built. Vast St Peter's was a particular headache and required constant repair. Unable to construct new buildings, the papacy resorted to reusing the old. In the late sixth century a vestibule of the old Imperial Palace was remade as the church of Santa Maria in Antiqua and the old office of the city prefect in the Forum became the church of Santi Cosma e Damiano. In the eighth century the former office of the Senate became the church of Santi Martino e Luca. Best of all, in the early seventh century Rome's most beautiful pagan temple, the Pantheon, became the church of Santa Maria ad Martyres, and so was saved from the slow ruin of other great temples.

The institutions of Rome were not so lucky. As we have seen, republican posts died away before the Gothic War began, but one ancient body had endured: the Senate. In 554 Justinian had it reconstituted, reducing the property qualification from 100 to 30 pounds of gold. He was obliged to do so, as by this time wealthy Roman landowners were an endangered species: most had fled to Sicily or Constantinople, while others lost the last of their fortunes paying ransoms to rescue relatives seized by the Lombards. Even Justinian's compromises, though, were not enough to stem the rot. The Senate died so quietly that we do not know exactly how or when it met its end. In the late 570s it was still sending embassies to Constantinople, begging the Eastern Emperor of the time for help against the Lombards. In 603 senators, along with the pope and the city's clergy, are said to have greeted the Byzantine emperor Phocas when he paid a brief visit to Rome, though the claim is questionable. Pope Gregory, who died the very next year, is said to have declared that 'The Senate is no more.' There is no question that the Senate had vanished by the time of Pope Honorius, who reigned from 625 to 638, as he transformed the old Senate House into the church of Sant'Adriano. An assembly that had once ruled the Mediterranean world, and had existed since the time of Rome's kings, 1,200 years ago, was gone.

Yet, as one set of institutions vanished, another rose to take their place. Ambitious, well-connected Romans followed the money. For a time they sought posts as officials or soldiers for the Eastern Empire. Then, as the Empire's influence faded, they turned to the Church, which, thanks to donations by wealthy Christians hoping to secure their places in paradise, was fast becoming Europe's greatest landowner. Within a century of the Gothic War Rome was ruled by a power order that was at once new and also rather familiar. At its summit, employing the title that emperors had done since the time of Julius Caesar – chief priest, or *Pontifex Maximus* – was the pope.

Beneath were his high clergy, who wore silk slippers, just as had Rome's senators.

Not for the last time, when it seemed that things could get no worse, Rome was helped by the misfortunes of others. The Lombard invasions of Italy caused such havoc that people flocked to the safety of its walls, repopulating the city, and by the end of sixth century the number of Rome's inhabitants is estimated to have swollen to between forty and fifty thousand. Four decades later the Byzantine Empire became a shadow of its former self as Muslim armies from Arabia snatched away half its territory, seizing lands from Tunisia to Syria. Around 636 Jerusalem fell and became all but unreachable to pilgrims. It was at this time that Rome's first guidebook for pilgrims appeared: *De Locis Sanctis Martyrum*, and Romans began to sell little phials of holy oil that had previously been a religious souvenir exclusive to Jerusalem. With its chief rival knocked out of the ring, Rome found itself Christendom's number one pilgrimage destination.

Rome, 1084

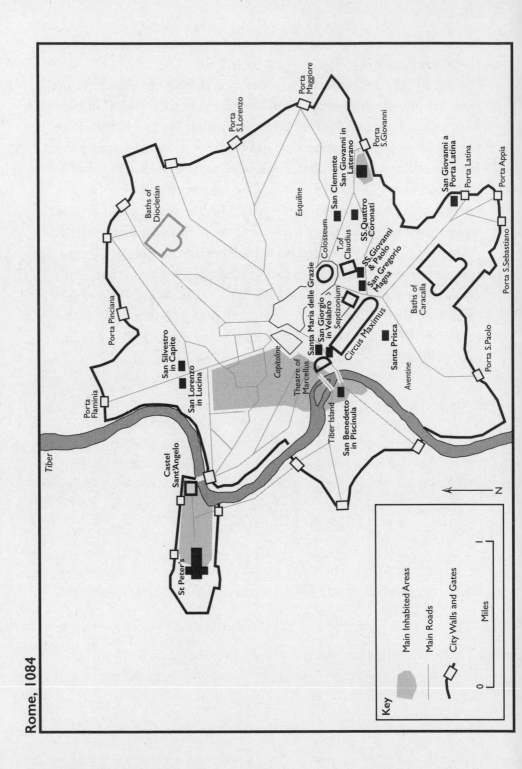

Porta Maggiore

Porta S.Lorenzo

Porta S.Giovanni

San Giovanni a Porta Latina

Porta Latina

Porta Appia

Baths of Diocletian

Esquiline

San Clemente

San Giovanni in Laterano

SS.Quattro Coronati

Colosseum

T. of Claudius

SS.Giovanni & Paolo

San Gregorio Magna

Porta S.Sebastiano

Porta Pinciana

Santa Maria delle Grazie

San Giorgio in Velabro

Septizonium

Baths of Caracalla

Porta Flaminia

San Silvestro in Capite

San Lorenzo in Lucina

Capitoline

Theatre of Marcellus

Circus Maximus

Santa Prisca

Aventine

Porta S.Paolo

Castel Sant'Angelo

Tiber Island

San Benedetto in Piscinula

Tiber

St Peter's

N

Key

Main Inhabited Areas

Main Roads

City Walls and Gates

0   Miles

CHAPTER FOUR

NORMANS

I

CANOSSA CASTLE, which sits on a rocky crag in the beautiful, rolling hills of Emilia Romagna in northern Italy, is a popular spot with visitors. Though most are local, some come from as far away as Germany, where, as we will see, the castle holds a special interest. In truth there is not that much to see. The summit of the crag was never large and has been further reduced by landslides. Part of a tower and the curved wall of a chapel survive but visitors spend most of their time in the modern museum building. Here they look at objects found at the site, dummies of historical figures and a large plaster model of the castle, which is dramatically shown off by the custodian. At the press of a button church music rings out and a section of the castle slides away in a mechanical landslip.

The castle has been destroyed and remade at least once, and little if anything remains from its moment of greatest fame, in the eleventh century. Then it was one of the strongest fortresses in this region of Italy and overlooked the main route to north-western Europe. It was the property of a formidable local ruler, Matilda of Tuscany, who was renowned for personally leading her troops into battle.

During the icy winter of 1077 Matilda had a house guest at Canossa: Pope Gregory VII, of whom she was such a strong supporter that their enemies maliciously claimed that they were lovers. And on 25 January 1077 Pope Gregory received a visitor, who had been so anxious to waylay Gregory that he had spent the previous weeks hurrying across frozen Europe. A chronicler of the time, Lambert of Hersfeld, describes how he and his little band of followers struggled over the ice-covered Alps:

> The men in the party did their very best to overcome this dangerous situation, now scrambling on their hands and feet, now leaning on the shoulders of their guides, sometimes slipping on the treacherous surface, falling over and rolling some way … The guides sat the queen and the ladies of her household on oxhides, led the way themselves and dragged them down behind them. They placed some of the horses on sleds, and led others with their feet hobbled, but many of these died as they were being dragged, and most of the others were in a very bad state … [1]

The party was led by King Henry IV of Germany, Burgundy and of Italy, and he had good reason to be in a hurry. Pope Gregory had excommunicated him, had orchestrated a revolt against him by his barons and churchmen, and was now on his way to Germany to preside over a council to depose him. Henry was fighting to save his throne. Gregory enjoyed the strong position he was in. Lambert of Hersfeld describes how he sat comfortably in the warm in Canossa Castle when Henry arrived,

> and since the castle was surrounded by a triple wall, he [Henry] was allowed within the second of these walls, leaving all his attendants outside, and there, stripped of his royal robes,

A contemporary illumination that depicts Henry IV asking Matilda of Tuscany and the Abbot of Cluny to intercede for him with the pope at the St Nicholas' Chapel at Canossa.

with nothing kingly about him, entirely without ceremonial, and with his feet bare, he stood, fasting, from morning until evening while he waited for the pope's sentence. He did this for a second, and then a third day. Finally, on the fourth day he was admitted to the pope's presence ...[2]

Lambert of Hersfeld, who was a staunch opponent of Henry and wanted to show him humiliated, probably exaggerates. Henry would have been unlikely to survive three days and nights outside, barefoot in the cold. Local people think it more likely that he spent the time negotiating from the nearby castle of Bianello and then came when Gregory had agreed to see him. Still, it was a remarkable event and one of the great shock moments of the central Middle Ages. Nobody had imagined a pope could wield power in this way, humbling Europe's most powerful monarch. Pope Gregory's triumph, though, would be short-lived. Four years later, in May 1081, King Henry appeared outside Rome at the head of an army, keen to enjoy a little revenge.

Yet something does not seem quite right here. The title of this chapter is *Normans* not Germans, Henricians or Imperialists. As we will see, this was a complex, three-cornered crisis involving three individuals whose characters could hardly have been more different. As well as puzzling, difficult Henry IV and controlling purist Gregory VII, the fate of the Romans lay also with Duke Robert Guiscard: a larger than life Norman military adventurer, as shameless as he was successful.

First the purist pope. Hildebrand, as he was known before assuming the papacy, was born in southern Tuscany and first came to Rome as a boy, probably at the invitation of his uncle, who ran a monastery on the Aventine Hill. He soon became a keen supporter of a new movement that was sweeping across Europe from France at this time and which sought to reform the Church. There was no question that the Church needed some shaking up as it had drifted far from early Christianity's ideals of humility, poverty and chastity. As Western Europe's greatest landowner it had become a magnet for those seeking wealth and power. Bishops were political players and simony – the sale of church positions – was common. Priests and monks enjoyed a much more comfortable lifestyle than the peasants whose tithes fed and clothed them. Nor did they deny themselves bedroom pleasures. By the ninth century married priests with large families were commonplace, and though in the early eleventh century, under the pressure of the Church reform movement, their marriages were less openly acknowledged than before, the change was largely cosmetic.

Nowhere was such unclergylike behaviour more evident than in Rome. Hildebrand arrived in the city at a low moment for the Roman Church, under Pope Benedict IX, whom chroniclers accused of every kind of monstrosity, from rape and murder to black magic. Medieval writers were often less interested in truth than in putting their patrons in the best light and assassinating the reputations of their enemies, so one frequently has to take their claims with a pinch of salt, but in Benedict IX's case there are signs that something really was badly amiss.

A member of a powerful family from the hilltop town of Tusculum, who had dominated the papacy for a generation – his two first cousins were popes before him – Benedict became leader of the Catholic Church at the tender age of twelve or fourteen. In 1044, when he had reigned for a dozen years, the Roman populace ended centuries of political docility and rose against him in armed revolt. Their rebellion was a transforming event that brought a new generation of aristocratic families to the fore. It also brought an almighty mess, even by Rome's messy standards. The rebels backed a new pope, Sylvester III, but Benedict maintained his claim. After a year he finally resigned the papacy and gave it – or rather sold it – to another candidate, Gregory VI, only to change his mind and claim it back. Rome ended up with three popes.

The chaos was sorted out by King Henry IV's father, Henry III, who – like his son thirty-six years later – wanted to secure his position by being crowned Holy Roman Emperor. Imperial coronation was a tradition that already stretched back two and a half centuries to

Charlemagne, but it required a plausible pope. Finding no such thing, Henry III created his own. In 1046 he journeyed to Sutri, just north of Rome, summoned a church council, had all three papal claimants dismissed and installed his candidate, who was German and strongly supportive of the reform movement.

It was a sea change moment. For the next half-century the papacy was in the hands of men determined to return the Church to the values of its earliest days, and who did so with a zeal that has been compared to that of Bolshevik revolutionaries. Rome's leading families lost their ownership of the papacy. Whereas for generations almost all popes had been Romans, for the next eighty years popes and most high churchmen were outsiders, either from elsewhere in Italy or from Germany. Hildebrand quickly became a key figure in the reformist new guard and in April 1073 he himself became pope. He took office determined not only to clean up the Church but to begin a moral reformation of all Europe, attempting to ban marriages of which he disapproved. Much of his controlling purism became focused on one unfortunate individual.

This was the second of the trio, Henry IV, king of Germany, Burgundy and of Italy. He was only 22 years old when Hildebrand became pope in 1073, yet he had already had a trying life. When he was just five years old his father died suddenly and unexpectedly, propelling young Henry on to the throne under the regency of his mother Agnes, who was another keen supporter of the Church reform movement. At the age of eleven he was kidnapped by one of Germany's powerful magnates, Archbishop Anno of Cologne – Anno invited Henry to see his river barge and then cast off – who supplanted Agnes and ruled the kingdom. When Henry finally assumed kingship for himself, at the age of fifteen, one of his first actions was to announce that he intended to divorce his wife by an arranged marriage, Bertha. Henry made no complaint against Bertha so it seems he simply did not like her. It was an unfortunate decision: Bertha was from a highly influential family and many German princes opposed Henry's move. So did the Church reformers in Rome who, worked up by the new moral climate, declared that such an action by a leading monarch would be a stain on all Christians. Henry was forced to back down and keep his wife. Worse, the incident left him badly damaged. During the crisis his enemies had accused him of every kind of sexual depravity, from taking concubines and fathering illegitimate children, to incest and child abuse.

As ever, it is impossible to know if these accusations were actually true. Nor, for the purposes of this account, does it much matter. What matters is that the claims were brought to the ears of Hildebrand and that he believed them. Hildebrand, who was some thirty-five years older than Henry, assumed the role of a disapproving father, a role that was more convincing because Henry's mother, Agnes, had moved to Rome where she was a close supporter of Hildebrand and the Church reformers. Agnes was as disappointed in her son as Hildebrand. Aside from his personal life there was also his attitude to Church reform. Henry was a supporter but, compared to his father, his zealotry was lukewarm.

Relations between the papacy and the German court, which were already strained, grew worse after Hildebrand became pope in 1073. The two clashed over power: Gregory objected to Henry's appointment of bishops in his kingdom and also his choice of advisors, whom Agnes and Gregory disapproved of. In late 1075, following several spats between the two men, Gregory demanded that Henry acknowledge his subservience to 'the empire of Christ' – in other words, to himself – and warned that if he did not do so, he would never crown him Holy Roman Emperor. Henry, furious, countered by demanding that Gregory resign as pope, claiming he had been elected illegally. The fates took Gregory's side. In early 1076 Henry summoned a synod of German churchmen in Utrecht who declared that Gregory was a false monk and excommunicated him. Just a month later on Easter Day Utrecht Cathedral was struck by lightning and burned to the ground and many Germans believed the disaster was God's way of giving his opinion on the dispute. Gregory, sensing victory, excommunicated Henry and began conspiring against him with German princes, one of whom, the reformist Rudolph of Swabia, was waiting in the wings as a replacement king. Gregory declared that he and Agnes would go to Germany, where, like a pair of punishing parents, they would together preside over an assembly of German princes to decide Henry's fate. As we have seen, Henry prevented him from doing so only by waylaying him at Canossa. There, to be released from excommunication, Henry had to swear an oath to Pope Gregory, accepting him as the arbiter in German politics, which meant he could decide Henry's future as monarch.

Yet if Canossa was a painful humiliation for Henry, it served him well. Having survived the crisis he returned to Germany, largely ignored the oath he had sworn and transformed his situation. He showed new skill at winning key figures to his side. Though Rudolph of Swabia tried to seize the German throne and Gregory excommunicated Henry again, this time most German princes and churchmen stayed loyal to their king. In October 1080, at the battle of Hohenmölsen, Rudolph of Swabia ceased to be a problem when he lost a hand and then his life. Henry, finding that he finally had some political room in which to manoeuvre, determined to negate the humiliation of Canossa and secure his political position once and for all. He would march on Rome and be crowned Holy Roman Emperor. He would not even have to endure his mother's disapproving looks as, conveniently, Agnes had died three years earlier.

In the winter of 1081 he gathered together a rather small army of Germans and Bohemians and crossed the Brenner Pass. Reaching Italy, where his forces were reinforced by some Italians, he then took a detour to Ravenna to collect the city's pro-reform bishop, Wibert. Wibert was Henry's fallback plan. If Gregory could not be persuaded or forced to crown him Holy Roman Emperor, then Henry would depose him and replace him with Wibert, his antipope.

Now it was Gregory who was in trouble. He scoffed at Henry's little army, predicting that it would never reach Rome, as nobody would provide it with victuals, but under the management of his antipope, Wibert – who proved an excellent military organizer – the force proceeded smoothly southwards. Gregory looked to his allies in Italy, of whom he had two. The first was Matilda of Tuscany. Firmly loyal to Gregory, she would have helped if she could have but the previous October her forces had been routed by an army of Henrician loyalists from Lombardy. She was powerless.

That left Gregory's other ally. So we come to the third of the trio, Robert Guiscard. He was Norman: a people who were eleventh-century Europe's great success story. If Alaric's Visigoths and Witigis' Ostrogoths had had a long journey to Italy, so had Robert Guiscard's Normans. It had begun in Scandinavia two centuries earlier, when shiploads of Danish Vikings set out to raid, among other places, northern France. Frankish rulers found their attacks so hard to deal with that they reluctantly granted them a piece of territory, which became known as the land of the Northmen, or Normandy. Here the invaders merged with the local population, took up the French language and French ways, fought violent feuds, were persecuted by their rulers, the dukes of Normandy, and sired huge families, creating numerous young Normans hungry to find opportunities somewhere else.

Many found them in southern Italy. Unlike the Normans who settled in England after 1066, the Normans of the south did not arrive as part of a grand, planned invasion but as small bands of adventurers. They probably first discovered the area when passing through it as pilgrims on their way to Jerusalem. By the 1020s Normans were working as mercenaries for all the various local powers in this fractured, politically complex part of Italy: for Lombard princes, for the Byzantine Empire and for the pope of the time, Benedict VIII. Feuding and political persecution in Normandy turned a trickle of immigrants into a flood. In 1030 a group of Normans was granted a small piece of territory at Averna, near Naples – the first of several – which they then extended, seizing land and building castles in villages.

The Normans were widely loathed for their brutality and greed yet there was no getting rid of them. The German reformist pope, Leo IX, tried his best, assembling a grand anti-Norman coalition

that included Lombard princes and the Byzantine Empire, only to
suffer a disastrous defeat at 1053 at the battle of Civitate, where Leo
himself was captured. Accepting that the Normans were now a major
force in Italy, the papacy made its peace with them and soon found
them useful. Norman soldiers were brought in to cow the old guard
of anti-reform Roman families and to prevent them from installing
their own papal candidates. So began an unlikely alliance, between
idealistic, purist Church leaders and self-serving Norman adventurers.

Of all of these adventurers, none rose faster than Robert Guiscard.
His father, Tancred, who was lord of the obscure Norman village of
Hauteville, had twelve sons by two wives, of whom Robert was sixth:
an unpromising start in life. In the mid-1040s, with no opportunities
at home, Robert journeyed to Italy. After struggling for a time as
a minor bandit leader in Calabria his breakthrough came when he
married a Norman heiress, Alberada, who brought him a dowry of
200 knights. With these at his side Robert's abilities soon showed
themselves. He was physically intimidating, he had a talent for
inspiring his followers and he was also very shrewd. The Normans had
a reputation for cunning among contemporary chroniclers – William
of Malmesbury memorably remarked that they 'weigh treachery by
its chance of success'[3] – while Robert de Hauteville, to give him his
full name, was regarded as tricky even by his fellow Normans. His
nickname, Guiscard, meant cunning or weasel.

By the time Henry IV set out on his march to Rome, Robert
Guiscard had been in Italy for thirty-five years and had made himself
one of the most powerful and feared rulers in the Mediterranean. The
sixth son of a minor Normandy squire now ruled most of southern
Italy and his little brother Roger controlled most of Sicily in his name.
His social rise had been equally spectacular. He was now a duke and,
having discarded the wife who had got him started, he was married
to a Lombard princess, Sichelgaita of Salerno.

And of course he was allied to the pope. As one might have guessed,
relations between the grasping amoral adventurer and a controlling
purist churchman had not been smooth. An initial meeting soon

after Gregory became pope in 1073 went badly wrong when Robert, like a suspicious Mafia don, rejected the meeting place Gregory had proposed, which lay outside Robert's territory. Robert's mistrust was matched by Gregory's pride and, as the chronicler Amatus of Montecassino reported, 'discord grew up between them, an ill-will and great anger'.[4] Later, when Robert permitted his nephew to raid Church lands, Gregory excommunicated him and the following year he excommunicated him again. Yet Robert does not seem to have been overly troubled. In contrast to Henry IV, Gregory's plotting did little to weaken his political position. The one who found he was vulnerable was Gregory. In June 1080, as his relations with Henry IV deteriorated, he realized he could not have an enemy to the south as well, and so he swallowed his pride and met Robert to make peace. Robert swore fealty to Gregory and gave him some gold, and in return Gregory released him from excommunication and accepted his claim to the latest territories he had seized.

Gregory had given more than he got. He had not even gained a useful ally, as it soon became apparent Robert had little interest in Gregory's problems. In the spring of 1081, as King Henry marched south across Italy, Robert Guiscard was already on the other side of the Adriatic, campaigning against the Byzantine Emperor, Alexius Comemnus, in his most ambitious project to date: the conquest of the Byzantine Empire. Pope Gregory had no friends to help him. As Henry's army set up camp in the Fields of Nero, just north-west of the city walls, they did so safe in the knowledge that nobody was likely to trouble them.

II

What kind of Rome awaited Henry IV and his army? Of the seven incarnations of the city that will be examined in this book, that of 1081 was certainly the strangest. It was a kind of *Gulliver's Travels* town, where tiny houses existed among vast ruins. Many Romans

lived actually inside the ruins, which they called *cryptae*, making their
homes in the broken remains of thousand-year-old apartment blocks,
in long dry baths, and in the storerooms and corridors of abandoned
theatres and stadiums. The Colosseum was now the city's largest
housing complex.

If a Roman had been transported from the 530s, just before
the Gothic War, he or she would have been struck by how sleepily
suburban – even rural – their city had become. In 1081 the most urban
area was a rectangular zone centred on the Pantheon, yet even this
was not crowded. Homes were one storey high, two at the most, and
many had a little courtyard between them and the street, and a garden
at the back. Outside this central rectangle, habitation was even more
diffuse and consisted of hamlets and villages separated by farmland.
Much of the outer edge of the city, including most of Trastevere, was
comprised of orchards and vineyards.

Rome was now a small city and its population in 1081 has been
estimated as somewhere between 20,000 and 30,000. Considerably
smaller than it had been prior to the Gothic War, it was a thirtieth
or fiftieth of its size at the height of the Empire. It was probably not
much larger than it had been in 387 BC, when Brennus and his Gauls
paid their visit, and when it was a fairly new town. Yet it was far from
alone in its reduction. Shrunk though it was, in 1081 it was still the
largest city in Western Europe and had been for several centuries.

In some ways it was not one city but three. To the left and right
of the central rectangle were two satellite towns, each of which was a
centre of the Church, and which were intense rivals. To the west was
the pilgrims' town, known as the Leonine City, that had grown up
around St Peter's. All pilgrims were required to stay here, including
the most powerful pilgrims of the age: the kings of Germany who
journeyed south, like Henry IV, to be crowned Holy Roman Emperor.
The German kings had their own palace that faced on to the Platea
Sancti Petri – St Peter's Square – which, when a royal visit turned
violent, as such visits frequently did, became the site of pitched battles
between royal followers and Romans. The Leonine City, which was a

wholly separate entity from Rome, was busier and more concentrated than any other area, and contained all of the city's shops. Lacking great ruins, its low, crowded streets would have seemed reassuringly familiar to medieval visitors.

At the eastern end was the Lateran, the papacy's political headquarters. Separated from the rest of the city by fields, it formed a kind of high-powered clerical village. Around the Lateran Palace, home to the popes, antiquities were displayed to give a sense of their authority. These included a bronze she-wolf and also, in the open area in front of the palace, the Campus Lateranus, an equestrian statue thought to be of that key figure in the rise of Christianity, Emperor Constantine. Except that it was not Constantine at all, but a thoroughly pagan emperor, Marcus Aurelius. Medieval Romans could be hazy about their past. Also on display were the head and hand of a vast statue, which really *was* Constantine's, but was widely believed to be of the biblical character Samson.

The Lateran was the departure point for an activity that, more than any other, lay at the heart of medieval Rome: religious processions. If emperors had met their Roman subjects in the circus, popes met them walking, and they met them far more often than other European monarchs. Thirty times a times a year popes embarked on great processions around their city. Sometimes on horseback, sometimes barefoot, and accompanied by crowds of high clergymen, nobles dressed in purple silks, ordinary Romans, and musicians playing cymbals, harps and trumpets, popes would journey for miles, performing masses along the way. Some of these grand processions were older than Christianity. One of the greatest, the Major Litany of 25 April, followed the route of an ancient pagan walk to honour the deity Robigus. Like many papal processions the Major Litany was quite a trek. Unusually, it began not at the Lateran but beside Augustus' vast, broken sundial in the Campo Marzio, then it headed north for several miles to cross Ponte Milvio, before turning back along the west side of the Tiber – where today crowds of Roma and Lazio football fans gather to watch their teams in the Stadio Olimpico

– and finally on to St Peter's. There were also night processions, when torches lit the way, lamps were suspended from roofs and chandeliers hung in the streets. One of the greatest of these celebrated the Feast of the Assumption of the Virgin Mary on the night of 15 August. During that season and at that hour the real feasting would have been by malarial mosquitoes.

These processions were not only an opportunity for the pope to meet his subjects. They were also a chance to pay them. The pope gave large sums to the churches where he said mass and, as emperors had had coins flung into the audience in the stadium, popes handed out money to select householders along the processional route, and gave to clergy and lay officials. They also gave to the poor. The greatest payouts were at Easter and Christmas, when the city's churchmen and lay officials received income, expenses and bonuses all rolled into one. A new pope, like a new emperor, was also expected to give generously when he took power.

He often needed to pay to *get* power. As in earlier times, papal elections were frequently contested. In 1058 the old guard of Rome's elite families, who had dominated the city before the revolt against murderous Benedict IX, attempted a comeback, thwarting the reformists and installing their papal candidate as Benedict X. It was a testing moment. Many would have resented the new non-Roman Church hierarchy and lower ranking churchmen were probably angry at the loss of their domestic and bedroom pleasures. Hildebrand, the future Pope Gregory VII, organized an energetic fightback. He persuaded the Norman prince Richard of Capua to lend him 300 knights and with the help of one of the city's leading moneymen, Leone di Benedetto Cristiano, he distributed extensive bribes to the Romans. Hildebrand's stick and carrot campaign succeeded. Benedict X was expelled from the city and replaced by the reform movement's man, Nicholas II.

It was the last gasp of Rome's old guard families but not the end of papal schism and, just four years later, on Nicholas II's death, another crisis arose. This time trouble sprang not from Rome's former aristocrats but from the royal court in Germany, which was then under the thumb of the young Henry IV's riverboat kidnapper, Archbishop Anno of Cologne, and which decided to put forward its own papal nominee, Bishop Cadalo of Parma. Hildebrand distributed money all through the night to set Romans against the German candidate, and again his efforts succeeded. When Cadalo was the first to run out of money his Roman supporters abandoned him and the reformists' man was crowned pope as Alexander II. Hildebrand's behaviour may seem surprising for a man determined to end the sale of Church offices yet he would have seen bribery as a justifiable means to an end. If reformists lost control of the papacy they would lose all hope of remaking the Church.

Besides, Gregory had little else to offer except cash. Europe's other monarchs won supporters by giving out grants of land or feudal titles, but though the Church of Rome owned plenty of land – both within the city and for 25 kilometres all around it – popes had no wish to give an inch of it away. They needed it. Like emperors in the past, medieval popes assumed responsibility for feeding Rome. Where emperors had arranged transport of food to Rome from all across the Mediterranean, diminished medieval Rome could be fed largely from the farmland immediately round about, just as it had been when Brennus and his Gauls attacked, a millennium and a half earlier.

Bribery was also an easy option for popes, who were cash rich. Money flowed to them from tolls charged at the city's gates, at the river ports, and at the market. It came from taxes, known as Peter's Pence, paid by Europeans to the papacy. It came from gifts given by monasteries or devout individuals. It came from the fees and bribes paid to international Church courts that Gregory had recently set up. It came from friendly rulers such as Robert Guiscard who, as we saw, handed over gold to seal his peace deal with Gregory VII. It came from German rulers who journeyed south, like Henry IV, to be crowned Holy Roman Emperor. But most of all it came from Rome's greatest money-spinner: pilgrims.

Under Gregory VII the city's pilgrim trade was booming. That Rome was enjoying a clean hands moment under the reformist popes doubtless added to the city's appeal. Pilgrims by the thousand came in the hope that Rome's famous saints would cure them of blindness, deafness or childlessness. Most of all they hoped the saints would intercede with God to forgive them their sins and award them a place in paradise. Saint Peter's key to heaven appealed as strongly as ever. Pilgrims to Rome, who were known as Romipetae, needed only to gain permission from their local church and to buy their scrip (a leather purse) and their staff, and they could set out on the long and sometimes dangerous journey to Rome. Devout pilgrims, who believed that suffering would help annul their sins, walked barefoot, but most travelled more comfortably on horseback. Along the way they could add to their heavenly credit by calling in at other holy shrines, such as that of the Tunic of the Virgin at Chartres, or of the Finger of John the Baptist at Maurienne.

When they finally reached Rome pilgrims did not only visit the city's great churches. They also played tourist and saw its classical remains. Though, as we saw with Marcus Aurelius' statue, these were not always remembered very precisely. Along with the supposed statue of Samson, highlights included Romulus' tomb, the remains of Julius Caesar's palace – on which, it was claimed, St Peter's had been built – and an old heap of stones that was said to have been Saint Peter's personal stash of grain, and which had become petrified when the emperor Nero inadvisedly tried to steal it away from him. The Colosseum was claimed to be a temple to the sun that had once been topped by a vast dome.

Popes, and especially reform popes, squeezed every penny they could from pilgrims. The Church charged taxes on the lodging houses where pilgrims stayed. It taxed the shops which now crammed the great portico that led them to St Peter's – which we last saw being used as cover by the Ostrogoths as they attacked Belisarius' troops on Hadrian's tomb – and where pilgrims could find every kind of service from boot repair to tooth-pulling, and could buy anything from straw for their beds and horses, to souvenir rosaries, and phials of oil from the lamps that burned above Saint Peter's tomb. Most of all, the papacy took the coins pilgrims threw on to the altar of St Peter's: a vast source of income, of which the reform popes greatly increased their own share, by sacking middlemen collectors who had filched half the proceeds.

The popes even made money from dead pilgrims. The Church claimed ownership of all property belonging to anyone who died during their pilgrimage. After a long and gruelling journey and with the city rife with malaria in the summertime these would have been plentiful. The reform popes took care to maximize income in this area and in 1053 Leo IX produced a papal bull that prohibited Romans from hiding the sick, hiding their possessions, or from advising them to leave the city. It was just such behaviour that gave Rome a reputation for being grasping and corrupt. By one account the very word Roman was a term of abuse in Europe and Geoffrey of Malaterra, the biographer of Robert Guiscard, was not unusual in his scathing view of the Romans.

> Your laws are wicked, full of falsehoods.
> In you all depraved things flourish: lust, avarice,
> The lack of fidelity, the absence of order, the disease
>   of simony,
> All these weigh upon your territory and everything
>   is for sale.
> Formerly the sacred order – like water pouring
>   forth – rushed through you.
> Now one pope is not enough; you enjoy having two
>   of such distinction.
> Your fidelity is purchased with sumptuous displays.
> When this one gives to you, you strike the other,
> When this one stops giving to you, you invite the
>   other one back.
> You threaten this one with that one, and thus you
>   fill your purse.[5]

In many ways it was an accurate assessment. Yet in Romans' eyes they were doing nothing wrong. They were simply trying to survive and to lead tolerable lives in the way they always had, by carefully harvesting the pickings that their city and its rulers offered them. One could hardly expect them to change their ways now, when Rome had existed parasitically for more than a thousand years. Rome was a city built from handouts and its architecture in 1081 exactly reflected when the tap of gold had flowed or run dry.

Of the two lean centuries following the Gothic War, when the tap had slowed to a drip, there was little to show, and the main vestiges of this bleak time were classical buildings that had been converted into churches, such as the Pantheon, and buildings that had collapsed through neglect. These included one of Rome's bridges, the Pons Agrippae, which fell down in the eighth century. Another casualty was the Colosseum, half of whose outer shell collapsed around the same time, leaving a vast heap of rubble. It used to be thought that this disaster was the result of an earthquake but it now seems likely that the Colosseum fell apart unaided. It had been built on two different kinds of sediment and as the building gradually settled under its own vast weight – and with many of the metal clamps holding the stones together stolen – it simply cracked apart.

The late eighth and early ninth century had left far more. It left Rome with churches, either new or rebuilt. Most were in the city centre, and were created to house martyrs' remains that were moved from the catacombs for greater safety. They included Santa Cecilia in Trastevere, San Marco below the Capitoline and Santa Prassede with its fine Byzantine style mosaics. Even some of the city's aqueducts were brought back to life at this time: the Acqua Virgo and probably three others. These were good times all across Europe, which was finally enjoying green shoots of recovery after the great collapse of the Germanic invasions, while Rome particularly benefited thanks to an alliance between popes and the powerful Frankish Empire: a special relationship that reached its zenith on Christmas Day 800, when Pope Leo III crowned Charlemagne the first Holy Roman Emperor.

The second half of the ninth century, though, had left Rome with hardly a single new building. The tap of gold had again slowed to a dribble. The reason why lay on the far side of the river in the Vatican, where a Roman transported across the centuries from the 530s would find the greatest single change to their city. The district around St Peter's was now enclosed by a new stretch of city wall, Rome's first since the Aurelian. It had been built in a hurry, and with good reason. On 23 August 846, a force from Arab Sicily landed at the mouth of the Tiber. Roman militiamen and foreign residents sent against them were quickly beaten back, and though the main part of Rome was safe behind its walls, St Peter's was not. The Arabs seized the basilica's many treasures and even took its bronze doors. Pope Leo IV began work on the new wall just two months later. This was Rome's greatest building project for centuries and the Frankish ruler Lothair lent a hand, calling for a special tax to be raised throughout his empire. Work gangs of Romans were employed, along with Muslim prisoners from a second fleet of raiders that was sunk in a storm, and the city's lime kilns were kept busy baking ancient pieces of marble into plaster. Finally, after four years, the new Leonine Wall was complete. Shaped like a narrow horseshoe, it was three kilometres long and had three gates. It also revealed how building standards had fallen during the previous four centuries: it was only half the height of the 22-kilometre Aurelian Walls. As will be seen, on a number of occasions it would be Rome's weak spot.

It was not only Rome that was struggling at this time. Most of Europe was assailed by a new trio of raiders – Arabs, Vikings and Hungarian horsemen – and rulers endeavouring to save their kingdoms from collapse had little gold to spare for Rome. As Rome's income dried up, Roman families fought over the little that remained, taking the city into mean, lawless days. For the first time it became acceptable – even commonplace – for popes to be murdered. A low point was reached in 897, when Pope Stephen VI organized a show trial for his dead predecessor, Pope Formosus. Stephen had Formosus' remains disinterred, dressed in full papal regalia and then placed on a chair so they could be tried by a Church synod. When Formosus' corpse failed to answer accusations that it had gained office illegally, three fingers were cut from its right, benediction hand and it was stripped naked and then thrown into the Tiber. Yet Formosus' bones soon had their revenge. Within months Stephen VI had been deposed and strangled.

The next era, the first half of the tenth century, would leave Rome a number of souvenirs, which included several monasteries and a new palace north of the Pantheon, built from the ruins of the temple of Serapis. This fresh spate of construction was the work of a power-playing dynasty, the Teofilatti, who employed an impressive variety of means to keep control of the city. The dynasty's founder, Teofilatto, a leading figure in Roman politics, strengthened his position by installing an ally as pope, John VIII. A fighting cleric, who personally led his troops in battle and permanently expelled Arab raiders from central Italy, John VIII assumed, when Teofilatto died, that Rome would be his, but he had not reckoned on Teofilatto's daughter, Marozia. Marozia had him suffocated and then augmented her power by marrying, in succession, two of southern Europe's strongest monarchs. The only one able to unseat her was her own son, Alberic, who locked her up in the fortress of Hadrian's tomb, ruled as king of Rome for twenty years, built the new palace in the old temple of Serapis, and then installed his son as pope. The Teofilatti may not have been gentle rulers yet under their reign Rome sparkled as Western Europe's greatest city.

Their glory days finally came to an end in 963 when the king of a newly powerful German state, Otto I, marched south to have himself crowned Holy Roman Emperor. So began a new era of interference in Roman politics by increasingly idealistic German rulers, thanks to whom, as has been seen, the papacy came into the hands of the reformers. The reformist popes were more interested in moral change than building churches and in 1081 they had left little mark on Rome's architecture, yet many new buildings appeared during the thirty-five years of their rule. These were part of a fashion that began to spread across Europe in the eleventh century, and which offered both status and protection from one's neighbours: fortress towers. By 1081 Rome's thirteen leading families had constructed a number of these, including several across the river in Trastevere. They also built fortresses in the city's ancient ruins, whose thick walls made them even more formidable than the towers. The Frangipani family, whose power centre was the old Forum area, had a fortress in the eastern part of the Colosseum. The Corsi had a fortified home built out of the old Roman records office on the Capitoline Hill. The family of moneyman Leone di Benedetto Cristiano, the Pierleoni, who were based on the Tiber Island, made a fortress of the old Theatre of Marcellus. An extension spur of the Palatine Hill, the Septizonium was fortified. The city's greatest strongpoint, though, was Hadrian's tomb – today's Castel Sant'Angelo – which in 1081 was known as the Castel dei Crescentii.

What was life like for members of Rome's thirteen leading families in their towers and fortified classical ruins? Evidence from archaeological work and studies of legal documents paints a picture of a city that a visitor from the 530s would have found dismal. Long gone were the delights of late antique Rome. Though it is not easy to know precisely what functioned when, in 1081 it appears that only one of the city's original eleven aqueducts was still operating: the Acqua Vergine, that brought water to today's Trevi Fountain area. The Vatican was supplied by the smaller fourth-century Acqua Damasiana. For washing and drinking most Romans relied on wells, small springs that flowed only in rainier seasons, or the Tiber. Pleasure bathing was a distant memory.

Compared to earlier eras, even wealthy Romans led a simple existence in the eleventh century. The city's housing was the best in Europe yet compared to the housing of classical times it was very basic. One of the most desirable residential locations was in the ruins of the Baths of Alexander just west of the Pantheon, that had homes with marble staircases and little gardens with apple and fig trees, but even here houses were poky and shoddily built from reused brick and stone. Further out, in the suburban hamlets around the centre, well-off Romans lived like farmers. They tended vegetables in their

gardens and made their homes in upstairs rooms that were reached by
a wooden outside staircase, while their animals lived below them. It
was a state of affairs that aristocrats of the Empire would have found
inconceivable. As for poor Romans, they lived in tiny, flimsy wooden
dwellings just two or three metres across that would have been little
more comfortable than the huts where the very first Romans had lived,
two thousand years earlier.

Yet there had been some improvements. A document from 1127
describes a house with a new medieval invention that probably already
existed in homes in the city in 1081: a cosy fireplace. And if Romans'
homes were basic, they could be well furnished. Dowries and wills
of the time list kitchenware, trousseaus of clothes, beds, bedding,
elaborate hangings, and walnut letter-holders. They also mention
parchment books (paper had yet to arrive from the East). Here was
another area where Romans were ahead of most Europeans. In the
eleventh century, when literacy outside the Church was very rare in
Europe, many leading Romans could read.

And their health will have been a little better than in earlier
times. Annoyances were worse than ever, and with the routine of
daily bathing gone Romans would have been constantly scratching
flea and lice bites, but the city's shrunken population was too small
for diseases such as measles to be endemic. Romans in 1081 probably
lived longer than they had done five or ten centuries earlier. As always,
they lived longest if they were rich enough to escape the city during
the malaria season.

If they did get sick, eleventh-century Romans' first response was
likely to be a guilty conscience. Christian medical thinking, which was
strongly accusatory, viewed plagues and madness as evidence of sin,
and leprosy as proof of sexual misbehaviour. Yet, in many ways, the
rise of Christianity had changed matters less than one might expect,
and Romans' health options were fundamentally no different than
they had been in pagan times. Like their sick ancestors, sick medieval
Romans could seek either a religious or a professional cure. Though
Rome now had several hospitals these were on the prayer side of

the spectrum and were staffed by churchmen. As hospitals were also centres of infection, devout Romans would have been wiser to avoid them altogether and go to a church. A leading choice was that of the two curing saints Cosma e Damiano in the Forum, which was built on top of the old healing temple of pagan deities Castor and Pollux. Medieval saints, like pagan Asclepius, proudly advertised how they had saved sufferers whose ailments had confounded every doctor.

If Romans did go to a professional they had better options than most Europeans. Much had been lost and forgotten since the Germanic invasions and European medicine had greatly declined since classical times, but it had declined less markedly in Rome and southern Italy, where doctors probably did little more harm, and almost as much good in 1081 as they had done a thousand years earlier. Many of the best Italian doctors at this time were Jews, who had greater contact with medical knowledge preserved in the Islamic world, where faith and medical practice had been kept more distinct.

There would have been a number of Jewish doctors to choose from in Rome in 1081, as the city had a sizeable Jewish population. Benjamin Tudela, a Jewish visitor to Rome three generations after 1081, wrote that the city had a community of two hundred. In a curious mirror of the Christian world, Rome was the centre of European Judaism. The high status of Roman Jews sprang from the fact that their community was so ancient – it was the oldest continuously in existence – and that the Roman Jewish liturgy was believed to have been brought directly from the Great Temple of Jerusalem, from a time when it had still been functioning. The city's Jews were often closely connected with the popes – in Tudela's time one was Alexander III's steward – and they sometimes persuaded popes to intercede on behalf of Jews who were being maltreated elsewhere in the Catholic world. In the late eleventh century Rome's Jews had a powerful friend in Leone di Benedetto Cristiano who helped Gregory VII bribe the Romans in papal elections, and who, as one can guess from his name, was descended from Jewish converts to Christianity.

Yet, aside from its Jewish community, Rome was not a place of great diversity. The streets of the Leonine City pilgrims may have echoed with numerous languages, spoken by visiting pilgrims, but across the Tiber one would have heard little else but Italian, along with some Latin, and German spoken by a few higher churchmen in the Lateran. Rome was probably more culturally monochrome in the eleventh century than it had been in the 530s, when at least there was a visible Gothic presence.

Roman food, though, was becoming more diverse. The city's lively market, which had moved only a short way from its ancient site beside the Tiber, to the slope of the Capitoline Hill, offered fish, every kind of meat, vegetable and fruit, along with vinegar, wines, and mustard oil. One could find black peppercorns, imported from the distant East, which were as popular as they had been in classical times, and so precious that they were sometimes used as currency. One could buy cheeses, which probably included buffalo mozzarella, as buffaloes had been introduced to Italy several centuries earlier, either by the Lombards or the Byzantines. Exotic new ingredients brought to Sicily by the Arabs were also to be found, including aubergines, spinach, pomegranates, almonds, rice and saffron, sugar cane and lemons.

By 1081 Roman cuisine was already moving away from its classical, Thai style incarnation towards something that is more recognisably Italian. Eleventh-century Romans enjoyed a vegetable sauce named *pulmentarium* that was the ancestor of pasta sauces and pizza toppings. However, there is no evidence that fresh pasta, which had existed in classical times, was particularly popular in the eleventh century, while dried pasta was a thing of the future and tomatoes remained undiscovered in the Americas. Though one culinary innovation had already reached Rome by 1081. It was first recorded in Venice in the tenth century, where it caused quite a stir when it was observed being used by a sophisticated Byzantine princess: the fork.

Romans were also less divided in terms of wealth than they had been for a long time. The thirteen leading families were nothing like the super-rich aristocrats of the past. They were not even landowners

– how could they be when the Church owned most land? – but were instead sub-letting tenants. Lacking dynastic prestige, as none could trace ancestors back beyond a few generations, they were an elite of the nouveau riche, whose power sprang from their fortresses, their gold and their connections.

Beneath them a whole crowd was pressing upwards, hoping for advancement. In marked contrast to Rome in 410 or even Rome in 530, Rome in 1081 had a sizeable middle class. This sprang from the city's dynamic economy as, for all its parasitism, eleventh-century Rome was a productive place. Following on from Belisarius' innovation, the Tiber now had a small fleet of floating mills. The city was filled with artisans' workshops and there were ironworkers and potters in Trastevere, carpenters and shield-makers over the river, and shoemakers, furriers and bronze workers in the old Forum area. Rome was also one of Europe's most important financial centres, whose moneylenders provided gold to popes, and to visitors who needed to bribe their way to a favourable result in the city's new international Church court, which had recently been established by Gregory VII.

Rome's middle-class clerks and minor clergy, builders and soldiers, artisans and shopkeepers enjoyed comfortable lives. The rents they paid were low and many leased two or three homes, along with a little land outside the city. Most owned a horse and a suit of chain mail and on the first Sunday of Lent, when throngs of Romans made their way to the hill of discarded amphorae, Monte Testaccio, to play games and kill a bear, a bullock and a cockerel – representing, respectively, the devil, pride and unchastity – the city's poor walked, but its butchers and clerks, along with members of thirteen great families, rode with the pope. Rome still had its poor, of course, about whom – as usual – we know relatively little, but the city was now largely free of slaves. In 1081, though slavery still existed in Western Europe, it was a rarity. Instead of slaves, Rome's wealthy were looked after by servants. Though the quality of servants' lives was probably little better than that of slaves of earlier centuries, at least they had marriage rights and could own property.

Finally, Roman society was a little less patriarchal than it had been in earlier eras. The Middle Ages is not a time that is usually associated with women's rights but in 1081 Roman females – or at least rich Roman females – were better off than one might suppose. In part, this was because their city followed Roman law, which was more generous to them than other legal systems in force in Italy at this time. Roman females could expect to inherit property alongside their male siblings. Like females in earlier ages they were usually married in their teens to Roman males in their twenties, which meant they had a good chance of becoming rich widows. The eleventh century saw a peak in female land ownership in Italy and a good portion of Roman property was passed down to children from their mothers. Some even passed on their surnames. In most cases this was probably because the children were born illegitimately or their father had been a churchman. In the century before 1081 more than a third of Romans who found their way into official records did not take their father's surname but their mother's. This was an era when Italian women could wield real political power, as did the formidable Matilda of Tuscany, who personally led her troops on campaigns.

As to Roman fathers, if, as is probable, they were like Genoese fathers a few decades later whose wills have survived, they would have been worriers. They worried they would be outlived by their young wives and that their children would be sidelined and lose their inheritance to children of a second marriage, a fear which led them to leave money incentives to discourage their wives from remarrying. They worried about their children who had died – of whom there would have been distressingly many in this era – and, fearing for their chances of reaching heaven, they left money to have masses said on their behalf. Even the childless were worriers. Afraid that there would be nobody to take care of them in their old age, they adopted.

When they were not worrying about their children or their health, or eating fine food with forks, the thirteen great families of

Rome spent their energies competing with one another, and by the reign of Pope Gregory VII this competition had grown increasingly violent. A split existed among them whose origins went back to the 1062 crisis, when Henry's riverboat kidnapper Archbishop Anno of Cologne and the German court tried to impose their own papal candidate. Though, as we saw, the German court was thwarted by Hildebrand's energetic bribery, the dispute opened up a new and lasting fissure between supporters of popes and emperors, which would grow into the Guelph–Ghibelline conflict that set Italian cities against one another for several centuries. It would also play a part in Henry IV's attack on Rome.

Most of Rome's leading families, including the Frangipani, the Corsi, and the family of Leone di Benedetto Cristiano, the Pierleoni, stayed loyal to the reform popes, but three took the German side of the squabble. In 1075 a spat grew up between one of the pope's officials and a member of one of these families, Cencio di Stefano. After di Stefano built a tower on Hadrian's Bridge to extort money from passers-by, Gregory's city prefect arrested him and was dissuaded with difficulty from executing him. The following Christmas Gregory VII, as was traditional, celebrated mass in Santa Maria Maggiore but a heavy rainstorm kept most Romans away and the church was almost empty. Di Stefano saw his chance for revenge. He ran into the church with a group of armed followers, seized Gregory by the hair, flung him on to his horse and kidnapped him, taking him to a nearby tower belonging to his family. The drama proved short-lived. The next day, when the weather had improved, a crowd of Romans freed Gregory, who forgave di Stefano on condition that he go on a pilgrimage to Jerusalem. Having agreed, di Stefano then reneged and fled to Henry IV's Italian capital at Pavia. It may seem a minor enough incident yet it seems to have had important consequences. Most of all it would lead Henry IV to make a bad miscalculation.

III

On 21 May 1081, Henry IV's army camped outside the walls of Rome. Once again, our picture of his forces is imprecise but we know that they included Germans, Bohemians and northern Italians. There were feudal levies and mercenaries, foot soldiers, archers and also Europe's new super-weapon: knights. Knights were a product of the stirrup, an innovation that had arrived several centuries earlier from the East. Thanks to stirrups a knight could ride full tilt at an enemy and spear him with his lance without being thrown backwards off his horse. With chain mail to protect both man and horse from archers' arrows, knights were the tanks of the medieval world and a charge by them could smash through the most determined resistance. Yet there would not have been many knights in this particular army. As has been seen, Henry's force was small. Compared to the hordes of Alaric and Witigis, it was tiny and it was probably a good deal smaller even than Belisarius' army of 5,000.

Henry seems to have assumed that his military strength was not of much importance. What mattered was that he was there. The ease with which Gregory VII had been kidnapped from Santa Maria Maggiore may have made him over-confident, leading him to assume that Romans loathed their pope as much as he did. Such thinking would certainly explain his woeful lack of preparedness. Though he had brought an antipope, Wibert, he had neglected to bring any siege machinery and his timing, too, was poor. To mount a serious siege of Rome before the summer malarial season began he should have left Germany in the autumn. Instead he had left in the late winter, reaching Rome only on 21 May. He expected to be crowned Holy Roman Emperor, whether by Wibert or Gregory, at Pentecost, which fell just a couple of weeks later. It seems Henry had hurried to Rome assuming he would be welcomed into the city by its citizens.

He soon realized his mistake. Members of Rome's pro-German families slipped out to join him but, whether from a sense of loyalty or in memory of his cash handouts, the great majority of Romans sided with their pope. The city gates remained firmly shut and the walls were well guarded by the city's militiamen, bolstered by a few Normans and some Tuscans sent by Gregory's ally Matilda. Thwarted, Henry did his best to put a good face on things, writing a friendly manifesto to the Romans in which he feigned puzzlement that they had not come out to welcome their soon-to-be Holy Roman Emperor. He appointed officials, church and lay, just as if he were already inside the city, and even held a Whitsuntide procession with his antipope. Then, in early June, he and his army packed up and left.

Gregory and the Romans must have been exultant. After barely two weeks their enemy had turned tail and gone. Yet any celebrations were premature. Henry was fully determined to be crowned and to enjoy some revenge for his humiliation at Canossa, and the following three years saw a series of sieges of Rome that were the most protracted since those of Totila five centuries earlier. With each, Henry came a little closer to getting what he wanted. During his second siege, which began in February 1082, he detached two of Gregory's last significant friends in the region, Abbot Desiderius of the monastery of Montecassino and southern Italy's lesser Norman ruler, Prince Jordan of Capua. Henry also began negotiating an alliance with the Byzantine emperor Alexius Comemnus, who, eager to halt Robert Guiscard's invasion of his empire, offered Henry a large cash payment if he would attack Guiscard's territories in Puglia. Yet Comemnus' gold also brought Henry new worries. Comemnus bribed a number of Guiscard's underlings in Puglia to revolt and in April 1082 Guiscard was forced to leave his Byzantine invasion in the hands of one of his sons and sail back across the Adriatic. For the moment Guiscard was fully occupied dealing with the rebels but Henry cannot have been pleased to see him back on Italian soil.

At the end of 1082 Henry camped outside Rome with his army, determined to throttle the city with a prolonged siege. As famine struck, Romans' loyalty to Gregory VII began to waver. Gregory did not help his own cause, as it was clear to all that he was the one preventing a resolution of the crisis. Regular negotiations were held between the besieged and the besiegers, in which Henry, eager to finish his campaign and get back to his kingdom, showed some flexibility, but Gregory would not give an inch. Starving Romans were paying the price for his high principles. Then Henry's position was further strengthened when he enjoyed a breakthrough. The city's famished defenders had become sloppy and on 3 June 1083 a force of Milanese and Saxons led by Wigbert of Thuringia scaled the low walls of the Leonine City, broke inside and opened one of the gates. After two days of fighting around St Peter's, Henry's army prevailed and he marched triumphantly through the gate with his knights, his bishops, his Roman allies and his antipope, to take up residence in the Imperial Palace beside St Peter's.

His victory was a limited one. Though the Leonine City was his, the rest of Rome across the river was still locked firmly against him. As for Gregory VII, he was tantalizingly close and Henry might have glimpsed him staring disapprovingly at him. As the Leonine City fell Gregory's Pierleoni allies had whisked him to safety in Castel Sant'Angelo, just a few hundred yards from St Peter's. Yet, even if Gregory was safe, his position was deteriorating. The loss of the Leonine City further undermined Romans' sense of loyalty. Henry increased his popularity by showering the Romans with gold that he had just received from his new Byzantine ally, Emperor Comemnus, which would have been very welcome to Romans who had been starved of income from the Church and the pilgrim trade. By the next year, as they endured yet another siege, and saw their pope as obdurate as ever – he insisted that Henry must humble himself again, as he had at Canossa – loyalty began to turn to loathing.

King Henry was unaware of their change of heart. Gloomily accepting that he would probably have to return to Germany crownless, he left Rome to honour his agreement with Alexius Comemnus and attack Robert Guiscard's territories in Puglia, until, his campaign having hardly begun, he was surprised to receive a delegation of

Romans inviting him into the city. In a letter to Bishop Theodoric of Verdun, Henry recounted his amazement:

What we did in Rome with ten men, so to say, the Lord wrought through us; if our predecessors had done it with tens of thousands, to all it would have been a miracle. When we were thinking of returning to German territory, behold, the Romans sent us envoys, asked us to enter Rome, and promised to obey us in all respects. And so they did...[6]

Finally, on 21 March 1084, after almost three years of trying, Henry entered Rome in full splendour. Against all precedent he took up residence not in the Imperial Palace but in Gregory's home, the Lateran Palace, together with his wife, Bertha, who he had tried to divorce, and his antipope Wibert. Within days a parliament of Romans met and deposed Gregory VII – safe but livid in the Castel Sant'Angelo – and Wibert was elected as Pope Clement III. On Easter Monday, in a ceremony of great pomp, Clement III crowned Henry and Bertha Holy Roman Emperor and Empress. He had achieved all that he had come to Italy for.

Except that it was not quite all. He also wanted to enjoy some revenge for his humiliation at Canossa Castle. Shortly after his arrival in Rome his troops launched an attack on Castel Sant'Angelo, but the smooth, high stones of Hadrian's old tomb proved as strong as they had to Witigis' Goths five centuries earlier, and the attack was fended off with high casualties. It was still only the beginning of April, so there was ample time before the malarial season threatened. Henry besieged the fortress to starve Gregory into submission. In the meantime, he turned his attention to those of the city's great families – the Frangipani, the Corsi, the Pierleoni – who had remained loyal to Gregory and had retreated to their fortresses. Henry besieged and took the Corsi's strongpoint on the Capitoline. He had less luck with the artificial spur of the Palatine, the Septizonium, that was held by Gregory's nephew Rusticus, where all he achieved was the destruction of some fine classical colonnades. His forces probably also attacked the Frangipani's fortress in the Colosseum, where fire damage has been found from this time. He does not seem to have attempted to seize the Pierleoni's fortress in the Theatre of Marcellus.

Then Henry's chance for revenge slipped away. In early May troubling news arrived. Robert Guiscard was marching on Rome. Having shown no interest in helping Gregory since he had returned to Italy, two years earlier, he had now decided to come to his rescue. In part this would have been because he had finally crushed his rebellious underlings. At the time same time, while he had been content to see his former excommunicator suffer a little in Castel Sant'Angelo, he probably did not wish to risk losing him for good. A papal ally, especially a papal ally who owed him, could be useful.

Henry had no intention of staying and defending his new friends the Romans. He had everything he had come for. Why risk facing Robert Guiscard in battle, or becoming besieged in Rome during the malaria season? So, on 21 May 1084, in some haste, he, his wife, his antipope and his army abandoned Rome. They left just in time. Three days later Robert Guiscard's army were camped outside the San Lorenzo Gate. If Guiscard hoped to be invited inside by Gregory's supporters he was disappointed. Aside from the families still loyal to Gregory, still besieged in their fortresses, Romans remained resolutely antagonistic to their pope. This would be a fight.

Having just defied repeated sieges by Henry IV the Romans would have been confident, but so was Robert Guiscard. His army camped outside the city walls was eleventh-century Europe's most formidable military machine, and Robert had defeated every major power in the Mediterranean, from Ibn al-Hawas of Sicily to the Venetians, to Emperor Alexius Comemnus of Byzantium. Now he had sent the Holy Roman Emperor fleeing.

As to what happened next, once again we find ourselves in the hands of highly partisan chroniclers. They even disagree on the size of Guiscard's army. Two sources – Bishop Guido of Ferrara and William of Apulia – claim he had a huge force of 30,000 to 36,000 men, while

Geoffrey of Malaterra reports, in his biography of Robert Guiscard, that he had only 4,000. Whom should we trust? Bishop Guido of Ferrara was on the imperial side of the squabble and so had good reason to exaggerate Guiscard's strength, as it would make Henry's flight more excusable. Besides, a force of tens of thousands seems implausible in an era when armies were rarely large, while it was even less plausible in the case of Robert Guiscard, whose main force was still on the far side of the Adriatic, battling with Alexius Comemnus' Byzantines. Geoffrey of Malaterra's small army seems the more likely.

As to how Guiscard's soldiers got into Rome, there is less disagreement. Geoffrey of Malaterra tells us that Guiscard camped his army outside the San Lorenzo Gate for three days, during which time he carefully spied out the city, and for once all the sources concur. Guiscard's forces successfully broke into the city without help from inside. It is a simple assertion yet it is also quite remarkable. All the attacks on a properly defended and walled Rome so far, from that of Alaric, to the Ostrogoths, to those of Henry IV, involved protracted and ineffectual sieges. Alaric took Rome after two years of trying, Totila after a year (twice) and Henry IV after three years. Witigis besieged the city for a full year and failed to take it at all. Alaric, Totila and Henry all managed to capture the city only with the help of those inside the walls. By contrast Robert Guiscard took Rome without any inside help, in just four days.

How did he do it? Sources and Roman tradition all agree that he camped his army to the east of Rome and then got in through one of the gates. Which gate, though, is less clear. The sources offer a series of possibilities, from the Pinciana and Flaminia gates on the north side of the city to San Lorenzo in the east, but it is almost certainly none of these. Archaeological work has uncovered both fire damage and repair work that dates from this period in a different location entirely: the Latina Gate to the south. The Porta Latina seems a highly plausible candidate. It still stands, and a glance is enough to show that the Aurelian Walls are lower here than at other locations. Geoffrey of Malaterra reports that, having left the main part of his army to the east of the city, where they would distract and pin down Roman forces, he used darkness to sneak a force of some 1,400 round the walls, which then launched a dawn attack where he 'sensed that the guard would be weakest, with nobody expecting anything to happen in that area.'[7] In the late eleventh century the Porta Latina was in a quiet spot, far from the more inhabited parts of the city. As to how the Normans got into the city, Malaterra tells us that, 'Once the ladders had been quietly positioned, he scaled the walls.'[8] Guiscard relied on the simplest tactics: darkness and surprise. Yet his strategy proved so effective that one wonders why it was never tried by Henry, or for that matter by Alaric or Totila? Having scaled the walls, the Normans opened the Latina Gate and let their comrades inside. The city lay open to them.

Robert Guiscard, a warlord whose name inspired fear across the Mediterranean, had Rome at his mercy. Did he exact a terrible revenge on behalf of his ally, Gregory VII, whom the Romans had just betrayed? Once again, chroniclers offer a series of very different accounts, though all are agreed on one point: a dose of arson was involved. William of Apulia tells us simply that Guiscard 'fired some of the buildings',[9] then rescued Gregory VII and left. The Liber Pontificalis claims Guiscard did great damage to the area north of the Pantheon, around San Lorenzo in Lucina. Leo Marsicanus looks to Guiscard's cunning side, claiming that he deliberately set alight the church of Quattro Coronati and then, when the Romans were distracted trying to put it out, darted across the city to free Gregory. Geoffrey of Malaterra reports that Guiscard rescued Gregory with little trouble and reinstalled him in the Lateran Palace, but then three days later the Romans treacherously rose against him, and Guiscard, in order to defend himself, damaged 'the greater part of the city'.[10] The goriest version is offered by Bishop Guido of Ferrara, who claims that Guiscard burned most of the city, destroyed churches, and violently seized many married women and simple people from the sanctuary of churches.

Once again, archaeology offers the only neutral source of information. No evidence has been found of widespread destruction, though eight important buildings were damaged, some of them wholly destroyed. All were churches and they are worth listing: San Giovanni in Porta Latina, Santa Prisca on the Aventine Hill, San Giorgio Velabro by the river, San Lorenzo in Lucina to the north of the Pantheon – the area that the Liber Pontificalis claimed was badly damaged – and Santi Quattro Coronati on the Caelian Hill.

It may seem odd that Robert Guiscard, who had come to rescue the pope, burned churches. In this era, though, they frequently had two functions: religious and military. As robust stone buildings – a rarity in eleventh-century Europe – they were natural citadels. When Guiscard entered the city his greatest concern would have been to create a safe escape route for himself so that, if things went badly wrong, he would not risk the nightmare scenario of becoming trapped in a hostile city. He could leave no enemies behind him to block his retreat and so needed to smoke out any opponents holed up in churches, by setting alight their doors or, more probably, by climbing on to their roofs, removing tiles and firing the beams below.

Rome's burned churches mark out the likely route the Normans took. Having caught the Roman defenders by surprise on the wall they then secured their line of retreat by smoking out two groups of resisters, in the tower above the Latina Gate, and in the church of San Giovanni in Porta Latina that was just below. Next they made their way north along the Via di Porta Latina, past the ruined Baths of Caracalla to the long-abandoned chariot-racing stadium, the Circus Maximus. Here they may have linked up with some of Gregory's allies in the city, as his nephew Rusticus was still holding out in the nearby Septizonium fortress and the Frangipani clan were just beyond in the Colosseum. Pausing to smoke out some more resisters in the church of Santa Prisca on the Aventine Hill, and some more in San Giorgio Velabro by the river, the Normans would then have linked up with the Pierleoni on the Tiber Island, before finally making their way along the river to rescue a grateful and livid Gregory VII.

The Normans had achieved their aim but they still had to get safely out. It may have been now that they damaged the church of San

Lorenzo in Lucina, north of the Pantheon, or the church could have been fired by a second raiding force that broke into the city through one of the northern gates, as some sources claim. But the worst damage was still to be done. On the Caelian Hill the church of Quattro Coronati was gutted. It is easy to see why. If churches were strongpoints, Quattro Coronati, whose high walls rose out of the ruins of an ancient Roman town house, was nothing less than a fortress, which dominated the northern approach to the Lateran. Quite a struggle appears to have taken place here as not only Quattro Coronati but the whole Caelian Hill area was devastated. Was it here that the Romans launched the ill-fated counter-attack on the Normans that Geoffrey of Malaterra describes? It seems unlikely. As Guiscard's eulogist Malaterra would have wanted to show that the Romans were treacherous and deserving of punishment. It is more likely that the church was fired so the Normans could seize the Lateran area, whose capture was essential if they were to prove that Gregory had truly triumphed. Control of the Lateran would also allow them to link up with the rest of the Norman army that was still waiting outside the walls.

So it seems that of all the accounts of the attack, the one that gives the truest picture is probably also the briefest: that of William of Apulia, who said only that Guiscard burned certain buildings, rescued Pope Gregory and left. His words hint at what seems to have been a distinctly modern operation. Robert Guiscard set himself a clear and limited mission that he undertook with great efficiency. He broke into the city, rescued Gregory and overcame Roman resistance in a very short time, probably a matter of hours. It was a search and rescue mission worthy of a modern special forces unit.

Not for the first or the last time, Rome had got off relatively lightly as the damage it had suffered could have been far worse. It was helped by its topography. As a garden suburb city, its buildings were too low and dispersed to fuel a firestorm. It was also fortunate to have been attacked in May when the air was still relatively damp and wood less combustible. Yet the destruction should not be understated, either. The Caelian Hill, which had been a busy artisan area, was largely abandoned after the sack. There would also have been other damage that no archaeology can reveal. If Guiscard's attack was something of a surgical strike, there was still the question of what followed afterwards. The Romans had turned against their pope and now he was back in charge. He may have shown forgiveness – the sources offer no information either way – but his allies, the Frangipani, Pierleoni and Corsi, would have felt strongly aggrieved by those who had besieged them in their fortresses. It is hard to believe there was not some score-settling.

Despite Robert Guiscard's success, the real victor in the whole messy business was Henry IV. Not only had he succeeded in having himself crowned Holy Roman Emperor, he also kept control of the papacy. Though he hurried back to Germany, his antipope Clement III retreated only as far as the nearby hilltop town of Tivoli, where, showing his military acumen once again, he foiled all efforts by Guiscard and Gregory VII to capture him. The majority of Romans did not waver in their hostility to Gregory – they really had grown fed up with the man – who, only weeks after being rescued, was forced to flee his state. Guiscard, recognizing the usefulness of having a pope as his house guest, took him to his capital, Salerno, where he quickly put him to work, and had him consecrate the fine new cathedral Guiscard had just built in the city. All in all, the Rome attack had been a highly successful operation for him, which had enhanced his status and given him guaranteed support from the rightfully appointed pope.

Yet Guiscard's triumph was short-lived. Within a year both Gregory and he were dead. Gregory VII, his papacy still in tatters, died in exile in Salerno in May 1085. Robert Guiscard followed him two months later, succumbing to fever on the Greek island of Cephalonia, where he was trying to restart his stalled conquest of the Byzantine Empire.

Henry and his antipope fared much better. Henry ruled for another two decades before finally being betrayed, imprisoned and forced to abdicate by his son, Henry V. As for Clement III, within months of Guiscard and Gregory abandoning Rome for Salerno, he was back in the Lateran Palace and, despite repeated challenges by

Clockwise from top left: Henry IV and the anti-pope Guibert; Gregory being expelled from Rome; Gregory VII's death; Gregory VII negotiates with the bishops about Henry's excommunication; from the Chronicles of Otto Freising, *twelfth century.*

rival candidates, he clung on to the papacy for another sixteen years until his death in 1100. Though he had his comeuppance in the end. After he died he received a *damnatio memorie* – a condemnation of memory – by his successor Paschal II, who had his bones dug up from their tomb and thrown into the Tiber.

As to Rome, after three years of sieges and with its legitimate pope flung out, it was left in an unstable state. If papal schisms had occurred from time to time in the past, they now became so commonplace that most incumbent popes were menaced by rivals' claims. And yet, somehow, in the city's calmer moments, repairs were made and the churches that had been burned down by Guiscard's troops, such as Santi Quattro Coronati, were rebuilt.

Two new churches were created thanks to the city's instability. Both of these could be described as revenge churches, as their construction was used by one pope to obliterate the building of a hated predecessor. San Clemente, near to the Colosseum, had been closely linked with Henry IV's antipope and military organizer, Clement III. After Clement III's death his successor Paschal II – who threw Clement's bones into the Tiber – had Clement's church entombed with earth and used as the foundation for a new San Clemente. A few decades later the same fate befell Santa Maria in Trastevere, which had been the church of Anacaletus II before he became pope, and was entirely demolished and rebuilt by his successor and enemy, Innocent II. Thanks to spite, Rome gained two of its most beautiful churches.

If Roman politics were not already complex enough, in the 1140s a new element was added. As happened in other Italian cities at this time, Rome's middle-ranking inhabitants created their own government – the Senate – as a secular answer to the papacy. That so much of early Rome has survived is partly thanks to the Senate. The new body looked back with nostalgia to Rome's early days, meeting on the city's old citadel of the Capitoline Hill, and reviving the ancient title SPQR. It also tried to protect the city's surviving antiquities. It prohibited damage to Trajan's Column on pain of death and senatorial officials, Maestri di Strade e degli Edifici, were created to protect ancient monuments. The Senate first met three years after Pope Innocent II began looting the Baths of Caracalla of stone to build his revenge church, Santa Maria in Trastevere, so its very existence may have been inspired by anger at the destruction suffered by the city's ancient remains.

Naturally the papacy was none too happy with the new power arrangement, and emperors, popes and the Senate soon became embroiled in a shifting, triangular struggle for power. The main victim of the resulting chaos was the pilgrim trade, as pilgrims, impatient with Rome's violent disorder and avarice, chose to go elsewhere. In the generations before 1081 Rome had gained a new rival in the form of Santiago de Compostela in Spain. Pilgrims to Compostela, like those going to Rome, enjoyed an exciting journey that included the adventure of crossing high mountains, and though Compostela could not offer Peter and his keys to heaven, at least it was not infested with malaria, while successful pilgrims could buy a badge – a scallop shell – to show off when they got home. (Rome offered none.)

If Compostela were not enough, a few years after Robert Guiscard's attack Rome had to endure a second great pilgrimage rival. A little surprisingly, this competition was largely created by the popes. In 1097 Pope Urban II, the nemesis of Henry IV's antipope Clement III, made a reality of an idea that Gregory VII had dabbled with, and called for a crusade to the East. Two years later Jerusalem was captured from its Islamic rulers and became open to Christian visitors as it had not been for more than six hundred years. Jerusalem trumped Rome in every way. Pilgrims were forgiven all their sins. They felt they were in the presence of Jesus himself. And they could also buy a badge that depicted a palm leaf. Rome lost out as pilgrims flooded eastwards.

As Rome struggled, competition between its basilicas increased. Pilgrims were often disappointed by St Peter's, where they found themselves kept at a distance from the saint's remains that were buried deep beneath the basilica. Even the area above the tomb, where one could lower pieces of cloth and have them imbued with blessings, was off limits to all but VIP pilgrims. The Lateran Basilica offered itself as a more exciting alternative. It had a large collection of excitingly visible relics, which included what were claimed to be the Ark of the Covenant, milk from the Virgin's breast, Jesus' bodily remains and blood, his foreskin, the remnants of five of the loaves and two of the fishes he had produced and, most popular of all, the heads of both Saint Peter and Saint Paul. The Lateran Basilica also housed a very popular cloth image of Jesus – the Uronica – that was claimed to have been painted by Saint Luke and the angels. It was said to cause instant blindness to anyone who looked upon it, and so was always kept carefully covered. In mid-August it was carried round Rome in a grand procession, had its feet washed and was introduced to an image of Mary from Santa Maria Nova.

The priests of St Peter's fought back. The cathedral already had a piece of the True Cross, which had been suddenly revealed to Pope Sergius I during restoration work in the seventh century. Now they discovered the chair on which Saint Peter had been enthroned as bishop (it was actually from northern France and was probably brought by Frankish ruler Charles the Bald for his coronation as Holy Roman Emperor). Most usefully of all they acquired their own image of Jesus – the Veronica – which was claimed to be on the cloth Veronica had used to wipe Jesus' brow.

Soon there was enough pilgrim gold for both basilicas. Within decades of the Norman sack Europe was booming, gold flowed freely and Rome entered one of its greatest eras of cultural achievement. New churches were built and artists came from all over Italy to produce magnificent mosaics, frescoes and statues. Rome also offered an enticing new pilgrimage product – indulgences – which reduced the amount of time one spent in hell before reaching heaven. Best of all, in 1187, Jerusalem fell to Saladin and so Rome lost a major competitor. The dynamic Pope Innocent III, who took papal power-playing to lengths Gregory VII had only dreamed of, capitalized on Rome's good fortune. He built a hospital for pilgrims in the Leonine City and introduced weekly processions of St Peter's Veronica image of Jesus, which proved hugely popular. And he finally gave Rome pilgrims a badge – the Signa Apostolorum – which depicted Saint Paul with a sword and Saint Peter holding his key to heaven. Heaving with crowds, the Leonine City resembled a vast bazaar, shopping stalls sneaked their way into the very nave of St Peter's, and innkeepers physically grabbed pilgrims from their rivals.

The good times reached a climax in the year 1300. In February of that year another power-player pope, Boniface VIII, announced that any pilgrim who reached Rome before the end of the year, who confessed, who was penitent and who stayed in the city for at least fifteen days would receive plenary indulgence, or forgiveness of all sins. Rome was now offering what had, until then, been a monopoly of Jerusalem. So began Rome's first Holy Year. It was a triumphant success and one chronicler reported that it was as if the whole world was rushing to Rome, whether rich or poor, old or young, male or female. By Christmas, the crowds were so great that a number of unfortunate pilgrims were crushed to death.

Nobody could have imagined what lay just around the corner. Within a few short years all building projects in the city had been abandoned, artists had left to find better prospects elsewhere and the pilgrim trade was a shadow of its old self. Rome became a depressed city of street battles between rival families, whose population fell by half, to some 17,000. This was the century when Europe was ravaged by the Black Death, yet the plague, though it added to Rome's decline, was not its real cause. Rome had been struck by something much more familiar. In 1309, encouraged by the king of France, the French Pope Clement V moved the papacy to Avignon. The popes had left.

CHAPTER FIVE

SPANISH AND
LUTHERANS

I

THESE DAYS, unless it is in the depths of the off season or you don't mind spending a few hours in a queue, it is best to book a visit to the Vatican Museums online. Even then it can be a trying business that may feel less like a cultural feast than a trip to the sales. Artworks are lost behind huge tour groups, selfie sticks and guides' batons brandished above them. Doors create bottlenecks where guards endlessly murmur, 'Don't stop, keep moving.' The worst spot, unsurprisingly, is the most popular: the Sistine Chapel. As you enter, guards call out, 'Silence', 'No photographs', and direct you to join the crush that fills the room, of people staring upwards, holding audio guides to their heads, or listening to their tour leaders through earphones. And yet, as you try to hold your space against the people shoving past, it is still a dazzling, overwhelming sight.

It was a very different scene in the middle of November 1523. At that time Michelangelo's ceiling paintings were new, having been completed only a few years earlier, while his vast portrait of Judgement

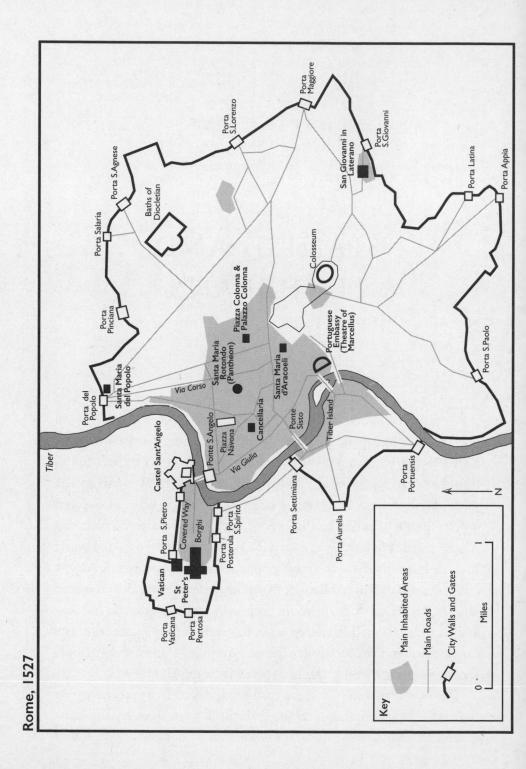

Rome, 1527

Porta Maggiore

Porta S.Lorenzo

Porta S.Giovanni

San Giovanni in Laterano

Porta S.Agnese

Baths of Diocletian

Porta Latina

Porta Appia

Porta Salaria

Colosseum

Porta Pinciana

Piazza Colonna & Palazzo Colonna

Porta S.Paolo

Santa Maria Rotondo (Pantheon)

Santa Maria d'Aracoeli

Portuguese Embassy (Theatre of Marcellus)

Porta del Popolo

Santa Maria del Popolo

Via Corso

Cancellaria

Tiber Island

Ponte S.Angelo

Piazza Navona

Ponte Sisto

Tiber

Castel Sant'Angelo

Via Giulia

Porta Settimiana

Porta Portuensis

Porta S.Pietro

Covered Way

Borghi

Porta Posterula

Porta S.Spirito

Porta Aurelia

Vatican

St Peter's

N

Porta Vaticana

Porta Pertosa

Key

Main Inhabited Areas

Main Roads

City Walls and Gates

0   Miles

Day remained a thing of the future. Several dozen hutch-like wooden cells lined the walls of the chapel, some painted red, others green, and each placed a little apart from its neighbours, to prevent those inside being overheard. There was no need to call for silence, as conversations would have been hushed and careful. This was a conclave of cardinals, meeting to choose a new pope.

It was deadlocked. For six weeks compromise candidates had been proposed and dropped (one of the first to go was England's Cardinal Wolsey) without success. Progress was blocked by the obstinacy of two rival factions, each of which had the backing of one of Europe's two great powers, who were in the midst of a grand struggle to dominate Italy. The group whose cells were painted red, whose candidate was Giulio de' Medici, was supported by Emperor Charles V. The other group, with green cells, was backed by the French king Francis I. De' Medici had fewer supporters among the cardinals – only 15 out of 39 – but, with some cardinals remaining neutral, he had enough to block the other side from winning. His cardinals were also dependable. Many were his relatives and had been appointed by his cousin, who until his death two years earlier had ruled as Pope Leo X.

By contrast all that held the other faction together was a shared desire to stop Giulio de' Medici. Its members included French cardinals, supporters of the popular Roman papal candidate Alessandro di Farnese, and also a group led by Cardinal Pompeo Colonna. Colonna had been a supporter of Charles V but had joined the French to thwart de' Medici, for whom he felt a strong dislike. The Medici were allies of the Colonnas' ancient enemies in Rome, the Orsini, while Pompeo had a personal grudge against them. Giulio's cousin, Pope Leo X, had imprisoned his relative, Cardinal Soderini, for several years on a false charge of plotting to kill him, and Soderini had only just been freed.

Six weeks was a long time for a conclave and impatience was rising, especially outside the Sistine Chapel. Until the cardinals made a decision the Papal States were in a state of paralysis and all public business was halted. The country was also vulnerable. The duke of Ferrara had already attacked its northern borderlands, seizing two towns. As was traditional when a conclave dragged on, Romans had rioted, shouting that the cardinals should hurry up and choose somebody, anybody, it didn't matter if he was a block of wood. The conclave guardians had been driven to making their worst threat, warning that if the cardinals did not reach a decision they would be put on a diet of bread and water. Still, the Mantuan envoy wrote despairingly that the cardinals seemed determined to spend the whole winter in conclave.

A resolution was nearer than he knew. On 16 November one of the anti-Imperialists finally cracked and switched his support to Giulio de' Medici. Rather surprisingly it was the one who most disliked him: Pompeo Colonna. That he had given way was largely the result of de' Medici's ingenious tactics. The French cardinals, growing weary of the deadlock, had thrown their support behind a new compromise candidate, Cardinal Orsini, and Giulio de' Medici, seeing his chance, said that he might also support him. Much though Pompeo Colonna loathed the thought of another Medici pope, the prospect of an Orsini pope was far worse. He and Giulio were publicly reconciled and eight days later Giulio was elected pope, taking the name Pope Clement VII.

The Romans were delighted. They had a pope; and a promising one, too. Leo X had been hugely popular, largely because of his lavish spending – which had contrasted strongly with the reign of his short-lived, stingy and much-loathed successor, the Dutch Pope Adrian VI – and everyone assumed Clement VII would be a big spender like his cousin. He was also expected to be an efficient pope, as it was well known that he had been the real statesman behind Leo's rule. Charles V's ambassador in Rome, the duke of Sessa, who had been working tirelessly in support of the de' Medici, was equally pleased. Triumphantly, he wrote to his master in Madrid, 'The pope is entirely your majesty's creature. So great is your majesty's power that you can change stones into obedient children.'[1] Yet, only three and a half years later, something that would have seemed unimaginable would occur. A huge, starving army would advance on Rome, sent by Charles V to exact revenge on Clement VII, his former protégé.

How had things gone so wrong? The answer lay largely with Clement himself. Clement has had a poor press over the centuries and his papacy is considered one of the most disastrous of any pope – which is quite a record to hold – yet it is hard not to feel a liking for the man. He was a private person, an unfortunate quality in a religious and state leader, and where his cousin had held lavish banquets with court jesters, Clement preferred quiet occasions with scholars. He was widely regarded as one of the finest musicians in all of Italy. He was a devoted admirer of Michelangelo, from whom he commissioned a number of projects, and with whom he kept up a regular correspondence, loudly reading out Michelangelo's jokes to the delight of the papal court.

He was also an unlikely pope. He was a love child. His mother was a Florentine woman of low birth while his father was the brother of Florence's ruler, Lorenzo the Magnificent. Being a Medici could be dangerous as well as advantageous as the family had many enemies, and baby Giulio's father was murdered shortly after he was born, causing him to be brought up in his uncle Lorenzo's home. Disaster then struck the whole family. When Giulio was fourteen the Medici were flung from power and exiled from Florence and it was almost twenty years before they were able to return as rulers, with the help of Emperor Charles V's grandfather, Emperor Maximilian. Throughout his life Giulio's first concern was to further his family's interests and those of their city, Florence.

After November 1523 he had two further interests to worry about: Catholicism and the city of Rome. His career in the Church owed everything to his cousin, who first promoted him into it, yet Clement had no wish to follow Leo's style, which had been closer to that of a Roman emperor than a pope. Leo held extravagant banquets and pageants, and he used papal troops to depose the duke of Urbino, in an unsuccessful attempt to create a new state for another of his cousins, Giuliano. In 1517 Leo falsely accused five cardinals, all of whom were old enemies of the Medici, of plotting against him. By doing so he both settled some old family scores – one of the cardinals was strangled in his cell – and, by selling their five vacant cardinal posts, he gained some spending money (one of the five was Pompeo Colonna's relative, Soderini). As has been seen, Leo also had no difficulty with nepotism and he made four of his relatives cardinals, one of them Giulio. Leo overcame the awkward matter of Giulio's illegitimacy by arranging for proof to be miraculously found that his parents had married in secret.

Clement, by contrast, was determined to be a good pope. He piously observed fasts and ate only bread and water during Lent. He tried to clean up the Church, at least in a modest way, and, despite the fact that, thanks to his cousin's extravagance, his papacy had inherited a huge financial black hole, he refused to sell cardinals' positions, or even to appoint new cardinals. That he tried to rein in spending won him few friends in Rome. Yet the disasters that struck his papacy sprang from elsewhere: when he tried to do the right thing in his foreign policy.

Foreign policy was never going to be easy. The previous three decades before Clement's election had been a violent and destructive time in Italy, when the peninsula was used as a battleground by Europe's great powers to settle their rivalries. That Italy was fought over was no accident. During this era Europe's rulers had grown accustomed to fighting with armies that were larger and more costly than their states could afford, and which could only be paid for with plunder. Italy was Europe's wealthiest region and so offered rich pickings. Until now Rome had not been a victim but an aggressor, as a series of powerful popes – including Clement's cousin Leo X – took advantage of the fighting to extend papal territory and to try and carve out new Italian states for their relatives. While other Italian cities had been wrecked, Rome remained unscathed.

At least till now. The papal conclave of 1523 had been contested so keenly because a new crisis was approaching between King Francis I and Emperor Charles V. Their personalities could hardly have been more different. Francis was something of a romantic, who viewed war in an almost medieval light, as an opportunity to show courage and gain honour. Charles V had much loftier ambitions. He was a one-man superpower, largely thanks to the poor health of his relatives. In this time Europe's ruling families frequently arranged marriages between their children, creating a complex web of royal cousins, and if enough of them died young or childless the result could be a kind of dynastic chain reaction. So it was with Charles. Born in the Netherlands, by the time he was nineteen the deaths of his uncle and aunt, a cousin, his father, a usurping uncle by marriage and Charles' highly placed grandparents, had left him ruler of most of modern Holland, Belgium and Austria, large parts of Germany, all of Aragon and its possessions – including Sicily and southern Italy – and finally Castile, which at that moment was in the process of conquering the Americas. He had also been elected Holy Roman Emperor.

One might think Charles would have been happy with his inheritance, but no. His mother was a depressive – possibly schizophrenic – who spent most of her life cloistered in a Spanish castle and Charles seems to have acquired her gloomy outlook. He was renowned for his chin, which was so large as to be almost deformed, and for his seriousness. Then again, he had much to be serious about. Ruling so many straggling territories meant there was more to go wrong. There was also the worry of the Turks, whose steady conquests in the Balkans and the eastern Mediterranean were causing alarm across Europe. Surveying his vast territories, which made him Europe's most powerful leader since Charlemagne, he decided that these had not come to him by chance, but that God had given them to him for a purpose. Accordingly, he set himself a short to-do list. First, he needed to unite all Europe (by defeating the French king, Francis, who was yet another of Charles' relatives). Second, he needed to unite Christianity (by crushing or winning round the supporters of a heretic challenging the Church, Martin Luther). Finally, he needed to save Christianity by defeating the Turks. His first task, of defeating the French, would begin in Italy.

To find his way through this minefield Clement VII needed luck and, above all, shrewd judgement. Both began to desert him even before he became pope. During the 1523 conclave a Venetian envoy reported that, in his eagerness to be elected, the future Clement had made an offer to the French to betray his supporter, Charles V, and remain neutral in any war, and possibly to support the French outright. Such a deal would explain a lot about his actions on becoming pope. At first neutral, within a year he had made a secret alliance with France.

He was far from alone. By 1524 Charles' vast empire and his sense of God-given destiny were causing unease across Italy, provoking Venice and Milan – which had also been imperial allies – to join the papacy in its secret alliance. Unfortunately, after only a few weeks, in January 1525, the alliance ceased to be secret. Charles was furious at this betrayal, especially by Clement, whom he had helped to win the papacy. He determined to gain revenge on 'that poltroon of a pope', adding ominously, 'Some day perhaps Martin Luther will become a man of substance.' The new anti-Empire alliance went awry almost at once. Within weeks Francis I was crushingly defeated at the battle of Pavia and he himself was captured. For a short time the disaster had an invigorating effect on Italians and, filled with patriotic fervour and determined to free their land of foreign invaders, most, but not all, Italian states joined a new alliance with France, the League of Cognac, but optimism quickly faded. The League's army became bogged down fighting Charles V's armies in northern Italy and opportunities were lost.

In the summer of 1526 Charles strengthened his forces. His commander in northern Italy, Constable Bourbon – a French renegade who had turned against his country after his king, Francis, tried to take his lands – was sent 5,000 Spanish, who at this time were considered the finest soldiers in Europe. Across the Alps, Charles' loyal underling in southern Germany, Georg von Frundsberg, was so keen to see Pope Clement hanged for his betrayal that he paid soldiers with his own money, pawning towns he possessed, his castle and even his wife's jewels. His efforts paid off and he managed to raise a force of 10,000 Landsknechte. Though mercenaries, the Landsknechte had an intense sense of collective loyalty, electing officers and court-martialling any soldier who dishonoured his comrades – each company had its own executioner – so their units have been described as military republics. They also held strong religious views. Many had been won over by Martin Luther's recent attacks on the papacy and were eager to kill some churchmen, the higher the better.

If he did not already have trouble enough, Clement also faced enemies from the south. Pompeo Colonna, who had extensive estates and castles south of Rome, was eager to avenge himself for, as he saw it, Clement's theft of the papacy, that had been rightfully his. Colonna allied himself with the kingdom of Naples – which was yet another of Charles V's territories – and it was he who struck the first blow against Clement. That he managed to do so was wholly Clement's fault as, though highly intelligent, Clement could be very gullible. In the summer of 1526 Pompeo had his cousin Vespasiano, whom Clement liked and – unwisely – trusted, convince him that the Colonna wanted only peace. Clement, struggling to deal with the financial black hole left by his cousin, decided to save money by standing down the troops he had guarding Rome from the south.

That it was a poor saving became painfully clear at dawn on 20 September 1526 when Colonna's troops seized Rome's San Giovanni and San Paolo gates and poured into the city. Compared to the other attacks on Rome that we have seen, this was more like a military parade than a sack. The Romans, who felt resentful towards Clement for having raised their taxes, refused to fight and instead went out to watch as Pompeo's troops marched across the town and then fought their way through the Santo Spirito Gate and into the Borgo, as the old Leonine City was now known. Pompeo failed in his main objective of capturing Clement, who saved himself at the last minute by fleeing along the raised escape passage to the Castel Sant'Angelo. The raid was still a humiliation for the pope. Worse, it showed his vulnerability. Clement was helpless against the raiders who pillaged the papal palace and stole every horse in the papal stables.

During the following months Clement gained his revenge. He raised armies, which, together with those of his League allies, destroyed Colonna fortresses south of Rome and captured a string of towns from imperial Naples. Unfortunately, Naples and the Colonna were no longer his real threat. In February 1527 Bourbon's 5,000 Spanish linked up with Frundsberg's 10,000 Landsknechte and, with Bourbon in command, the huge combined army, whose camp followers and prostitutes outnumbered its soldiers, began moving slowly southwards. Emperor Charles V made his intentions clear. He wanted to hold a general council of the Church, which could mean only one thing: he intended to see Clement replaced as pope. If Frundsberg's Landsknechte had not already hanged him.

First, though, they had to reach Rome, which was no easy matter. Though it contained the most formidable soldiers in Europe, Bourbon's army was, like any army of this era, highly unstable, being less an arm of the state than a kind of rogue state in its own right, loyal only to itself. Having entered papal territory in early March it then had to stop outside Bologna to shelter from atrocious late winter weather. Idleness soon led to trouble. The Spanish troops, who were owed more back pay than the Landsknechte, mutinied, and Bourbon saved his own life only by fleeing to the Landsknechte and hiding in a horse stall. The Landsknechte then rebelled too, and when their commander Georg von Frundsberg tried to control them he became so worked up that he had a stroke and was forced to abandon his soldiers and return to Germany.

It was not a promising start to the campaign. To Pope Clement, though, the simple fact that a large imperial army had crossed into papal territory had a demoralizing effect. In mid-March, without consulting his League allies, and despite the fact that his forces were making good progress in the south, Clement made a unilateral peace with Charles V's ruler in Naples, the imperial viceroy Charles de Lannoy. Clement's allies were furious. Yet one can see why Clement was tempted as it was an excellent deal. Lannoy agreed that all imperial troops would leave papal territory at once, while Clement's ally, the duke of Sforza of Milan – who was at the heart of the whole conflict – would regain his lost dukedom. The war was over and Rome and

Florence were safe. As his part of the truce, Clement agreed to end his attacks on Naples and also to hand over 60,000 ducats, which would be given to the Landsknechte to persuade them to go home to Germany. Happy in the knowledge that he had nothing further to worry about, Clement, for a second time in less than a year, saved money by standing down his troops.

But he had been gulled again. In Charles V's rickety empire it was often unclear who had authority over whom, an ambiguity which Charles and his commanders found very useful. That Clement had made peace with Charles' man in Naples, Lannoy, did not mean he had made peace with the commander of Charles' army in northern Italy, Bourbon. Lannoy, who was known for his double-dealing, probably intended to trick Clement all along, though he made a pretence of acting in good faith. He sent an envoy to Bourbon's army, which was still sheltering from the weather outside Bologna, who handed over Clement's 60,000 ducats and ordered Bourbon to leave papal territory. To Bourbon, though, retreat was not an option. Charles V had secretly instructed him to take Rome if he could, while even the pope's ducats were not enough to cover his troops' back pay. Bourbon knew they would be satisfied only if they plundered a large city: either Florence or Rome would do. Accordingly he had his soldiers fake a second mutiny and then told Lannoy's envoy that he was unable to leave papal territory as his army was now out of control.

Finally, at the beginning of April, having slimmed down his forces, reducing the camp followers to a meagre three prostitutes per company, Bourbon and his army resumed their march south, sacking and burning small towns along the way. The weather was as bad as before, with heavy snow and driving rain that left rivers so swollen that Bourbon had to leave behind his three heaviest guns. On 15 April he was met by the perfidious viceroy of Naples, Lannoy, who brought another stash of money. This had been extracted from the Florentines, who had melted down treasures from their churches in the belief that this would convince Bourbon to leave. The invasion was being financed by its victims. Bourbon pocketed the money and marched on, his army larger than ever, as it had now been joined by several thousand Italian adventurers, eager to gain some plunder.

On 25 April, Clement, who had finally seen the worthlessness of his truce with Lannoy, changed his mind yet again and rejoined the League of Cognac. Though he had stood down most of his troops he was not entirely at the mercy of Bourbon's forces. The Venetians, in spite of Clement's treacherous unilateral peace, had ordered the League's army, which was commanded by the duke of Urbino, to march south, shadowing Bourbon's forces. If this was good news for Clement, it was not that good. The duke of Urbino, who was violently short-tempered, and had personally murdered two people by the age of 21, one of them a cardinal, was the very same duke of Urbino who Clement's spendthrift cousin, Leo X, had tried and failed to rob of his dukedom. The League army's commander-in-chief was no friend of the Medici.

Urbino soon showed his priorities. In late April, Bourbon's army neared Florence, where a large anti-Medici faction was ready to welcome them into the city. Urbino saved the day, reaching Florence before the Imperialists, cowing the anti-Medici rebels and keeping Bourbon's army at bay. His actions, though, were intended as a favour not to Clement but to himself. In exchange for Urbino's help, the pro-Medici Florentines handed back a small area of territory that Urbino had failed to regain since Leo X tried to steal his dukedom. Urbino might be commander of the League army but he was working strictly for himself.

Worse, the saving of Florence put Rome in greater danger. Bourbon, fearful that the League army would foil him again, began a rapid, forced march. At Siena, which was an imperial ally, he slimmed down his forces again, dismissing more camp followers and abandoning all his remaining artillery. His army, its load lightened, then began a dash southwards. The weather was still terrible and the river Paglia was so swollen that to avoid being swept away, his cavalry clutched the manes of their horses and his soldiers clung to one another's shoulders. Despite this the army made rapid progress, covering 30 to 50 kilometres each day.

As they drew closer to Rome, Bourbon received word from Clement's other enemy, Cardinal Pompeo Colonna, who proposed that he and Bourbon should attack Rome together. On the night of 9 May Colonna would have his supporters in the city rouse the populace in revolt against Clement, and at dawn the next morning they would open the Porta del Popolo to Bourbon's troops. The plan made a good deal of sense. Bourbon's tactics, as far as he had any, were strangely out of time. During the battles that had been going on for the previous thirty years in Italy, European warfare had become transformed. Medieval tactics involving knights and pikemen had given way to methods that looked ahead to those of the Napoleonic era, in which artillery and soldiers armed with arquebus guns were the key to winning battles. Campaigns were frequently decided by sieges, around which a new science was evolving, of elaborate bastions, of trenches and counter-trenches, and of underground mines and counter-mines, and in which defenders had a strong advantage over their attackers. It was unheard of for a city to be attacked by storm.

Yet, without artillery, Bourbon had no other options. His army raced on to Viterbo, past Lake Bracciano and to Isola Farnese, carried forward by its hunger, its momentum and its fear of the League army that its soldiers knew was close behind them. On the afternoon of 5 May, four days before Colonna's proposed uprising, the army reached Rome. Though his soldiers were exhausted, cold and starving, Bourbon did not wait but immediately sent out a force to cross the Tiber, and another to skirmish at the walls of the Leonine City. Neither achieved anything but high casualties. Reluctantly, Bourbon had his soldiers set up camp on nearby Monte Mario while he himself rode out to make a careful inspection of the Leonine Wall looking for weak spots. He soon found one.

II

What kind of Rome lay waiting for him? Compared to our earlier glimpses of the city, some of which have been a little hazy, Rome in 1527 can be seen in sharp detail as we are almost spoiled for information. Where before we have relied on archaeological discoveries, legal documents or perhaps a telling line in a letter or a satirical poem, there are now paintings of the city, sketches, maps and city guides for visitors in different languages. There are numerous buildings that have survived comparatively unscathed across the ages. There is also a new form of writing that was unheard of in the unegotistical Middle Ages, and was rare even in classical times: the personal account. With the rise of printing a century earlier and with more people able to read and write than ever before, the literary selfie had arrived. At times it seems as if everyone who was anyone produced their version of great events, to exaggerate their own roles and smear their enemies.

If a Roman from 1081 had found himself transported forwards four and a half centuries, his greatest surprise would have been the discovery that their city had moved. By 1527 Rome had completed a process that had been going on for more than a millennium, as it shifted slowly westwards, pulled by the river and the magnet of Saint Peter's tomb. By the sixteenth century, Romans had abandoned their ancient heartland – the seven hills – for the malarial lowlands beside the Tiber. This change had brought another. The suburban, garden city of the eleventh century had been replaced by two sharply distinct landscapes. Most of the area within the old city walls was now countryside. The *disabitato* – which meant the uninhabited part – was made up of fields and vineyards, along with occasional churches, farmhouses and country retreats for wealthy Romans. The Forum, which had been the Frangipani's power base, was now called the *Campo Vaccino* (the cow field), and the southern part of the Capitoline, the Tarpeian Rock, was *Monte Caprino*, or Goat Hill.

As to the smaller, inhabited, *abitato*, a visitor from 1081 would have found it oppressively crowded. Packed into its streets were more Romans than the city had contained for a thousand years. Since the popes had returned to Rome from Avignon in the 1420s Rome had boomed. In May 1527, as chance would have it, we know precisely how many Romans there were, as the city's first ever census had been taken only a few weeks earlier. In early 1527 Rome had a total of 54,000 inhabitants, excluding infants. Six years earlier, prior to a series of troubles – which we will come to – the population had been considerably larger, and may have been as high as 85,000. And of course there were also pilgrims who, as in medieval times, were a constant presence. In jubilee years Rome had more visitors than inhabitants, thronging the Borgo, staying in the city's hundreds of lodging houses and, as ever, buying straw for their bedding in St Peter's Square. St Peter's itself was something of a disappointment – it was a building site – but pilgrims who came at Easter, Ascension or Christmas could watch the pope appear on the portico above the church's entrance to bless the Veronica cloth. And there were the other great churches to visit, with their famous relics. San Giovanni, despite having burned down twice, still displayed Peter's and Paul's heads.

Yet if Rome was larger than it had been for many centuries, it had slipped behind other cities. To visitors from northern Italy, or northern Europe, whose towns had mechanical clocks and a new sense of time and precision, Rome was old-fashioned. It was also falling behind economically. Unlike other great cities in Europe and the Middle East, Rome had comparatively few artisans. Most Romans worked as shopkeepers or innkeepers in the pilgrim trade, or as bankers, jewellers, painters, medal makers or silversmiths. Directly or indirectly, almost everyone in Rome now worked for the Church.

The Church could pay well and its gold had had a striking effect on the city's population. In the early sixteenth century few Romans were really Romans. Less than a quarter of them had been born in the city or even in the Papal States. Rome in 1527 was the most cosmopolitan city in Europe, and its people were more diverse than they had been since imperial times, a thousand years earlier. More than half came from other Italian states and almost a fifth from outside the peninsula. Rome had Lombard builders, architects, artisans and labourers. Rome's river port was worked by Genovese sailors. There were Tuscan bankers, jewellers, shopkeepers, printmakers, painters and sculptors, German bakers and cooks, and German and French innkeepers. To warm the nights of the city's numerous Spanish churchmen there was a thriving colony of Spanish prostitutes, one of whom inspired a play that was a huge hit in Spain. One of the few European countries that was hardly represented, curiously enough, was England, though there had been a sizeable English colony only a century earlier. It was as if the English were already preparing themselves for their break with the Catholic Church.

As well as economic migrants, the city was home to refugees escaping violence. Lombards fled the endless wars fought over Milan by Europe's great powers. Albanians and Balkan Slavs fled Turkish occupation. Jews fled a new wave of persecution in Portugal, Spain, and Spanish-conquered Sicily and southern Italy. For the most part they found Rome a welcoming sanctuary. The two Medici popes, Leo X and Clement VII, were known for their tolerance and in 1527 Rome had a thriving Jewish community of almost 2,000, which included every profession from doctors, bankers, musicians and rabbis to the poorest artisans and traders. When Michelangelo painted the Sistine Chapel he sought out Jewish Roman models for Old Testament figures. Though life for Rome's Jews could be precarious at certain seasons. Easter passion plays in the Colosseum could work Christians into violence and Carnival, in the last days before Lent, also had its dangers. Races were held on the long Via del Corso, in which Jews old and young were made to run semi-naked, as crowds, many of whom had placed bets on the runners, jeered and threw filth. Jews were not alone in having to run the gauntlet on the Corso. There were also races for young Christians, old Christians, for donkeys and for water buffalo. Pope Alexander VI, formerly Rodrigo Borgia, introduced a new race for Rome's prostitutes.

Most of the city's immigrants lived in areas that a visitor from the eleventh century would have found dimly familiar. They were medieval and, thanks to medieval city planning, their inhabitants lived cheek by jowl in permanent chaos. Compared to those of classical times, homes in 1527 were still small – a few had four floors but most had only two – yet they were festooned with balconies, outside stairways, overhangs and porticoes that encroached on every free inch of space. Below them lay a labyrinth of courtyards, archways and dark, winding alleys that were congested with obstacles and, most of all, congested with Romans: Romans doing their laundry or cutting up animal carcasses; Romans selling their wares or cooking their dinner. Rome in 1527 stank as it had not done since the glory days of Empire: of rubbish, offal and fish bones, of filthy water from tanneries and dyers, and of dung, both animal and human.

Rome was also a city of that most medieval of constructions, fortress towers. A visitor from the eleventh century, if he or she climbed one of the city's hills, would have been astonished by the city's appearance. Rome now had a pincushion or porcupine look. In 1081 it had possessed a dozen fortress towers. Now there were hundreds. Offering both status and security from one's neighbours, during the high Middle Ages towers had become a must for every Roman who was anyone, and even shopkeepers built them. Some sprouted from ancient triumphal arches. The Church soon joined in and spindly bell towers, or *campanili*, sprang up beside churches across the city. One even appeared on the portico of the Pantheon. Rome also had a new skyline. Where it had once been overlooked by the temple to Jupiter Best and Greatest on the Capitoline Hill – now a quarry for stone – from the 1250s it was dominated by a large new church that stood on the other, northern end of the Capitoline: Santa Maria in Aracoeli.

Fortress towers did not stand alone but rose up from medieval palaces that were built around courtyards, and had outside stairways, often covered to keep their inhabitants dry. To Romans of the High Middle Ages these homes were a vast improvement on the ad hoc homes of their eleventh-century ancestors, which had been built out of the city's crumbling ruins. These had long ago fallen out of fashion and in 1527, aside from the pope's fortress, the Castel Sant'Angelo, the only classical building that was still inhabited was the old Pierleoni fortress, the Theatre of Marcellus, which had lately been converted into a palace and was now the home of the Portuguese ambassador.

By the 1520s fashions had changed once again, and if many rich Romans remained in their families' medieval palaces, with small windows and dark, poky rooms, few wanted to do so. They wanted to live in a new Renaissance palace – still relatively rare, though steadily growing in number – whose rooms were spacious and filled with light. Rome's new housing was designed with a new sense of the rational, with each level assigned a clear role, from the storerooms and stables on the flood-prone ground floor, to the halls, dining rooms and owners' bedrooms on the temperate first floor – the *piano nobile* – to the servants' quarters that, just as in ancient Roman mansions, baked beneath the roof.

One of Rome's first new palaces was the Palazzo San Marco, which was begun in 1455, and is better known by its later name of Palazzo Venezia (it was here that, almost five centuries later, Mussolini would appear on the balcony to address huge crowds of supporters). Two decades later, Rome's palace boom really took off, when Pope Sixtus IV introduced a new law that allowed high clergy, who until then had been required to bequeath any palace they built to the Church, to leave palaces to their relatives. It would not be the last time that Rome's architectural beauty would be nourished by dubious financial arrangements. Palaces and grand new houses sprang up across the city. One of the largest was built by Sixtus' nephew, Cardinal Raffaele Riario, who had money to spend, having won a huge sum gambling with the son of Sixtus' successor, Pope Innocent VIII, and who demolished a fourth-century church to build his grand new home, the Palazzo della Cancelleria. In 1523 it would be given to Pompeo Colonna by Giulio de' Medici, as part of the deal he made for Colonna's support in the conclave.

The greatest Roman home, naturally, was in the Vatican. In the 1520s the Vatican Palace was in the midst of becoming Europe's largest palace. It had accomplished this feat in a complex series of stages. At the beginning of the thirteenth century a palace was built here which gradually supplanted the Lateran as the main papal dwelling. In the 1480s Pope Innocent VIII built a modest second palace on the Vatican hill, which overlooked its medieval predecessor several hundred yards below and was named the Belvedere for its fine views. Two decades later the syphilitic warrior Pope Julius II had his architect, Bramante, draw up a plan to link the palaces by two immensely long wings. By 1527 one wing was already complete and overlooked what would become a gargantuan courtyard that occupied three levels as it climbed the hill.

Beneath its Renaissance palaces Rome had new Renaissance streets. An eleventh-century visitor would have found these puzzlingly alien: straight, wide and uncluttered, with high, clean-lined buildings. It was almost as if Rome's ancient ruins had come back to life. And, in a way, that was exactly what had happened. In 1527 the Italian Renaissance was at its height and classical design was much admired. The architecture of Rome's new buildings emulated that of Rome a millennium and a half earlier.

Rome's new streets, and especially their names, could be read like a book that recounted Rome's violent and nepotistic recent history. Just as Roman emperors had left their mark with a new set of baths or a new forum, Renaissance popes – who could behave very much like Roman emperors – did so in more functional ways. The habit was inspired by a disaster. One evening during the 1450 Holy Year, when the Sant'Angelo Bridge was crowded with people leaving the Borgo for their inns across the river, a mule started bucking. In the panic that followed almost two hundred pilgrims were crushed to death or fell into the Tiber and drowned. Afterwards a number of measures were taken to remove the city's worst bottlenecks and to make it more easily traversable for pilgrims. In time for the 1475 Holy Year, Sixtus IV – a worldly, power-player pope, whose nephew was the assassin of baby Giulio de' Medici's father – built Rome's first new bridge for more than a thousand years. It was intended to ease pressure on the Ponte

Sant'Angelo and, naturally, Sixtus named it after himself, as the Ponte Sisto.

After the Ponte Sisto came new roads. For the 1500 Holy Year, Pope Alexander VI (previously Rodrigo Borgia) built the Via Alessandrina, which cut through the Leonine City. Alexander VI's successor, Pope Julius II, was in many ways even more alarming than his Borgia predecessor. The nephew of the Sixtus IV who had built the Ponte Sisto, he had a foul temper, suffered from syphilis and dressed in armour to lead his troops in battle. Julius built the Via Giulia, that linked the Ponte Sant'Angelo with his uncle's Ponte Sisto. Across the river Julius built another new road, the Via Lungara, which linked the Vatican with Trastevere, each of which had their own walls, and which until then had only been reachable from one another by passing across the river twice and going through the main part of Rome. Finally, Julius' successor, Clement's cousin, Leo X, built the Via Leonia that extended halfway across the city, from Porta del Popolo in the north to the centre of the city.

Yet if Renaissance Rome's popes built new bridges, palaces and streets, they were responsible for comparatively few new churches. In the 1470s Pope Sixtus IV built Santa Maria del Popolo, a traditional Renaissance design – octagonal with a small dome – which, like his Ponte Sisto, had pilgrims in mind: it lay just inside the city's northern gate where most of them first entered Rome. Sixtus also built the beautiful Santa Maria della Pace, near Piazza Navona. However, most churches of this era were built not by the papacy but by professional guilds or fraternities of foreign nationals. The city's German community built Santa Maria dell'Anima, close to what is now Piazza Navona, and the Spanish of Rome created San Pietro in Montorio on the Gianicolo Hill.

The great majority of Rome's churches in the 1520s were still medieval. Many dated from the glory days of the twelfth and thirteenth centuries when the city had thrived and drew Italy's finest artists, from Pietro Cavallini to Jacopo Torriti, to create magnificent mosaics, frescoes and statues. Yet there was something a little odd about Rome's high medieval churches. When they were built the Gothic style held sway and across Europe churches rose up with tall, pointed arches; but not in Rome. Roman church builders refused to bow to fashion and remained uniquely conservative. Arches stayed Romanesque and mosaics were so closely modelled on the city's earliest church decoration that they included imagery that had nothing to do with Christianity: shepherds, dolphins, and rural scenes. Today's visitors to Rome's medieval churches may struggle to find a sense of passing time, as their decorations seem strangely alike.

If early sixteenth-century popes built few churches at least they had a good excuse: they were engaged on building one church that was Europe's greatest construction project since classical times. It is a change that a visitor from 1081 would have found profoundly shocking. In 1527 Rome's greatest and most famous church, St Peter's, which had drawn pilgrims from across Europe for more than a thousand years, was half demolished. Only the cathedral's frontage, which faced on to Saint Peter's Square, and the eastern part of the nave, remained standing. The rest was in chaos, with giant new pillars rising out of a construction site. In its midst, a temporary building had been put up to shelter the altar and Saint Peter's tomb beneath.

In some ways St Peter's was a victim of its own success. Three centuries earlier it had quashed its old rival the Lateran Basilica once and for all, when Innocent III had 'Mother of all churches' – a title the Lateran had long claimed – written in giant letters on the archway above in its nave. As if stung by its demotion the Lateran Basilica burned down not once but twice, in 1308 and 1361. Saint Peter's corpse had won a crushing victory, drawing the whole city westwards towards it, while his head, allegedly in the Lateran, was left increasingly remote, exiled to a kind of village with a cathedral and a palace surrounded by empty fields. Naturally, Renaissance popes wanted to be buried near Saint Peter's body, and they also wanted to be buried in proper style. The demolition of St Peter's, which many Romans regarded as an act of gross vandalism, was first set in motion by the warrior pope, Julius II, who claimed the old building was unsafe. It was true that a leaning nave wall was cause of concern, but Julius' real reasoning seems to have been less selfless: demolition allowed him to build himself a splendid tomb.

The building that was to replace the old St Peter's had been designed, like many of Rome's new buildings in the early sixteenth century, by Bramante, who declared it would be as if the Basilica of Maxentius – one of the largest buildings of the late Roman Empire – were topped by the dome of the Pantheon. Romans replied by naming him *Bramante Ruinante* (Bramante the wrecker). It was not by chance that no building on this scale had been attempted since late antiquity. Bramante used moulded concrete techniques that had remained forgotten or misunderstood for a thousand years. It was only in the previous decades that Renaissance scholars had studied these methods, which had been described by the classical architect and writer Vitruvius, and brought them back into use.

The popes had, of course, also completed another great church, though this was not for the Romans but strictly for their own private use: the Sistine Chapel. Constructed rather hurriedly between 1477 and 1481, its walls were then decorated with paintings by some of the greatest artists of the era: Sandro Botticelli, Pietro Perugino and Filippino Lippi. As for the chapel's ceiling, it might never have been touched if the building had been better constructed. In 1504 a huge crack appeared in the roof above the altar. It was made safe by placing large metal rods beneath the floor and the roof. Pope Julius II was not prepared to leave his uncle's Sixtus' chapel ugly and so, for a huge fee, he hired a 33-year-old artist named Michelangelo Buonarroti to paint over the mess. At first Julius wanted Michelangelo to depict the twelve apostles but when Michelangelo complained that this would be 'a poor sort of thing', Julius – at least according to Michelangelo – let him paint whatever he liked. The result, twelve years later, was 1,200 square metres of extraordinary imagery, most of it by Michelangelo's own hand, that revolutionized Western art.

That Renaissance popes had devoted their resources to a private chapel is not surprising. Compared to their medieval predecessors, who were constantly rubbing shoulders with their Roman subjects, Renaissance popes were aloof and princely. The great processions of the Middle Ages, in which popes rode or walked barefoot among crowds of Romans, mostly vanished during the Avignon years, when the popes abandoned Rome for Provence. By 1527 only one or two processions were still held, such as those that marked the lavish feasts of Corpus Christi and Saint Mark. The most splendid procession was the rarest: the *possesso*, where a new pope paraded through the city to claim it as his own. Likewise, most papal ceremonies were now held behind closed doors before a select audience of high churchmen and foreign ambassadors. In medieval times popes had frequently celebrated mass and preached but in the Renaissance they became increasingly mute. Monks now did most of the preaching and services were dominated by laborious rituals, such as the vesting – dressing – of the pope.

Yet, if the Sistine Chapel had been costly to build and decorate, its expenses were dwarfed by those of rebuilding St Peter's. It was this vast outlay, in fact, that was largely to blame for the dire predicament in which the Romans found themselves in 1527. Julius II's successor, Leo X, who had numerous other expenses, from banquets and elephant pageants to predatory wars, began a fund-raising campaign to pay for the building work. In 1517 he sent a monk named Johann Tetzel to tour Germany selling indulgences, which supposedly had the power to release one's dead relatives from purgatory, or reduce the length of one's stay there. Tetzel's salesmanship – he used the memorable catchphrase, 'The moment a coin in the coffer rings, a soul from purgatory springs' – caught the eye of another monk, named Martin Luther, who was so incensed that he wrote a denunciation of Church corruption, the *95 Theses*. It was the first of a series of memorably pithy, irate pamphlets which, thanks to printing, rapidly went viral across Germany. As has been seen, Luther's writings had inspired the Landsknechte with loathing for the Roman Church. Luther also gave them a sense of divine destiny by prophesying that it was God's will that Rome should be destroyed.

It was not only Tetzel's marketing campaign that had offended Luther. Luther had visited Rome in 1510, arriving full of idealism and departing thoroughly disillusioned. It was not very surprising. Romans were expert at fleecing every kind of visitor, including German monks, while the papal court was very far from the Christian simplicity Luther admired. It was a place of superficiality and fashion, where success came to those who could charm the right people, or had a talent for ad-libbing poetry in Latin. Life at the pinnacle of the Church was also luxurious. The two papal dining halls employed a wine steward, three bakers, five chief cooks, six stewards and numerous assistant cooks. As well as the pope, the Vatican Palace was home to several dozen high churchmen, each of whom had his own large household of servants.

The papacy was gaudily splendid abroad, too. Like Europe's princes in this era, popes had to spend big and look the part, to be heard. The papacy operated a network of nuncios, legates and revenue-seeking apostolic collectors, who travelled to every corner of Europe and whose lifestyle was calculated to impress. The papacy even had its own postal system, which, at least by Renaissance standards, was fast and efficient, and made Rome Europe's communications centre.

Naturally, all of these arrangements were expensive, and eleventh-century church reformers such as Gregory VII would have turned in their graves had they known how their successors raised money. The rot began at the end of the Avignon years, during the Great Schism, when Europe had three rival popes, each of whom was painfully short of funds. By the sixteenth century highly dubious money-raising techniques had become the norm. As well as taxing the Papal States to the hilt, and borrowing vast sums from a network of bankers – whose relatives they appointed as cardinals – Renaissance popes, like Renaissance princes, made an art of selling Church positions, and there was hardly a post, religious or bureaucratic, that was not up for sale. Bishoprics and cardinals' posts were routinely sold. So was the income from profitable abbeys, cathedrals and churches. One reason the papacy needed an efficient postal service was so that it could learn quickly when some distant bishop had died, whose post the papacy could give to a supporter or sell. When short of cash – as they always were – popes created new positions that were sold like a modern annuity: the buyer would pay a large sum and then be reimbursed with annual income over time. There were even low-ranking posts calculated to appeal to small investors, and places in the papal police force, the *servientes armorum*, were bought by Rome's smiths, bakers and barbers.

Almost everyone in the papal court had rights to the income of an abbey or cathedral or church that kept them financially afloat. Favoured high churchmen sometimes had as many as two dozen, which yielded huge sums. Having purchased positions, courtiers were entitled to sell them or bequeath them to their relatives. This leads us to something else that medieval church reformers would have found profoundly disturbing. If in the eleventh century the Church had a problem with procreating priests, in the Renaissance it had a problem with procreating popes. Under the reign of Innocent VIII in the 1480s it not only became acceptable for popes to have illegitimate children, but for popes to openly acknowledge and promote their progeny. Alexander VI – previously Rodrigo Borgia – legitimized his son Cesare, made him a cardinal and then helped him conquer an Italian state for himself (which Cesare was prevented from doing only because his father died before he could finish the job). Alexander's daughter, Lucrezia Borgia, married members of no fewer than three of Italy's best families: Giovanni Sforza, Alfonso of Aragon the duke of Bisceglie (murdered by Cesare in the Vatican) and finally Alfonso d'Este, son of the duke of Ferrara.

By comparison the two Medici popes were examples of virtue, as neither had children. Claims that Clement VII was the real father of his nephew Alessandro were almost certainly false, while rumours at the time suggested that his cousin Leo X's main interest was in his own gender. However, childlessness was no safeguard against nepotism. Leo made four of his close relatives cardinals and, as we saw earlier, he used papal forces to expel the duke of Urbino from his lands to try and provide a state for his cousin, Giuliano. Clement, who wanted to be a good pope, refused to appoint any new cardinals, despite the fact that he was desperately in need of the cash, which a sale or two would have provided. Yet, as will be seen, when he was in deep trouble even Clement weakened.

That the Church was run along these lines cannot be defended, but from its very earliest days Western European Christianity had always been something of a nut of two halves. For every self-denying austerity churchman there was another who was happy to enjoy some worldly pleasures, and the Church went through regular cycles in which each of these forces gained ascendancy over the other. The real difference between Christianity in the eleventh century and five centuries later was one of power. In the eleventh century, thanks to the intervention of the Church reformer Emperor Henry III, purists took control of the Church. By contrast, in the 1520s the new purists – Martin Luther and his supporters – remained firmly outside. If Charles V had intervened and made Martin Luther pope, as was not inconceivable, there would have been no Reformation.

The Romans had no illusions about their rulers. They frequently became the subject of that scathing, world-weary humour which was so distinctively Roman, and which – thanks to the wealth of documentation available – becomes visible at this time. In the 1520s a high-class Roman prostitute was referred to as 'an honest courtier'. Popes and members of their court were routinely reviled in foul-mouthed writings placed on a battered ancient statue, which Romans called Pasquino, in the Parione district. In one of these Pasquino complained that he had been insulted in a most offensive way. Another talking statue asked what the insult had been. Had he been called a liar or a thief? A cuckold or a forger? A fornicator who had knocked up some girl? No, replied Pasquino, the insult was far, far worse. He had been called a cardinal.

Yet it was not papal extravagance that aggravated the Romans, but rather its absence. High-spending Leo X was immensely popular, so much so that on his death he became the first pope to have his statue set up on that bastion of civic, anti-papal Rome, the Capitoline Hill.

By contrast his short-lived successor, the Dutchman Adrian VI, who tried to clean up the Church and cut extravagance, was loathed, and his death was greeted with a classic example of Roman black humour. The morning after Adrian died a note appeared on his doctor's door, thanking him for saving the nation. One can see the Romans' point of view. Austere popes may have been good for the reputation of the Catholic Church but they were no use to the Romans. Adrian's brief reign saw a halt to all the city's building projects and caused an exodus of scholars and artists. By contrast under high-spending Alexander VI, Julius II and Leo X, the city thrived.

After Adrian VI, the news that another Medici had been elected was greeted with excitement but well-meaning Clement soon disappointed. Conscious of the financial black hole his cousin had left, Clement spent frugally and taxed heavily, even taxing clergymen, who had previously been exempt. Clement, like Adrian VI, was unlucky in having inherited a huge financial mess, but both popes were also plain unlucky. Leo X's eight-year reign had been free of sudden and unexpected disasters but he was hardly cold in his grave when things started going wrong. The humanist Piero Valeriano joked grimly Adrian VI arrived in August 1522 with the plague, which was almost true: the disease preceded him by three months. It struck again two years later, now under Clement, and again in September 1525, when it ravaged the city for five months. These outbreaks may have been less lethal than the earlier and far greater bubonic plague epidemic – the Black Death – but they still caused numerous deaths, especially among children who had no immunity, while the city was struck by other problems too. Clement's war with Charles V caused food prices to leap in 1526 and in the same year the Tiber broke its banks and Rome was disastrously flooded. Plague, war and famine – three Apocalypse horsemen out of four – caused Rome's population to fall sharply in the years before 1527, perhaps by as much as a third.

These disasters tell us a surprising truth about Renaissance Rome. A visitor from 1081 would have found that in many respects the city had been far more comfortable to live in during the eleventh century.

Certainly, its infrastructure had been in a far better state. Many of Renaissance Rome's sewers, which had been one of the city's first achievements, had become blocked and, as the street level rose thanks to fires and floods, were all but unreachable to repair. A stinking open sewer, the Chiavica di San Silvestro, ran right across the city, from the Trevi area to the Tiber. The aqueducts were no better. In the 1520s, when Rome had far more inhabitants than it had had for a thousand years, only a single aqueduct still worked – the Acqua Vergine – and it produced a feeble flow of water. Attempts to repair it were hampered by the fact that the Romans appeared to have to have forgotten where its underground course began.

As Rome's aqueducts declined, so did Romans' drinking habits. Though a couple of springs supplied water to the Leonine City and a few lucky Romans had wells, in 1527 most Romans washed with, cooked with and drank Tiber water. It was decanted for a week to allow sediment to fall away and was then considered clean. Visitors from elsewhere in Italy were appalled, and rightly so. The Tiber was Rome's main sewer, rubbish dump and morgue and classical Romans would never have dreamed of drinking its water. Yet Renaissance Romans not only drank it but claimed to enjoy its taste. Clement VII, when he paid a visit to Marseilles in 1533, insisted on taking several barrels of it with him so he would not have to risk drinking the local supply.

Then there was the question of hygiene. To put it simply, Renaissance Romans stank. Classical Romans would have been disgusted, as even their household slaves smelt far sweeter. By 1527 it was standard practice for most Romans – like most Europeans – to enjoy a full body wash only during major life events: in other words, when they were born, before their wedding night, and when they died. For all other occasions a quick dab at appropriate areas would do. Romans' clothes were cleaned hardly more often than their owners and their outer garments were given a thorough wash only once a year. Romans in 1527 would have itched and scratched as constantly as they had in 1081, if not more so.

Renaissance Romans also lived less long than their eleventh-century predecessors. As well as measles, typhus and tuberculosis, early sixteenth-century Romans had a constant fear of plague, while malaria was as lethal as ever, especially – as always – to poor Romans who could not escape the city in late summer. Romans' love of Tiber water would have afflicted them with waterborne diseases. Finally, if this were not already enough, there was a wholly new health threat: the French Disease, also known as the Great Pox, the French Pox and – by the French – the Neapolitan Disease. Today we call it syphilis. It seems to have originated in the Americas and first became known in Europe in 1495 when it was contracted by French troops besieging Naples. Within months it was causing alarm and intense discomfort across Italy. It produced rubbery growths on the genitals that could grow as large as a bread roll, as well as the pustules that devoured skin and bone, and purple rashes to the face that marked out sufferers. As well as Pope Julius II, celebrity victims included Cesare Borgia, three sons of the duke of Ferrara, Charles V's grandfather, Emperor Maximilian, and a good number of cardinals. Observers at the time noted that it seemed especially fond of priests.

If there were more diseases to catch in 1527 than five centuries earlier, one might hope that medicine had improved. It was undeniably more impressive. In 1527 a sufferer could pray to specialist saints or could seek help from a whole array of professionals, including street tradesmen selling quack remedies, apothecaries who had shops filled with drugs, surgeons who patched up wounds – and who doubled as barbers – while, for those who had money to spend, there was a wealthy and educated elite of professional physicians who looked with scorn on all of the rest.

Yet these professionals were not justified in their disdain. Italian medicine may have grown as an industry but its thinking had barely changed since 1081, or for that matter since 408. Renaissance doctors still followed the ideas of classical Hippocrates and Galen, to which had been added a little further wisdom from Arab medical writers such as Avicenna. They still viewed bad health as stemming from an imbalance of the four humours. Many accepted that sickness might be caused by sinfulness or evil spells and did not question Aristotle's claim that women were defective males. A visit to the doctor in 1527 was hardly more likely to cure you than it had been five or fifteen centuries earlier, and though Rome had more hospitals in 1527 than it had in 1081, they were so infested with sickness that it was usually wiser to stay at home.

Romans were certainly safer staying at home rather than stepping into the street outside. Rome, like other Italian cities at this time, had a murder rate that was four times higher than that of crime-ridden late 1980s New York. Serious crimes often sprang from the prevailing honour system, under which a show of disrespect could bring a quick and violent response. The system, which extended across the Mediterranean – and in a gentle way still does – was nothing new and had been present throughout Rome's long history. What was new in 1527 was that interrogations of suspected criminals by Roman magistrates were carefully documented and the records have survived. For the first time we have a clear picture of the city's crime.

The worst honour crimes usually involved seduction of females. The honour system had no sense of gender fairness and male promiscuity won little disapproval, but if an unmarried Roman's sister or daughter opted for night-time pleasure her whole family was shamed. The disaster could be overcome if the seducer then married the girl – and preferably handed over a cash payment by way of an apology – but if he did not do so, or if, horror of horrors, a Roman's wife were seduced, then injury or murder could well follow.

Fortunately, most honour crimes were less dramatic. Romans frequently insulted one another – quick, biting repartee was much admired – and these insults could inspire all kinds of petty trouble, from brawls among washerwomen by the Tiber, to a prostitute's rejected client daubing her door with excrement. The honour system was also responsible, in an indirect way, for legal suits concerning injuries brought about by rampaging bulls. By tradition, Renaissance Romans who wanted to impress a girl would rent an ox from the city's slaughterhouse, together with a pack of specially trained dogs. If all went well the dogs would bite at the unfortunate ox's ears, causing it to become so demoralized that it would let itself be led tamely by a rope to the home of the girl who – as the suitor hoped – would then applaud from her window. If all did not go well, the city authorities had to deal with the denunciations of irate shopkeepers and injured passers-by.

Yet Romans had little fear of the authorities. In Rome, as throughout Italy, police were despised as a useless, crooked force that tyrannized the helpless and kowtowed to the strong and there was a certain amount of truth in this view. Magistrates, too, inspired little terror. They could torture suspects but, compared to those of classical Rome, when slaves could be lacerated with whips, ripped apart on racks and burned with scalding hot plates, Renaissance Roman tortures were feeble. Males had their hands tied behind their backs, were hauled up by a rope, held for a short time and then dropped (a process known as the *strappado*). Females were more likely to have their fingers or toes pinched. Transgressors often regarded their torture with a certain pride. As for the city's jails, these were used less to inflict punishment than to remove those who disturbed the peace or who were found tiresome: incurables, cripples, vagabonds, drunks, people with mental problems, and epileptics. Many were held in the Carceri di Tor di Nona by the Tiber, which was built from the ruins of the classical-era river port (inmates of lower cells occasionally drowned). VIP prisoners were held in the city's maximum security jail, Castel Sant'Angelo. Only in extreme cases were Romans taken up to the city gallows, which, appropriately enough, appear to have been placed on the Tarpeian Rock, from where citizens had been thrown in Rome's earliest days.

One phenomenon against which Renaissance Rome's authorities were noticeably helpless was mobs of stone-throwing boys. These were a plague in many Italian cities but especially in Rome, where the problem became acute from the 1480s. Youths and small boys, wearing heavy coats to protect themselves, would unleash showers of stones against one another. Sometimes hundreds became involved, fighting battles that might be local (Trastevere versus the Monti area across the river) or political (pro-French versus pro-imperial) or religious (Christians versus Jews). As well as one another, the boys would attack anyone who seemed vulnerable or different, from poor farmers just in from the countryside, to foreigners, to Jews. In tough times the rich were also targets, and prostitutes were frequent victims.

These terrible mobs exacerbated a change that had been going on for several centuries. A visitor from 1081 would have been surprised by how few females – or at least respectable females – they saw on the streets. In Renaissance Rome, much as in classical Rome, respectable women, if they were visible at all, were usually to be found looking out from the safety of their doorway or peering down from a window. They had been forced from the streets not only by stone-throwing boys but also by fears for their own reputation. The city's streets were now seen as places of immoral, honourless prostitutes.

Respectable Roman women found their lives were also restricted in other ways. Renaissance Italy had no powerful female rulers: no Marozia or Matilda of Tuscany. The daughters of leading families disappeared from sight after marriage, vanishing into an indoor life of domesticity and pregnancy. Women who did try to exert influence were criticized or ridiculed. Pope Leo X's sisters, who lobbied Clement VII for favours to their husbands and sons – the kind of lobbying that everybody at the papal court was engaged in – became, quite unfairly, scapegoats for Clement's financial troubles. This diminution of female independence had been growing across Europe for several centuries. It was caused in part by another change: the replacement of female inheritance by dowries. Yet not all women accepted their lot. Intriguingly, it was Renaissance Italy that saw a visible fightback, in the form of two of the world's first true feminist writers, both of them from Venice: Modesta Pozzo and Lucrezia Marinella, who wrote the strikingly titled *The Nobility and Excellence of Women*.

Some Roman females were self-employed and financially independent, but not from choice. In 1527 the city had a thriving population of prostitutes that has been estimated at between 700 and 1,000: a good number for a city of 55,000. They were highly visible, dressing up – like their classical forebears – in men's clothing, and loudly calling out to passers-by. During Carnival they were known to hurl perfumed eggs at potential customers. Their presence may seem a little surprising in the capital city of Catholic Christianity, a religion that venerated virginity and chastity, but Rome was also a city of single males, whether members of the male papal court, or wifeless immigrants. Male Romans outnumbered female Romans by six to four. Besides, in this era Christianity was fairly tolerant of prostitution. No Renaissance pope acted against prostitutes, and though there were attempts to restrict their presence to the district around Augustus' tomb, many roamed wherever they chose, even seeking out custom in churches.

A select few had access to Rome's most desirable locations. These were Rome's courtesans: high-class prostitutes who, like Japanese geishas, were valued both for their bedroom skills and for their wit and intellect (qualities which were considered a little unseemly in respectable women). Roman courtesans, who were famous for their large, circular beds discreetly enclosed by hangings, included fine poets and letter-writers who could recite beautifully in Italian and Latin. Some were celebrities of their time and one, known as *Imperia*, had a string of high-ranking admirers, including the painter Raphael, the Tuscan banker Agostino Chigi – who accepted Imperia's daughter as his own – and also Cardinal Giulio de' Medici, the future Pope Clement VII.

Spending time with an alluring, witty courtesan on her circular bed was by no means the only pleasure to be found in Rome. Despite the city's failing infrastructure, life could be sweet, especially for wealthy Romans, and early sixteenth-century Rome would be remembered as something of a golden age. Rich Romans' drinking water may have become fouler over the centuries but this was not true of their food, which, for those with money to spend, was lavishly sophisticated. Ingredients were now to be found in Domitian's old athletics stadium, the Circus Agonalis – which by 1527 had been paved and was beginning to evolve into the Piazza Navona – and to which the city's main food market had recently moved from the Capitoline Hill (the fish market was still beneath the arches of Portico d'Ottavia). Along with a wide selection of meats, vegetables and fruit, Romans could enjoy a good number of items that are still favourites today, from ricotta cheese and buffalo mozzarella to mushrooms, truffles and artichokes. Dried pasta, though it was expensive compared to fresh, could also be found, and fresh pasta came in many of the forms it does now, from macaroni and pappardelle to tortelli and ravioli.

As ingredients grew more varied, so did the dishes made from them. Eleventh-century Romans may have enjoyed a good diet but their meals were fairly simple, consisting largely of roasts or stews that were mopped up with bread. By contrast, great Renaissance banquets would have impressed a Roman emperor, though he might have found it a little sweet. Luxury Renaissance Roman dishes were highly flavoured with spices from the Orient: ginger, nutmeg, cinnamon and above all, sugar, which, as a novelty, was added to almost everything, including meats. Dentists thrived. Salty flavours were despised as food of the poor, who used salt as a preservative. Renaissance Rome, like classical Rome, had star chefs whose names were known throughout good society. One of these was Bartolomeo Scappi, who in April 1536 held a famously vast banquet in the home of Cardinal Campeggio in Trastevere, whose 200 dishes were recorded. Highlights included lamprey pie, cold roast carp in sugar and rice water, and hake in mustard sauce. The finale was intended for effect rather than taste: a gigantic pie was brought to the table and when the pastry was cut open a flock of live songbirds flew out.

Wealthy Renaissance Romans also enjoyed intellectual pleasures. After a fine dinner a host might take his guests to see his collection of ancient Greek vases, classical statues and antique manuscripts. This was the age of humanism and the rediscovery of the classical past. Humanists were very much products of new technology: the printing revolution that had begun three generations earlier, which had made books and education more affordable than they had ever been. Humanists, who called themselves *literati,* or men of letters, were brought together by a shared fascination with classical times, and also a desire to produce written works in good Latin. Most were not from wealthy families, so they struggled financially. These days they might be described as perpetual students.

In the early sixteenth century humanists were found all across Europe – the most renowned was Erasmus of Rotterdam – but many were drawn to Rome and its antiquities. They formed associations, which met in the gardens of leading members to discuss antiquities and read out Latin writings. They also set themselves the task of trying to correct medieval myths and rediscover the city's ancient topography. To this end they scoured monasteries for forgotten texts, sifted through the city's ruins, and deciphered ancient inscriptions. Poggio Bracciolini pointed out that the ancient pyramid beside Porta San Paolo was not, as had long been claimed, the tomb of Romulus' brother Remus, but of a classical Roman named Cestius (not such a hard discovery, seeing as the name Cestius was written on its side in huge letters). By 1527 humanists had discovered that the equestrian statue of an emperor was not Constantine but Marcus Aurelius, that Rome's ruined baths were not ancient palaces, and that the Colosseum was an amphitheatre rather than a temple to the sun.

The more fortunate among them had some form of income from the Church. Some were hired as spin doctors or diplomats and Alexander VI, the Borgia pope, employed them to write eulogies of himself: a task in which their classical knowledge proved invaluable, as they could look back to ancient poets' fawning praise of their emperors. But for every humanist who earned a decent living there were others who were on the breadline and whose stories reveal much about how Roman society functioned. Piero Valeriano, a humanist who came to Rome from Venice, endured four hungry years before finally enjoying a breakthrough. It came when Clement VII's high-spending cousin Leo X was elected. It was Valeriano's good fortune that his old Greek tutor was a friend of the new pope, and through his lobbying, Valeriano gained income from enough Church benefices for a comfortable life. Eight years later, when Leo died and was replaced by the stingy Dutch Pope Adrian VI, Valeriano, like many humanists, appears to have left Rome and it was he who made the cutting observation that Adrian had arrived with the plague. Yet he soon landed on his feet, becoming tutor to Clement VII's illegitimate nephews, Alessandro and Ippolito de' Medici. Valeriano was luckier than many other humanists, who struggled on tiny incomes from Rome's university, La Sapienza, and struggled even more when, as was often the case, it was closed because of building repairs or an outbreak of the plague.

Artists, or at least those of them who were successful, had a much easier time. Popes such as Julius II and Leo X were generous patrons and under their rule renowned artists, who in the past had been treated as social inferiors, were welcomed into Rome's highest society. A few, such as Raphael, became so rich they built themselves palaces. In the first decades of the sixteenth century Rome was the greatest artistic centre in Italy and though some artists left when the stingy Dutch Pope Adrian VI cut spending, many stayed, including Sebastiano del Piombo and Parmigianino. Another Roman resident in 1527 was the Florentine silversmith and sculptor Benvenuto Cellini, famous for his outrageously self-aggrandizing autobiography. Rome's artists had their own club and Cellini describes attending one of its dinners, to which every guest was required to bring a city prostitute as his guest. One of the leading artists of the era, Giovanni Antonio Bazzi openly used his gay nickname, *Sodoma*.

If Rome could be a delightful place for the rich, though, life for less wealthy citizens was a different matter. Their existence was little better than it had been for their poor forebears five or twelve centuries earlier. Their homes frequently lacked kitchens, so they relied on inns and street stalls, and ate what poor Romans had always eaten: a mush of vegetables, cheap grain and beans, perhaps garnished with a little pork fat, tripe or some pigs' trotters. The very poorest Romans lived in homes that would have been hardly more comfortable than Romulus' hut. One stood right by St Peter's. Struggling females enjoyed one privilege that their eleventh-century predecessors had not had: they could anonymously give away unwanted newborn babies. They used a twelfth-century invention, the *ruota*, a cylindrical device built into the walls of orphanages. Mothers placed the newborn into the device from the street, rang a bell and the baby was then taken by those inside.

If rich and poor Romans led very different lives they had one thing in common: all were less politically independent than their twelfth-century ancestors, and more under the thumb of the papacy. The days were long gone when the city's great and middling citizens rode out with their pope to Testaccio Hill for the carnival games, or walked barefoot with him on one of his processions around the city. Compared to the medieval papacy, the papacy of 1527 was aloof, private, and above all powerful. If the Romans had learned anything from the bleak decades when the popes abandoned them for Avignon, it was that they needed their popes. The hundred years since the popes had returned saw steadily rising papal control. The last attempt by Rome's leading families to challenge papal power, in 1511, was easily swatted away by Julius II. Thereafter Rome's leading families were excluded from the papal court, which, as in the late eleventh century, was filled with Tuscan and German outsiders. Rome still had great families, such as the Barberini and Farnese and, most formidable of all, the Medici's allies the Orsini and their enemies the Colonna, but even the latter two were now a much diminished force. The Colonna posed a threat to Clement only because they had Charles V's empire behind them.

Likewise Rome's civic government, which had been dominated by the city's old families, had seen its powers steadily whittled away. Its officials who, as in medieval times, struggled to defend the city's ruins from papal stone theft, found themselves increasingly sidelined. This was an era when the city's antiquities were pillaged on a grand scale, as the Colosseum, the forums, the Palatine Palace, and ruined classical temples were denuded of stone, which was used to build palaces, the Ponte Sisto bridge and, most of all, the new St Peter's. By the 1510s destruction was intense. Among its casualties was Rome's other pyramid classical tomb that had stood near St Peter's, and also a triumphal arch near the Baths of Diocletian, the Temple to Ceres on the Via Sacra, and part of the Forum Transitorum, which was burned for lime. The only restraint to the destruction was papal conscience, which led popes to try to preserve at least the more interesting remnants.

III

In the early spring of 1527 Pope Clement must have wished he had made more of an effort to woo the Romans, as now he badly needed their help. While Bourbon's army made its dash for Rome, Clement belatedly appealed to his subjects at a great council of Rome in the church of Santa Maria in Aracoeli on the Capitoline. Clement begged them to fight, assuring them that they would only need to hold out for three days as they would then be rescued by the League army.

On the afternoon of 5 May Romans could see the threat facing them as a huge force advanced towards the city. It was larger than any that had approached Rome for many centuries, containing 700 lancers, 800 light cavalry, 3,000 Italian adventurers, 5,000 Spanish and 10,000 Germans. At almost 20,000 men it was five times the size of Robert Guiscard's army. Yet the Romans' situation was better than it might have been. The Romans, who only eight months before had happily watched Pompeo Colonna's soldiers process through the city, responded to Clement's call, declaring that they would live or die beside him, like the sons of Mars of ancient times. Their change of mind seems to have been inspired by Colonna's raid. The humiliation Clement had suffered left his subjects more sympathetic towards him.

The city was fairly well defended. Its walls were antiquated, it was true, but they still formed a formidable barrier to an army with no artillery. Despite Clement's disastrous decision to stand down his troops once again, Rome had a good-sized force of defenders. As well as a mixed bag of civilians from the city's various districts – those who had not been stolen away by the city's wealthy to defend their palaces – there were 4,000 regular soldiers and 2,000 Swiss troops. Most formidable of all, there were a further 2,000 members of the elite Italian Black Bands force, which had been led by Clement VII's cousin Giuliano until his death a few months earlier. Rome also had a highly competent commander, Renzo da Ceri. Only three years earlier Renzo had thwarted another imperial army, also commanded by Bourbon, which besieged Marseilles for a month, only to be humiliatingly forced to retreat. Everything suggested that Renzo was now about to enjoy an even greater triumph. Without food or shelter the imperial army could not survive outside the walls for more than a few days and the League army was expected to arrive shortly. A desperate imperial retreat to Naples beckoned.

Renzo organized the city's defences as skilfully as he could in the short time left to him. Aware that, as well as Bourbon's army to the north and west of the city, he might also have to deal with a Colonna attack from the south, he manned the south and eastern Aurelian Walls, though with his worst troops: Roman civilians and even some monks and priests. He placed his best soldiers in the parts of the city that were directly threatened by Bourbon's armies: in the Borgo, in Trastevere and along the north section of the Aurelian Walls. Renzo recognized that the Borgo was the city's weakest spot, and that the greatest part of the Borgo was by the Santo Spirito Gate, where the walls were lower than elsewhere and faced on to high ground, and where Pompeo Colonna had broken through eight months earlier. Renzo placed artillery at a number of locations, which between them fully covered the danger area. His heaviest guns he placed in Castel Sant'Angelo. He also wanted to cut the bridges over the Tiber so that, if the Borgo and Trastevere fell, the city beyond the river could be saved, but this was prevented by the Romans, who had no wish to see their city disrupted. It was a decision they would soon regret.

On the night of 5 May 1527 Roman defenders could see the campfires of the 20,000 imperial troops on Monte Mario. On the Capitoline Hill, Rome's ancient citadel, the great bell rang, tolling

the alarm and the streets below rang with shouts of, 'Arms, arms!'
The Romans' greatest fear was of betrayal: an understandable concern
with so many Colonna supporters in the city. But, as events would
soon show, danger would come in quite another form, which neither
Rome's defenders nor the Imperialists had foreseen.

Outside the walls in the small hours of the morning, Bourbon
made the traditional speech to urge on his troops. He ordered them
to build scaling ladders from fences and any other wood they could
find. His hope was to break into the city in the same way as Robert
Guiscard had four and a half centuries earlier. His soldiers were to
scale the walls and make for the weak spot that Bourbon had noticed
when he made his inspection hours earlier. It was close to Santo
Spirito Gate in a part of the Leonine Wall that had been constructed
around a poorly camouflaged private house, and in which a gun port
had been made from a window that was too large for safety. Yet,
compared to Bourbon, Robert Guiscard had had a great advantage:
surprise. Bourbon's troops were to assault the exact area that the
Roman commander, Renzo, had anticipated would be attacked.

Sure enough the Imperialists soon found themselves struggling.
After a firefight between arquebusiers on both sides, Bourbon, wearing
a white cloak over his armour, urged his soldiers to hurl themselves at
the walls. In the face of arquebus and artillery fire the attackers suffered
high casualties and before long the defenders had captured five of their
battle standards, which they carried in triumph back to the Borgo. But
then, just when things were going well for the Romans, the battleground
became quietly and gently transformed. Luigi Guicciardini, who ruled
Florence for the Medici at this time, and later wrote an account of the
1527 disaster in Rome, described how, 'about this time a heavy fog began
to appear, which spread itself thickly over the ground and became
increasingly dense as the day approached. This often happens in the
middle of spring, and this fog was so thick that people could not see
each other at a distance of six feet.'[2]

Thanks to the fog, which was made denser by gun smoke, those
on the city walls and in the Castel Sant'Angelo could not see to aim

and they were forced to fire blind, aiming towards the sound of the enemy. Before long the Imperialists' superior numbers began to tell. Renzo, who had been on a section of the Aurelian Walls, hurried to the Borgo to take personal command and ordered in reinforcements, but there were none to be found. But then, just as the Imperialists were gaining ground, they were struck by a disaster: one that would have grave consequences for the Romans. As Guicciardini tells us: 'Monseigneur de Bourbon was to be seen encouraging the troops ... holding onto one of the ladders leaning against the wall with his left hand, and with his right hand signalling and urging the men to ascend it. Suddenly he was shot through by a ball from an arquebus ...'[3]

Struck in the forehead, Bourbon died instantly. Benvenuto Cellini, the silversmith and autobiographer, who was never one to let the truth spoil a good story, offered his own version of the event. Encouraged by a friend who wanted to see what was happening, he found himself on the walls by Campo Santo in the midst of the fighting. Though his friend panicked and wanted to run, Cellini would have none of it:

> I checked him and shouted, 'Now you've brought me here, we must show that we're men.' At the same time I pointed my arquebus towards the thickest and most closely packed part of the enemy, taking direct aim at someone I could see standing out from the rest ... We all fired, twice in succession, and I looked cautiously over the wall. The enemy had been thrown into the most extraordinary confusion, because one of our shots had killed the Constable of Bourbon. From what I learned later he must have been the man I saw standing out from the others.'[4]

News of Bourbon's death spread rapidly on both sides of the walls. For a brief time the defenders imagined they were saved, but then the imperial commanders rallied their forces, transforming their soldiers' shock into hunger for revenge. The attack was renewed more fiercely than before and the Romans, seeing they might be defeated,

BORBONE OCCISO, ROMANA IN MOENIA MILES
CAESAREVS RVIT, ET MISERANDAM DIRIPIT VRBEM.   *1527.*

At the death of Charles Bourbon, the troops of Charles V storm the walls of Rome, from a sixteenth-century engraving.

desperately flung burning liquids over the wall and fired into the fog. It was no use. Around ten o'clock a small band of Spanish troops were seen inside the city. Whether they had got in through the oversized gun port or by scaling the walls is unknown. As to what happened next, all the sources are broadly agreed, though they differ as to who was most to blame. Guicciardini, whose brother was leading papal troops under the League commander, the duke of Urbino – and leading them very ineffectually – had no wish to let any other papal commander look good. Accordingly, he portrayed Renzo da Ceri as both incompetent and cowardly, saying that he shouted out, 'The enemy are within! Save yourselves, retreat to the strongest & safest places!'[5] Other sources report that Renzo resisted bravely, trying to kill any who fled from the walls. Whatever he did, his efforts were to no avail. Panic swept through the defenders and resistance collapsed.

Before long the gates had been opened and Imperialists were pouring into the Borgo, shouting 'Spain! Spain! Kill! Kill!' So began an event that still has the power to cause great shock even five centuries later, and which has been described as the sixteenth century's 9/11. In every regard it seems to have been far more terrible than any of the other sacks the city had suffered. Of course, this may be in part because the others have been remembered in less detail. Yet the situation on 6 May 1527 was undeniably horrific. The imperial army was not only fired up by desperation and by religious passion; it also lacked the restraining influence of authoritative commanders. Georg von Frundsberg was in Germany, having never recovered from his stroke, and Bourbon was dead. Even had he lived, it is highly doubtful that he would have been able to exert much control over his troops during the first hours, but he might have later. Without him his soldiers felt freer, and also had cause to seek revenge.

Many Romans had assumed that if Rome fell the result would be much as it had been eight months earlier when they watched Colonna's troops process through the city. Instead the Borgo became a slaughterhouse. A few defenders managed to save themselves in the initial confusion by merging with the attackers, but most were not so lucky. Some tried to flee across the river in boats and many drowned. Only a handful of the elite Black Bands survived. The Swiss made a stand by the obelisk in front of St Peter's, where they were torn apart. The imperial soldiers, with nobody left to oppose them, then went through the Borgo like a scythe, killing all they met. The commander of the Swiss Guards, Röust, who had been carried heavily wounded to his quarters nearby, was cut to pieces in front of his wife. A monk from the monastery of San Salvatore reported that 'Everyone in the Santo Spirito hospital was killed apart from the few who managed to flee.'[6] A good number were thrown alive into the Tiber. The same monk also reported that all the orphans in the La Pietà orphanage were killed and that many 'were thrown from windows into the street'.

As the slaughter began, people tried to flee to the safety of the Castel Sant'Angelo, including Pope Clement VII. He had been praying and attending mass in St Peter's and, as during the Colonna raid, was persuaded to leave just in time. As he hurried down the papal escape passage to the castello, he and his entourage were spotted by Spanish troops, who took pot shots at him from below. A large crowd of soldiers, churchmen, merchants, nobles, courtiers, women and children soon formed outside the castello, pressing so tightly that they prevented the gate from being closed. By the time the portcullis was finally dropped a large number had got inside. As Archbishop Pesaro of Zara reported, the situation brought out Clement VII's ruthless side: 'The pope was told that there were many people in the castle, most of them of no military use, and there was little grain, so many of the useless ones were thrown out.'[7] Their fate is unknown. Yet there was still room inside for the right sort of person. Elderly Cardinal Pucci, who had hurled abuse at the attackers during the fighting on the walls, and who was knocked down and trampled in the ensuing panic, was hauled up by rope through a window. Another cardinal, Armellino, was pulled over the battlements in a basket.

Among those who had managed to get into the castello was Benvenuto Cellini. As fearless as ever, he went directly up to the guns where, as he recounts in his autobiography, he found their commander, Giuliano the Florentine, 'tearing at his face and sobbing bitterly'. Giuliano did not dare fire in case he hit his own house, where he could see his wife and children being set upon. Fortunately, Cellini was made of sterner stuff:

> I seized one of the fuses, got help from some of the men who were in such a sorry state, and lined up some heavy pieces of artillery and falconets, firing them where I saw a need. In this way I slaughtered a great number of the enemy. If I had not done so the troops who had broken into Rome that morning would have made straight for the castle and could easily have entered, as the artillery was not in action ... Anyhow, all I need say is that it was through me that the castle was saved that morning.[8]

The imperial forces had captured the Borgo but not the rest of the city. The Castel Sant'Angelo Bridge that led to it was impassable, as it could be raked by the fire of the large guns in the castello itself. After a hurried discussion the imperial commanders decided to launch an attack on Trastevere, which lay behind its own defensive walls half a mile south of the Borgo. By now the fog had lifted so the defenders had a clear view, but the heart had gone from them and resistance was feeble. Imperial forces broke through the walls by San Pancrazio Gate on the Gianicolo Hill and, seizing control of the district, gorged themselves on food they found there.

Ponte Sisto, Rome's new bridge that connected Trastevere to the main part of the city, was beyond the range of the guns on Castel Sant'Angelo, and the imperial forces advanced cautiously, only to find it was all but undefended. By then it was evening and the Romans had fled back to their homes. The army crossed the river and split into its two main elements: the Landsknechte made their way to Campo de' Fiori and the Spanish to the Piazza Navona. For a time both contingents kept formation, ready to fend off an attack. Then, when none came, soldiers began to slip away.

It was now that the city's trials truly began. One observer remarked that Rome made hell itself look a place of beauty. Another told how the imperial soldiers, 'threw the bodies of little children out of doorways into the street. And women were dragged out and outraged on the ground … crying and wailing so loudly that all the city could hear.'[9] A third reported that ' large numbers of the priests are naked and that it is a terrible thing to see the great number of dead, and most of all the little children younger than ten years old', and that the soldiers 'are exhausted from lack of sleep, drunk on blood, killing everything'.[10] Guicciardini, though he did not witness events himself, also gave a graphic account, which, since he thoroughly disliked both Rome and the Romans, has a discernible whiff of *Schadenfreude*:

> In the streets there were many corpses. Many nobles lay there cut to pieces, covered with mud and their own blood, and many people only half dead lay miserably on the ground. Sometimes in that ghastly scene a child or man would be seen jumping

The Germans plunder Rome, from a nineteenth-century engraving.

from a window, forced to jump or jumping voluntarily to escape becoming the living prey of these monsters and finally ending their lives horribly in the street.[11]

It is unclear how long the violence and destruction lasted. Guicciardini claims that the imperial commanders, concerned that their soldiers were beginning to turn on one another, managed to restrain them after three days: the traditional amount of time allotted to a sack. Another source, Buonaparte, though, writes that after three days the Prince of Orange – who had assumed command after Bourbon's death – ordered the soldiers to stop sacking the city and begin taking prisoners instead, but the soldiers replied that as Bourbon was dead they no longer had a commander, and carried on more brutally than before. In view of difficulties Bourbon and Frundsberg had had in controlling their troops, Buonaparte's account seems all too plausible.

The sack was unusual in that clergy were not spared. Alaric and Totila had treated them with respect but now if anything they were treated more cruelly than non-churchmen. The cardinal of Como reported that the soldiers killed monks and priests on the altars of churches and took prisoner or raped many young nuns. One priest was killed because he refused to administer the sacraments to a mule that the Landsknechte had dressed in clerical vestments. The 80-year-old cardinal of Gaeta and Ponzetto, who could hardly walk, was forced to parade around the city in a Landsknechte cap and uniform. A group of Landsknechte put the cardinal of Aracoeli – who was still very much alive – in a coffin and carried him around the city singing funeral dirges, before stopping at a church to give him a funeral speech, in which they ascribed every kind of monstrosity to him.

Not everyone was sorry at the churchmen's fate. Guicciardini, who, as we saw, was no lover of the Romans, recounted with a certain glee how:

many of these men wore torn and disgraceful habits, others were without shoes. Some in ripped and bloody shirts had

German Landsknechte ridiculing the pope, engraving from Gottfried's Historical Chronicle, *1619.*

cuts and bruises all over their bodies from the indiscriminate whippings and beatings they had received. Some had thick and greasy beards. Some had their faces branded, and some were missing teeth; others were without noses or ears. Some were castrated and so depressed and terrified that they failed to show in any way the vain and effeminate delicacy and lasciviousness that they had put on with such excessive energy for so many years in their earlier, happier days.[12]

Church property fared no better than churchmen. The altar of St Peter's was piled with the corpses of those who had fled there in hope of finding sanctuary. Even the tomb of Julius II, who had been a firm ally of the Empire, was looted. Rome's churches were robbed of their silverware, their chalices and vestments. Guicciardini reported that

The sumptuous palaces of the cardinals, the proud palaces of the pope, the holy churches of Peter and Paul, the private chapel of His Holiness, the Sancta Sanctorum, and the other holy places, once full of plenary indulgences and venerable relics, now became the brothels of German and Spanish whores.

and that the Landsknechte

committed shameful acts on the altars in the most sanctified places.[13]

Churches, including St Peter's, were used as stables for horses of the imperial cavalry. Relics likewise fared poorly. St Peter's and St Paul's heads were flung into the street. The head of John the Baptist was stripped of its silver decoration and thrown to the ground, only to be saved by an old nun. The Veronica cloth that for centuries had been a symbol of Rome, copies of which innumerable pilgrims had taken home as souvenirs, was lost. By one account it was burned, by another it was sold in an inn.

After five days of carnage a new force of marauders appeared: on 10 May, just as he had promised, Cardinal Pompeo Colonna arrived with a further 8,000 troops, who quickly joined in the looting. Colonna settled some private scores with Clement VII for destroying his properties outside Rome, by burning down Clement's vineyard by Ponte Milvio and also the Medici Villa Madama on Monte Mario. Yet compared to the other Imperialists, Colonna and his army were angels of restraint. Pompeo stopped his troops' rampage after a short time, while he himself was distraught when he saw what was happening to Rome, his city.

After a few days the soldiers' focus began to alter, from simple violence and destruction to something more profitable. By all accounts the Spanish were the first to look to self-enrichment, though the Landsknechte – who were described as being less worldly but more violent – soon followed suit. Not that the change brought much of an improvement to the Romans. Having been slaughtered, they now found themselves imprisoned and tortured, as their captors forced them to agree to high ransoms, and to reveal where their valuables were hidden. Guicciardini describes their fate with his usual *Schadenfreude*:

> Many were suspended by their arms for hours at a time; others were led around by ropes tied to their testicles. Many were suspended by one foot above the streets or over water, with the threat that the cord suspending them would be cut. Many were beaten and wounded severely. Many were branded with hot irons in various parts of their bodies. Some endured extreme thirst; others were prevented from sleeping. A very cruel and effective torture was to pull out their back teeth. Some were made to eat their own ears, or nose, or testicles roasted; and others were subjected to bizarre and unheard of torments that affect me too strongly even to think of them, let alone to describe them in detail.[14]

Buonaparte tells of how some Romans had sticks pushed beneath the nails of their fingers and toes, or had melted lead poured into their throats. Castration appears to have been common and one source claims that numerous testicles could be seen lying in the streets.

Artists and humanists were not exempt. The painters Perino del Vaga and Giulio Clivio were tortured and had all their possessions taken. Gianbattista Rosso lost all his property and was forced to act as a kind of porter for his captors, heaving their loot about. Parmigianino was luckier, though not much. When the imperial army broke into the city he was working on a painting of the Madonna and Child, which so impressed the soldiers who captured him that instead of demanding money they ransomed him for watercolour portraits of themselves. Unfortunately, he was then caught by another less art-conscious group of soldiers who took everything he had.

Parmigianino's experience was common, and many Romans paid out one extortionate ransom only to find they then had to pay again to another set of captors. A Florentine, Bernardo Bracci, was taken by some cavalrymen to the German Bartolomeo bank (the imperial forces took care not to sack the banks, especially the German banks, so hostages could borrow money for their ransoms), but as he was led across the Ponte Sisto, he was stopped by one of the imperial commanders, the marquis of Motte. On learning that Bracci was going to borrow 5,000 ducats for his ransom, Motte declared, 'This is a very small ransom. If he won't pay another 5000 ducats to my account, I order you to throw him into the Tiber immediately.'[15] So Bracci doubled his debt.

For some the pain of torture proved too strong to bear. One hostage, Girolamo da Camerino, crept slowly towards the window of his house, where he was being held, and leapt out and killed himself. Another hostage, Giovanni Ansaldi, had agreed to a ransom of 1,000 silver ducats, only to be tortured for a second time because his captors had changed their minds and decided they wanted gold ducats instead. When they were not watching, Ansaldi grabbed a dagger from one of them, killed him and then killed himself.

Even those who assumed they would be left in peace were not safe. The home of the Portuguese ambassador, who was also the king of Portugal's nephew, in the old Theatre of Marcellus, became filled with fleeing Romans and their valuables. Unfortunately, word then reached the imperial forces and two Spanish captains soon appeared, who offered to fly their flag over the residence and protect it in exchange for a large sum. To the dismay of the Romans hiding inside, all of whom wanted to pay off the Spanish, the ambassador haughtily sent the officers away, telling them that to fly any flag would be a dishonour to his king. The two officers left, but returned soon afterwards with a large force of Spanish and Landsknechte armed with artillery. The ambassador then opened the palace gates and within a short time his residence had been wrecked; all those inside were taken prisoner and he found himself being dragged naked through the streets. The vast sum of half a million ducats was eventually extracted from him and his guests.

Not even pro-imperialists were safe. One of the very first palaces to be sacked was that of Pompeo Colonna, which was invaded after his servants forgot to hang out a banner saying to whom it belonged. Four cardinals who were well-known supporters of Charles V, and who had crowds of pro-Imperialists sheltering in their palaces, avoided the mistake made by the Portuguese ambassador and took in Spanish officers as protection, though it did them little good. As days passed their Spanish guests, observing the wealth of valuables all around them, demanded huge pay-offs, not from the cardinals themselves but from their refugee guests. Having got their money, the Spanish then informed the cardinals that their comrades the Landsknechte were keen to sack their palaces and that they could only be stopped by a further large payment.

At this point the cardinal of Siena, who had close links with the Landsknechte, decided it was time to make a stand and he announced he was not paying another penny. Within hours his palace had been stripped, his guests were either dead or taken prisoner, and he himself had been beaten up and dragged to the Borgo to raise a 50,000-ducat ransom. The other three pro-Imperialist cardinals crept out from their palaces late in the night and hurried to Pompeo Colonna's palace. Yet, as Cardinal di Como reported, a group of women with Cardinal della Valle did not get into Colonna's palace quickly enough and were taken, screaming, crying and begging. Even the marquesa of Mantua, whose son Ferrante was a commander in the imperial army, found herself endangered. Together with some 2,000 Romans who were crowded into her palace, she paid out 52,000 ducats to the Spanish, only to be threatened by the Landsknechte. Twice her son Ferrante persuaded them to leave her in peace but she had no confidence in their promises and eventually fled with her guests to Ostia. The moment she left, her palace was sacked.

The most distressing details of what happened in 1527 often do not come from written accounts but, a little surprisingly, from legal documents. Roman notary records show how, as well as enduring attacks, robbery, rape and torture, Romans were also struck by the plague, which, in the chaos of the sack, soon grew into a full epidemic. Even before the sack began, one notary, Pietro Paolo Amodeus, lost eight children to the disease. Another document tells of how a Paduan priest, Paolo de Caligariis, came to take possession of his new church, Santa Cecilia de Turre in Campo, only to find that he could not get upstairs as the upper level was filled with the corpses of plague victims.

Notary documents also show how ordinary Romans tried to preserve some sense of normality in the horror, by having legal contracts carefully drawn up between themselves and their tormentors, as receipts for ransoms paid. Most were with Spanish soldiers, as it seems the Landsknechte were unwilling to be troubled with paperwork. Some Romans also drew up legal protests. One couple made a complaint against the pro-empire cardinal, Enckenvoirt, and also to an Imperialist captain, Aldone. The couple had placed their three children in Enckenvoirt's palace for safety but they had then been taken prisoner by Captain Aldone, along with all the others sheltering in the palace, despite the fact that under imperial army rules no one under the age of fourteen was to be taken. Though the parents paid ransom money, Enckenvoirt still handed the three children over to Aldone. Whether the parents ever retrieved their children is unknown.

High above the nightmare in the Castel Sant'Angelo, Pope Clement, surveying a disaster that he was largely responsible for, decided to grow a beard as a sign of mourning for Rome. Other churchmen followed his example and, before long, beards would become a new fashion across Italy. As time passed what remained of Clement's hopes fell away. The League army that he had believed would come to the rescue in three days never appeared. Its commander, the duke of Urbino, who, as has been seen, had little love for the Medici, was enjoying a little revenge. Instead of hurrying to Rome he took a detour to Perugia, where he set about removing the city's ruler, Gentile Baglione: a papal appointee who Urbino considered an enemy of his own small state. Afterwards, Urbino marched his army towards Rome, only to come up with a series of reasons why he should not attack and snatch Clement to safety, including the claim that he

Landsknechte mercenaries besieging Castel Sant'Angelo, sixteenth-century engraving.

required a whole army of Swiss troops. After 27 May he no longer needed excuses as the Spanish had surrounded the castello with siege works. There was no hope of reaching Clement.

Bad news filtered into the castello from the outside world. The papal state was haemorrhaging territory. As well as Perugia, papal authority had been lost in Rimini, the duke of Ferrara had taken Modena and Clement's supposed ally, Venice, had occupied Ravenna and Cervia. The worst news, though, came not from papal territory but Tuscany. When they heard of Rome's fall the Florentines had risen up against the Medici, forcing out Clement's two illegitimate nephews, Alessandro and Ippolito. Clement's eight-year-old niece, Catherine, was held in the city as a hostage. The Medici had lost their heartland.

Yet despite all the discouraging news life could have been worse for the thousand-odd soldiers, cardinals, prelates, ambassadors, merchants, bankers, wives, children and courtesans who were hiding out in the Castel Sant'Angelo. When imperial troops first burst into the Borgo there had been a rush to seize provisions from nearby shops and, as the archbishop of Zara recounted, the effort had paid off:

We had grain and wine to last a month, as well as some salted meat and cheeses, around 40 bullocks had been brought in, which we got through in less than eight days, and then we had the salted meat and a little ham and cheese and some rice, and we had good bread and excellent wine, all of it Greek.

The archbishop appears to have quite enjoyed himself:

I was always well in myself and I was neither fearful nor exhausted, nor had nightmares. Thanks be to God! Every day we said litanies and day and night we read the psalms, leaving none out. And the pope often celebrated mass and gave a generous indulgence, a copy of which I brought here … And in truth, we were so many in the castle that it truly seemed like there was religion with us, and many cardinals and prelates celebrated.[16]

The one who was enjoying himself most of all, naturally, was Benvenuto Cellini, who confessed that, 'My drawing, my wonderful studies and my lovely music were all forgotten in the music of the guns, and if I told all the great things I did in that cruel inferno, I would astonish the world.'[17] Cellini described how he took a shot at a Spanish officer who, thanks to the sword he was wearing across his front, was instantly sliced in two. The pope was so impressed that he personally gave Cellini his blessing and forgave him all the killings that he had committed or might commit in the future in the name of the Church. Cellini – in one of the few incidents he describes that actually rings true – was then ordered by the pope to remove precious stones from his golden tiaras and other treasures, so they could be sewn into the linings of his clothes. Cellini built an improvised oven to melt down the remaining gold. He described how, during a break from his work, he took a shot at a man riding on a mule below the castello, and 'hit him with one of the projectiles I was using, right in the face. The rest of the shot struck his mule and the animal fell down dead …

The man I had hit was the Prince of Orange.'¹⁸ Cellini, at least by his account, had bagged his second imperial commander of the conflict.

The Prince of Orange really was hit by a shot from the castello, though he suffered only a grazed cheek. It was as well he survived, as he was responsible for saving a large part of the Vatican library, which he did by commandeering it as his wardrobe. Nor was he the only imperial commander who tried to restrain the destructive efforts of his troops. Legal documents also show there were instances of individual kindness by soldiers. Two Spanish officers gave the nuns of Campitelli 30 ducats as a dowry for an eleven-year-old orphan, and after the sack a Spanish officer with a bad conscience returned several valuables he had taken to the canons of St Peter's, for the salvation of his soul. But such acts seem to have been sadly rare.

Cellini's enjoyment of the music of the guns could not go on indefinitely. With food running short and plague breaking out in the castello, the holdouts knew they had to strike a deal. So did the imperial commanders, who wanted to end matters before their army dissolved into chaos. Negotiations between the parties stalled. The Spanish captains insisted Clement must leave Rome and become their prisoner in the Spanish-ruled town of Gaeta down the coast. Clement prevaricated with cunning and a great deal of prayer. The deadlock was eventually resolved, rather unexpectedly, by Pompeo Colonna. On 1 June Clement invited him for an audience. The occasion became an emotional one for both men, who broke into tears at what had happened to Rome, and within a week an agreement was reached. Clement avoided being taken to Spanish territory but agreed to provide, in stages, 400,000 ducats as ransom for himself and everyone else in the castello. As collateral he handed over seven of his closest associates, none of whom, understandably enough, was very keen to go. On 7 June the Castel Sant'Angelo's garrison marched out through the gate, flags flying, accompanied by almost all of the churchmen, artists, bankers, wives, children and courtesans who had been sheltering there. Clement remained with a handful of colleagues, guarded by imperial troops.

A late nineteenth-century vision of the Gallic sack of Rome. *Brennus and His Share of the Spoils* by Paul Joseph Jamin, 1893.

She-wolf suckling Romulus and Remus. The wolf statue was believed to date from Rome's earliest centuries until 2006, when carbon dating revealed it was in fact medieval.

Section of the Aurelian Walls between Porta Latina and Porta Metronia. Built more than a century before Alaric's Visigoths appeared and strengthened shortly before they arrived, the walls were effective against armies but not betrayal.

Fabricius Bridge. Rome's oldest surviving bridge, it was built in 62 BC, during the last decades of the Republic.

Stilicho, military commander of the Western Roman Empire during its great crisis in the early fifth century, with his wife Serena and son Eucherius. Ivory diptych, Monza cathedral, Lombardy.

A glimpse of classical Rome. Fresco detail, National Museum of Rome, Palazzo Massimo alle Terme.

The Colosseum. To this day it is thought to be the world's most concentrated killing ground, where between a quarter and half a million people lost their lives. It was also surprisingly fragile.

(*Above left*) The interior of the Pantheon, classical Rome's greatest architectural gem, which is also one of the city's great survivors. It remains largely intact since imperial times.

(*Above right*) Trajan's Market: a classical Roman shopping mall which was part of a vast complex that included a basilica hall, two libraries and the famous column depicting Trajan's conquests.

Porta Salaria, where Alaric got in. Or rather a section of wall next to where it used to be. The gate itself was demolished in 1871.

Mosaic of Emperor Justinian and his retinue, Basilica of San Vitale, Ravenna. Belisarius, the Byzantine general who saved Rome and then failed to save it, is to the left of Justinian, with the Rolling Stones haircut.

Santo Stefano Rotondo: one of Rome's most exquisite fifth-century churches. In this era the only new buildings were churches and the rest of the city decayed.

Porta Asinaria, where Totila got in. The windows above the gateway were added during the gunpowder age but otherwise the gate has changed little since Totila's time.

(*Bottom left*) Pope Nicholas II invests Robert Guiscard as duke of Apulia, Calabria and Sicily, 1059: an unlikely alliance, between zealous, purist reformer popes and ruthless, self-serving Norman adventurers.

(*Bottom right*) Section of the Leonine Wall. It was built 846-50 AD to protect the Vatican, after an Arab raid during which the St Peter's lost all of its many treasures and even its bronze doors.

Porta Latina, where Robert Guiscard got in. It remains all but unchanged from Guiscard's time.

San Giovanni a Porta Latina. The present church was extensively repaired after being burned by Guiscard's Normans, to smoke out Roman defenders who threatened their retreat.

Santa Maria in Trastevere. One of Rome's most beautiful churches, it was built out of spite, after Pope Innocent II demolished its predecessor, which was associated with his hated rival, Pope Anacletus II.

A view of the pincushion Rome of the high Middle Ages, with its numerous fortress towers. From a 1459 copy of St Augustine's *City of God*.

Rome three decades before the 1527 sack. Aside from a few classical and
Renaissance patches it was a largely medieval city. (Woodcut from the 1493
Nuremberg Chronicle by Hartmann Schedel.)

Pope Julius II ordering Bramante, Michelangelo and Raphael to construct the
Vatican and St Peter's. The decades before the 1527 sack were a cultural high point for
Rome when the city drew Italy's greatest artists. (Emile Jean Horace Vernet, 1827)

The Pasquino talking statue, still talking to this day.

A nineteenth-century view of the papal citadel where Pope Clement VII and others fled imperial troops. (*Castle of San Angelo* by Joseph Turner, 1775–1851.)

(*Below*) The sack of Rome, 1527, by Holy Roman Emperor, Charles V, work attributed to Pieter Brueghel the elder. Dramatic though it is, the painting captures little of the true horror of the event.

(*Right*) Tor Sanguigna, a medieval tower hidden away among later buildings. One of many medieval towers that have survived in Rome.

(*Below*) Porta San Spirito, where the Imperialists got in. The gate was wholly remade when the Vatican and Trastevere were given new defensive walls, following the 1527 sack.

View of the Piazza Navona, Rome by Canaletto (1697–1768). The new Baroque Rome of palaces, domes and fountains that delighted nineteenth-century tourists.

La Festa dei Moccololetti (Festival of Tapers) by Ippolito Caffi (1852). The finale to Rome's uproarious carnival celebrations, when Romans and tourists let their hair down together.

Dome of St Peter's, dusk. After classical Rome's temple to Jupiter Best and Greatest, and medieval Rome's church of Santa Maria in Aracoeli, both on the Capitoline Hill, the skyline of Baroque Rome was dominated by the Vatican.

View from the dome of St Peter's. The wide Via della Conciliazione, leading away to the river, had been a warren of medieval streets until it fell victim to Mussolini's campaign of demolitions.

(*Above*) The Fountain of Four Rivers, Piazza Navona. Artwork fountains were part of the remaking of seventeenth-century Rome, intended to make the city into a weapon of the Counter-Reformation.

(*Top right*) Columns of Bernini's vast, curving arcades. Thanks to them St Peter's Square finally became a place to awe pilgrims.

(*Middle right*) Street corner religious image, one of many dozen that appeared under the intensely conservative popes of the earlier nineteenth century.

(*Bottom right*) Statue of Garibaldi, Gianicolo Hill. Part of the anti-papal propaganda that filled Rome after it became capital of the unified kingdom of Italy.

(*Above*) Palazzo della Civiltà Italiana. Part of Mussolini's planned permanent exhibition area south of Rome, E-42. The building, which was nicknamed the Square Colosseum, had six vertical and nine horizontal arches, to represent the letters of Benito and Mussolini.

(*Left*) Obelisk at the Foro Mussolini (now the Foro Olimpico). Weighing over 300 tons it still stands by the stadium of Roma and Lazio football teams.

(*Right*) Equestrian relief of Mussolini in the Palazzo degli Uffici dell'Esposizione Universale di Roma, E-42. Mussolini's nose was broken off during the Second World War but was quietly repaired in 2001.

American officers lined up for flag-lowering ceremony in front of the Vittoriano after the liberation of Rome, on 5 June 1944.

Romans unload sacks of flour to feed the starving population after liberation.

It seemed that, after a long and terrible month, the dreadful business was finally over. Unfortunately, Clement did not have anything like 400,000 ducats to give, while the imperial soldiers, who by now were regularly mutinying and were all but ungovernable, would not leave until they had been paid. It was a new impasse. The imperial commanders, who were as eager to be gone as Clement was for them to go, appealed to Charles V for money but the emperor felt his army should be able to pay for itself and he sent a mere 100,000 ducats, not in gold but in bills of exchange.

On 10 July, as plague raged through the city and food became scarce, the imperial army, aside from a couple of thousand left to guard the pope, marched off to pillage the nearby countryside, where they caused such devastation that it remained an unproductive wasteland for years to come. In September, the Landsknechte who had been left in Rome built a gibbet and were dissuaded with difficulty from hanging the seven hostages Clement had handed over as collateral. In early October their comrades returned from the countryside to their quarters in Rome, again mutinying and demanding their pay, which their commanders did not have and the pope could not give. The imperial army was slowly wasting away and deaths and desertions had already cut its numbers by almost half. As the weather grew colder its remaining soldiers began to destroy the city in a new way, ripping out doors, door frames, panels and the timbers of houses to burn as firewood.

In the depths of autumn Clement was approached with an unexpected request. William Knight, envoy to King Henry VIII of England, had completed a long and unhappy journey through terrible weather, at the end of which he had almost been killed by hungry locals outside Rome. He had brought Henry's appeal to declare invalid his marriage to Catherine of Aragon. Henry's timing could hardly have been worse. Catherine of Aragon was yet another of Charles V's relations; in this case his aunt. Henry had set in motion the annulment just eleven days after imperial troops first burst into Rome. If he had asked for a divorce a year or two earlier, Clement – then an ally of England at war with Charles V – would have agreed without a murmur. With great difficulty William Knight managed to smuggle his request into the Castel Sant'Angelo via the chamberlain of a Venetian cardinal. Knight offered Clement two possible papal bulls. One gave permission for Henry to marry Anne Boleyn. The second, rather surprisingly, offered a compromise, under which Henry would take Anne as his second wife while keeping Catherine as his first. At this moment, when Lutheranism was a rising force and Christianity was in flux, polygamy – which had a strong presence in the Bible – had a number of enthusiasts. Clement, a master at prevarication, told Knight that it would take a little time to complete the paperwork.

Knight soon enjoyed easier access to the pope. In early December the deadlock in the Castel Sant'Angelo was finally ended. It was broken when imperial commanders, who by now lived in terror of their own soldiers, conspired with Clement to sneak him out of the city. A new deal, the latest of many, was struck. Of the seven hostages Clement had handed over in June, and who had nearly been lynched by the Landsknechte, two had recently managed to escape by getting their guards drunk. Clement said he would replace them with his two illegitimate nephews, the Medici heirs, Ippolito and Alessandro. As neither nephew was anywhere near Rome, Clement offered in the meantime three of his remaining associates in the castello, including two cardinals. It was a disingenuous offer, as Clement had no intention of handing over his nephews, yet it was enough to break the impasse. On 6 December 1527 the guards in the Castel Sant'Angelo were withdrawn and in the small hours of the night the imperial commanders, who had kept their soldiers in the dark about the whole business, had the pope, disguised in the clothes of his own chamberlain, smuggled out of the city.

Yet even with Clement gone Rome's misery was not over. For a further two months what was left of the imperial army continued to mutiny, to raid nearby towns and to use the city's buildings as a source of firewood. Finally, in February 1528 the prince of Orange and another imperial commander, del Guasto, managed to extract 100,000 ducats from the viceroy of Naples, which was enough to give the soldiers two months' back pay. They had wanted far more but they were in no mood to argue as for once they needed their commanders. A French force had linked up with the army of the League and was making rapid inroads into imperial Naples. If they were not careful the Spanish and Landsknechte would have no friendly territory to flee to.

Finally, on 15 February, the Italian and Spanish troops marched out of Rome. The Landsknechte left the next morning. The exodus was surprisingly orderly. Within hours of their departure, members of the Colonna's old enemies, the Orsini family, burst into the city and avenged themselves on any Imperialists who had been unwise enough to linger. A few Romans managed to get something back from their tormentors: among legal documents of the time, one is a contract between a certain Bernardino del Bufalo and several Spanish officers in the Santo Spirito hospital, whom del Bufalo agreed to sneak out of the city unharmed in exchange for the officers' looted valuables. After eight months of occupation, destruction, plague and innumerable deaths – one Spanish soldier claimed he threw 2,000 bodies into the river and oversaw burial of another 10,000 – Rome was finally free.

Clement VII, cautious as ever, did not come back to his capital till the following October, returning in the midst of a violent thunderstorm. The lowest point of his papacy came three months later, in January 1529, when it seemed he had lost almost everything he held dear. A series of cities had been stolen from the papal state, Rome lay in ruins and the papacy was threatened with a new schism as the French and English urged cardinals to meet in Avignon, presumably to choose a new antipope. The Medici had lost Florence. And on top of everything else, Clement, as everybody knew, was dying. Rumours claimed he had been poisoned, though it is more likely he had either malaria or a malingering cold that had got out of hand. In his desperation he finally did what he had been so determined to avoid, and made both his illegitimate nephews Alessandro and Ippolito cardinals.

But Clement did not die. Instead, over the next five years he achieved a remarkable turnaround in his fortunes. He did this by swallowing his pride and doing what he would have been wiser to do years earlier: he formed an alliance with Charles V. Charles added the Medici to his many relations by marrying his illegitimate daughter, Margaret, to Clement's illegitimate nephew, Alessandro. The new alliance soon proved highly beneficial to both parties. Charles squeezed some funds from Clement in the form of church taxes from the kingdom of Naples, and he also improved his reputation, which had taken quite a battering as news of Rome's sack spread across Europe. The new entente reached a high point in Bologna on 24 February 1530, when Clement crowned Charles Holy Roman Emperor. By then peace had been agreed between the Empire and France. Charles had won the struggle and his empire was accepted as the controlling power in Italy.

In return, Charles gave Clement almost everything he had lost. Both through force of arms and diplomatic pressure he rebuilt the papal state, retrieving the cities that had been snatched away by its neighbours. Best of all, in Clement's eyes, in September 1529 imperial troops under the prince of Orange marched on Florence. Despite ingenious fortifications designed by Michelangelo the city fell after a terrible siege lasting eleven months. The next summer Clement's nephew Alessandro rode into the city to be installed as its first openly acknowledged hereditary ruler. The Medici had regained their heartland.

Alessandro, like Clement's other nephew, Ippolito, proved a poor ruler and Florence soon passed to another branch of the family, under Cosimo, but it remained in the hands of the de' Medici, while Clement scored a big success for another of his close relatives. In September 1533, he journeyed to Marseilles. Along with his barrels of Tiber water, which saved him from the risk of drinking the local supply, he also brought his young niece, Catherine, who we last saw being held hostage by Florentine republican rebels. The next month Clement himself married Catherine to King Francis I's second son, Henri, and so restored his relations with France. Clement, who knew only too well how monarchs could oil their way out of a

properly constituted marriage, is said to have intended to witness the
consummation personally. Fourteen years later, after the fortuitous
death of her brother-in-law, Catherine became queen of France.

Within a year of his niece's marriage, Clement was dead. He died
still wearing a beard in mourning for Rome. His papacy would be
remembered as a disaster, yet it could have been far worse. He had
managed to salvage all that he most cared about. The papal state,
Florence and the Medici were restored in their fortunes. Rome had
been wrecked, it was true, Luther's doctrines continued to spread
unchecked and Henry VIII's England had broken from the Church
of Rome, but faraway England was low on Clement's list of priorities.

And Rome? Francesco Gonzaga, who visited the city soon after
the sack, described it as a city of abandoned houses without doors,
windows, attics or roofs. Of the many people he had known there
before the sack, he recognized hardly one and when he asked about
old friends he heard that most of them were dead, a great many from
the plague. For two years the city suffered famine and the starving
inhabitants in the surrounding countryside resorted to banditry. It was
hard to imagine that things might get any worse but then, in October
1530, they did. The city was struck by the worst flood ever recorded:
it inundated most of the city centre to above head height, destroying
hundreds of houses, drowning several thousand Romans and bringing
a new famine. Commentators wondered whether Rome had finally
reached the end of its days.

But of course the city went on. Houses and churches were repaired.
The city had a scare in the spring of 1536. Emperor Charles V had
finally reached the third part of his to-do list – making war on Islam
– and, in an effort to crush North African pirates, he had seized Tunis.
He was now with his army in Naples and his next destination was
Rome. Romans prepared to flee the city but, fortunately, Charles' visit
was to be a friendly one. Clement VII's successor, Paul III, decided to
make a grand show of the city to impress the emperor. He demolished
a number of churches and hundreds of houses to create new vistas
and make Rome's antiquities more visible.

Paul's efforts succeeded. Though some Romans were horrified to recognize the faces of soldiers who had tortured them nine years earlier, no destruction was done and Charles, as he rode along a new Via Sacra, passing beneath triumphal arches both ancient and newly built for the occasion, was greatly impressed. He would not have realized it but he had helped preserve some of the antiquities he saw, as his sacking of the city had halted their being quarried for stone. That his troops had wrecked Rome and raped and tortured its inhabitants was discreetly passed over by Pope Paul, and Charles was hosted in grand style. The vast Renaissance banquet in Trastevere that included 200 dishes cooked by the great Bartolomeo Scappi was held in his honour. Charles had such a good time that he decided to extend his stay. Enjoying fine food and a grand tour of the city's antiquities, he was one of Rome's first true tourists.

Slowly the city recovered. Money seeped back through the rickety system of papal finances, and Rome was rebuilt. The destruction of wooden houses in the sack, and Pope Paul III's clearances, accelerated its transformation from a medieval to a Renaissance city. Though most artists, and humanists too, had fled or died in 1527, some returned. One of Clement VII's last acts as pope was to commission Michelangelo to decorate a wall of the Sistine Chapel. The result, his *Last Judgement*, showed how times had changed. By comparison with the confidence and optimism in his ceiling paintings, the *Last Judgement* was a disturbing, gloomy masterpiece that reflected some of the horrors of Rome's sack. In 1542 work was finally resumed in earnest on the new St Peter's. Paul III hoped to have it completed in time for the 1550 Holy Year. He was over-optimistic and St Peter's would not be finished for more than a century.

If Rome was growing again, it was growing in a direction that took it ever further away from the easy-going, tolerant city it had been under the Medici popes. As the schism between the Church of Rome and Protestants in northern Europe grew more bitter and permanent, the Catholic Church came under the spell of a new purism that was far more invidious than that of the eleventh-century reformists. Its greatest enthusiast was Cardinal Gian Pietro Carafa, a Renaissance Senator McCarthy who became determined to cleanse the papal court of, as he saw them, subversives. In 1542 he supported the creation of a new Inquisition in Rome, and he was so impatient for it to begin work that he bought chains and locks for its new jail with his own money. Thirteen years later, in 1555, Carafa was elected pope as Paul IV and used his position to embark on a witch-hunting campaign against suspected heretics, gays and sellers of Church offices. Romans, many of whom would have been included in at least one of these categories, learned to live in fear of being informed upon, arrested, secretly interrogated and tortured. It was Paul who brought to the Church a new Index of prohibited books, which included those of the Renaissance's greatest humanist scholar, Erasmus.

If these terrors were not enough, under Paul IV Rome seemed destined to relive the disaster it had endured a generation before. Paul, who was a passionate Italian patriot and who had never forgiven the sack of 1527, formed an alliance with France against the Empire, which went wrong almost as rapidly as Clement's had done. In 1557 a Spanish army under the duke of Alba advanced on the helpless city. Fortunately, Alba was reluctant to repeat the public relations disaster of three decades earlier and Paul IV realized his error just in time. On 14 September, in a rare display of good judgement, he signed a treaty of complete surrender and the duke of Alba let the city be. But Rome had no luck that month. The very next day, on the night of the 15th, the Tiber burst its banks in the worst flood since 1530.

As Romans looked about them that September, their city ruined once again, with disease breaking out, an enemy threatening outside the walls and a witch-hunter pope inspiring fear on every street, one would forgive them for thinking that Rome was cursed. They would never have imagined that they were just two years away from a new pope, a new and lasting peace and the start of one of Rome's greatest eras, when their city would grow and thrive as it had not done since classical times.

Rome, 1849

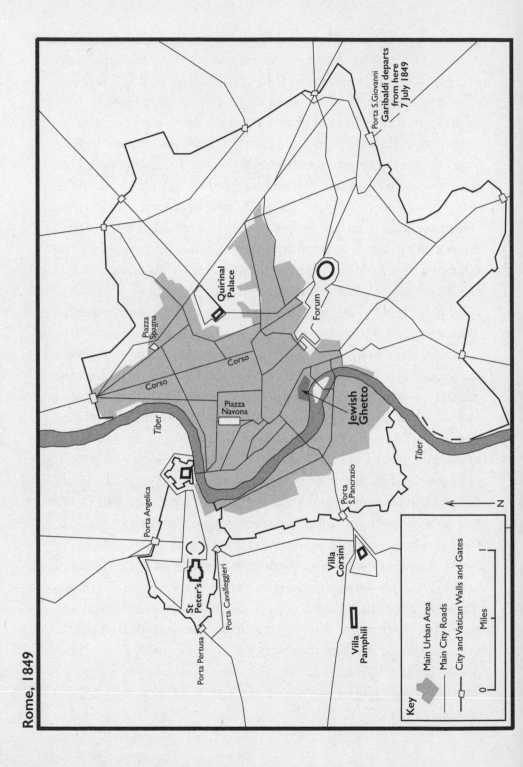

Porta S.Giovanni
Garibaldi departs
from here
7 July 1849

Quirinal
Palace

Forum

Piazza
Spagna

Corso

Corso

Piazza
Navona

Jewish
Ghetto

Tiber

Tiber

Porta
S.Pancrazio

Porta Angelica

St
Peter's

Villa
Corsini

Porta Cavalleggieri

Porta Perusa

Villa
Pamphili

N

Key

Main Urban Area

Main City Roads

City and Vatican Walls and Gates

0   Miles

CHAPTER SIX

FRENCH

I

THESE DAYS THE QUIRINAL PALACE in the heart of Rome is a busy place. Tall uniformed Corazziere – the personal guards of the president of Italy – shepherd tourists and school groups through security checks and into the state rooms, to the gardens and the stables, to see the palace's paintings, its grand chandeliers, and its collection of antique plates and clocks. If they are lucky, visitors may catch a whiff of haute cuisine prepared for foreign dignitaries, or even glimpse the president as he passes through the courtyard in his official car.

It was a very different place on the evening of 24 November 1848, when the French ambassador, the duc d'Harcourt, approached in his carriage. Then it was not a presidential but a papal palace. It was also a place where something bad had happened recently. One of the main doors was scorched black and a good number of windows had been shattered. There would have been a discernible tension in the air as Harcourt's carriage was stopped and he presented himself, not to members of the pope's Swiss Guards, as would have been the case only a few days earlier, but to soldiers of the National Guard. These were Rome's citizens in uniform and they were less concerned with protecting the pope than with making sure he did not leave. They were his jailers. Harcourt, as a friend of the pope, would have been viewed with suspicion.

But they let him into the palace. He was escorted up the grand stairway to the papal apartments where Pope Pius IX was waiting. Considerately – and unwisely – the National Guards allowed the door to be closed so Harcourt and the pope could talk in private. It was a strange sort of discussion. For a short time the National Guardsmen outside would have heard the voices of both men, but then only Harcourt's, speaking loudly enough for them both. By now Pope Pius had slipped into an adjoining room, where he hurriedly changed from his papal robes into the vestments of an ordinary priest. Putting on a pair of dark glasses he, together with a papal servant, Benedetto Filippani, left Harcourt talking to himself and as Filippani lit the way with a small, flickering candle they hurried through the shadow-filled halls of the palace. John Francis Maguire, who wrote an account of events a few years later, describes what happened next:

> As they passed through one of the apartments, the taper was suddenly extinguished, and both the pope and his attendant were left in total darkness. To proceed further without light was impossible; so Filippani was obliged, in order to re-light the taper, to return to the same cabinet in which the French Ambassador had been purposely left waiting. On seeing Filippani return, the Duke was seized with astonishment and terror, believing that some untoward occurrence had occasioned the extinction of the taper, and deranged the entire plan of escape.[1]

But the duc d'Harcourt need not have worried. Filippani relit his candle, hurried back to Pius and led him to the oval stairway on the far side of the palace. In the courtyard below, where a horse-drawn city cab was waiting, the pope had another scare, when a servant recognized him and went down on his knees to be blessed. Fortunately, the National Guards, who kept up a poor sort of watch that night, did not notice. Pius climbed into the cab, which rattled out of the palace. After taking a roundabout route through Rome's streets to avert suspicion, Pius exchanged his cab for the carriage of the Bavarian ambassador, who was another conspirator and who gave Pius his doctor's passport. In the middle of that same night Pope Pius IX crossed the frontier to the kingdom of the Two Sicilies. He had successfully escaped from his kingdom. Only five months later a large, modern and professional French army of between eight and ten thousand soldiers advanced towards the walls of Rome, determined to put him back.

The mid-nineteenth century was an age of revolutions, when Europeans longed for or dreaded the sudden overthrow of their established orders. These dreams and fears had their origins half a century earlier, in France's revolution, which, with the help of French armies, was then exported across Europe. France's radical new vision of a forward-looking, rational, meritocratic world reached Italy in 1796, brought by France's new star general, Napoleon Bonaparte. Napoleon did his best to free Romans of their antiquated aristocratic ways. A liberty tree was planted in the Forum and the pope, Pius VI, was kidnapped and dethroned to die in exile. A decade later, now as Emperor of the French, Napoleon proclaimed Rome the second city of his empire and capital of a kingdom of Italy. The country, though occupied, was more united than it had been for a thousand years.

Most Romans had little liking for the French during these years and remained strongly loyal to their pope. In 1798 the poor of Trastevere rebelled and were subdued only with violence. Yet after the French left Italy in 1814 many Italians found they were nostalgic, not for French occupation but for some of the changes the French had brought. Educated, bourgeois Italians were blocked from advance by exactly the entrenched aristocratic elite that French revolutionaries had so reviled. Politics, too, went into reverse. Italians, like other Europeans, found themselves ruled by absolute monarchs who imposed strict censorship and suppressed any sign of dissent. No Italian government was more reactionary than that of the Papal States, whose jails became crowded with political prisoners. In the 1830s and '40s Pope Gregory XVI even rejected technological change, banning the telegraph, gas lighting and also railways. The latter, whose French name was *chemins de fer*, he denounced as *chemins d'enfer*, or 'the ways of hell'. Italians also felt national humiliation. The French had been replaced by new occupiers: Habsburg Austrians. After 1815 several Italian states were ruled by members of the Habsburg family, and Venice, which had been an independent republic for more than a thousand years, was now a province of the Austrian Empire, as was Milan. The desire of Italians to unite and end foreign occupation of their country, which we saw flare briefly in 1525, burned again.

Italian opposition began through art. Italians became captivated by a wave of romantic novels, histories, paintings, plays and operas in which patriots battled to defend the honour of their wives and daughters from defilement by brutal foreigners. Next came rebellion. Revolts broke out in northern Italy in 1820 and again in the early 1830s. Though all failed, by 1847 an expectation had grown up that a great revolutionary upheaval was coming. This belief was first inspired, rather surprisingly, by the same Pope Pius IX who we just saw scurrying down dark corridors to flee his own state.

Pius began his career as a radical. His family, the Mastai, were supporters of Italy's revolutionary national movement and his predecessor as pope, the reactionary Gregory XVI, complained that even Cardinal Mastai's cat was a Freemason (a supporter of liberal reforms). Mastai, whose Church career had been outside Rome, and who knew little of Vatican politics, was something of an innocent: approachable, informal and very devout. Having been elected in June 1846 as a compromise candidate between two high-profile cardinals, he quickly showed his political colours. He freed political prisoners and allowed political exiles to return, removed censorship, created an elected advisory council, and even established a French revolutionary style National Guard of Roman citizens. He also announced his intention of modernizing his state by introducing the telegraph, gas lighting and railways.

Reform-starved Romans were ecstatic. When Pius freed political prisoners people wept with joy and a huge crowd marched to the Quirinal Palace to give thanks. Thereafter, when Pius passed through the city people threw flowers from balconies, knelt down by the roadside, and even removed the horses from his carriage and pulled it along themselves. A patriotic fervour seized the city as festivals were held, bands played revolutionary hymns and churches were illuminated with the Italian tricolour. It was not only Romans who were excited by the strange spectacle of a radical pope, and by 1847 his reforms raised expectations across Europe. These hopes became self-fulfilling and in early 1848 uprisings broke out in Palermo, Naples and across the Kingdom of the Two Sicilies, whose intensely reactionary king, Ferdinand II, was forced to offer his people a constitution. In February and March revolutions engulfed mainland Europe. In Paris, Vienna, Berlin and across Germany and Italy, governments teetered as monarchs fled their palaces and offered constitutions to their peoples. After five days of street fighting the Milanese flung out a 19,000-strong Austrian garrison and King Carlo Alberto of Piedmont declared war on Austria. To Romans it seemed it could only be a matter of time before Pius IX was president of a free and united Italy.

Their pope, though, had rather different ideas. Pius enjoyed his popularity but he had no intention of losing his kingdom, even to become president of Italy. He also feared that if he provoked the Habsburgs, Austria might secede from the Catholic Church, as England had under Henry VIII. Stresses grew as Romans began to doubt his revolutionary convictions. On 29 April 1848, against the advice of his cabinet, who resigned en masse, Pius shocked Romans by announcing that he would not join other Italian states in going to war with Austria.

Greater disappointment followed. Over the next few months Italians, disunited and poorly led in battle, saw their hopes of a free, unified Italy slipping away. At the battle of Custoza in late

July, Carlo Alberto's Piedmontese army was routed by a smaller Austrian force and, shamefully, Carlo Alberto abandoned the Milanese to the Austrians. The revolutionary tide was turning all across Europe as conservatives rediscovered their confidence. In Naples, Ferdinand shelled his rebellious subjects into submission, earning himself the nickname, 'King Bomba'. It seemed Rome was doomed to go the same way as everywhere else. Pope Pius, who was now detested for his betrayal of the national cause, tightened his grip on power. He appointed a conservative chief minister, Pellegrino Rossi, who purged the Roman police of radicals, exiled two leading revolutionaries and reintroduced censorship. By the autumn there was a widespread expectation that Rossi was about to launch a *coup d'état* and that the constitution that Pius had recently granted would be annulled.

The Romans, though, were in no mood to be suppressed. In the early afternoon of 15 November Rossi set out to meet the legislature of the Papal States, which was meeting in the Palazzo della Cancelleria. The American writer Margaret Fuller, who lived in Rome throughout these times, recounted what happened. Rossi's

> carriage approached, attended by a howling, hissing multitude. He smiled, affected unconcern, but must have felt relieved when his horses entered the courtyard of the Cancelleria. He did not know he was entering his place of execution. The horses stopped; he alighted in the midst of a crowd; it jostled him as if for the purposes of insult; he turned abruptly and received as he did so the fatal blow.[2]

He had been stabbed in the throat and within moments he was dead. It was a measure of his unpopularity that papal troops watched the killing without a word, while neither they nor anybody else made any attempt to seize his assassin. Soldiers later joined a large crowd which, cruelly, gathered beneath the house of Rossi's new widow to sing, 'happy the hand which rids the world of tyrants'.

The Quirinal Palace under siege, contemporary engraving.

The following day the pope's powerlessness was fully revealed. A crowd gathered in the piazza in front of the Quirinal Palace to demand the appointment of a radical, pro-nationalist government. When the tiny force of Swiss Guards inside the palace fired, causing injuries, the piazza filled with the pope's own troops, from papal regiments and also the new National Guard of Roman citizens. After they shot at the palace windows, killing one cleric, the pope accepted defeat and appointed revolutionaries to his government. He also replaced his Swiss Guards with members of the National Guard, becoming a prisoner in his palace. One week later he made his escape to the territory of King Bomba of Naples. On 6 January 1849 any last hopes of reconciliation were extinguished when Pius excommunicated the Romans for their 'monstrous act of undisguised felony and of actual rebellion.'[3]

Popeless, the Papal States proceeded down the revolutionary path they had chosen. Elections were held for a constitutional assembly

Proclamation of the Second Republic from the balcony of the Capitoline,
9 February 1849.

and on 9 February a new Roman Republic was declared. The Italian
tricolour flew from the Senatorial Palace on the Capitoline, the
equestrian statue of Marcus Aurelius wore a tricolour garland round
its neck, bells were rung, cannon fired and even beggars wore red
liberty caps. After the defeats of the year before, Rome's revolution
gave new hope to Italian republicans and nationalists, many of whom
made their way to the city.

Notable among these were two of the greatest figures in the history
of Italian unification, Giuseppe Garibaldi and Giuseppe Mazzini.
Superficially the two men had much in common. Both came from
the same part of Italy. Mazzini was born in Genoa, where he grew up
reading patriotic romantic novels and dreamed of becoming a literary
critic. Garibaldi was brought up just along the coast at Nizza – now
French Nice, but then a half-French, half-Italian city that belonged
to the Italian kingdom of Savoy – where he spent his younger years

working aboard sailing ships trading to the Black Sea. Both men took part in the failed revolutionary uprisings of the 1830s and both were arrested. Garibaldi – always the more dramatic of the two – was sentenced to death but escaped.

In terms of their characters, though, the two men could hardly have been more different, as was revealed by how they spent their years of exile. Mazzini quickly assumed the mole-like existence of a revolutionary conspirator. He hid himself away in an apartment in Marseilles, hardly leaving the building, though his enemies managed to discover him nonetheless, causing him to move to Switzerland, and then, in 1837, to London. Here he became accustomed to the city's dirt, bedbugs and drunkenness and led an austere, monk-like existence, working day and night and keeping himself awake with coffee and cigars. At times he was so short of money that he was forced to pawn his watch, to walk rather than pay for omnibus fares, and he struggled to buy postage stamps for his coded letters. Yet he gradually built up a revolutionary organization, the Young Italy Movement. Creating a network of informants and supporters across Europe, Mazzini became the PR man of Italian nationalism, cultivating contacts among English liberals and producing a stream of journalistic pieces. It was a measure of his success that the leader of European conservatism, the Austrian chancellor Prince Metternich, considered him the most dangerous man in Europe.

By contrast, Garibaldi's exile was exhilaratingly outdoors. He fled to newly independent South America where he soon became involved in a doomed separatist struggle, fighting for the Republic of Rio Grande that sought to break away from Brazil. Garibaldi was shipwrecked, captured and tortured yet remained largely unscathed. He learned how to ride a horse, how to fight guerrilla warfare and, from free-living gaucho ranchers, he acquired his distinctive look, which he would make famous, including the felt hat and poncho. He also found the love of his life, Anita, whom he stole away from a dull husband, and who, fortunately, was no less adventurous and fearless than he was.

Losing hope in the struggles of the Republic of Rio Grande, Garibaldi and Anita made their way to Montevideo, which was also embroiled in war, against the dictator of Buenos Aires, Juan Manuel de Rosas. Garibaldi created an Italian Legion of like-minded exiles who took as their uniform a consignment of red shirts intended for abattoir workers. In early 1846 the Italian Legion defeated Rosas' forces at San Antonio del Salto. Afterwards Garibaldi and his followers enhanced their reputation by refusing to take any reward from the Uruguayan government. The battle of Salto was a turning point in Garibaldi's career. Thanks largely to Mazzini's tireless journalistic promotion his name began to be known in Europe. He was eminently promotable. His public persona – the courageous, self-denying patriot – perfectly matched a hero from the pages of one of the romantic novels that Italians had been reading for decades.

News that revolution had broken out in Italy brought both him and Mazzini hurrying home and in the summer of 1848 they finally joined forces. It was an unhappy collaboration. By then the Italian national cause was already struggling. After Piedmontese armies were defeated by the Austrians at Custoza, Mazzini joined Garibaldi's volunteers, who were harassing Habsburg troops near Lake Maggiore. Mazzini's mole-like existence had left him poorly prepared for the life of a foot soldier and a few days of forced marches were enough to send him hurrying across the frontier to Switzerland. Garibaldi's volunteers defeated an Austrian unit, in one of the few Italian successes of that disastrous summer, but he was soon forced to follow Mazzini to Switzerland, where the two had a bitter falling-out over tactics.

The flight of Pope Pius IX and the declaration of the Roman Republic took them both south, and each assumed a key role in Rome's new revolutionary state. In March 1849 Mazzini, riding high on his name as a revolutionary organizer, became the Roman Republic's effective leader, so dominating the ruling triumvirate that its decisions were largely his. Garibaldi led his legion of volunteers. It was clear to both men that the Roman Republic was unlikely to survive for long. By early April 1849 Europe's revolutionary tide had ebbed to the point where Rome, Venice and Hungary were the last holdouts in a sea of reaction. Four powers – Austria, Spain, Naples and France – had announced their determination to defeat Rome's Republic and place Pope Pius back on his throne. Austria was in the process of seizing towns in the northern Papal States and Ferdinand of Naples – King Bomba – was threatening from the south and east.

Yet, doomed though it seemed to be, Garibaldi and Mazzini were agreed that the Roman Republic was of immense importance, as it might breathe new life into the national cause by offering an inspiring example. As ever, they had different ideas as to what kind of example this should be. Garibaldi wanted the Romans to show their courage and prove, after the humiliations of the previous year, that Italians would fight bravely for their country. To Mazzini, the public relations man, Romans needed also to show their moderation so the national cause could win foreign friends. To this end he acted quickly against any attacks on churchmen, Church property or the rich. Mazzini was not a traditional Catholic – his beliefs were mystical – but he was careful to show that, though he was at war with the pope, he was not at war with Catholicism. During the popeless Easter of 1849 he found a pro-revolutionary churchman to bless the crowd from the balcony of St Peter's as Mazzini stood beside him.

Mazzini also tried to impress with his own lifestyle. He lived as frugally as ever in a single room, unguarded and approachable, and he dined simply at a nearby trattoria. His efforts may not have held much sway with Europe's great powers but they did with foreign writers, such as Margaret Fuller. They also impressed Romans and Mazzini gained the support of a key local figure, the wine merchant Angelo Brunetti, who was known by Romans as Ciceruacchio (and whose son Luigi had assassinated the prime minster, Rossi). With Ciceruacchio's support Romans, though they were at first doubtful of Mazzini, were won round. The new and fragile Republic had grown some roots.

Mazzini saw Garibaldi as something of a liability. For all his popularity, Garibaldi was unpredictable and his views could be radical. His loathing of priests had led him to declare himself an atheist: a stance that was seen as beyond the pale by most Europeans at this time. There were also his views on marriage. He had famously stolen Anita from her legitimate husband and they did not marry until after the birth of their first child. Accordingly, Mazzini declined to appoint Garibaldi as the Republic's military commander, instead choosing a plodding and stodgily respectable Roman, Pietro Roselli. Garibaldi was sent to the hill town of Rieti, to train his legion and guard the Republic's eastern border against possible Neapolitan attack. Garibaldi, who knew full well why he had been sent there and was struck by a bad bout of rheumatism, became frustrated and moody, one moment excitable, the next grumbling that his volunteers were a generation of hermaphrodites.

It was not from the east, though, that danger would come. On 25 April General Oudinot landed a large, well-equipped and professional French force at Civitavecchia, just forty miles west of Rome. It was discouraging news yet Mazzini remained optimistic, sure his publicity talents might yet carry the day. Of the Republic's four declared enemies, France was the least obdurate. Its new president, Louis Napoleon, was an unlikely reactionary as, like Mazzini, he had spent most of his life as a radical conspirator, plotting and enduring time in jail. In his youth he had dabbled in Italian nationalist revolutionary politics, and Mazzini had met him in London when they were fellow political exiles. Nor did Louis Napoleon seem a leader who would have much stomach for conflict. One of the few women close to him with whom he had not had an affair, Hortense Cornu, offered a memorable assessment of his character. He was kind and loyal, she said, but also lazy and lacking in any kind of principle. 'Everything wearies him,' she reported. 'He gets up bored, he passes the day bored and goes to bed bored.'[4]

Mazzini had hopes also of winning round French public opinion. Only a year before, France had been a beacon of revolution, and though the country had been moving steadily to the right since then, it was still a republic and elections to its new assembly were approaching. Mazzini had posters printed that displayed, in French, the fifth article of France's new republican constitution – 'The French Republic will never employ its forces against the liberty of any other people' – which he had placed on walls along the road from Civitavecchia to Rome.

Mazzini's hopes, though, were misplaced. Most of the French population outside radical Paris admired the pope and they believed him when, from his exile in Gaeta, he declared that Rome was 'a forest of roaring beasts, overflowing with men of every nation, apostates, or heretics, or leaders of communism and socialism'. (The foreigners were Mazzini, Garibaldi and their supporters.) General Oudinot's officers were not republicans and nor were his troops, most of whom were farmers conscripted from France's conservative countryside. They paid no attention to Mazzini's posters but marched straight on towards Rome.

II

As to what kind of Rome awaited the French, one change to the city since 1527 was immediately evident. Oudinot and his army were advancing on a wall that had not existed in the early sixteenth century. In a classic example of shutting the stable door after the horse has bolted, it had been built in the decades after Spanish and Lutheran attack, to protect the western side of the city that had proved so vulnerable. Starting at Castel Sant'Angelo, it encircled the Vatican and its feeble Leonine Wall, then ran along the top of the Gianicolo ridge, encompassed the district of Trastevere, before finally descending to the river. By nineteenth-century standards it was already antiquated but, supported by a thick barrier of earth and containing a series of bastions for cannon, it was far superior to the Aurelian Walls on the other side of the river, which had hardly changed since Alaric's time. Oudinot was marching towards the one part of the city that could put up a good fight.

Within the walls Rome had, for once, not swelled or shrunk or moved. The *abitato* had encroached a little on the empty *disabitato* but not greatly, and a good half of the area inside the city walls was still green. Yet, if the city had not changed much in size, a visitor from the early 1520s would still have found it largely unrecognizable. Most of all they would have been impressed. Rome was vastly transformed for the better.

It was now a city of fountains, and the tinkling of water could be heard everywhere, flowing from hundreds of street taps and dozens of great fountains, some of which, like the Trevi and the Four Rivers, were great works of art. In the 1840s fresh, clean, drinking water was available to all. Rome was also a city of dazzling architecture. Among numerous new palaces and great houses, the most spectacular was the Quirinal Palace, which overlooked the city from the Quirinal Hill, and which had already been the main home of the popes for 250 years, after they turned their backs on the malaria-ridden Borgo. Vast and with fine gardens, the Quirinal Palace was almost as impressive as the older Vatican Palace. Rome was also filled with new, striking churches with ornate Baroque facades and, inside, ceilings covered with gold leaf, or paintings depicting crowds of saints looking down from heaven. Even the city's medieval churches had been gaudily refurbished, their ancient columns encased in colourful marble. Rome was now a city of beautiful piazzas of every shape and size, from the small and intimate to St Peter's Square, with its two vast, curving colonnades.

A visitor from the early sixteenth century would have had her greatest surprise, though, if she climbed one of Rome's hills and looked back at the city's skyline. In 1527 Rome had been a pincushion city bristling with towers. In the 1840s it was a city of domes. It had some six dozen of them, large and small. The greatest, of course, was St Peter's. A building site in 1527, the cathedral was now complete, having been consecrated in 1626, just a century behind schedule. Rome was also now a city of vistas, with some long straight streets that culminated in an ancient Egyptian obelisk (and, occasionally, a fake new one). These grand views were carefully framed, and nowhere better than in the Piazza del Popolo, whose twin churches (not identical though they seemed so, thanks to an ingenious optical illusion) perfectly set off the mile-long Corso to the Capitoline Hill.

Looking at this visual feast, a visitor from 1527 would probably have imagined that the Catholic Church had been thriving since his day. In fact much of what they saw had been inspired by the Church's failures. In the 1550s, as the Council of Trent led Catholicism down the road of purism and intolerance, the papacy belatedly responded to the disaster of the Protestant Reformation, as popes Pius IV and Pius V attempted to renew both Catholicism and its capital. They set in motion long overdue work to clean up the city's drains and ordered the repair of Rome's one functioning classical aqueduct, the Acqua Vergine, which produced only a dribble of water. In 1570, for the first time in centuries, it became a torrent, which was used to power fountains that were then built all across the Campo Marzio. More fountains followed when, in 1587, a second ancient aqueduct, the Acqua Felice, was brought back to life. On the other side of the Tiber the Damasiana was repaired and then, in 1612, the ancient Acqua Paola flowed once again, bringing quantities of fresh water to Trastevere and the Borgo. Romans no longer had to drink Tiber water, though some continued anyway, claiming they preferred it.

Improvements were also made above ground. The Capitoline Hill was slowly remade to Michelangelo's design, with the Senator's Palace and two others facing one another around a trapezoid piazza. Seventeenth-century Rome's transformation accelerated under the influence of two architects in particular. Francesco Borromini produced intense designs that included the twizzle-shaped tower of Sant'Ivo alla Sapienza and the intricate pattern work of the church of San Carlo alle Quattro Fontane. His great rival, the prolific artist and architect Gian Lorenzo Bernini produced the Tritone and Four Rivers fountains in Piazza Navona and the immense bronze canopy – the *baldacchino* – in St Peter's.

Yet Rome's real transformation would require a further dose of Catholic sense of failure. A visitor from 1527 would have been surprised to learn that a great number of the city's new sights were the work of a single pope, Alexander VII, who reigned for just twelve years from 1665 to 1677. Prior to his election, when he was Cardinal Fabio Chigi, he had worked as a papal negotiator at the peace negotiations at Münster that ended the carnage of the Thirty Years War. The resulting treaty accepted for the first time that Protestant churches were a permanent part of Europe's religious landscape. Catholicism's greatest setback, the Reformation, which had lost it a large portion of its European parishioners, was now official. Chigi, who was left traumatized, was determined to restore the Church's prestige. At the start of his reign the former queen of Sweden, Christina, came to Rome, having renounced her throne and converted to Catholicism. Alexander VII, hopeful that he might win more high-ranking converts, sought to return the city to its former glory so it could become a showcase of Catholicism.

Alexander had Rome's most renowned antiquities cleared of detritus, replacing several columns of the Pantheon that had been lost to medieval violence and relandscaping the Piazza della Rotunda to make the building more visible. He tidied up streets and piazzas, forcing owners to rebuild the frontages of their houses so they were properly aligned. He restored old churches and built new ones. He gave Rome new vistas and framed those that existed, as with the twin churches in Piazza del Popolo that set off the Corso. He remade Rome's squares, from Piazza Collegio Romano to Piazza Venezia and Santa Maria in Trastevere. He gave Rome what became among its most popular sights, such as Bernini's elephant in Piazza della Minerva. Most of all he and Bernini – his chief collaborator – gave St Peter's Square its vast curving colonnades.

Even the *disabitato* was transformed. In 1527 it had been working countryside, made up of fields and vineyards with the occasional church or country home. In the 1840s it was largely comprised of holiday homes for Rome's rich: country villas surrounded by ornamental parkland. One of the largest of these, the Villa Borghese, had its own lake. The Villa Doria Pamphili, which lay outside the city walls, just beyond the new fortifications above the Vatican – and through which General Oudinot's soldiers marched towards Rome – had two lakes, each with a small waterfall.

If he had been able to look into the future, Alexander VII would have been disappointed. His efforts did not cause a flood of foreign VIPs to convert, and northern Europe remained obstinately Protestant. Yet his beautified Rome succeeded in other ways, becoming a must-see city for Catholics and Protestants alike. So we come to another change that would have surprised a time traveller from 1527. Rome in the 1840s was crowded with a wholly new kind of visitor. These were not pilgrims (though there were still plenty of these as well) but sightseers. The new Grand Tour had arrived.

It had been building up for some time. As we saw in the last chapter, Emperor Charles V could be considered one of the first cultural tourists. Many more would follow. Barring occasional hiccups, such as when Pope Pius V excommunicated Queen Elizabeth I, or when French revolutionaries invaded Italy, the Grand Tour became ever more popular with wealthy northern Europeans, for whom it was the accepted way to round off one's education. When Napoleon's occupation of Rome ended, tourists poured south, much to the annoyance of Lord Byron, who complained that the Continent was 'pestilent with English – a parcel of staring boobies who go about gaping, wishing to be at once cheap and magnificent. A man is a fool who travels now in France or Italy, till this tribe of wretches is swept home again.'[5]

Byron would be in for a long wait. In 1846 Rome had 300,000 visitors, or double the city's population. Tourists were the most visible foreign element on the city's streets, as pilgrims stayed for only a week or two while tourists would often remain for a whole season, from October to the spring, when the city was largely malaria free. They came for the culture, for the sunlight, and in some cases to save money. The earl of Shrewsbury boasted that by spending his summers in Rome – rashly, in view of the malaria risk – he saved himself £2,000 a year. Rome became their home away from home and, as well as seeing the sights, they would call on one another, have their portraits painted by resident artists – who were mostly northern Europeans like themselves – and dabble in a little painting and writing.

Writers were especially drawn to Rome. Dickens and Byron, Ruskin and Lear, Irving, Cooper, Emerson and Nathaniel Hawthorne all spent time there. Elizabeth Gaskell claimed her days in Rome were 'the tip-top point of our lives. The girls may have happier ones – I never shall.'[6] The American sculptor and writer William Wetmore Story spent much of his life in the city. Keats, though he was in Rome for just a few months, became a kind of honorary Roman after dying there. He was far from alone. In 1849 the non-Catholic cemetery, just below Cestius' pyramid, was crowded with the bones of eminent foreigners who had succumbed to typhoid, tuberculosis, malaria or riding accidents.

Tourists still happily alive set themselves to work on the serious business of sightseeing. As well as the city's classical ruins, palaces and churches there were its paintings, and it was all but obligatory to see the portrait of Beatrice Cenci – whose authenticity is now questioned – and lament the injustice of her fate (she was abused by her monstrous father and, after she and her siblings killed him, was executed). Though there were numerous guidebooks to the city, John Murray's, first published in 1843, quickly became *the* guidebook for English-speakers, causing William Wetmore Story to observe that, 'Every Englishman carries a Murray for information and a Byron for sentiment, and finds out by them what he is to know and feel at every step.'[7]

As well as describing the sights, Murray offered practical advice on where to stay, where to eat and how to avoid being cheated. Most of his suggestions concern the area around Piazza di Spagna. A relatively new neighbourhood – the Spanish Steps and Trevi Fountain had been built the previous century – its housing was less cramped than that of other districts and its straight streets were wide enough to take a carriage. By the 1840s the area had become a foreign – and especially English – colony; so much so that Romans called it the *Ghetto degli Inglesi*. Aside from the Anglican Church, which thanks to papal sensibilities had to remain outside the city walls, almost every service that English visitors might need was to be found here, frequently offered by other English people. There was an English livery stable, an English reading room, an English circulating library and an English club (proposal strictly by existing members). Among numerous English tradesmen – whom Murray recommended above locals, 'as they are more to be relied upon for punctuality, good articles and honesty' and who refrained from, 'bribing servants to obtain their masters' custom'[8] – there were English tailors and wine sellers, English bakers, hatters, boot- and shoemakers, English saddlers, dressmakers, hairdressers and booksellers, and even an English greengrocer. The English, together with other resident foreigners, had their own *passeggiata* on the Spanish Steps. Teams of the English played cricket against one another in the gardens of Villa Pamphili. The English even had their own pack of hounds – maintained by subscription – for hunts outside the city.

With tourism came souvenir shops. William Wetmore Story found these distasteful, complaining that 'Pictures and statues have been staled by copy and description, until everything is stereotyped,' from the *Dying Gladiator* to *Beatrice Cenci*, who 'haunts one everywhere with her white turban and red eyes'.[9] Tourism also brought crowds, especially during Holy Week at Easter when hotels were packed and the price of a city cab doubled or tripled. Dickens, watching the pope convey the sacrament from the Sistine Chapel to the Capella Paolina noted that, of the crowd watching this sombre Catholic ceremony, three-quarters were Protestant English.

We owe much to the Victorian tourists. The accounts they wrote of their visits provide a far more vivid portrait of the city than those of any previous era. Rome in the 1840s excited strongly partisan responses, as it still does today. Many loathed it. Nathaniel Hawthorne complained of its 'sour bread … enormous prices for poor living, beggars, pickpockets, ancient temples with filth at the base', and its 'shabby population smoking bad cigars'.[10] Young John Ruskin both loathed and loved it. He despised ancient Rome, declaring it to be 'a nasty, rubbishy, dirty hole – I hate it'. But he adored the city's landscape, observing that there was 'not a single corner of a street which if studied closely and well would not have been beautiful'. Then he loathed it all again, deciding that it was 'the bluest place conceivable. Everybody in it looks like a vampyre; the ground is cold and church-like; the churches are full of skeletons; the air is sulphurous; the water is bilge; the sun is pestiferous; and the very plaster of the houses looks as if it had got all the plagues of Leviticus.'[11] William Wetmore Story adored it all, even the stink: 'It was dirty but it was Rome, and to anyone who has long lived in Rome even its very dirt has a charm which the neatness of no other place ever had.'[12]

The tourists came, above all, to enjoy a dizzying sense of time past and greatness lost – though it was now much harder to appreciate Rome's lost glories as a good portion of them had disappeared. A visitor from 1527 would have been disappointed to see how many of the city's ruins had vanished, their stone recycled and their marble baked to make plaster. The new St Peter's was the worst culprit and a large part of it had been constructed from the collapsed portion of the Colosseum. But at least what remained was more visible. Thanks to the city's Napoleonic rulers, who sought to prepare for Napoleon's triumphal progress through his second capital (which never happened), centuries of detritus had been removed from the Forum and the buildings and market stalls encroaching on the Pantheon were demolished.

Although there was a little less to see in Rome there were new possibilities outside the city. Adventurous tourists could now explore a quite new kind of ruin: Etruscan cities and tombs. For a century these had fascinated northern Europeans, so much so that English aristocrats had Etruscan rooms installed in their country homes, and Josiah Wedgwood's copies of Etruscan pottery (most of which were in fact Greek) became so popular that in 1769 he named his new factory Etruria. Etruscomania led to an interesting rediscovery. In 1839 Elizabeth Gray paid a visit to a ruined city north of Rome, whose walls she found were in the process of being eaten away as, 'every peasant has been at liberty to carry off the stones, destroy the remnants of walls and buildings and dig up the ancient highways, in order to fence round his own sheepfold, or patch of corn land; to build his conical hut'.[13] The vanishing city was Rome's ancient rival, Veii. Rome's first victim was finally back in the limelight.

When not describing Rome's cultural sights, tourists complained – and there was much that annoyed them. Rome may have improved beyond all measure since 1527, yet when compared to other nineteenth-century European cities it was old-fashioned, even bewilderingly so. Visitors were irritated by its antiquated bureaucracy, and by its main post office where they went to collect their letters, and which would close for no reason anyone could understand. They grumbled about the city's numerous feast days when cafés and restaurants were only permitted to serve plain, light food (though Protestants could sometimes get round the rules). They were confused by the city's clocks, whose hours were numbered from one to six, and whose hour hand (there was no minute hand) made a full circuit of the clock face four times a day. And they were baffled by Rome's incomprehensible time system, under which each day began at the Ave Maria (half an hour after sunset) though the exact moment was set officially, with adjustments announced every few weeks in the official papal almanac, the *Diario Romano*.

Protestant tourists also loved to complain of what they saw as the strange superstitions of Catholicism. Despite the ravages of Charles V's Landsknechte, many of these still remained. In St Peter's, hidden in repositories and shown to the public only on special feast days, were part of Longinus' lance, with which he had stabbed Jesus' side, as well as Saint Andrew's head and even the Veronica cloth, which had supposedly been burned or sold in an inn in 1527. However, these days the popularity of all three was eclipsed by a new miraculous object: the Bambino of the church of Santa Maria in Aracoeli, which was a wooden figure of Jesus, dressed in satin, gold lace and precious jewels. It was widely believed to have healing powers and was brought to sick patients accompanied by physicians, who – fortunately – were able to give actual medical advice. When the Bambino passed through streets, often in his own carriage, Romans would kneel, cross themselves and women would cover their heads. Dickens described it as 'a little wooden doll, in face very like General Tom Thumb, the American dwarf'.[14]

The greatest number of tourists' grievances, however, were reserved
for their lodgings. Though they might spend a day or two in a hotel
on their arrival, most then moved to a rented apartment that was both
more spacious and less costly. Yet, living as the Romans did could be
a sorry experience. Sir George Head described dirty stairways, poorly
fitting doors, badly made locks and draughty windows, observing that
many properties were 'so questionable that, in any other place than
Rome, one would think it disreputable to enter'.[15] It did not help that
the tourists visited Rome in the autumn and winter, although the
buildings they stayed in were designed to keep out the intense summer
heat. Nathaniel Hawthorne found himself sitting by a smoking,
cheerless fireside wearing more clothes than he had ever worn in his
life. Fleas were a constant problem as they infested almost all rented
housing, from the poorest to the best.

There was also the noise. Ceilings were anything but soundproof,
while apartments were often reached through a labyrinth of different
entrances, so 'one may hear one's fellow lodger stamping continuously
for weeks or months', without ever being able to catch him at the door
and ask him to be quieter. There was also an infuriating device that was
used all over Rome to carry water to upstairs rooms, which involved
'a copper vessel suspended by a ring to a slanting wire, and drawn up
and down to an upper window, which process is an extraordinarily
noisy one'. The copper vessel was so small that it had to be hauled
up repeatedly; and as there were half a dozen or so such wires in
every piazza, 'the same disagreeable, grating, rattling and splashing
disturbance is repeated continually'.[16]

And of course there was the stink. Despite plaques placed all over
the city threatening dire penalties to anyone who deposited rubbish, it
was dumped everywhere, along with worse things. All grand tourists
concurred that Rome smelt terrible and they disagreed only as to
where, if anywhere, smelt even worse. August von Kotzebue thought
Naples was worse, James Johnson picked Lisbon and John Ruskin
favoured Edinburgh. Lady Morgan claimed Rome had no paragon,
while she considered the approach to St Peter's Rome's vilest spot,

declaring grandly, 'Here the streets of the filthiest city in Europe are found filthiest.'[17] Hawthorne warned anyone passing through the Forum that 'you must look well to your steps or they will be defiled with unutterable nastiness'.[18]

Rome's streets had annoyances other than dirt. Most were unpaved. Some had large elliptical-shaped openings to drains below, through which valuables could easily fall. Though, as Sir George Head recounted, a remedy was usually at hand: 'Some small lean boy, trained by frequent practice to squeeze his carcass through the aperture is invariably to be found ready to redeem the lost treasure.'[19] In hot weather the drains became refuges for colonies of cats, whose faces could be seen peering out of the openings.

Most of all though, thanks to Gregory XVI's distaste for gas lamps, Rome's streets were dark, and at night they were far from safe. A common ploy of robbers was to ask for a light for their cigar. When the victim reached out obligingly they would find a dagger pressed to their chest. Odo Russell, the unofficial British representative to the Vatican (no official one being acceptable from a heretic, Protestant country), was told by his Roman servant, 'to offer no resistance if I am attacked, but to give up my money as he promises he will get it all back from the police the next day. But he says if I resist they will run a long knife into me and then run away.'[20]

Romans might seem alarming to foreign tourists but they posed little threat to the wider world. A visitor from 1527 would have been disappointed to find how much of a kitten their home town had become on the world stage. In the early sixteenth century, as the headquarters of Europe's religion, and as the capital of a second-tier, yet significant, military power, Rome was still a city of consequence. By the 1840s it was a fascinating and picturesque oddity. It is hard to think of a moment since Brennus' Gauls attacked when the city had been more of a backwater. The world had moved on and left it behind, small and provincial. Between 1520 and 1849 its population had not quite doubled, from around 80,000 to 150,000, while during the same period London's population had grown over forty times and it was now in excess of two million. Hardly a single building of consequence had been constructed in Rome for a century and some things had not changed in a thousand years. Watermills were still moored to the Tiber Island. Rome was in a rut even when it came to art. In the 1840s most of the city's artists were second-rate foreigners scraping a living by painting portraits of tourists. The nineteenth century's Michelangelos were in France, Spain, Germany or England but not Rome.

The city's economy, too, was far sleepier than it had been three centuries earlier. At a time when Europe's northern cities were powerhouses of industry, the French political economist Jean Charles de Sismondi offered a damning assessment of Rome's productiveness: 'In Rome, with the exception of artists, hoteliers, coach drivers and shopkeepers selling trinkets to foreigners, everyone languishes, everyone struggles, every project fails, every industry is regulated into poverty, except that of begging.'[21]

As the city had declined, so had its aristocracy. By the 1840s there were only a dozen or so families who, like the Pamphili, owned tracts of land, villas, palaces and art collections, and who could look rich northern Europeans in the eye. Far more common were Romans who, though they had a title and a decent-sized house, were rentiers, struggling to make an income from letting out an apartment or two to tourists. John Murray warned his readers that they should be sure to obtain a rental contract, 'however respectable the landlord may appear.'[22]

If most of Rome's aristocrats suffered reduced circumstances, at least they enjoyed a warmer family life than their predecessors. In the past, Italy's urban nobility lived in large, extended families, but from the late eighteenth century aristocratic newly-weds emulated the bourgeoisie, setting up their own homes. They also became more intimate with one another. Aristocratic mothers brought up their children themselves rather than handing them over to wet nurses, and there was less reserve between husbands and wives and parents and children. Italian family life had reached the elite. Rome's nobility also enjoyed better food, at least to our taste buds (a visitor from 1527 would have found it a little bland). From the seventeenth century Eastern spices ceased to appeal to Europe's wealthy, in part because they had become too cheap to give status. Sweet and sour sauces lost their popularity and sugar – which had been added to almost everything – was relegated to desserts. In the 1840s Rome's wealthy preferred delicate-tasting local foods, such as beans, artichokes, broccoli, pasta, potatoes, and fish or veal in a white sauce. They also enjoyed tomato sauces, whether on pasta or meat. Roman food was finally emerging as the cuisine we know today.

All these dishes were also popular with the poor, though, unsurprisingly, their tomato sauce was poured on to different cuts of meat. Choice parts went to the rich while the poor made do with tripe, liver and other remnants, which were becoming the basis of many classic Roman dishes. Life for Rome's poor was as tough as in previous ages, if not tougher, and many made their living from odd jobs or busking. The nineteenth century saw a sharp rise in the number of illegitimate births in Italy and more Italians than ever made use of the *ruota*: the device built into the walls of orphanages that allowed mothers to leave their babies anonymously. The prospects for abandoned newborns were not good. With more foundlings and fewer wet nurses, infant mortality in Italian foundling hospitals was higher in the nineteenth century than it had been in the Middle Ages.

Not many tourists took time off from their cultural tours to see how Rome's poor lived, but William Wetmore Story did. In classical times Rome's poorest had lived in the highest part of apartment blocks but now they were in the lowest, right by the noise and stink of the street. Story found them crouching over a little earthenware pot of coals to keep warm, in rooms with cheap brick paving, stains on the walls and shabby, rickety furniture, though there was 'no place so mean as to be without its tawdry picture of the Madonna, with a little onion-shaped lamp burning below'.[23]

Rome's struggling economy was not the people magnet it had been in the past. Immigrants drawn to the city were mostly from rural areas of the Papal States where prospects were even worse. But at least these days a Roman had a better chance of finding a wife. As immigration shrank, so did the city's gender gap. In 1600 men had outnumbered women by three to two, but by the 1840s the difference was barely one in twenty. It did not take long for arrivals from the country to take on Roman ways and they were soon largely indistinguishable from the rest of the population. As a consequence, tourists usually assumed they were all locally born and – despite the fact that the city had enjoyed eighteen centuries of immigration from all over the Mediterranean – they romanticized them as the direct descendants of the ancient Romans. Many claimed to see a clear resemblance between their faces and those of classical statues. They were particularly fascinated by the Trasteverini whom they found delightfully picturesque. Story described them, 'going home with their jackets hanging over one shoulder. Women in their rough woolen gowns, stood in the doorways, bare-headed, looking out from windows and balconies, their black hair shining under the lantern.'[24]

Tourists even romanticized poor Romans' violence. Knife fights were common, and though they were usually caused by disputes over women and honour they could erupt over the most trivial of things. In one incident in 1866 a street musician was thrown a coin from an upstairs window, which a bystander then covered with his foot. When the musician complained and forcibly tried to move his foot the other man stabbed him in the neck. Tourists liked to see such incidents as a debased resurfacing of the fighting spirit of Livy's republican heroes but their real cause was more prosaic. Romans fought one another not because it was their nature but because they had no faith in papal justice and preferred to take matters into their own hands. Culprits vanished into the crowd and were protected by friends and neighbours. Few were caught.

Then again, the Church authorities were not too concerned by such crimes. They were much more interested in another form of transgression: adultery. Here was a change which would have greatly surprised a visitor from the easy-going days of the early sixteenth century. Rome in the 1840s was a city of intense moral policing. Though its roots lay in the strictures of the Council of Trent, the new approach came fully into effect under the conservative popes who ruled after the French revolutionary era. This was the age when ornate images of Jesus, the Madonna and flying cherubs appeared above every Roman street corner, and the Roman dialect poet, Giuseppe Gioachino Belli wrote that SPQR stood for, '*Solo Preti Qui Regnano, e Silenzio*' (Only priests rule here, and silence).

Reaction reached a high point under Pope Leo XII, who reintroduced an antique and grisly form of execution – *mazzolatura* – in which the condemned was struck on the head with a large hammer and had his throat cut. He also banned inoculation on the grounds that it caused a dangerous mixing of the human and the animal, closed Rome's drinking houses, forbade wine except with meals, and prohibited card-playing, coffee and dancing the waltz. During the Holy Year of 1825 (which drew disappointingly few pilgrims) he ordered daily religious processions and banned all non-sacred music. Leo XII was greatly concerned with extramarital sex and, as well as having his Swiss Guards patrol the streets watching for women in tight-fitting clothes that might excite lustful thoughts, he sometimes took off his papal robes and personally toured the streets as a plain-clothes pope, sniffing for sin.

Inevitably these strictures had quite an effect on Romans' sex lives which, in the late eighteenth and early nineteenth centuries had been notoriously open, at least for the rich. The French general, Marmont, who visited Rome in 1790, wrote that, 'The freedom of women passes all belief, and their husbands permit it, speaking cheerfully and without embarrassment of their wives' lovers.'[25] Extramarital affairs had their own traditions, and it was accepted that married women could be attended to by their lovers – termed *cicisbei* – during the day, so long as they returned home to their husbands at night. As for the husbands, they were said to be happy with the arrangement, as it meant they were free to indulge in daytime affairs of their own.

Naturally such arrangements were no longer possible when Leo XII ruled. Rome's eternal sex-workers, too, found life increasingly hard. Long gone were the days when elegant, educated courtesans were regular visitors to the papal palace, or one might, at Carnival, find oneself struck by a perfumed egg thrown by one of the city's many prostitutes. A growing number of restrictions against them were introduced in the eighteenth century, and in the nineteenth they were banned altogether: Pius IX denounced prostitution as a sin and so a crime. Yet this did not mean it disappeared. In the middle of Pius' reign, the chief medical officer of the French army in Rome, Dr Jacquot, observed that though prostitutes faced imprisonment, fines, torture and every kind of harassment, Rome remained 'a notorious centre of European prostitution where women solicit openly in the streets, in dark corners, in brothels, under deserted porticoes and along remote thoroughfares'.[26]

Then the papacy's chief moral concern was not prostitutes so much as misbehaving Romans. To prevent them from transgressing, Rome's streets were patrolled each night by priests, police and *sbirri* – a kind of papal beagle – who kept a close watch on suspect individuals. Priests drew up maps of parish sinfulness and sent reports to higher church authorities, such as this one, recorded on 23 May 1823:

> I took myself during the night to the house of Maria Gertrude Armezzani to see if she was alone and to observe if she was in an enjoined state. I found her with the bolt shut, together with a young man who was dining with her. I once again admonished her and though she sought to give me various excuses, her confusion made it easy enough to see her life.[27]

The Church was especially concerned with secret adulterers who lived in 'a state of concubinage as if they are cohabiting legitimately'. Lapses in paperwork were no excuse and priests were told, 'If you have any doubts address yourself as to where they came from, and if foreigners, require them to give proof of their marriage, treating them with much suspicion ...'[28] Though Church authorities were kept in the dark over street knifings, they found ample collaborators when it came to rooting out adulterers and prostitutes. Romans enjoyed the sport of spying on their neighbours, and wives were happy to report prostitutes or local seductresses who might tempt their husbands. And yet, despite all the risks, a good number of Romans still flouted the law and lived together outside matrimony. Some did so because they could not afford to marry, others found themselves blocked by paperwork, while some simply did not get round to it, or loathed the Church. Parish priests sought out couples who went to elaborate lengths to appear married, dining together, walking out together, but who were ready to move away if a priest came knocking at their door.

The Church's zealousness in this area could even affect foreign visitors, though it was rare, as they generally arrived with their own strong sense of keeping to the rules. Odo Russell, the unofficial British representative to the Holy See, had to deal with a young Englishwoman who left her chaperone and moved alone into an apartment on the Corso, where a Roman man paid her regular visits. Russell decided to leave her to the mercies of the Church authorities, and a visit by a squad of papal police scared her so much that she fled back to her chaperone. Foreign trespassers were unlikely to get into real trouble. Then the same was true of Romans, a fact which highlights the strangeness of papal justice, which was run on wholly different principles from justice anywhere else. It was less concerned with just punishment than with the confession of sins and forgiveness. Once an unmarried couple had been caught they were often not punished at all but were forced to marry, frequently in jail. Adulterous couples in which both parties were married to somebody else posed more of a problem, yet they too were treated mildly. They were usually given light sentences, made to confess and then warned never to speak to one another on pain of a much longer spell in jail.

Even condemned murderers were treated with a kind of gentleness. Before being delivered into the hands of Giovanni Bugatti, Rome's long-lived executioner, who had been dispatching papal subjects since 1796, the condemned spent their last night with two comforters from the Fratelli della Arciconfraternita di San Giovanni Decollato, who would try to cheer them up with pictures of the Virgin and Jesus on the cross. The next morning, as they were led to the city guillotine – a souvenir of French revolutionary rule – that was set up by the river, close to the church of Santa Maria in Cosmedin, other comforters would encourage them to have good thoughts. Executions were frequently delayed for hours until the condemned confessed. Luckier murderers escaped execution, spending time in jail or pulling oars on a papal galley, and ended their days working as gardeners in one of the city's parks. Sir George Head observed a group of them on the Pincio, watched by a soldier, and was struck by how relaxed they were, remarking, 'no other class of the Pope's subjects appear more thoughtless and lively than these galley-slaves', while their guard was 'on the easiest terms with them, all laughing and conversing'.[29]

Rome was forgiving to many who were treated harshly elsewhere. Begging was not frowned upon and though competition could be intense, the life of a beggar in Rome was better than in London or Paris. The Church had kept up its responsibility of helping the poor, so Rome's beggars were fed by the city's monasteries. If sick they could go to one of the city's many hospitals. As a result Rome was crowded with vagrants and William Wetmore Story graphically describes how they would brandish their infirmities: 'every kind of withered arm, distorted leg and unsightly stump. They glare at you out of horrible eyes that look like cranberries.' Yet they could also charm, especially foreign females 'on the cold side of thirty', addressing them as, *'bella, illustrissima'* and, *'principessa'*. They particularly targeted foreigners, chanting, *'Signore, povero stroppiato, datemi qualche cosa per amore di Dio.'* ('Sir, for God's love, please give a little something to a poor cripple?') The only way to be free of them, Story advised, was 'to be black-haired, to wear a full beard, to smoke in the street … and shake the forefinger of the right hand when besieged for charity'[30] – in other words, to be Italian. Though he added that Italians gave more generously than visitors.

Tourists found Rome's beggars infuriating but also fascinating. Their persistence knew no bounds. Tourists visiting country fairs miles outside Rome found familiar Roman beggars lying in wait for them. One Englishwoman who had removed herself to Tuscany for the malaria season discovered that one had come all the way to Lucca. This was King Beppo, the most famous of all Rome's beggars, who appears in numerous accounts of the city. Strongly built, aside from his crippled legs, he pushed himself around on a wooden platter and was sometimes found begging from a donkey, which he could mount without help by hauling himself up with a rope. Charming and good-humoured, he ruled all Rome's beggars like an emperor and was said to be so wealthy that he acted as their moneylender.

The Church had not always been so tolerant of beggars. In the late seventeenth century, at the height of the Little Ice Age, when harvests were poor, the city became so overwhelmed that an establishment was set up to turn them into useful members of society. San Michele a Ripa still existed in the 1840s: a huge institution, somewhere between a poorhouse, a jail and an academy, that towered above the Tiber in Trastevere. Influenced by seventeenth-century French ideas, in many ways it was ahead of its time and it won much praise from the English prison reformer John Howard when he paid a visit in the 1790s. Entrance requirements were strict. Older residents had to have been residents of Rome for at least five years and to have no family to support them. Younger ones had to be between seven and eleven and had to prove they were fatherless, and that their mothers, if alive, had had at least three children. The restrictions were necessary because places at San Michele were much sought after. Young residents were taught a whole range of skills, from carpentry and shoemaking to printing, tapestry, metalwork, dyeing, medal-making and clothes-making, to architecture and art. Promising young painters were taught by the best artists in Rome. In 1835 San Michele held a public show of its young residents' work. The institution was so highly regarded that richer parents of non-orphans paid for their children to go there, though they endured the same simple living conditions as the orphans.

If the papacy showed humanity towards the poor, orphans, and even to criminals, it was less kindly to those it regarded as its enemies, or as being outside its world. Until Pius IX released them, the papacy's political prisoners were kept far from sight in the popes' gulag, the fortress of Civita Castellana forty miles north of Rome. Females could find themselves badly received if they failed to fit the Church's ideal of womanhood: modest, sexless baby-makers who spent their days at home. Rape was included in a blurred legal category that included both seduction and adultery, and women who had been sexually attacked often found that instead of winning justice, they were cautioned against misbehaviour while the attacker was let be.

And of course there were Rome's Jews, who in the 1840s were still locked away in their Ghetto. A visitor from 1527 would be confused. The idea of a ghetto in Rome would have seemed unthinkable in the early sixteenth century, when popes acted to protect Jews from Spanish persecution, and when Michelangelo found models among Rome's Jewish inhabitants for his Old Testament figures in the Sistine Chapel.

That such a place existed was thanks to Paul IV, the Senator-McCarthy-like pope whom we met at the end of the last chapter. When elected pope in 1555 he quickly set about restricting the lives of Rome's Jewish inhabitants. Their property was confiscated and they were required to rent properties in their new Ghetto, located in a low-lying area north of the Tiber Island that was vulnerable to flooding. The zone was sealed off from the rest of the city with walls and Jews were only allowed to leave it during the day. Ten synagogues were closed down and worship was permitted in just one. Jews had to wear distinguishing clothes – caps for men, shawls for women – in obedience to humiliating and long-ignored medieval rules. They were banned from employing Christian servants or wet nurses, or from having commercial dealings with Christians, while Jewish doctors – who had included many of the city's best physicians – could no longer treat Christians. Jews who had owned fine businesses were forced to become rag merchants, who could trade only in second-hand or discarded goods. Soon after Paul IV's reign all Rome's Jews were required to attend a weekly sermon in the church of San Gregorio della Divina Pietà, to be lectured on the errors of their religion.

These restrictions were not only mean-minded. They had a clear purpose: to extinguish the city's Jewish community once and for all. Thanks to a ruling by Gregory I, a thousand years earlier, which prohibited forced conversion, misery was the only means available to the papacy to persuade the Jews to abandon their religion. As an experiment, the Ghetto was a colossal failure. Rome's Jewish community, which had led European Jewish learning in medieval times, became steadily degraded and by the 1840s, unusually in Western Europe, half its members were illiterate, yet it did not disappear but survived and grew. At a ceremony during the carnival festivities before Lent, the latest Jewish converts were put on parade and in the 1840s tourists were amused to note that there was only one, who had to be shown year after year.

Still, failure proved no discouragement to those who had created the Ghetto. During the two and a half centuries of its existence, popes tightened and loosened regulations but none questioned that Rome's Jews should lead separate – and more degrading – lives from the city's Christians. Rome's Jews had tantalizing glimpses of freedom, when Rome was occupied by French revolutionary and Napoleonic forces, but from 1815 the old restrictions were again enforced. By the 1830s, as Jews gained full civic rights elsewhere in Europe, the existence of Rome's Ghetto appeared increasingly barbaric, and, in 1836, France, Austria and the Rothschild family all urged that reforms should be made. The railway-hating Gregory XVI reluctantly allowed the Ghetto to be enlarged a little, to include the Palazzo Cenci, but that was all.

In the 1840s the Ghetto was a popular tourist sight and its gloomy lanes and cramped courtyards were a must-see for adventurous tourists. A number of writers left descriptions, which often manage to disparage papal cruelty while also throwing in a little anti-Semitism. Thus William Wetmore Story wrote that the Rome's long-suffering Jews had a 'greasy, anointed look', with their 'thick peculiar lips, narrow eyes set close together, nose thin at the junction with the eyebrows and bulbous at the end'.[31] All were agreed that the Ghetto was dirty and crowded. Dickens said it was 'a miserable place, densely populated and reeking with bad odours'.[32] Story felt the Jews were lucky to live in an area at high risk of flooding as it meant that 'Old Father Tiber washes out this Augean Stable'.[33]

Yet life in the Ghetto was not all bad. Cruelty from outside brought its inhabitants closer together, and if their culture had grown rougher and less literate it had also grown stronger. Rome's Jews developed their own version of Italian, which had an important impact on Roman dialect. Containing a good number of Hebrew words, it was full of richly graphic phrases, such as, 'A black bargain' (a bad deal), 'A real serpent' (a long queue), 'A mirror' (someone whose mood reflects that of the person they are with, and who is cheerful on the street and scowls at home) and 'Better king of a hovel than a slave in a palace'. They also developed their own food, which included dishes such as salted cod, courgette flowers filled with mozzarella and anchovies, and deep-fried artichokes, all of which became classics of Roman cuisine.

Rather surprisingly, the Ghetto was a relatively healthy place to live in. Thanks to Jewish religious concerns with cleanliness it may have been far less dirty than tourists assumed, and its inhabitants were relatively unaffected by the cholera epidemic that struck Rome in the 1830s. And though it was in a low-lying area right by the Tiber, it was malaria free. The mystery of how such a thing could be perplexed many foreign visitors. Tourists imagined malaria was caused by emanations from the earth, and claimed that visitors put themselves at risk if they moved too quickly from a hot and sunny spot to a cool damp one (which tourists regularly did when visiting a crypt or catacombs on a warm spring day). Consequently, some claimed the Ghetto was malaria free because, as William Wetmore Story observed, it was a place where 'the air is much beaten by a constant concourse of people'.[34] Though wrong, Story was not as wrong as one might think. The Ghetto had no malaria because there was no room for gardens, which meant there were no puddles or pots filled with standing water where mosquitoes could breed.

For all the tourists' comments, it is doubtful that Christian Romans were any cleaner than their Jewish neighbours. Though Rome in the 1840s had some public bathhouses these were few, and Story thought them poorer than those in any other city he knew. He claimed that ordinary Romans 'are not a bathing people', and showed 'a common horror at the Anglo-Saxon idea of a cold bath each morning'. Even wealthy Romans, like wealthy Anglo-Saxons half a century earlier, 'wash themselves but they do not take baths. They use the wash bowl, but the bathing-tub and the shower-bath frighten them.'[35]

When it came to their health, 1840s Romans had some advantages over their Renaissance ancestors. Surgery techniques had improved and diagnosis had advanced with the development of the stethoscope. Smallpox had been much reduced by campaigns of vaccination (despite Pope Leo XII's ban) while the city's improved drains reduced outbreaks of typhoid, and its aqueducts and fountains did the same for waterborne diseases. Though malaria was still a major worry, especially for people who could not leave the city in the summer – and who did not live in the Ghetto – there was now a remedy, at least for those who could afford it. Since the beginning of the seventeenth century rich Romans could take doses of the bark of the Peruvian cinchona tree, which helped combat the disease.

In its fundamentals, though, 1840s medicine had advanced remarkably little since the 1520s, or for that matter since the days of the Roman Empire. Doctors still followed the theories of Hippocrates and Galen that claimed sickness resulted from an imbalance in the humours. As with the French Disease in the 1520s, early nineteenth-century physicians failed to comprehend, let alone treat, the new disease of their age, cholera, which they believed was caused by stinking air. That Romans could expect to live longer than their ancestors was largely down to good luck. Since the late seventeenth century Rome and all of Europe had been free of bubonic plague, which had vanished as mysteriously as it had first appeared.

Yet, outside the malarial season, Rome's health dangers did not put off the tourists and, for all their grumbling, many adored the city. As well as being fascinated by its ruins and paintings, they found Rome a visual feast. Many commented on the food stalls and shops to be found in streets around the Pantheon, which, at the end of Lent, were filled with highly elaborate displays of all the delicacies Romans would shortly be able to eat again. At dusk on the last day of Lent the city produced one of its great sights, when St Peter's was illuminated by scores of paper lanterns, acquiring, as Story described it, 'a dull furnace-glow, as of a monstrous coal fanned by a constant wind, looking not so much lighted from without as reddening from an interior fire'.[36] There was the spectacle of Easter pilgrims, many of whom came from the nearby countryside dressed in local costumes, chanting psalms as they passed. In addition there were also more traditional-looking pilgrims dressed in oilcloth, with long staffs, scallop shell badges and rosaries, and whose 'dirty hands held out constantly for, "*una santa elemosina pel povero Pellegrino*".'[37] Though, as Story explained, most of these were not real pilgrims at all but Rome's usual army of beggars trying a different tack.

Visitors found Rome's street life endlessly fascinating. When they strolled through the city they saw Romans playing the same ball games that they had in classical times. They saw washerwomen beside the city's fountains passing time by insulting one another, and passers-by, in rhyming verse. Charles Dickens described a strange procession he saw, that was '…preceded by a man who bears a large cross; by a torch-bearer; and a priest: the latter chanting as he goes': it was the dead cart, filled with bodies of the poor, on their way to be thrown into a pit outside the walls.[38] Story saw a Roman funeral that looked like it should for a pirate, its black banners 'gilt with a death's head and crossbones', and its group of accompanying friars, 'shrouded from head to foot in white, with only two holes for their eyes to glare through'.[39]

Or one could spend an evening at one of the city's theatres: a popular passion for Romans, who crowded in to see a new play and became so involved that they would cheer the hero and hiss the villain. Though productions could be hard to follow. Until the election of Pius IX, papal censors went through every scene, striking out anything they considered subversive, and some plays were so badly cut they made little sense. Even operas were mauled. Any with a religious or rebellious theme was prohibited, as were any that depicted a wicked pope. Heckling was banned and Lady Morgan described how anyone who hissed was immediately seized by soldiers, 'with which the theatre is filled, (for the most military government in Europe is the Pope's) and then taken to Piazza Navona, mounted in a sort of stock and flogged. Then carried back and placed in his seat, to enjoy the rest of the opera, with what appetite he may.'[40]

And of course there was always the city's religious spectacle. Experienced tourists became adept at recognizing orders of friars from the colour of their robes. Story's favourites – and most Romans' – were the Franciscans and Capuchins, Rome's other army of beggars, who went from house to house asking for donations. As Story writes, 'They are very poor, very good-natured and very dirty. They seem to have a hydrophobia.' Another order, the Saccone, was filled by wealthy men who had chosen to live in poverty and who also begged for alms, going about in pairs, dressed entirely in white. 'They often amuse themselves by startling foreigners … Many a group of English girls, convoyed by their mother, and staring into some mosaic or cameo shop, is scared into a scream by the sudden jingle of the box, and the apparition of the spectre in white who shakes it.'[41]

There was always the hope one might catch a glimpse, in a carriage clattering by, of a cardinal in his scarlet robes, or even the pope himself. Yet a visitor from the 1520s would be surprised at how remote and invisible popes had become. Even the tradition under which a newly elected pope rode through the city on horseback, distributing silver and gold, had been watered down: after an accident in 1769, popes now travelled in the safety of a carriage. Popes blessed crowds from the balcony of the Quirinal Palace and they celebrated mass at Christmas, usually in Santa Maria Maggiore, but in the 1840s there was only one papal procession. This was held on the feast of Corpus Domini on the first Sunday of Pentecost and was a huge event. The parade included church scholars, attendees of charity schools and hospitals, the city's friars – chanting and carrying candles – then the chapters, canons and choirs of Rome's seven greatest churches, followed by monsignori, bishops and cardinals, and finally the pope himself, carried on a splendid platform. Yet, compared to the marathon processions of medieval times it was very modest, managing just one circuit of St Peter's Square.

If Rome's religious processions were a little dull these days, the city was justly famous for its popular holidays. The October Festival held on Monte Testaccio – the last remnant of Romans' medieval holiday – included dancing and games, for which poor Roman girls would dress up in their best finery and hire a carriage, as many as fourteen of them cramming inside, all 'shouting, screeching and playing the tambourine, like a party of wild Indians'.[42] Before Christmas the city filled with *Pifferari*: musicians from the mountains of Abruzzo, one of whom played a pipe while another played the bagpipes. On Christmas Day, after celebrating mass, Romans would walk through the city eating quantities of *torone* and *pangiallo*: a cake made with plums, lemon and almonds. At the beginning of January the area around the church of Sant'Eustachio became crammed with stalls selling noisy toys, and children – and their parents – would enjoy making a huge din with whistles, tambourines and trumpets.

But the greatest festival of all – greater even than Holy Week – was Carnival. Held during the last two weeks before Lent, it was a mix of colour, chaos and nineteenth-century animal cruelty, at which Romans showed their capacity for letting themselves go, and normally strait-laced northern visitors enthusiastically joined them. It took place on the Corso, which by mid-morning would already be crowded with carriages and pedestrians. People wore elaborate costumes. Small boys dressed and walked like old men, and Romans with bushy beards strode about in white dresses and straw bonnets. Sir George Head describes a man who claimed to be a professor of music who had taught cats to sing. On his shoulders he carried a large wooden box containing six cats and from time to time he would launch into a song, pulling the cats' tails until they squealed.

Some costumes were elegant, though they did not stay so for long. All around the Corso portable stalls sold nosegays – bunches of wild flowers held together with string – and comfits: pea-sized pellets made from lime or plaster of Paris. The Corso became a battleground as nosegays were hurled and comfits burst on people's clothes, powdering them white. Attacks were launched from all directions: by pedestrians, by people in carriages and others on balconies. Some carriages were like wooden fortresses, filled with young Romans who kept up a steady fire on all around them, while if they passed another gang a huge fight ensued. Occasionally disaster struck, as when a young English girl on a balcony threw a handful of comfits at a papal policeman. The *carabiniere*, furious, marched up to the balcony – from which the girl had already fled – though fortunately he 'was a good natured fellow and consented very willingly to drink the Pope's health with a glass of rosolio'.[43]

Each day of Carnival culminated in a race. Fourteen unfortunate horses were brought to the Piazza del Popolo, decorated with coloured ribbons and large flapping pieces of tinfoil. Each horse had four large patches of pitch stuck to its flanks from which hung four heavy pear-shaped spurs, covered in half-inch spikes. When released, the horses, which were riderless and terrified by the roar of the crowd and the jabbing of the spikes, hurtled down the Corso, the crowd opening and closing around them as they went, as everybody wanted to see (occasionally someone wrongly assumed all the horses had passed and was run down), till they reached the Piazza Venezia, where they were forced down a side street and collided with a barrier of blankets.

Finally, on the last evening of Carnival there was the festival of tapers. The Corso became thronged with people holding tiny candles, all joining in a game of trying to extinguish everyone else's while keeping their own lit. Anyone who doused another's candle would shout in triumph, '*senza moccolo!*' (without light). Some tried to improve their chances by tying bunches of candles together or bringing torches.

Struggles grew intense. Pedestrians leapt on to carriages to try and put out their occupants' lights. Battles broke out between upper and lower balconies, as people hurled sopping handkerchiefs or tried to behead candles with wire loops on long sticks. Ladies' bonnets were crushed in the melee, and strange sights were witnessed, as when Sir George Head saw, together on one balcony, an Italian priest, an English clergyman and a princess from the House of Brunswick, all fighting furiously and 'engaged like children at blind man's buff'.⁴⁴ All the while, for anyone able to stand back and watch, the Corso was an extraordinary sight of constantly twinkling lights, from which the cries of *senza moccolo* produced, 'a sound indescribable – an earthly moaning, which can be compared to nothing better than the howling of the wind in a ship's shrouds in a hurricane'.⁴⁵

In the heady days of the spring of 1847 Rome saw new kinds of celebration. After Pius IX's cardinal secretary announced that elections would be held to choose a council to advise the pope, a huge crowd with torches assembled in the Piazza del Popolo and then streamed slowly down the Corso to the Quirinal Palace, where they lit fireworks. When Pius appeared on the balcony they shouted *vivas* and went down on their knees to receive his blessing. A few days later an open-air popular dinner was held in the ruins of the Baths of Titus, overlooking the Colosseum, where an effigy of Romulus, Remus and the she-wolf was set up. There was music and speeches, including one by a novelist who recounted events in Rome's history and made particular reference to the moment when, at the castle of Canossa, the ruler of Germany, King Henry IV, was forced to beg forgiveness from the pope. (The Austrians afterwards complained.)

The following July, after trouble broke out between cowherds and some of Rome's Jews, there was an equally notable celebration. The inhabitants of Regola and Trastevere, who were old enemies of the city's Jews, wanted to avenge the cowherds but the populist leader Ciceruacchio persuaded them instead to make a pact of friendship with the Jews. That same night 2,000 Romans entered the Ghetto singing and carrying torches in what was, by all accounts, a remarkable moment of reconciliation. The following spring there were more celebrations in the Ghetto, after Pius ordered the walls to be demolished.

During the months that followed Rome was on a political seesaw. In October, as Prime Minister Rossi tightened the reins of Pope Pius' power, the mood changed and *sbirri* – the papal beagles – led an attack on the Ghetto which saw three days of plundering and burning. Within weeks Rossi was dead, the pope had fled and in February Romans joined in celebrations of their new republic. Two months later, on 30 April 1849, it seemed all was about to change again, as General Oudinot led his army towards Rome.

III

The French did not expect much trouble. As has been seen, Louis Napoleon had been following papal pronouncements from Gaeta and he assumed that the Romans were impatient to be freed from oppressive rule by foreign revolutionaries such as Garibaldi and Mazzini, and that they would welcome French troops as liberators. Wary of antagonizing French radicals, his instructions to General Oudinot were both optimistic and unclear, as he hoped to pull off something of a magic trick by installing a reactionary prince without himself seeming too reactionary. Oudinot was not to recognize either the Roman Republic's ruling Triumvirate or the Roman republican assembly, yet he was to treat members of each with polite respect. The task of the French was to bring about reconciliation between the Romans and their pope, who was to be reinstated but was to keep the constitution he had granted his people. If the Romans resisted, though, Oudinot was to use force.

General Oudinot, like his president, anticipated a quick and easy policing operation. Revolutionary movements had crumbled with little resistance everywhere else in Europe and this one promised to be no different. Oudinot felt the best tactic was to strike quickly before the Romans had had time to respond to his arrival. He organized his forces at Civitavecchia as quickly as he was able and then marched them east towards Rome. According to his intelligence reporters he had many supporters among the clergy in the Borgo. His map of the city showed there was a gate in the walls – Porta Pertusa – at the top of the Vatican Hill, which would be the perfect place to break in and unite with his Roman allies. If there were a hitch, his soldiers would march down to the Porta Cavallegieri where his intelligence told him that friendly clerics would open the gate. He did not bother to bring scaling ladders, or heavy siege guns that would slow him down, making do with light field guns that would be enough to break open Porta Perusa's doors. He did not waste time stopping to examine the city's defences but marched straight for the Vatican. Military professionalism led him to send out a column of troops to protect his right flank, though it seemed doubtful they would be needed. The whole business should all be over in a few hours and Oudinot looked forward to dining that evening in Rome.

On the other side of the walls that same morning the American sculptor and writer William Wetmore Story took a stroll round the city and would have agreed with Oudinot's assessment. He wrote in his notes, 'All the streets deserted, gloomy and morose, as before some terrible thunderstorm.' There were no women to be seen and the shops were all closed, 'with here and there a door half open and revealing the form of a soldier peering out'. Story had heard rumours that the Roman National Guard 'are nearly unanimous in desiring the return of the pope and the abolition of the Triumvirate and the Republic, and that they will not fight'.[46]

One could understand the Romans having a sense of buyers' remorse, as their situation was far from promising. The city's defenders outnumbered the French army but not greatly, while compared to Oudinot's disciplined, well-trained troops they were a very mixed bag, and most had little or no military experience. Included among them were 1,400 Roman volunteers who had fought the Austrians the previous year and so had some battle experience, though it had largely consisted of defeats. Others did not even have this. There were 2,500

Garibaldi in Rome with his servant, Aguyar.

Papal troops and *carabinieri*, and also recent Roman volunteers: 1,000 National Guards – the citizen army created by Pius IX – together with 300 students and several hundred Trasteverini, armed with knives and shotguns. A force of Lombards led by Giacomo Medici who did know how to fight were unable to do so. They had fallen into the hands of the French at Civitavecchia and to extricate themselves had given their word of honour that they would not take up arms against them, at least for the present.

It is doubtful how well any of these elements would have fared without the help of another force that arrived just three days before Oudinot appeared outside Rome. If Garibaldi was viewed with suspicion by Mazzini, he had an ally in the Roman Republic's minister of war, Giuseppe Avezzana, and when news came that the French had landed at Civitavecchia, Avezzana hurriedly sent word to him at Rieti. Two days later Garibaldi and his legion of 1,300 entered Rome. They quickly caused a stir as, with their long hair and beards and their small felt hats, they looked like no ordinary soldiers. Some of the officers, who had accompanied Garibaldi all the way from

Montevideo, had American saddles and wore their famous red shirts. Most striking of all was Garibaldi himself in his trademark poncho, accompanied by a giant freed Brazilian slave named Aguyar who was his helper and bodyguard. And yet, even though the new arrivals had an invigorating effect on Rome's defenders, few of them had much fighting experience. Several hundred were students and artists.

Fortunately, luck was with the Romans. It came in the form of Oudinot's plan of the city. When French scouts came in sight of the walls of Borgo they were greeted with two surprises. The first was a sharp blast of gunfire, which told them they were not going to be welcomed as liberators after all. The second was the fact that Porta Pertusa, which Oudinot intended to break open with his light field guns, was walled up, which it had been for years. Oudinot's plan was badly out of date.

Still Oudinot was not discouraged. He sent a column of troops down the hill towards Porta Cavalleggeri, which, his intelligence told him, would be opened by friendly clerics. For good measure he sent another column around the walls on the north side in the direction of Castel Sant'Angelo. His decisions were poor. His soldiers were already tired, having been marching all morning in heavy uniforms beneath the hot spring sun, and now they had to pick their way down steep paths, heaving their field guns under withering fire from the walls. Those who managed to reach the Porta Cavallaggeri discovered no friendly clerics, and the gate remained firmly closed, while they found themselves caught in an indent in the walls, exposed to fire from both the north and the east. Lacking scaling ladders, a few tried to climb the walls using spike nails before Oudinot ordered them back. The assault had lasted barely an hour.

Yet the battle was far from over. To the south, in the grounds of the Villa Pamphili gardens, just in front of the city walls, Garibaldi learned of Oudinot's setback and decided to attack. Three hundred students and artists, none of whom had experienced battle till now, clambered over the wall of the gardens into a deep lane beyond. Just as they did so a column of a thousand French troops, which Oudinot had

French troops under Lieutenant–General Charles Oudinot make their first attack on Rome near the Porta Angelica, engraving from Illustrated London News, *19 May 1849.*

sent out to cover his flank, came into sight. The artists and students charged, briefly pushing the French back before themselves being chased out of the lane and back into the park.

So began a furious struggle. The rest of Garibaldi's legion joined in but were repelled, and clusters of the students and artists took refuge in outhouses in the gardens, where they struggled to hold out. Garibaldi, realizing that the fight was going against him, sent word to Colonel Galletti, who commanded 800 troops in the Gianicolo walls just to his rear. These were the Roman volunteers who had fought the Austrians the previous year. Eager to make up for their earlier defeats they joined the fray and their numbers and enthusiasm soon told. Garibaldi, whose presence had an inspirational effect on his troops, personally led charges through the woods and copses of the gardens. The French were forced to retreat to an area of vineyards beyond the lane and for a time each side fired at the other. The deadlock was finally broken by the Roman side, in their most courageous action of the battle. They jumped down into the lane into a fusillade of French fire and then charged up to the vineyard. After a hand-to-hand struggle with bayonets the French turned and ran. Several hundred were captured.

After the battle came disagreements. Garibaldi, who was injured by a bullet to his side, had wanted to pursue the French and drive Oudinot into the sea, but he was overruled. Mazzini did not want to aggravate the French, with whom he still hoped to reach an accord. Garibaldi was left feeling resentful. Yet there was no denying that the Roman Republic had had a great victory. Its mixed bag of forces had defeated a professional army and Rome was saved, at least for now. The Romans were exultant and a little surprised at themselves. That night the city was lit up with candles burning in every window and the streets were filled with cheering crowds. They had reason to be proud. Despite the pope's claims that the Republic was ruled by a dictatorship of foreigners, the great majority of the soldiers who had defeated the French were Romans.

For a time it seemed Mazzini's republic might have saved itself. The French threat had barely been staved off when an even larger enemy force advanced on Rome – 10,000 Neapolitan troops led by King Bomba – but after suffering two crushing defeats by Garibaldi they fled back south, and in the middle of May there was new cause for hope. Oudinot offered a truce and a French envoy, Ferdinand de Lesseps, arrived in Rome to negotiate an accord with the Triumvirate. De Lesseps, who had expected to be dealing with radical, anticlerical terrorists, was impressed by Mazzini's moderation. The French soldiers who had been captured in the battle in the Villa Pamphili Gardens were treated kindly and were given a sightseeing tour of Rome before being returned without condition to Oudinot. Church property and clerics had not been harmed and even those who Mazzini knew were plotting against his Republic were left at liberty. After two weeks of talks De Lesseps and the Triumvirate reached a deal. The question of the restoration of the pope was put off for the moment, but it was agreed that the French would occupy positions around Rome to protect the city from the Austrians.

Unfortunately the negotiations were a sham. Louis Napoleon saw it as a matter of national pride that French arms be vindicated and, unknown to De Lesseps, his talks were intended all along to distract the Romans while Oudinot waited for reinforcements. The very day after the De Lesseps accord was agreed Oudinot declared the truce was over. By now his forces had doubled and he had 20,000 men backed by engineers and siege guns, with more on the way.

Oudinot, determined not to be caught out in another attack, then played a second trick on the Romans. He had noticed – as had Garibaldi – that Rome's Gianicolo defences hinged on a single spot: a four-storey country retreat, the Villa Corsini, that lay just inside the Pamphili Gardens. Situated on a high knoll, it overlooked the city walls from only a few hundred yards away. In the weeks since the victory on 30 April Villa Corsini should have been fortified with earthworks and guns, and that it had not been was the fault of General Roselli, Mazzini's ploddingly respectable military commander. When Oudinot ended his truce he promised, with deliberate vagueness, that he would not attack 'the place' before Monday 4 June, so that any French still in the city would have time to leave. On the evening of Saturday 2 June, Roselli paid a visit to the garrison around the Villa Corsini – a pitiful 400 troops without guns or trenches – and told them to get a good night's sleep as there would be no attack on them that night.

Just a few hours later French soldiers poured through the Pamphili Gardens. General Oudinot had employed a verbal trick that would cause lasting bitterness on the Roman side. He claimed he was free to attack the Villa Corsini as it was outside 'the place'. Despite brave resistance by the defenders the villa was quickly taken. Garibaldi, who had only just returned from campaigning against King Bomba's Neapolitans, and was convalescing from the bullet wound he had received on 30 April, hurried up the Gianicolo Hill to organize a counter-attack. So began the second battle for Rome, though in effect

it was over before it began, as everything was against the Italians.
To attack they had to make their way to a small gate in the wall of
the Pamphili Gardens, beyond which they found themselves at the
pointed end of a funnel-shaped space with no cover of any kind,
where they faced furious French fire from the Villa Corsini. It was a
killing ground.

Matters were not helped by Garibaldi, whose skills lay in open,
guerrilla warfare rather than close fighting of this kind. He would
have been wiser to wait until his guns had had time to batter the
Villa Corsini to rubble, but instead he ordered wave after wave of
attacks, that were more like suicide assaults. Still those involved did
not flinch from doing as they were ordered. Among them were the
Lombardy Bersaglieri who had been unable to fight in the previous
battle because they had given their word of honour to the French. Torn
apart as they charged the villa, they knelt down in the open and fired
at the building, towards enemies they could not see, yet each one kept
his place till their losses had become so great that their commander,
Manara, sounded the retreat. Several times the Italians managed to
drive the French from the villa but the building was impossible to
defend from the other side and was soon retaken. By the end of a
day in which the Italians lost many of their finest troops, they had to
accept that the position too was lost.

From this moment anyone with the faintest military knowledge
could see that the city faced certain defeat. It could only be a matter
of time before the French would break through, while the Roman
Republic could expect no help from outside. Along with France,
Austria and Naples, its declared enemies now included Tuscany, and
Spain had landed troops south of the city. Britain and the United
States both regarded Mazzini's republic warily and had no desire
to become involved. Even *The Times* was no friend. The newspaper's
correspondent, who was embedded with Oudinot's forces at
Civitavecchia, took his hosts' view of the conflict and told his readers
that Mazzini's Rome was in the hands of dictatorial foreigners, 'who
rob and assassinate under the name of liberty', and that 'three or four

priests who had the courage to appear in public have been butchered in open day, and their flesh, cut up in morsels, thrown into the Tiber'.[47]

Hopeless though their situation was, the Romans fought on. Their battery on the ancient hill of broken amphorae, Monte Testaccio, fought artillery duels with French guns on the Gianicolo. From a bastion beside Porta San Pancrazio a band played the Marseillaise to shame the French, though without success. Oudinot's forces tried to distract the Romans by lobbing shells into the city from batteries south and north of the Aurelian Walls. Fortunately, the damage done to Rome's buildings was relatively light and the greatest victim of the bombardment was Pope Pius IX, who would be resented for it for many years. Two balls that struck St Peter's were sent to him in Gaeta and when a shell came down Romans shouted, *Ecco un Pio Nono* ('Here comes another Pius the Ninth'). Romans put out fizzing shells with pans of water and threw them into the Tiber.

At times the bombardment could be beautiful. In a melancholy moment towards the end of the siege, the American writer Margaret Fuller, who had become a passionate supporter of the Roman Republic and who helped tend wounded soldiers in the Quirinal Palace – now being used as a hospital – described watching shells fall at night: "Tis pretty, tho' a terror, to see the bombs, fiery meteors, springing from the horizon line upon their bright path to do their wicked message. 'Twould not be so bad, meseems, to die of one of these ...'[48]

Margaret Fuller showed the lie of Pius' claims that Rome was in the hands of militant foreign terrorists. She had never known the city so safe, she wrote, and had often walked through its streets alone without once seeing violence. Bar occasional hissing, even the French in the city were left in peace. Romans were content to mock their enemies, which they did, as ever, via their talking statue Pasquino, who now spoke through a satirical magazine, *Don Pirlone*.

The French slowly pressed forward. Their easiest option would have been to move against the Gianicolo walls head on but they were prevented by the survivors of Giacomo Medici's Lombardians who, despite constant shelling and repeated bayonet charges, held out in a

small but strategically placed villa just beyond Porta San Pancrazio –
the Vascello – which they defended almost to the end. As a result the
French were forced to focus on a bastion to the south, slowing their
progress. But they had all the time they wanted. Gradually, their siege
guns reduced the ramparts to rubble and their trenches zigzagged
forward. Almost three weeks after they took Villa Corsini, Oudinot's
soldiers broke through and seized a section of the walls by today's
Villa Sciarra park, yet they still found themselves held. Garibaldi had
established a new defensive line a few hundred yards further back,
using a stretch of the 1,400-year-old Aurelian Walls.

Here, heavily outnumbered and outgunned, the Romans showed
a courage that would have impressed Livy, holding out for another
nine days. In the midst of the fighting Garibaldi's pregnant wife Anita
appeared unexpectedly from Nice, determined to be at her husband's
side. By now he was fighting Mazzini as much as he was the French.
As usual, the two fell out over strategy. Garibaldi the guerrilla fighter
wanted to take what remained of the Republic's forces and lead an
insurrection in the hills of central Italy. Mazzini the spin doctor wanted
to fight on in Rome to the last so that the Republic would be seen
never to have surrendered. Matters were finally decided on 30 June after
another French breakthrough. Garibaldi, who had just learned that
his bodyguard and friend Aguyar had been killed by a shell, appeared
before Rome's assembly stained with dust and blood, his sword so
buckled from use that it would only fit halfway into the scabbard. The
assembly offered him three options. The Republic could surrender, it
could continue to fight on in Rome, or it could take the battle to the
hills. Naturally Garibaldi chose the hills, declaring, *'Dovunque saremo,
colà sarà Roma'* – 'Wherever we go, there will be Rome.'

Two days later his army assembled in St Peter's Square. Garibaldi
was so besieged by well-wishers that he could hardly get through to
his troops. The moment inspired one of his most celebrated speeches:

Fortune, who betrays us today, will smile on us tomorrow. I am
going out of Rome. Any who wish to continue the war against

the foreigner come with me. I offer neither pay nor quarters
nor provisions. I offer hunger, thirst, forced marches, battles
and death. Let him who loves his country in his heart and not
just with his lips follow me.[49]

After two months of resistance and almost a month of continuous
fighting the battle for Rome was over. Later that same day Garibaldi
and some 4,000 volunteers gathered by San Giovanni. They included
most of the survivors of the city's defence, as well as Ciceruacchio and
his two sons, and Anita, wearing the red shirt of her husband's legion.
Slowly they marched out of Porta San Giovanni and left the city
behind. Garibaldi's offer of the morning would prove all too accurate.
His resistance in the hills quickly became a flight to escape, in which
his army was steadily whittled away. Ciceruacchio and his two sons –
the youngest only thirteen years old – were captured and shot by the
Austrians and pregnant Anita died of exhaustion and disease. Only
Garibaldi survived to fight again.

The day after he and his army left, the French entered Rome, and
so began two decades of restored papal rule. Of the seven attacks
described in this book, without doubt this one was least like a sacking,
and the city suffered little or no material damage, yet it was terrible in
its way. The French broke up the elected Roman assembly with fixed
bayonets, disarmed the population, tore down all emblems of the
Republic, expelled foreigners who had served it, and began hunting
down leading figures in Mazzini's government. Many were saved by
the British and American consuls who, to the disapproval of their
governments, issued passports by the hundred. Mazzini, who was too
well known for the French to arrest, stayed in the city for several days,
hurriedly setting up an underground resistance.

He was probably behind the Romans' response to the French
occupation. Margaret Fuller saw a resistance pamphlet that appeared
the day after the French entered the city and which called on Romans
to treat them with icy disdain. They were to ignore any French soldier
who addressed them; when they entered a cafe or restaurant all

A French visitor is set upon by patriotic citizens and their dog, engraving from Illustrated London News, *6 October 1849.*

Romans were to leave; windows should be closed when they passed, and any Romans who fraternized with the French – especially any Roman females – would be cursed. As the pamphlet declared, 'Let the liberticide soldier atone in solitude and contempt for having served priests and kings.'[50]

Yet it soon became clear that the Romans' worst oppressors were not the French but papal officials. A month after they took Rome the French handed power to three cardinals who Romans named the Red Triumvirate, in reference not to their politics but their scarlet vestments. So began a prolonged struggle between the French who, for the sake of their own reputation, tried to steer the papacy towards a moderate course, and the papacy, which sought revenge and absolutist control. The papacy usually prevailed. One of the first actions of the Red Triumvirate was to offer an amnesty which excluded so many that it seemed more like a proscription. Among those denied papal forgiveness were all former members of the Roman Republic's government and assemblies, all its high-ranking military officers, and all those whom Pius had amnestied when he had first been elected, in 1846. Margaret Fuller commented, 'It seems he cannot rest or his counselors cannot rest till he had recanted every good thing he ever did.'[51] During the first eight months after the Republic fell, an estimated 20,000 Romans – or an eighth of the city's population – left Rome, half of them expelled.

Pius did keep one of the promises of his early radical days. Over the next years Rome became linked with the rest of Europe by telegraph and by railway and the city was finally lit with gas lamps, which were fuelled by a smoke-belching gasworks on the old Circus Maximus chariot-racing course. In every other respect, though, Rome returned to the reactionary days of Pope Gregory XVI. Once again the Papal States became a land of informers, of surveillance, of opened letters and of political prisoners. By 1853 there were more than a thousand of these, many of them held in a special wing of the huge San Michele workhouse in Trastevere. Executions resumed, as did censorship. Theatre and opera productions were meticulously controlled and books on the papal Index of prohibited books were publicly burned on church steps.

For Rome's Jews, too, life had an unwelcome sense of déjà vu. In October 1849 the papal beagles – the *sbirri* – claimed that the Ghetto was full of stolen treasure and induced French soldiers to join them in a three-day search, which, though it unearthed no stolen goods, involved looting, destruction and arbitrary arrests. The restrictions that Pius had lifted were enforced again and Jews were banned from almost all trades. In theory they were still permitted to move out of the Ghetto but bureaucratic obstacles and delays made setting up home elsewhere in the city almost impossible. Like Gentiles, many Roman Jews voted with their feet and by 1853 a quarter of the Papal States' Jewish population had left. By 1860 over half of Rome's Jews had no property and lived by begging.

Romans, Christian and Jewish alike, sullenly resisted. William Wetmore Story wrote that the city was 'stricken with a morose silence'.[52] Romans secretly passed one another copies of satirical cartoons from their brief revolutionary days. They protested when they saw a chance. In November 1849 Margaret Fuller was in the church of Sant'Ignazio for the annual service for the dead when '… a deep voice sounded from the crowd the words, "Peace be with those who perished for their country!" and at the same time a shower of roses and myrtles was thrown upon the catafalk [sic], while the crowd shouted a fervent, "Peace. Peace. Amen."'53 Though the authorities tried to find the culprits, the crowd would not give them up. The papal authorities frequently found themselves frustrated and plans to purge Rome's administration of disloyal elements had to be abandoned, as nobody would inform on their fellow officials.

Pius himself was left in doubt as to how he was regarded by the Romans. On the day he finally returned to Rome from the kingdom of Naples, in April 1850, an attempt was made to burn down the Quirinal Palace. Shortly afterwards he moved to the Vatican Palace, which – with its escape walkway to Castel Sant'Angelo – was safer. There he received foreign dignitaries, including Odo Russell, the unofficial representative of heretic Britain. Russell considered Pius a vindictive and bloodthirsty old man who was increasingly divorced from reality. In one of their meetings Pius assured Russell that Italians had merely been led astray by foreign, revolutionary agents, and that, 'When they have suffered more they will repent and return to us.'54 He was also convinced that the British were about to abandon Protestantism and return to the Catholic fold.

Romans had reason to hope that they would see an end to their troubles. In part this was because of what they themselves had achieved. Their defence of Rome had been undeniably courageous and it soon attracted notice, being seen as an example of brave patriotism, just as Mazzini and Garibaldi had hoped. Written accounts of the city's defence appeared and one was translated into English by W. E. Gladstone. Mazzini's years of patient spin-doctoring came good and Italian unifiers found they had powerful new friends. Among them, rather surprisingly, was the same Louis Napoleon who had brought about the Roman Republic's defeat. In early 1859, now Emperor of

France, he helped Piedmont to eject the Austrians from Italy. His change of heart was caused less by conscience and more by fear. During the late 1850s he survived no fewer than three assassination attempts by Italian patriots determined to avenge the Roman Republic. The third, which took place in January 1859, was the most dramatic. Organized by a former follower of Mazzini, Felice Orsini, it was carried out as the emperor and empress arrived at the opera. Three bombs were thrown, blowing out gas lamps and plunging the street into darkness and chaos. Louis Napoleon's carriage was destroyed and a number of people were injured, though not the imperial couple. Just two months later Louis Napoleon had French officials hold secret meetings with those of Piedmont to discuss a joint attack on Austria.

Mazzini's refusal to let Garibaldi pursue Oudinot's retreating army may have been the right decision after all, as a crushing French defeat would have made support for the Italian cause far harder to justify. Louis Napoleon's change of heart was a turning point. Within months the Austrians had been ejected from Lombardy and Prime Minister Cavour was organizing plebiscites in Tuscany and other Italian states, that joined them to a new kingdom of Italy in the north. Garibaldi then doubled its territories. Having landed in Sicily with a thousand poorly armed volunteers, he managed, through strategy and enthusiasm, to overcome the professional armies of the kingdom of Naples. His reputation as the nineteenth century's revolutionary superstar was made. When visiting London a few years later he was greeted by the Victorian equivalent of Beatlemania, mobbed by vast crowds, and scandalous scenes took place as respectable Englishwomen 'flew upon him, seized his hands, touched his beard, his poncho, his trousers, any part of him they could reach', conducting themselves in 'an indecent manner'.[55]

As Italy became unified and the pope saw most of his kingdom break away and join the new state, expectations rose in Rome. Crowds held up pictures of Garibaldi, hissed papal police, and puzzled them by chanting *'Viva Verdi'*, by which they meant not the operatic composer, but *Vittorio Emanuele Re d'Italia* (Victor

Emmanuel, king of Italy). When they were charged by papal dragoons Romans answered with boycotts, ceasing en masse to smoke, or to buy papal lottery tickets, even refusing to go to the carnival. The Corso was left deserted as crowds instead gathered outside the city walls, near the Porta Pia. Pope Pius replied by trying to scare them into submission, sending the city's veteran executioner, Giovanni Bugatti, to ride among them.

Pius held on, at least for now. Louis Napoleon may have helped Italian nationalists against Austria but he had no wish to see the pope defeated, so the French garrison stayed. Yet even Pius could see the end was coming. Increasingly he turned his back on the physical world and concentrated on realms from which he could not be deposed. In 1864 he published *The Syllabus of Errors*, which set the Church against every kind of new thinking, from pantheism and naturalism to materialism, rationalism, socialism, communism, secret societies, Bible societies, liberalism and Masonic sects. Yet if Pius rejected rationalism and science, science proved rather useful to him. Thanks to the telegraph, railways and steam travel, in the late 1860s he was able to summon a council of bishops from all across the Catholic world. It was the first time such an assembly had been held since the sixteenth century and Pius used it to establish a new principle within Catholicism, of papal infallibility, according to which the pope was the only true interpreter of the Church.

At the very moment Pius made himself a dictator of dogma his actual kingdom fell apart. The doctrine of papal infallibility was agreed in July 1870. Days later the French army mobilized for war with Prussia and within weeks Louis Napoleon had withdrawn his garrison from Rome. In September, at the battle of Sedan, he suffered a disastrous defeat and was himself taken prisoner. With no French to guard it, Rome was ripe for the taking. Pius refused to negotiate a compromise with King Vittorio Emanuele and now it was his turn to find himself alone: no great power would come to his aid and when he appealed to the Romans only 200 offered to fight for their pope. Pius looked for help from elsewhere. Though old and overweight he took himself to the Santa Scala steps near the Lateran, which, like innumerable pilgrims before him, he climbed on his knees, praying.

It was of no use. On 20 September 1870 Italian guns blasted a modest-sized hole in the Aurelian Walls close by Porta Pia and soldiers swept into the city. Of the many invasions Rome had experienced this one was unquestionably the mildest and the only casualties were Romans who succumbed to stray bullets, or to a few shells lobbed into the centre by an overenthusiastic Italian commander. Within hours, papal troops had surrendered and were escorted to the Vatican by Italian soldiers, who protected them from angry crowds.

The Italian authorities had envisaged Pius retaining a miniature kingdom that would include the Vatican, the inhabited Borgo area beside it, and also the green stretch of land beneath the Gianicolo walls, but in the end even this was not possible. The population of the Borgo had no wish to remain under papal rule and angrily demonstrated, forcing Pius into the humiliating position of having to ask the Italian authorities to send troops to protect him. The occupation became permanent after plebiscites were held to approve Rome's union with the rest of Italy. The main part of Rome voted yes by 40,785 to 46 while the Borgo, whose inhabitants had a separate vote, agreed by 1,566 votes to none at all. Pius replied, a month later, by excommunicating everyone who had helped take away his kingdom.

Romans had a final chance to show their feelings towards their former ruler in the early hours of 13 June 1881. Pius, having spent his last years sequestered in the Vatican plotting for the reconquest of his lost state, had died three years earlier, leaving a problem. He had given instructions that he wanted to be buried not in the Vatican but in the church of San Lorenzo on the far side of Rome. After three years of delay the Italian prime minister Agostino Depretis decided the moment had come to move Pius' corpse to its new home. Depretis decided it should be done in the middle of the night, in the hope that nobody would notice.

He was mistaken. Word spread and by midnight a crowd of 100,000 thronged the area around St Peter's Square. The burial procession, which included devout Catholics, chanting and carrying candles, became a moving battleground as it was set upon by Romans, who had not forgotten or forgiven the shells fired on their city in Pius' name. Stones were thrown and when Pius reached the Ponte Sant'Angelo there were shouts of, 'Into the river with him.' His bones eventually made it safely to San Lorenzo, but without much dignity. To escape the crowd his cortège had to speed up and cross the city at a brisk trot.

It was the first time Pius had left the Vatican for eleven years. Had he been able to see the city, he would have found it was changing so fast that some areas were already barely recognizable. Rome was undergoing yet another great metamorphosis, now as the capital of Italy.

CHAPTER SEVEN

NAZIS

I

THE VILLA ADA SAVOIA, in the affluent north-east suburbs of Rome, does not look like a place where anything important would have taken place. Today it is the embassy of the Arab Republic of Egypt and a couple of bored-looking soldiers keep watch over the main entrance. It lies at the edge of the Villa Ada, one of Rome's great parks, where locals enjoy Sunday picnics and walk their coiffured dogs. The building is not old, dating from the later nineteenth century, nor is it especially grand. Square in shape and with a fake medieval tower just beside it, it could be a game show host's Tuscan holiday home. A glance around the area, however, soon offers clues that it once belonged to someone of significance. An abandoned building just behind, now boarded up and covered with graffiti, was once a stable filled with pedigree horses. Also nearby is an ornamental garden, a tiny amphitheatre overlooked by a dilapidated summerhouse and, most telling of all, a large underground bomb shelter. If one had not already guessed from the building's name, all is made clear from the coat of arms

Rome, 1930s

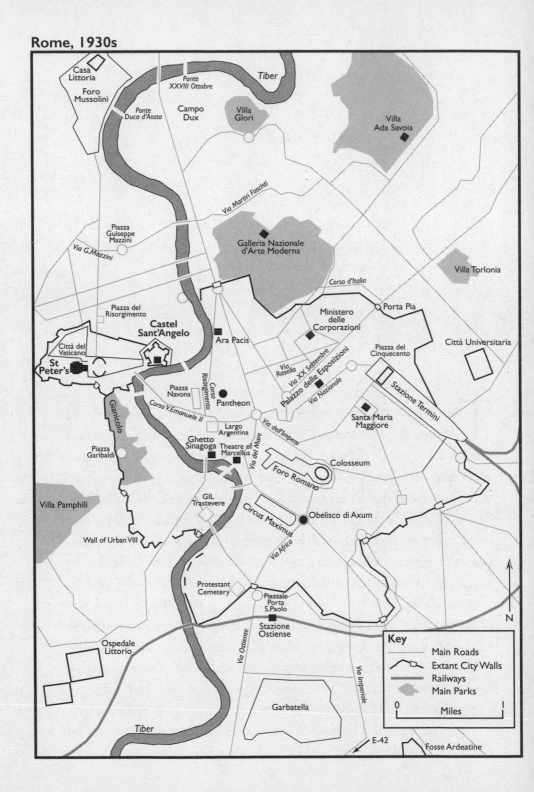

Casa Littoria
Foro Mussolini
Ponte XXVIII Ottobre
Tiber
Ponte Duca d'Aosta
Campo Dux
Villa Glori
Villa Ada Savoia
Via Martiri Fascisti
Piazza Guiseppe Mazzini
Via G.Mazzini
Galleria Nazionale d'Arte Moderna
Villa Torlonia
Corso d'Italia
Piazza del Risorgimento
Ministero delle Corporazioni
Porta Pia
Città Universitaria
Castel Sant'Angelo
Ara Pacis
Città del Vaticano
St Peter's
Piazza del Cinquecento
Via Rasella
Via XX Settembre
Palazzo delle Esposizioni
Stazione Termini
Corso Risorgimento
Piazza Navona
Pantheon
Via Nazionale
Corso V. Emanuele II
Largo Argentina
Via dell'Impero
Santa Maria Maggiore
Gianicolo
Piazza Garibaldi
Ghetto Sinagoga
Theatre of Marcellus
Via del Mare
Foro Romano
Colosseum
Villa Pamphili
GIL Trastevere
Circus Maximus
Obelisco di Axum
Wall of Urban VIII
Via Africa
Protestant Cemetery
Piazzale Porta S.Paolo
N
Ospedale Littorio
Via Ostiense
Stazione Ostiense
Key
Main Roads
Extant City Walls
Railways
Main Parks
0   Miles
Tiber
Garbatella
Via Imperiale
E-42
Fosse Ardeatine

on the fake medieval tower: that of the royal House of Savoy. In the summer of 1943 this was the private residence of the king of Italy, Vittorio Emanuele III.

At five in the afternoon on Sunday 25 July he had a visitor: Benito Mussolini. A small convoy drew up to the building. The three escort cars full of guards and adjutants drove back to the entrance to the park, leaving Mussolini and his secretary, Nicola De Cesare, who was carrying a large portfolio full of documents, to climb out of their sedan. The king was waiting at the entrance of the villa to welcome them, which he did with some warmth, greeting Mussolini as *Duce*, a term he had avoided during twenty years of Mussolini's leadership. The door to the villa closed behind Mussolini and his secretary, and *carabinieri* (police officers) had their driver park the sedan in a quiet corner of the grounds. He might have noticed, as he drove, that hidden from sight beside the villa was an ambulance.

Mussolini looked tired that afternoon and according to one source his chin was covered with stubble because – uncharacteristically – he had forgotten to shave. Then he had had a long and trying night. He had presided over a meeting of the Fascist Grand Council, the first held for several years, which had lasted for ten hours and became increasingly rancorous as leading Fascist leaders blamed one another – and especially blamed Mussolini – for Italy's disastrous conduct of the war. A few days afterwards a Swiss journalist, M. de Wyss, who lived in Rome throughout this time and left an account of all she witnessed, pieced together what happened from some of those who had been present:

> Furious personal attacks and violent invectives poured forth. For instance, De Vecchi shouted at Frattari: 'You are kept by this prostitute' – for Frattari was backed by Mussolini's notorious mistress, Petacci. Everybody screamed. Some pounded the tables with their fists. Some cried. The Minister Pareschi even fainted.[1]

The meeting finally ended at three in the morning when the council voted to strip Mussolini of his powers and to place the king in charge of Italy's armed forces. Mussolini had been deposed. But, waking up the next morning, he decided to ignore the whole business. After all, the Grand Council only had a consultative role. He would carry on as usual, quietly arranging a little revenge on his treacherous colleagues. He arrived at his office in Palazzo Venezia at nine, just as usual, and in the early afternoon he went home to the Villa Torlonia in the north-east of the city. Here he learned that the king had summoned him to the Villa Ada Savoia. A little oddly, Mussolini was instructed not to come in the military uniform he habitually wore, but to wear civilian clothes. His wife, Rachele, was suspicious and told him not to go, but Mussolini ignored her and, in a blue suit and black hat, he set out through the heavy summer heat.

M. de Wyss wrote an account of Mussolini's meeting with the king, which she described as a bitter one, in which each furiously denounced the other. Her contacts, though, seem to have exaggerated and reports gathered months later from those who had been present offer a less dramatic picture. The king told Mussolini that he knew what had taken place at the Grand Council meeting. Mussolini, who had anticipated that this subject would be raised, hurriedly leafed through the portfolio of documents his secretary had brought, looking for one to show that the Grand Council's role was purely advisory. The king insisted the vote showed that confidence in Mussolini's leadership had collapsed, and then announced that he had decided to appoint a new political leader: Marshal Badoglio. Fearing that Mussolini might become violent, he had an adjutant concealed in the next-door room, ready with a loaded pistol, but the precaution was not needed. Mussolini seemed to crumple.

The interview over, the king conducted Mussolini and his secretary to the villa entrance, calling out, 'Where's the Duce's car?' Instead of their sedan, though, it was the ambulance that had been hidden behind the palace that appeared. As the king disappeared into the villa Mussolini found his path blocked by a carabiniere officer, Captain

Vigneri, who told him that, for his own protection, he must go with him. At this moment the rear doors of the ambulance opened to reveal a squad of well-armed carabinieri. Mussolini took a step away, murmuring that he did not need any protection, but Vigneri took him firmly by the arm and led him towards the ambulance. By one account, as Mussolini climbed inside he pissed himself.

King Vittorio Emanuele was an unlikely figure to have deposed the country's dictator in a coup. Known for his tininess – Queen Victoria, herself no giant, remarked of him, 'he is dreadful short'[2] – he had never wanted to be king and in his youth he tried to persuade his father to nominate his dashing cousin the duke of Aosta in his place. When his father was assassinated in 1900, Vittorio Emanuele accepted his role without enthusiasm. He was far happier breeding horses, hunting and finding new items for his large coin collection – or, during the First World War, spending time with Italian troops at the front – than performing public duties. Frugal, even stingy, he used the Quirinal Palace only for state events, preferring to live in the far smaller Villa Ada Savoia. When Mussolini seized power in 1922 Vittorio Emanuele was grateful to him for, as he believed, having saved both Italy and the monarchy from Bolshevism. For the next two decades he left decision-making to Mussolini and kept a low profile.

The backseat monarch was transformed into a man of action by the disastrous war Mussolini had brought upon their country. By 1943 it was clear that it would be lost, and as early as January the king's advisors urged him to depose Mussolini and sue for peace with the Allies. The king, who was by nature cautious and fatalistic, prevaricated. Then, on 19 July 1943 Rome was bombed for the first time. A huge day raid that involved more than 600 US aircraft showed up Italy's lack of preparedness with painful clarity. The king, watching from Villa Ada Savoia, saw that there was not a single Italian fighter in the skies, while the city's anti-aircraft guns lacked the range to reach the American planes. Unopposed, the bombers approached in perfect formation. As the dust cleared from the destruction more scandalous failings emerged. Shelters had been inadequate and no teams were ready to begin digging out survivors. In the San Lorenzo district, where most bombs fell, some 1,500 Romans died.

The attack also revealed what Romans thought of their monarchy. When the pope, Pius XII, visited San Lorenzo after the attack and distributed money he was met with cheering and tears of gratitude. When Vittorio Emanuele and his wife Elena appeared a little later, they were hissed. Vittorio Emanuele was called a cuckold and Queen Elena a whore. One woman tried to spit on her. When the king offered people money they tore it up and threw it back.

Six days later the king had Mussolini arrested and appointed the career soldier Marshal Badoglio in his place. When they heard the news of Mussolini's fall late that evening the Romans burst into the hot summer streets to celebrate, some of them still in their pyjamas. Pictures of Mussolini were thrown from shops and offices, firemen brought down Fascist insignia, the Fascist Party headquarters was attacked, the offices of the city's main Fascist newspaper *Il Tevere* was set alight and prisoners were freed from Regina Coeli prison. Police looked on, grinning. A few Fascists caught on the street were beaten up and one or two killed – the local party boss in Trastevere was said to have been chopped into small pieces in a butcher's shop – but, as de Wyss observed, 'taking it all in one cannot imagine a quieter and smoother overthrow of a dictatorial rule after twenty-two years of its abuses'.[3]

Badoglio, in his first broadcast as leader, insisted the war alongside Germany would go on, but few took him seriously and Romans were hopeful they would soon have peace. Sadly, it would not be so easy as that.

Badoglio was a great survivor. As one of the Italian army's commanders he had endured the First World War, despite being blamed for Italy's greatest defeat of the conflict, at Caporetto. Next he had made it through Mussolini's rise to power, despite having urged that Fascism should be resisted. Mussolini, who rather liked to have something damning hanging over the heads of his close colleagues in case he chose to be rid of them, entrusted him with Italy's invasion

of Abyssinia. Now, as Fascism fell apart, Badoglio had survived once
again, jumping from the sinking ship just in time: he had taken a
leading role in the king's coup d'état. But he was more than seventy
years old and as cautious as his king. Though from the first he intended
to switch sides, instead of doing so swiftly he delayed, negotiating
with the Allies.

All the while Hitler, who never for a moment believed Badoglio's
assurances of loyalty, poured troops into Italy. After 45 days Italy
announced an armistice with the Allies. Within hours German troops
began to advance on Rome.

II

As to what Rome awaited them, to see it in anything like a state of
normality we should step back a few years, to before the war began. If
a Roman from the 1840s had been transported almost a century into
the future, to the late 1930s, the first thing that would have struck him
or her was how huge the city had become. In 1939 there were almost
one and a half million Romans. The population had increased tenfold
since we last saw it and, finally, there were more Romans than there
had been in classical times.

The city was vastly busier and noisier. In place of a few sleepy
cabs and carriages it now had buses, electric trams and no fewer than
30,000 cars clogging its congested streets. The city had more bridges
than ever before: ten (in classical times there had been eight). It
had begun to extend beyond the old Aurelian Walls and, in another
first since classical times, its empty areas, the *disabitato*, had largely
disappeared. With it had gone most of Rome's elegant Baroque parks
and villas, though fortunately not all of them. The Villa Borghese had
survived, as had the vast Villa Pamphili, where Garibaldi's volunteers
had fought the French in the spring of 1849, and also the Villa Ada,
where, as we saw, King Vittorio Emanuele had his residence. The
disabitato had succumbed to a construction boom of the 1870s and '80s

when Rome, as the new capital of Italy, became a vast building site. Plans of the city's remaking were frequently ignored and numerous ancient relics were lost in the frenzy of development.

It could have been even worse. During this same era medieval Paris was largely razed to the ground by Prefect Georges-Eugène Haussmann. In Rome some especially outrageous proposals were seen off, such as plans to demolish a section of the Aurelian Wall, to destroy a stretch of the older Servian Walls near Termini railway station, and to remake the Appia Antica as a tramway. And some good came out of the destruction. Under the guidance of the archaeologist Rodolfo Lanciani the Colosseum was given a spring clean and the Pantheon – once again – was cleared of accretions, including two seventeenth-century bell towers that Romans referred to as *ass's ears*. If much was lost to development, much was also found. By the late 1880s, 192 marble statues had been unearthed along with 266 busts and heads, a thousand inscriptions and more than 36,000 coins. Eventually, belatedly, the city's antiquities became properly protected. Shortly before the First World War the city's socialist mayor, Ernesto Nathan, ring-fenced the Theatre of Marcellus, the Baths of Diocletian and the Portico of Octavia from development and transformed the Forum, the Palatine and nearby areas into an archaeological park.

Along with the city's vastness, a visitor from the 1840s would have been astonished by its political display. In the earlier nineteenth century Rome had been a city of the popes that was dominated by churches, Catholic institutions, papal insignia and street corner images of Mary and Jesus. In the late 1930s these still existed but alongside them was a new layer of symbols that celebrated everything the Church detested. The Liberal governments which ruled Rome after 1870 had made their new capital into a vast theatre of propaganda in their cold war with the papacy. Unified, royal Italy celebrated itself with new main streets that cut across the city: Via Nazionale, that led from the Piazza Venezia to Termini railway station; Via Settembre XX, that led to the Quirinal Palace from the spot where royal troops broke through the wall in 1870 (and was named after the day when they did so) and Corso Vittorio Emanuele II. This last, which sliced through the maze of lanes across the river from the Vatican, and had been the dream of past popes and of Rome's Napoleonic conquerors, finally made the city traversable from the Tiber to the start of the Corso. Destructive though it was, it could have been worse, twisting and weaving so the finest buildings of the area were preserved.

To papal fury the city centre was now home to non-Catholic churches: Anglican All Saints' Church on Via Babuino, American Episcopal St Paul's within the walls on Via Nazionale, and, close to Piazza Venezia, a church belonging the Waldensians, whose members had once been burned as heretics. And there were the statues. These now crowded Rome as they had in classical days and hardly an enemy of the popes was absent. As well as Liberal politicians, in Trastevere there was now a statue to the early nineteenth-century Roman dialect poet Giuseppe Gioachino Belli, who had enjoyed taking a dig at priests. On the Capitoline Hill, ancient seat of civic resistance to papal rule, stood a statue of Cola di Rienzo, the unstable fourteenth-century would-be founder of the new Roman Republic, now reinvented as a national hero. In the Campo de' Fiori towered a statue of Giordano Bruno, the philosopher and mathematician who in 1600 had been burned in that very spot by Pope Clement VIII, while panels on the statue's plinth honoured celebrity rebels against the papacy, from John Wycliffe to Jan Hus.

The Gianicolo Hill, where Garibaldi and his volunteers fought, had become a vast open-air shrine to the battles of 1849. Streets around the hill were named after those involved: Via Emilio Dandolo, Via Emilio Morosini, Viale Aurelio Saffi, among many others. In pride of place, naturally, was Via Garibaldi, which snaked its way up the hill. Around Piazza Garibaldi on the hill's summit were busts of dozens of those who had fought for Italy's unification, and in the square stood a huge equestrian statue of Garibaldi himself, staring out over Rome in his trademark fez and poncho. A short distance away an ornamental lighthouse flashed out the green, white and red of Italy's national flag, and every noon a gun was fired to wake up Romans to the need to defend their country. To the ire of the popes, Garibaldi and his horse's backside were clearly visible from the windows of the Vatican Palace.

Yet the Gianicolo was not Rome's greatest tribute to the victory of Italy's unifiers. Far more imposing was a monument Garibaldi and his horse peered out towards: the vast, glaringly white Vittoriano, or monument to Vittorio Emanuele II. Overlooking Piazza Venezia, it had swallowed up the whole northern slope of the Capitoline Hill. Loathed by many – Romans called it the wedding cake or typewriter, and one described it as a luxury pissoir – its making had involved extensive destruction, including the Tower of Paul III and the cloisters of the church of Santa Maria in Aracoeli. Opened in 1911 after twenty-six years of planning and work it was 135 metres wide and 70 metres high. It supported sixteen vast statues that represented each of Italy's provinces, and a gargantuan equestrian statue of King Vittorio Emanuele II, which was so huge that twenty-one of those involved in its making were famously photographed sitting at a table enjoying a drink of vermouth inside the horse. As intended, it offered a riposte to the equally vast bulk of St Peter's across the river.

Other slights to the papacy were marked by what had vanished. A visitor from the 1840s would be surprised to find that the jumble of medieval housing, alleys and courts of the Ghetto had gone. With the exception of a small section that had been added only in the earlier nineteenth century, it had been demolished in the 1880s, replaced by high apartment blocks and a towering new synagogue. Most Jewish Romans had been happy enough to see it go, though many, by force of habit, continued to live there or close by. Most were strong supporters of the new national state that had freed them, and under which Italy's small Jewish population, numbering only a few tens of thousands, had thrived, particularly in the professions from which they had previously been excluded: politics and the military. In 1910 Rome was governed by a Jewish mayor, Ernesto Nathan (whose family had helped Mazzini during his exile in London, and who moved to Italy in Ernesto's youth). 1910 was also the year in which one Jewish prime minister of Italy, Sidney Sonnino, was succeeded by another, Luigi Luzzatti. Five years later, when Italy entered the First World War, there were three Jewish admirals and fifteen generals. Though, as we will see, by the late 1930s life for Jewish Romans had greatly changed.

Another part of Rome that had vanished was its riverside. This transformation, for once, did not represent a slight towards the popes, but had been a practical measure to save Rome from further disastrous floods. The last of these struck on New Year's Eve 1870, and was gleefully seized on by Pope Pius IX as divine judgement on the seizure of his kingdom. Garibaldi, as a member of the Italian Senate, became involved in the debate over what should be done, proposing that a Tiber canal should be built to divert floodwater, in a vast work project that would toughen up decadent Italians. He also urged that the Tiber be paved over to create a roadway where the New Italy could be celebrated with huge military parades. It is probably as well that he did not get his way on the last proposal, though the run-off canal might have served Rome well. Instead, following the example of London and Paris, high embankments were built on either side of the river. Rome was made safe from floods, but at a cost. Riverside sections of the Aurelian Walls disappeared along with three churches, a theatre and four palaces. The greatest casualty, though, was Rome's dreamy riverfront, whose houses had reached to the water's edge, hanging above the stream.

From destruction emerged a new Rome. Under four and a half decades of Liberal rule from 1870 to 1915, the city was remade as a European capital, with a monumental new law court, a national bank, a military academy and numerous ministries. Outside the old city walls Rome had a new power station on Via Ostiense and it was guarded by fifteen new forts and three gun batteries. It had new sports associations, a horse racing track and even a velodrome. Most of all, Rome was filled with new housing. Already by the late 1880s the city had more than 3,000 new apartment blocks, which formed a series of new districts whose squares were named – naturally – in honour of the new Italy: Piazza Cavour, Piazza Mazzini, and Piazza Risorgimento. Even street plans could be political. The new residential area of Prati was constructed directly beside the Vatican yet locals point out that the papal city can be very hard to see. They claim that ingenious developers ensured that most streets would point away from St Peter's and the Vatican, so it was visible to few, except servants washing laundry on their masters' and mistresses' rooftops.

Yet all of this was only one part of the propaganda in stone that filled 1930s Rome. There was also another, which a visitor from the 1840s would have found altogether more alien. If Liberal Rome was designed to blend in with the buildings of the past, and did so reasonably well, the next stratum of the city made no such compromises. Its plain columns and hard frontages with undecorated windows had a faintly barracks-like appearance, as well they might. They had been created by a movement of Italy's First World War veterans: Fascism.

As Fascist Rome was largely created by a single individual, Benito Mussolini, we should know a little about the man. He was brought up in a small village just outside the sleepy town of Predappio in Emilia-Romagna in north-east Italy, where his mother was a devoutly Catholic schoolteacher and his father was a sometime blacksmith and sometime drunk, womanizer and layabout, who was drawn to radical politics. Benito followed in the footsteps of his father but with far more success. Charismatic, egotistical and restlessly ambitious, he was allegedly expelled from two schools for stabbing his fellow pupils. A talent for political journalism and oratory made him a rising star in Italy's socialist party, and he became editor of its main newspaper, *Avanti,* but then the First World War changed his political direction. Soon after the conflict broke out, when Italy was still neutral, he abandoned pacifism and socialism and – possibly financed by the British secret services – he urged Italians to join the Allies against Austria and Germany. After serving in the war for two years without great distinction he discerned an element in Italian society that could prove a powerful political force: embittered ex-soldiers who returned from the front to find their families struggling and their jobs gone. Mussolini urged them to seize power as a new elite: the *trincerocrazia,* or trenchocracy. He led them against his former socialist colleagues.

Benito Mussolini in a satirical cartoon published in a weekly antifascist magazine,
Il Becco Giallo, *which ran from 1924–26.*

As squads of ex-soldiers violently broke up left-wing demonstrations and strikes, Mussolini became the darling of Italy's wealthy, who saw him as their best defence against Bolshevik revolution. With their help, on 28 October 1922, as Fascist squads descended on the capital in the March on Rome, he became national leader.

In his early, radical days, Mussolini had had little time for Rome, which he described as 'a parasitic city, full of landladies, shoe shine boys, prostitutes and bureaucrats'.[4] Romans returned the compliment and showed negligible interest in Fascism until it overwhelmed them. From 1922, though, as his capital and his home, Rome became one of Mussolini's chief preoccupations. Like many an emperor and pope before him, he was determined to make it a showpiece of his thinking that would be passed on to future generations as a legacy of the Fascist era.

Naturally this transformation would involve a good deal of destruction. Mussolini was concerned to preserve Rome's medieval,

Renaissance and, most of all, classical heritage, all of which dated from times when Italy had been a major force in the world, but he had little time for the Baroque, when the country had been in decline, and he positively disdained anything from the Liberal era. In his eyes Fascism was the antithesis of Liberal rule, which he despised as disorganized, selfish, feeble, indolent, amoral and decadent. To him the nineteenth century had been the age of the individual and the twentieth century would see the triumph of collectivism and the state. If Liberals had made Rome into a propaganda weapon against the popes, Mussolini used it as a weapon against Liberalism, even in terms of people's homes. Liberal-era Romans had lived in dark, dusty old buildings on narrow, winding streets. Fascist Romans would live beside wide, straight roads, in apartments filled with air and light, and that would help remake them as a tough, dynamic people. (Some new boulevards would also help alleviate Rome's chronic traffic problems.)

Destruction began on 21 April 1926: Rome's 2679th birthday. Mussolini, who was never one to miss a photo opportunity, began the process himself, appearing with the pickaxe that would become a familiar sight over the next few years. His target was the neighbourhood of Piazza Montanara just by the Theatre of Marcellus, which had been a favourite haunt of nineteenth-century tourists seeking the picturesque and which, in the 1920s, was one of the few spots where that side of Rome could still be found. It was a place where country people gathered to seek a day's work, where salesmen traded in old coins and where scribes wrote letters in the open air for illiterate customers. The area represented everything Mussolini loathed: a backward Italy, patronized as quaint by foreign tourists, whom Fascists blamed for having turned the country into a land of servants.

Yet the liquidation of Piazza Montanara was not only undertaken to reverse past humiliations. Like all of Mussolini's grand schemes in Rome it was intended to alleviate unemployment, and demolition work was done not by machinery but by hand to create more jobs. The demolished area also provided land for the first section of a new boulevard, the Via del Mare, which would eventually stretch all the way from the centre of Rome to the sea. As well as easing traffic jams, the road was intended to make Romans look to the oceans, inspiring them to once again become a world-conquering people. It also took them to the beach, where they could enjoy sunlight, air and healthy exercise. Finally the destruction would allow Romans to be inspired by their past. The classical Theatre of Marcellus, the Arch of Janus, several temples and the medieval church of San Giorgio al Velabro all emerged from the destruction, isolated and visible as they had not been for centuries.

Many neighbourhoods – or slums, as the Fascist authorities preferred to call them, regardless of what treasures they contained – went the way of Piazza Montanara. In 1932 work began on a second great thoroughfare, the Via dei Monti, which was to take Romans into the healthy air of the hills. Its first stretch was a wide avenue, the Via dell'Impero, which, lined with flagpoles and statues of emperors, passed across the old classical fora, slicing through a low ridge and destroying an entire neighbourhood. The Basilica of Maximus was newly revealed and the Colosseum became pleasingly visible from Mussolini's office in the Palazzo Venezia, but churches and palaces vanished, along with housing that had contained 6,000 bedrooms.

By 1933 almost 100,000 Romans had lost their homes to the destruction yet it continued apace. In 1934 Mussolini's interest turned to the tomb of Emperor Augustus, whom he regarded as an example to Fascist Italians. Augustus was a logical choice as he had destroyed constitutional government and replaced it with his own dictatorship. The tomb, which had been concealed for a thousand years beneath, variously, a medieval fortress, hanging gardens, a bullring, the artist's studio where the vast equestrian statue of Vittorio Emanuele had been made and, most recently, Rome's main concert hall, proved disappointing when it finally emerged into the light, lower in height and more ruined than was expected.

In October 1936 it was the Borgo's turn. Mussolini appeared with his pickaxe on a rooftop above the area of narrow streets between St Peter's and the river known as the Spina. Its demolition was to celebrate one of Fascism's greatest coups. In 1929 the poisonous enmity between Italy's rulers and the popes was finally brought to an end by the Lateran Treaties. The new peace was celebrated by the creation of the wide, straight Via della Conciliazione, which would make the facade of St Peter's visible from afar. It was not a new idea. It had been proposed by French occupiers for Napoleon's procession through the city, and before them it had been suggested by Rome's leading architect of the Baroque era, Bernini. Even in his time the idea had had its critics and Cardinal Pallotta commented that at the end of a wide, long avenue, St Peter's would shrink away to nothing. He was quite right and the drama of walking through a narrow lane and being suddenly confronted by the vastness of St Peter's Square was lost. It was a pattern that was repeated across the city. The French writer André Gide observed that under Fascism Rome had become grand but it had lost its allure. Previously everything had needed to be discovered. Now it was glaringly displayed.

Not all that Mussolini did was deleterious to the city. His enthusiasm for classical Rome brought about some preservation, such as of ruined republican temples in what is now Largo Argentina, which had been about to be lost to development. Nobody missed the removal of Pius IX's gasworks, along with a scrap iron heap and a pasta factory, which had covered the old Circus Maximus. It was thanks to Mussolini that Augustus' Temple to Peace – the Ara Pacis – which contained some of classical Rome's finest reliefs, was reconstructed. Visitors to Rome enjoyed being able to see the city's ancient buildings more clearly, while some Fascist buildings had a kind of stark beauty. Yet the remaking of Rome diminished the city's texture: its layers of the past crowded one on top of another. Rome also became more disjointed. As Mussolini demolished areas to reveal early treasures, it gained a series of soulless bald patches between its warrens of narrow streets.

Out of destruction rose the new. By the late 1930s Rome had new Fascist bridges, a new university, four new post offices and a number of new ministry buildings, which included, on Via Veneto, the Ministry of Corporations, that were to be Fascism's answer to capitalist exploitation and Marxist class hatred. Following the conquest of Abyssinia, work began on a new Ministry of Africa next to the Circus Maximus, in front of which stood an ancient Ethiopian obelisk taken from Axum. All across Rome there were new apartment blocks up to ten floors high, where Romans were to enjoy air and sunlight. There were new schools where young Romans were taught about Italy's victories in the First World War and Fascism's triumphs. One, on the Aventine Hill, was named after the schoolteacher who was presented as an inspiration to all Italy: Mussolini's mother.

There were new centres for the Fascist youth organization, the GIL. An especially lavish complex by Porta Portese in Trastevere included a cinema, on its wall emblazoned the slogan: NECESSARIO VINCERE PIV NECESSARIO COMBATTARE (*You must win but above all you must fight*). Here, and in their schools, young Romans gathered each Saturday afternoon in their uniforms – which looked much like those of the Boy Scout and Girl Guide movements, on which the GIL was modelled – to shout patriotic slogans, vow loyalty to their *duce*, Mussolini, and take part in calisthenics and, for the boys, military drill. More fortunate GIL members could go skiing, horseback riding and spend time at summer camps by the sea or in the mountains. And of course they could sing the anthem of the movement, the hymn of the Balilla:

> Up little wolves and eagles
> Like Sardinian drummers
> Let your spirit beat in your breast
> Full of virtue
> The flag of Italy flutters
> And you are part of that fluttering
> Proud of eye and quick of step

Each year in May tens of thousands of GIL members from across Italy gathered at Camp Dux, a huge sports area by the Ponte Milvio where for a week they competed and learned to put selfishness behind them, and lost themselves in Fascist collectivism. The luckiest 25,000 paraded past the Colosseum in front of Mussolini himself. For adults who sought healthy exercise there was the Foro Mussolini below Monte Mario. A vast complex, it included an Olympic tennis stadium, the headquarters of Italy's Olympic Committee and a sun therapy camp on the slope of Monte Mario. Its main arena, the Marble Stadium, was surrounded by statues of sixty-four athletes, each of which was made in and represented a different Italian city. On the edge of the complex stood a 20-metre-high obelisk made of 300 tons of Carrara marble, on which was written in bold capital letters, MUSSOLINI DUX. Yet a good part of the Foro Mussolini – like many of Mussolini's projects – remained unfinished as the 1930s drew to an end. The new National Fascist Party headquarters, the Casa Littoria, was still under construction, while work had barely begun on a towering statue that was to stand two and a half times higher than the obelisk, which it would face. It was to represent Fascism and the head had already been completed. It bore a strong likeness to Mussolini.

Under Fascism Rome became a city of exhibitions: about Fascism, naturally. The first of these, the Mostra della Rivoluzione Fascista, opened on the tenth anniversary of the March on Rome, in October 1932, and was a kind of temple to the new Fascist religion, designed to transform all who passed through its rooms into true believers. The building it was held in, the Palazzo delle Esposizione on Via Nazionale, dated – embarrassingly – from the despised Liberal era, and its frontage was concealed behind a fake facade with four huge metallic fasces as pillars. The display inside recounted Fascism's brief history, culminating in the dimly lit Hall of Martyrs, which contained a seven-metre-high cross and a thousand electric lights in the walls. The English hiker Roland G. Andrew, himself a keen Fascist, was impressed:

Little pennants hung there in the twilight, each bearing the word presente and the name of the man who had died to save his country from the international disease that was gnawing at her vitals. From a distance came the strains of music: the Giovanezza hymn played softly for those who had died for the Cause, but were still present, hallowed in the memory of the New Italy they had anointed with their blood.[5]

Some five million visitors passed through the exhibition, though some will have been motivated less by ideology than by the chance of enjoying a cheap trip to Rome. A stamp at the end of the exhibition entitled one to 70 per cent back on the cost of one's train tickets. Even left-wing French writers Simone de Beauvoir and Jean-Paul Sartre, who came to Italy to deride Fascism in 1932, shamelessly took the discount.

The Mostra della Rivoluzione Fascista, which continued for several years, marked the beginning of a Fascist obsession with displaying itself. After it was cleared of gasworks and the pasta factory, the Circus Maximus became the site of a series of Fascist showcases: on the Fascist women's movement; on how to raise healthy Fascist children; on Italy's national minerals; on Italy's textile industry and on the Fascist after-work leisure organization, Dopolavoro. On 23 September 1937 – Emperor Augustus' 2000th birthday – Mussolini opened an exhibition of Augustus and Romanness. At a militaristic and highly choreographed opening, Mussolini was presented with a live eagle. On the very same day a second Mostra della Rivoluzione Fascista was opened across the city in the Museum of Modern Art. The biggest display, though, was yet to come. In the late 1930s, a few miles south of Rome, work began on a permanent and truly vast exhibition of Fascism, in an area designated E-42, for 1942, the 20th anniversary of Fascism, when it was to be opened.

As well as exhibitions, Fascists also had a strong fondness for grand public gatherings and Rome became filled with processions and demonstrations. Military parades processed through the city, and especially along the wide Via dell'Impero between the Colosseum and Piazza Venezia. Huge crowds were summoned to Piazza Venezia to applaud Mussolini's great campaigns: the Battle of the Births, which was to inspire Italians to increase their numbers; the Battle of the Grain, which was to increase Italy's wheat production; the Battle of the Lira, which was to restore the currency's value; the project to drain the Pontine marshes and cleanse the country of malaria; the invasion of Abyssinia that would create a new Italian empire, and – when the League of Nations replied by imposing sanctions on Italy – the Autarky campaign for economic self-sufficiency.

Fascism was everywhere in Rome. It was in fasces and eagles carved into buildings. It was in slogans on posters: *Mussolini is always right! The Fascist does not take the elevator!* Most of all it was in the face of Mussolini whose cult, by the late 1930s, was little less than a religion, in which he was presented as something between a saint, a film star and a superhero. When he appeared on cinema screens, the audience rose to their feet as one. Mussolini, who claimed he had remade himself as a kind of machine who needed almost no sleep as he watched over the Italian nation, looked down from the walls of offices, shops, hairdressers', tobacconists' and railway waiting rooms. He could be purchased on postcards in dozens of different poses: Mussolini the orator, Mussolini the statesman in a frock coat, Mussolini the uniformed soldier, Mussolini the yachtsman, the flyer, the horseman; fashionable Mussolini driving a sports car, fit Mussolini leaping over an obstacle, rural Mussolini harvesting wheat or planting a tree in Calabria, fearless Mussolini stroking a wild beast, cultured Mussolini playing the violin, history-making Mussolini marching on Rome, or simply Fascist Mussolini doing a Roman salute. The French novelist and journalist Henri Béraud observed: 'Wherever you go, whatever you do, his gaze follows you everywhere ... Mussolini is omnipresent like a God.'[6]

Even Rome's time had become Fascist. On newly built monuments there were now two dates: the familiar Christian one and also another, much shorter, marked A.F. for Anno Fascista: 1922, when Mussolini took power, was Italy's year zero. Rome's calendar, too, was Fascist. The city's great holiday of Carnevale was gone. Wearing fancy dress in

Propaganda poster featuring Benito Mussolini.

public was now illegal and the only trace of the old festivities was that the Corso became a little more crowded in the days before Lent. In 1930, the key holiday for Liberal, Risorgimento Italy, of 20 September – the day when Rome was conquered and the country fully unified – was quietly dropped. New civic celebrations included 23 March (when the Fascist movement was founded in Milan in 1919); 21 April (Rome's birthday); 4 November (Italy's First World War victory at Vittorio Veneto) and of course, in pride of place, 28 October: the anniversary of the March on Rome.

Yet the Fascists did not have it all their own way. As well as possessing Christmas and Easter, in 1925 the Church under Pius XI promoted the celebration of the Feast of Christus Rex: a new anti-socialist cult whose feast day fell on the last Sunday of October, and so clashed directly with the anniversaries of both the March on Rome and the battle of Vittorio Veneto. At Easter 1933, when the Mostra della Rivoluzione Fascista was in full swing, Pius XI brought crowds of his own by inaugurating an extra Holy Year, to celebrate the 1,900th anniversary of Jesus' death. The papacy competed also through architecture, creating large new churches in Fascism's new urban areas.

The word *totalitarian* may have been an invention of Fascist Italy yet the country was never as totalitarian as Fascists would have liked. From the start Mussolini had to share Italians with two other leaders. The king was content to take a political back seat but he had the loyalty of many in the armed forces and the police, and if peace with the Vatican made Fascism more popular with many Italians, it also meant the Catholic Church was more demanding. One of the papacy's first requests after reconciliation was that Mussolini remove the statue of Garibaldi that was so irritatingly visible from the Vatican. Mussolini, determined to show who was in charge, refused, and instead added a new statue of Garibaldi's wife, Anita: depicted in a heroic pose, on a galloping horse, a pistol in one hand and a baby in the other.

Mussolini saw Rome as a kind of huge machine of brick and stone, which had two functions: to glorify Fascism to the world and to help re-forge Italians as an aggressive, conquering people. How far his

efforts changed Italians we will come to later. As to the impression
Fascist Rome made on foreigners, there were relatively few of them
to offer a judgement. In the 1930s they had a modest presence in
the city, which was less cosmopolitan than it had been in most eras
we have looked at. Rome had many immigrants but almost all were
Italian, while most, as usual, came from provinces close to Rome. In
1931, of a million Romans only 5,000 were foreigners, of whom the
largest two groupings were Americans and Germans. The Ghetto
degli Inglesi was a poor shadow of its 1840s self and only a few vestiges
survived. As well as the Anglican Church on nearby Via Babuino, the
Piazza di Spagna still had the Union Club, an English chemist's and
Mrs Wilson's bookshop and lending library. For most of their needs
English-speaking residents in Rome now had to resort to shops run
by Romans. It was also no longer the home of the city's great hotels
and in the 1930s the most luxurious of these – the Ambasciatori, the
Excelsior and the Grand – were all on the Via Veneto, which had not
existed in the early nineteenth century.

That Rome had lost its allure for foreign writers, poets and artists
was largely the result of its success. As we have seen, after it became
Italy's capital in 1870 it became a building site filled with crowds and
traffic, and it soon lost the eccentric charm of its papal days. And after
the Wall Street Crash few northern Europeans or Americans could
afford to idle away half a year abroad, especially in Italy, which, thanks
to Mussolini's campaign to push up the value of Italy's currency – the
Battle of the Lira – had become an expensive destination.

Even short-term tourism struggled. Aside from the question of
expense, some visitors were put off by Fascist rhetoric, which railed
against foreigners who sought out antiquities and art rather than
coming to see the new Fascist Italy. Some radical Fascists urged that
all foreigners who carried a copy of Baedeker and a Kodak camera
should be turned back at the frontier. Even when, in the hungry '30s,
the government tried to encourage tourism, the regime's preferred
visitors were those who showed interest in Fascism's revolution, which
some did. Many, such as the English hiker Roland G. Andrew, came

pre-converted and, like Andrew, wrote accounts of their visits to spread the word of their new faith.

Even Fascist Rome, with its construction sites and traffic jams, won praise. There was no denying that there had been improvements. The traffic might be bad but at least drivers were agreed as to which side of the road to drive on: prior to the First World War Romans drove wherever they liked. Quality Roman hotels might be expensive but they were spotless, well managed and they were required to display room prices clearly, so cheating was impossible. Tipping was now illegal (though the 1930 Baedeker guide claimed it was still expected by porters and cab drivers). The city was clean and, thanks to hundreds of new lavatories, Romans were no longer seen relieving themselves in the street. Rome was safer and, with squads of Fascist militiamen patrolling trains, trams and railway stations, one ran no risk of being robbed of one's luggage. Prostitutes, who had been firmly removed to state-licensed brothels, no longer assailed one on the street. Most remarkable of all, Rome was, for the first time in many centuries, beggar free. Fascist hiker Roland Andrew passed a whole week in the city without being asked for money once.

Rome was also easier to reach. Italy's roads, which had been famously bad, were transformed under Fascist rule. The same was true of the rail network, with new stations, new and faster lines, electric services and, famously, trains that ran on time. Those in a real hurry could even reach Rome by air. After the opening of a seaplane port at Ostia one could travel from London to Rome with Imperial Airways in a mere 27 hours. As the 1930 Baedeker guide explained, the luggage allowance was 100 kilograms, which may seem generous by today's standards, but which included the weight of the passenger.

Rome in the 1930s was also healthier than it had ever been. True, the city was still rife with tuberculosis and trachoma and there were regular typhus epidemics, but the city's worst scourge, malaria, had finally been defeated. Thanks to developers' destruction of Rome's great Baroque parks, with their ponds and puddles and pots full of water, the disease had disappeared from Rome by the end of the nineteenth century and, after Mussolini's campaign to drain the Pontine marshes, all of Italy was largely, if not entirely, free of the disease by the end of the 1930s. As in most of Europe, Italians' life expectancy, which had changed relatively little over previous centuries, soared after the 1840s, as death rates halved.

Romans were more literate than they had been even in classical times, with the majority able to read and write. And some aspects to life under Fascism were undeniably popular. Young Romans enjoyed taking part in Fascist sports events and Saturday afternoon patriotic assemblies of Fascism's equivalent of the Scouts. For grown-ups, the dopolavoro leisure movement offered unadulterated Fascist fun. To the annoyance of more militant Fascist leaders, dopolavoro was never used to indoctrinate its members. At their local dopolavoro clubhouse Romans could play darts or cards or football, listen to the radio, enjoy a glass of wine or grappa at the refreshments bar, and perhaps watch a film, or put on an amateur theatrical production. Dopolavoro holidays included cultural bus tours, sea cruises with ballroom dancing, and jaunts to Riccione on the Adriatic, which was Italy's answer to Blackpool or Atlantic City. Such trips may have been scorned by educated, middle-class Romans but they were immensely popular with dopolavoro members, of whom there were almost four million in 1939.

Fascism could also be cosy. For those who did not question it, and especially for those Romans who benefited the most – the city's middle classes – the world felt reassuringly safe thanks to the regime's rigid control of information. Mussolini, whose own career had begun in political journalism, was intensely concerned with what news reached Italians, even to the detriment of more pressing political matters. All foreign newspapers were banned, with the exception of the Vatican's paper, *L'Osservatore Romano*, while even it sometimes had to be sold under the counter. Though most newspapers were not directly Fascist-controlled, all were intimidated into obedience within the first few years of the regime and their journalists were required to join the Fascist Party. The information that reached them was tightly restricted, coming from a single Fascist-controlled news agency, Agenzia Stefani. If anything untoward did slip through, a stream of censorship orders was sent out each day, detailing what could not be written.

As a result of all of these efforts, Italians who knew the world only through Italy's news coverage existed in a state of happy reassurance. For them Italy was a land without political demonstrations or crime, where there was no corruption, no embezzlement and no train crashes. They were spared the pain of reading about the 1930s Great Depression. Little happened even outside Italy as Mussolini, wary of reducing his diplomatic options, insisted that other regimes should also be treated with respect. Even Fascism's supposed foe, Bolshevik Russia, was not criticized until Mussolini threw in his lot with Hitler in 1936. Radio news was equally bland, as were the newsreels shown in Rome's sixty-odd cinemas, most of which were viewed personally by Mussolini before release. Typically these included a story from abroad, one or two sports items, and another that showed a member of the royal family, the Fascist Party Secretary, or most usually Mussolini himself, announcing a new campaign or inaugurating a new ship or bridge or building. A newsreel's final story was designed to leave watchers in a good mood, and might be about a celebrity from the world of entertainment, or something amusing involving children or pets. Violence, crime, sex and women in short skirts were noticeably absent. Even Italy's wars could go largely unreported. Though the conquest of Abyssinia was well covered, and was presented as an impressively modern operation in which Ethiopian faces were rarely seen, Italy's extensive involvement in the Spanish Civil War was hardly mentioned.

Feature films were equally mild. Along with some patriotic romps and foreign imports, which only became subject to censorship in 1939, Romans were treated to endless romantic comedies involving wealthy, fashionable people – dubbed *the white telephone set* – which, to take them further from reality, were usually set in Budapest. One might have imagined Romans would have become frustrated at living in this bubble of blandness and comfort, but no. Though a large number of them had their own radios in the 1930s and could easily have listened to foreign channels, including some that broadcast in Italian, few did.

Of course, in spite of the newsreels, for many Romans life under Fascism was anything but cosy. This was especially true for those who fell short of the Fascist ideal: tough, patriotic, law-abiding, respectable in appearance, unquestioningly loyal and – preferably – male. Intellectuals and artists, who often found it hard to remain unquestioning, were regarded warily by the regime. Compared to their equivalents in the Soviet Union or Nazi Germany, Italy's intelligentsia were treated fairly gently, but their world became ever more inward-looking and parochial, while some individuals suffered badly. Arturo Toscanini, one of the greatest conductors of his age, who had supported Fascism but then grew disillusioned, was beaten up by Blackshirts for refusing to play the Fascist anthem 'Giovinezza' before a performance.

In Rome, as in all Italy, the ones who fared least well under Fascism were the poor. For all the ideology's boasts that it had created a harmonious society free of class hatred, the truth was rather different. The corporations system, loosely modelled on medieval guilds, claimed to have created a new *third way*, under which employers and employees, guided by Fascist trade unionists, worked harmoniously together for the good of the nation. In reality it was a sham under which employers were free to exploit their employees as they wanted. Fascist trade union leaders did not represent their members but bullied them like little Mussolinis. At meetings there was no room for debate and any who protested were reported to the police as subversives. The much-vaunted Fascist welfare system was no better. Though employees paid high contributions towards their healthcare, pensions and unemployment benefit, the funds they paid into were regularly raided by the state to pay for its wars and its grand projects, such as Mussolini's remaking of Rome.

Fascism was very much a dictatorship for the affluent and respectable. Even Rome's old aristocracy did well. During the 1920s and '30s all but one of Rome's governors were from the city's nobility:

the Cremonesi, the Potenziani and the Ludovisi. In 1936 the city was ruled by a member of the Colonna family. At the end of the 1930s only one-sixth of Italians made it past primary school and most of these had educated, affluent parents. In Rome the best new housing – apartments with elegant balconies and marble foyers – was theoretically available to all but it almost always ended up in the hands of Fascist officials, or wealthy Romans with Fascist connections. Poorer Romans were likely to find themselves in suburban Case Popolari, up to ten floors high. The flats they contained were mostly small and crowded, so much so that the only moment when parents had a chance to do their bit for the Battle of Births was on Fascist Saturday, when their children were away shouting slogans at their youth organization meeting. Life in the Case Popolari was simple, to say the least. Cooking was done on a coal or wood stove. In 1931 nine out of ten Rome apartments lacked their own bathroom and residents shared lavatories in the corridors outside, which usually had nothing but a hole in the concrete floor, and a hook on the wall on which were speared scraps of newspaper. Young and old made use of chamber pots at night, which were emptied into the communal loos the next day.

Romans in the 1930s may have been cleaner than Romans of the 1840s but they were not much cleaner. Many apartments lacked piped water, which had to be carried in by bucket. Most Roman men did not shave every day and when they did so it was in the evening, using warm water left over from cooking. They washed themselves in the kitchen sink with laundry soap so they smelt like their clothes. Women, most of whom did not work and – as we will see – were discouraged from doing so, washed the next morning, using water from large, cylindrical bed warmers that still had a little faint warmth. They washed standing up with the help of a curious contraption, which consisted of an iron frame with a mirror at the top and two bowls beneath: one for soapy water and another with clean water for rinsing. As electricity was exorbitantly expensive, piped hot water was an impossibility for almost everybody, and even middle-class Romans managed to bathe properly only during warmer weather.

But there was much worse than the Case Popolari. There were the *borgate*: Rome's new outer suburbs. By the late 1930s a fortunate few of these, such as Tiburtina to the east of the city, had managed to evolve into fully functioning parts of the city – Tiburtina had an open air school (chilly in winter but better than nothing) as well as a gym, a Fascist Party office and even a swimming pool. But most *borgate* were slums that lacked drainage or roads. They were a Rome that very few visitors saw. One who did was the French writer Maurice Lachin, who in 1935 toured the *borgate* of Garbatella and Sette Chiese, where he found families crowded into tiny spaces, and some living in caves that had been designated as accommodation by the authorities. The *borgate* were Fascism's dumping grounds. Far from the city centre, they were hard to escape. As well as unfortunates who had lost their homes to Mussolini's demolitions, their inhabitants included all those whom the regime wanted out of the way: the unemployed, the criminal, beggars and unlicensed freelance prostitutes. And of course there were people who were opposed to Fascism who could be more easily watched in such places.

Yet the *borgate* were not Rome's only slums. The city also had others that were not officially sanctioned and had grown up of their own accord, built by those who had nowhere else to go, many of them refugees from acute rural poverty. Homes consisted of shacks that the Romans called *barruché*, after Abyssinian huts. In 1933 there were as many as 6,000 of these in the area beyond Termini railway station. They lacked water, electricity and drainage, and life for their inhabitants would not have been much more comfortable than it had been for Rome's earliest hut-dwelling inhabitants, 2,500 years earlier.

Life under Fascism was not always easy even for affluent Romans, especially if they happened to be female and aspirational. In some ways Roman women had enjoyed better career possibilities in the eleventh century than they did under Fascism. As early as 1920 Mussolini declared that, 'Women are a charming pastime, when a man has time to pass … but they should never be taken seriously.'[7] It was a view he kept. In the early years of Fascism Italy's feminist groups were quickly abolished and though one women's organization was sanctioned by the regime – *Fasci Femminili* – this was not intended to mobilize women but to dispense propaganda to them. In Fascism's view a woman's national duty was to stay at home, support the workforce (their husbands) and raise young Fascists-to-be.

The Church fully agreed, if for different reasons: Fascists wanted women to help them win the Battle of the Births while the Church saw any restraint on procreation as sinful against God. Both stood vehemently against abortion and under Fascist rule any doctors or midwives suspected of offering it were sent into internal exile on a prison island. Both shared the same ideal of womanhood, as sensible, virtuous, plain-living, unadorned – even unsexy – and of course firmly shackled to the home. Fascism especially loathed women with short hair, and derided as neurotic all women who were fashionable, sociable or wore lipstick. Newspapers were forbidden to include photographs of women with small dogs, on the grounds that women should be devoting all their affections to baby Fascists. By contrast prolific mothers were honoured by the state. On 24 December, which was designated Mother and Child Day, mothers with seven, or ideally as many as eleven, children were presented with awards. Fathers of large families gained promotion in state jobs and they and their families enjoyed free medical care, free school meals and free tram tickets. By contrast, men who failed to marry were required to pay a special bachelor tax.

Roman women were positively discouraged from working. In 1934 Mussolini warned them that work was not only dangerous to them but could leave them sterile. As early as 1923 women were banned from being heads of middle schools, or from teaching history or philosophy. In 1939 the state took firmer action, announcing that henceforth women were barred from all management positions, and that a maximum of 10 per cent of professional workers could be female. Yet some opportunities for females continued right through the Fascist years. Roman women could join one of the city's dozens of brothels, which Fascist leaders – nostalgic for their soldiering days – approved of, on the grounds that they toughened up Italian males and provided harmless release for husbands, who might otherwise endanger marital stability by embarking on affairs.

If brothels were permitted, little else was. Here was an aspect of Roman life that a visitor from the 1840s would have found very familiar. As it had been under the train-hating pope Gregory XVI, Rome in the 1930s was a city of moral policing. In the 1840s its streets had been patrolled by priests watching for sexual misbehaviour. In the 1930s they were patrolled by Fascist militiamen. As Maurice Lachin observed in 1935, Rome was no place for lovers: 'True love and sentimental walks have become perilous … It is not wise to venture through the streets of Rome in the company of a woman as there are roundups, in which zealous agents often see wickedness where it does not exist.'[8] Even holding a conversation with a woman could put one in trouble with the militiamen, who patrolled their localities from dusk to dawn. Women required a chaperone to visit the cinema or to go dancing and were excluded from bars. Visitors to dopolavoro clubhouses were almost wholly male. Embracing and kissing in public were strictly prohibited and any woman who seemed to be lingering alone in a public place was likely to be questioned and, even if her papers were in order, might find herself spending a night in jail. Unmarried or separated women about whom gossip circulated, which suggested they were sexually loose, could find themselves arrested and removed to one of the country's prison islands.

As well as unromantic, 1930s Rome had next to no nightlife. When Simone de Beauvoir and Jean-Paul Sartre visited the city in 1932 they found the night-time streets almost empty. Feeling rebellious they decided to provoke Fascism a little and to stay up till dawn. At midnight they sat chatting beside one of the fountains of a deserted Piazza Navona, till they were approached by two Blackshirts. As Simone de Beauvoir recounted, 'That we were tourists won their indulgence but they told us firmly to go to bed.' Undaunted, the couple moved to the Colosseum, where at three in the morning they were approached again: 'A light shone on us. What were we doing?

This time it seemed that our behaviour was indecent even for tourists. Sighing at the thought of a long, Madrid night, we ended up going back to the hotel.'⁹ It was as if Mussolini had transformed Rome into a vast version of the local town where he had grown up: sleepy, respectable, dull Predappio.

Yet if it was dull, Rome could also be dangerous. As a foreigner, Simone de Beauvoir knew she was unlikely to get into trouble, but Romans had no such confidence. In the 1930s many of them imagined they were being watched and often they were. Between 1926 and 1943 some 40,000 Italians were placed under surveillance, monitored by three separate spying agencies, which were also bitter rivals. Between them they ran hundreds of informers who operated networks of sub-informers. Post was opened, houses searched and 400 stenographers diligently typed out tapped telephone conversations. Hoteliers were required by law to report on guests, doctors had to report on patients who suffered from alcoholism or mental illness, and bar owners lost their licences if they refused to spy on their customers. Even architecture was put to use: the Case Popolari were given few entrances so it was easier for police to keep watch on their inhabitants.

Fascism's surveillance was so successful that it almost put itself out of business. By the early 1930s its main targets, anti-Fascist groups, were largely broken. New targets were found in anyone the regime found un-Fascist or distasteful. Homosexuality was not illegal under Fascism, as the regime refused to admit it existed, but gay men were watched and arrested, along with the mentally ill, alcoholics, pimps, loan sharks, child abusers, drug dealers and Jehovah's Witnesses. Rome of the 1930s was an anxious city where people were careful what they said in public. Though some were more anxious than others. As was usually the case with Fascism, life was much easier if one was respectably wealthy and had Fascist connections. In 1936 George Mosse, a Jew who had recently escaped from Germany to Italy, found himself on a train when, to his alarm, his well-dressed fellow passengers began telling Mussolini jokes, though a carabinieri officer was within easy earshot. As Mosse had feared, the officer walked over to them, only to begin telling Mussolini jokes of his own. The situation would probably have been very different if jokes had been told by someone who was poor or drunk, who had mental problems, or was known to be idle, a loudmouth, or an old leftist. In other words, someone with an anarchist streak like Mussolini's father, or for that matter like Mussolini himself in his younger days.

Such people could find themselves in deep trouble over the most trivial of matters. Late on a hot summer's night in 1937 a middle-aged tinsmith and former anarchist named Ruggeri Leggi was enjoying rides with friends on a roundabout in Piazza dei Coronari in the centre of Rome. When a killjoy civil servant fetched a squad of militiamen to have the roundabout shut down for the night, Ruggeri, who had been drinking, grumbled to the militiamen that he would do whatever he wanted as he was free and couldn't care less about the law. He was given three years of internal exile. In the north of Italy another known troublemaker was sentenced to a year's internal exile because he placed his pet rabbit on a restaurant table and told it, 'Move it, Mussolini.'

In October 1938 a whole new group of Romans found they were now viewed with suspicion by the state: the Jews. In previous years, the regime, though it contained several vehement anti-Semites, had been tolerant of its Jewish citizens. Then, Fascism had many Jewish supporters. Among Rome's Jewish community was the city's deputy police chief. Everything changed when Mussolini, eager to keep up with his ally Hitler, introduced the 1938 Racial Laws. For a brief time these were harsher even than those of Germany, and they became more restrictive the following year. Jews were banned from holding positions in the army, the police and from teaching in universities or schools. Jewish children were excluded from Italian state education, forcing Jewish Romans hurriedly to improvise a school of their own. Some restrictions were small-minded and mean, such as the ban on Jews from taking holidays by the sea or riding in trams. Others were grimly familiar. As they had been in previous centuries, Jews were prohibited from professions and from managing shops. They were allowed only to sell goods from small, portable stalls and

Announcement in a Fascist magazine explaining the activities from which Jewish people are excluded, from La Difesa della Razza, *5 November 1938.*

eventually not even from these. But, as ever in a country where most arrangements were personal and complicated, there were exemptions, notably for Jews who had been wounded in the First World War. As Jewish Romans had felt strongly patriotic towards the state that had freed them, there were a good number of these.

When it came to those who got on the wrong side of the government, Fascism liked to boast that, when compared to the Soviet Union, it was not a murderous regime, and in some ways this was true. The death penalty was used sparingly and between 1926 and 1943 only twenty-five people were executed in Italy for political crimes. Yet if Fascism did not take many Italian lives, it wrecked many. In this same period 10,000 Italians were sent into internal exile, the great majority of them male and breadwinners, whose absence left their dependent families in a desperate state. Numerous letters from internal exiles have survived – many addressed to Mussolini himself – praising the regime in lavish terms and with their writers begging to be released, or for their families to be given support.

Even lesser punishments could be devastating. Fascism grew out of violence – squads of ex-soldiers beating up their political enemies – and for all Mussolini's attempts to make the movement respectable, violence was never far from its heart. In the late 1930s militiamen of the MSVN – an organization that evolved directly from the squads of the early days – routinely beat up people who failed to take off their hats when a Fascist procession went by. They raided districts – Rome's working-class area of San Lorenzo was a favourite choice and, after 1938, the Ghetto – where they smashed up shops and bars. They took people back to their headquarters to beat them up again, or force-feed them castor oil or petrol. Some victims died or were left with permanent injuries, while in a land obsessed with status to soil oneself in public after a dose of castor oil was a kind of death – of reputation.

Fascism could cause havoc to people's lives simply by exclusion. People who offended the regime, by failing to enrol their children in the Fascist youth movement or by making a joke to the wrong person, could find that their party membership, their work permit or their Fascist Trades Union card was withdrawn, and that they had no job, no livelihood and no social benefits. Fascism extinguished people's very joy of life. One of the regime's most surprising achievements was that it made the Romans – a people who were famously loud – go quiet. The French writer Béraud lamented the silence of Rome, where even singing a song could be dangerous if, like one that had the refrain, 'don't get angry, life is short', it was regarded as anti-Fascist. By the late 1930s spies employed to inform the government on the state of the nation complained that their work was becoming impossible as people refused to speak in public. On trains and trams if someone started badmouthing the regime – usually one who was drunk or had mental problems, as nobody else would be so rash – others would quickly shut them up, fearful that simply hearing this could put them in trouble.

One of Fascism's many victims was Fascism itself. Beyond the law and beyond criticism, Fascists high and low quickly became corrupt.

Militiamen engaged in theft, extortion, confidence tricks, violence and sometimes murder. Leading Fascists who had been born poor grew mysteriously wealthy. Local Fascist leaders were seen eating in the best restaurants – often without paying the bill – and went on lavish holidays. Their wives used official cars to go shopping for the latest fashions. People waiting in the interminably slow bureaucratic offices saw Fascists and their friends and relatives jump the queue. The lower a Fascist's rank, the more pompous and bullying his or her (it was almost always his) behaviour. Fascism could also be used. People denounced their neighbours, sometimes to win favour with the regime, sometimes to settle old scores.

The pattern was set at the very top and part of the problem lay with Mussolini himself. He was not himself avaricious but he was willing to tolerate failings, including corruption, in his close colleagues if it gave him scandalous information on them that might prove useful. Fascists further sullied their reputation by hurling dirt at one another. When fighting local power battles they would publicly accuse one another of sexual transgression with prostitutes, mistresses, other Fascists' wives, and occasionally with men. By the late 1930s even honest Fascists were widely assumed to be corrupt.

Some Romans saw that, for all its boasts, Fascism was also incompetent. Aside from the draining of the Pontine Marshes, most of its great campaigns were failures. The Battle of the Births had no discernible impact on the country's declining birth rate. The Battle of the Grain increased wheat production but had a woeful effect on all other farming. The Battle of the Lira made exports and tourism less competitive, helping to push Italy into a deep economic crisis two years before the Wall Street Crash. Under the elected Liberal governments that Mussolini so despised, Italy had had one of Europe's fastest-growing economies, ahead even of Germany's. Under Fascism it was one of the slowest. By the end of the 1930s even the new African Empire was in trouble, as local guerrilla insurgencies began to turn Abyssinia into an Italian Vietnam.

Finally, Fascist propaganda was a failure. By the late '30s few

Italians believed it or took any notice. Despite a dozen years of state hectoring, in 1937 young Italian females had no wish to spend their lives siring eleven children: most felt one or two would be enough. Nor did they intend to stay at home cooking: most wanted to work, ideally in a good profession. In October 1938 when the state turned against its Jewish citizens, Romans remained thoroughly unconvinced. By 1939 spy reports to the Fascist leadership reluctantly admitted that Romans had been 'conditioned by an unrelenting compassion for the Jews',[10] who they felt had done nothing wrong. Priests attacked the Racial Laws and Romans were overheard saying that the city's Jews were better than many Christians, being often more able in business, more honest and more compassionate to the poor. Another report stated that 'everyone said the government was wrong, everyone said that this nastiness will soon be over'.[11] Even high Fascist officials insisted the Jews were no danger to the state and some gave shelter to Jews fleeing from other countries.

Yet, arguably Fascism's greatest failure was in the very campaign that Mussolini had most set his heart on: to remould the Italians as a driven, aggressive nation. In the 1930s, in the hands of the pedantic Fascist Party Secretary Achille Starace, the project became not inspirational but irritating. Italians were told not to wear slippers, in an anti-bourgeois campaign to shake them from their complacency. State officials were forced to buy and wear Fascist uniforms that were expensive and itchy. Instead of shaking hands, which was denounced as unhygienic, Romans had to greet one another with the raised right arm of the Roman salute. And they were told to stop addressing one another with the traditional *lei*, instead using the plural *voi*, which was seen as tougher and more formal. Spy reports admitted that almost nobody used *voi*, while those who did often did so facetiously, with a smirk.

By the late 1930s it was evident that Fascism was in deep trouble. On paper it was more successful than ever. It faced no opposition and between 1931 and 1938 party membership had swelled from 800,000 to five million. Italians assembled in huge crowds for the ever-growing number of Fascist meetings and Fascist marches. Yet it was a hollow triumph. Spy reports to the regime's leaders warned that enthusiasm for Fascism was largely dead. Rather than making Italians dynamic, Fascism's control had made them apathetic. They joined the party and turned up for marches and meetings because they had no choice. At the entrances to Piazza Venezia, where Mussolini made his famous speeches from the balcony, Fascist militiamen set up tables to collect people's party cards so they could see who had failed to appear. In October 1935, when demonstrations were organized to cheer his announcement of Italy's invasion of Abyssinia, arriving demonstrators panicked when they found the militiamen had not turned up.

By the end of 1938 apathy turned to loathing, and largely because of coffee, or rather the lack of it. The government's latest campaign, for national self-sufficiency or Autarky – a riposte to League of Nations' sanctions against Italy for invading Abyssinia – had caused a grave economic crisis. Prices rose and the government, short of money, became grasping, increasing the costs of union dues. As exports struggled, imports became unaffordable and the country grew short of oil, sugar and, most of all, coffee. Romans found themselves taking their morning break in coffee-less bars or queuing for hours for their supply. As they queued they complained, if quietly. Until then senior figures in the regime such as Starace had been hated but Mussolini had remained largely above criticism, the Teflon dictator. In May 1939 government spies noted an alarming rise in Mussolini jokes, such as, *What does M stand for? Misery.*

Not that the regime was in danger. For all its unpopularity Fascism's machinery of control remained intact and was staffed by people who had much to lose if the government fell. Left to itself, the dictatorship would probably have endured for many more years. To discover the reason why it did not one can go to a spot just to the south-east of Rome's ancient Aurelian Walls. Here in the spring of 1938 a gleaming new railway station had just been built to impress a visitor to the city: Adolf Hitler. Having stopped at Florence to enjoy the art, he arrived in Rome on the evening of 3 May. He had quite a welcome. Thousands of citizens had been organized to cheer

and wave along the railway route. Ostiense station, which was hung
with vast eagles and swastikas, was decorated with two gigantic
murals, one representing Mussolini and Fascism, the other Hitler and
Nazism. Even street names offered a welcome. The short road from
the station to Porta San Paolo was now Viale Adolf Hitler and the
adjoining square, which contained his statue, was Piazza Adolf Hitler.
Hitler's motorcade took him along Mussolini's new boulevards: past
the Colosseum, across the fora to Piazza Venezia and then to the
Quirinal Palace. During Hitler's stay, which lasted several days, he
and Mussolini visited the Foro Mussolini to watch young Fascists
mass into a huge M and then a swastika.

The new alliance, though, was never popular in Italy. Germany,
and especially Austria, were the country's traditional enemies, against
whom the struggle for national unification had been fought. To make
matters worse, by 1938 it was clear that Mussolini was very much the
junior member of the partnership. Hitler did as he liked – shortly
before his visit to Rome he had, without a word of warning, annexed
Mussolini's client state of Austria – while Mussolini emulated and
tried to impress, commanding Italians to goosestep, to do Roman
salutes and to turn against their Jews.

Almost no Italians wanted war. They had enough trouble paying
bills and finding coffee. But on 10 June 1940 – nine months after his
ally Hitler – Mussolini went to war with France and Britain. His
chief motive was fear. With France on the verge of capitulation he
was worried he would lose his place at the peace conference and miss
out on his share of the spoils. American Colonel J. Hanley watched
the huge crowd summoned to Piazza Venezia to cheer Mussolini's
declaration of war and he observed that people seemed glum and
subdued. Later he heard that Italian newsreels of the event had
had to be dubbed with cheering from sports events. According to
government surveillance reports some Italians accepted that one had
to be on the winning side but many felt ashamed at stabbing their old
ally France in the back. Only a few students and keen Fascists showed
any enthusiasm for the conflict.

The instincts of the Piazza Venezia crowd were soon proved right. Romans blacked out their windows and Fascist militiamen yelled *Luce* if they saw a glimmer of light, but Mussolini never did take his place at the peace conference. Three years later Italy was still fighting, now against Free France, Brazil, Britain, the Soviet Union and the United States. Newspapers reported regular German and Italian victories in Russia and North Africa yet these victories crept obstinately closer to home. By early 1943 it was clear to all that the conflict would be lost. As to what had gone wrong, the subject of this book is Rome, not Italy in the Second World War, yet one myth is worth disposing of: that Italians were somehow incapable of fighting. They had fought bravely in the First World War and with some success, despite facing enemies who were wealthier and better equipped. Even during the Second World War one Italian unit, the Folgore Parachute Division, proved highly effective in the North African war against the British, who regarded it with great respect. But it had been trained by Germans.

The Italians did poorly in the Second World War for two reasons: because it was a war they did not believe in and because they were disastrously let down by their rulers. Though Fascism had poured money into the military it got very little for its lira. Poorly supervised industry produced submarines that were dangerous to their crews, bombers whose engines regularly failed (and whose test data was falsified), a fighter plane that was considered the worst in Europe and tanks that were so tiny and thinly armoured that Italians called them sardine cans. Italy's military was bloated with too many officers and too many empty boasts. In 1939 the air force claimed it had 8,500 aircraft ready for war when it actually had a tenth as many. Mussolini was no better. As war approached he claimed that Italy had twelve million bayonets in 150 well-equipped divisions when in fact the country had ten divisions, all of them below strength and none properly equipped. Some had guns that had been captured from the Austrians in 1918. Once again Fascism compared poorly with the elected, Liberal governments Mussolini so despised. Italy had been far better prepared when it went to war in 1915.

Finally there was the problem of Mussolini himself. Hitler has been accused of disastrously overruling his generals. Mussolini, who was minister of war, of the air force and the navy, would not even allow them to attend his strategic meetings. As a war leader he was both too aggressive and too timid, he vastly overestimated his country's capabilities and, most of all, he kept changing his mind. In the autumn of 1940 when Britain was beaten and vulnerable, he sent his bombers to Belgium to raid London (which it emerged they did not have the range to reach) and dispatched his trucks to Trieste in readiness for an invasion of Croatia, only to decide that he would attack British Egypt instead. Lacking trucks, proper air cover, and protected by their feeble sardine can tanks, Italian soldiers had to walk across the desert, to be overwhelmed by a British force a tenth their size.

Defeat followed defeat yet Fascism staggered on, zombie-like. By the spring of 1943 it had lost the power even to frighten its own citizens. Government spies wrote despairingly that in theatres and cinemas, on trams, trains and in air raid shelters people denounced the regime quite openly, blaming Mussolini as readily as the rest. As they turned their backs on their government, Italians looked to their pope. The population of Rome, which, unlike other Italian cities had not yet been bombed, grew to two million as people fled there, hoping Pius XII's presence would keep them safe. The number of people who applied to join the priesthood, and so could avoid being called up, likewise swelled.

Even now Rome hardly felt like a city at war. Unlike in Britain or Russia there was no mass mobilization of the nation. When M. de Wyss visited the beach at Ostia she found Rome's coastline was guarded by two soldiers who had to share a pair of boots. Mussolini's great construction projects had all ground to a halt, and the opening of the vast E-42 exhibition of Fascism was indefinitely postponed, but the regime did its best to keep up its propaganda war, celebrating its 20th anniversary with a third (and last) *Mostra della Rivoluzione Fascista* in the Museum of Modern Art. Its main purpose was to promote the war effort and the racial campaign. A *Sala del*

Cinema displayed carefully selected film stills of well-known actors in military roles: Americans and British looking scared or foolish and Italians looking tough. Other exhibits and caricatures warned of the danger to the nation posed by Africans and Jews, and photographs of classical statues and lookalike modern Italians were placed side by side to show the enduring purity of the race. On 10 May 1943, as in previous years, Empire Day was celebrated, and posters appeared depicting Italians in colonial helmets, despite the fact that every inch of Italy's African Empire had now been lost. Optimistically the posters declared, 'Torneremo!' (We will return!) though some were rewritten by Romans as 'Perderemo!' (We will lose!)

III

Romans' prediction came good on the evening of 8 September 1943, when Marshal Badoglio announced the country's surrender to the Allies. Romans celebrated in the streets, if more warily than they had when Mussolini had been deposed six weeks earlier. They hoped that the Allies would appear quickly and that their war would be over.

When she woke the next morning M. de Wyss was cautiously optimistic. Everything seemed much as usual. Walking through the city centre she saw a young Roman striding off to a tennis party with his racquet. True, from the early hours of the morning she had heard the faint sound of guns, which seemed to be growing gradually louder, but there was no knowing whose guns they were. The newspapers were no help. They had announced the armistice but regretfully, like a spouse who is leaving a marriage but hopes that the separation will be amicable. To add to the confusion some papers also offered stirring – and quite untrue – reports from the Calabrian front, describing how German and Italian units had pushed the Allies back. Romans were told to remain calm as the Italian authorities negotiated the transfer of German forces to the north. As the well-informed de Wyss knew, Rome was ringed by large numbers of Italian troops, including a well-equipped motorized division, who should have been able to keep the Germans at bay till the Allies appeared.

Leading figures on the German side fully agreed. The Allies were landing forces at Salerno and Hitler worried that his troops in the south of Italy would be cut off unless they retreated without delay. His commander in southern Italy, Albert Kesselring, who had his headquarters just south of Rome at Frascati – in chaos after a devastating American bombing raid – concurred. He expected the Allies to drop parachutists in Rome and perhaps make a further sea landing near the city. The Italian forces around Rome far outnumbered his own and Badoglio, Kesselring assumed, would already be moving them against him. Kesselring ordered his troops near Rome to advance on the city and test the water. In the city centre German diplomats burned documents and sent their families away. Neither de Wyss not Kesselring knew the shameful truth. In all the previous attacks on Rome examined in this book, its defenders were sometimes incompetent or ineffective, yet the city was never so badly served as it was by the former Fascists, and those who had risen high under Fascism, who governed in early September 1943.

Italy's armistice with the Allies had been secretly signed on 3 September at Cassabile in Sicily and was to be announced five days later. The Allied commander in the Mediterranean, Eisenhower, sought to make good use of the time left to him before the news broke. As Kesselring had guessed, Eisenhower had arranged that 2,000 parachutists would descend on Rome on the evening of 8 September to secure the city's airfields and help Italian forces defend the city from German attack, and the next day his troops would land at Salerno. To prepare for the parachute drop two US generals, Taylor and Gardiner, were smuggled into Rome the evening before. Arriving in the city late they soon became concerned by what they found. They were taken to the Palazzo Caprara beside the Ministry of War where, instead of being introduced to key figures engaged in Rome's defence as they had expected, they were brought a splendid meal from the nearby Grand Hotel, which included consommé, veal with vegetables, crêpe suzette and vintage wine. Losing patience, they demanded to see Badoglio and were driven to his grandiose home. It was a discouraging meeting. Badoglio, who the Americans had supposed would be frantically preparing for the next day's events, was fast asleep and had to be woken. While they waited his nephew explained that the announcement of the armistice would have to be delayed by a few days as nothing was ready, and the parachute drop should be cancelled as the Germans had taken all the available fuel. Badoglio, when he eventually appeared, looked scared. 'I'm an old general who has won two wars,' he told the Americans. 'Don't leave me to the Germans. If they catch me …'[12] He made a sign of his throat being cut.

He and Vittorio Emmanuele had had five days to prepare for Italy's surrender yet all they had done was look after themselves. Vittorio Emanuele sent his daughter-in-law to Switzerland and Badoglio sent relatives both there and to Tangiers. It was only in the afternoon of 8 September, when the announcement of Italy's armistice was imminent, that the king finally held a meeting with his ministers and military chiefs at the Quirinal Palace to consider what to do. The Minister of War, Antonio Sorice, and General Carboni, both of whom were nervous of the German response to Italy's unilateral surrender, proposed that the Italians should pretend that they had not surrendered after all. Major Marchesi, the assistant to the king's chief minister, Ambrosiano, who had been present at the surrender in Sicily, scotched the idea, pointing out that the Americans had filmed the whole ceremony. Then discussion became irrelevant, as news arrived that Eisenhower was speaking on the radio and announcing the armistice. The king declared, 'Now there's no doubt,'[13] and Badoglio hurried to Rome's broadcasting centre on Via Asiago, to announce it, too.

From that moment Italy's rulers behaved less like a government and more like a theatre audience wondering what would happen next. Badoglio, the king and a number of high ministers assembled at the Ministry of War on Via XX Settembre. At this stage reports suggested that the Germans were retreating north. After a modest dinner, Badoglio and the royal family, who were all early sleepers, went to bed. The king and queen took the precaution of sleeping in their clothes. When everyone woke shortly before dawn they were told that the Germans had cut off all routes out of Rome except one, which led east to the Apennines and the Adriatic.

There was little or no discussion as to what should be done. Then again, this was a moment that Vittorio Emanuele had been anticipating for some time. Ever since he had deposed Mussolini he had kept a naval vessel at Civitavecchia ready to whisk him away. Just after five in the morning he, his family, Badoglio and their helpers assembled with their luggage in a courtyard of the Ministry of War and a convoy of seven cars took them on to Via Napoli, made its way up the Via Nazionale, past Termini station, San Lorenzo and out of the city. So fled Italy's royal family and head of state. The only one who was troubled was the heir to the throne, Prince Umberto, whom everyone called Beppo, and who said, 'Dio Mio! Che figura!' ('My God, how bad we'll look'.) His mother, Queen Elena, told him sharply in French, 'You're not going back, Beppo. They'll kill you.' Badoglio, pale and nervous, kept murmuring to himself, 'If they get us they'll cut all our throats.'[14]

Some seventy more cars followed soon afterwards and that afternoon the small port of Ortona on the Adriatic was crammed with royals, government ministers and generals, anxiously waiting for a boat to take them away. Though not everyone of high rank was there. In Rome a group of anti-Fascist partisans paid a visit to the Ministry of Trade and Industry. The main door was wide open and there were signs of a chaotic departure. In the main meeting room they found the minister, Leopoldo Piccardi, with his head in his hands. 'I'm all alone,' he told them despairingly. 'They left me. They ran.'[15]

Yet fleeing Rome and abandoning their people was not the worst thing that the king and his government did that day. Worse were the instructions they left. Two clear orders were issued. First, the navy was told to send the cruiser *Scipione* and two corvettes to collect a group of 'high personages' (the king and his government) and take them south to Allied territory. Second, the army commander Roatta ordered the armoured division outside Rome – the most effective Italian unit – to proceed to Tivoli, east of the city, to establish an eastern front. As there was no enemy to establish a front against (the Germans were behind them, advancing on Rome) Roatta's purpose was obvious. The division was to cover the country's rulers' flight. Rome was denuded of its most capable defenders to help its leaders escape.

Changing sides in the middle of a war was never going to be easy but it was not even attempted. A few of the more fanatical Fascists favoured the Germans but most Italian troops felt little liking for them and would, if clearly instructed, have fought to defend their country. Their orders, though, were anything but clear. Even Badoglio's announcement of the surrender had been murkily ambiguous. He told Italian forces to 'Cease all hostile acts against the Anglo-Americans,' and to 'Oppose attacks by all hostile forces.'[16] During the night of 8 September, as the king slept in his clothes in the Ministry of War, his chief minister Ambrosiano sent out an order forbidding Italian forces from taking hostile action against the Germans, and instructing them that if Germans advanced without aggression they were to let them pass through their positions. Ambrosiano evidently hoped that if the Italians did not aggravate the Germans they would go away. By contrast there was nothing ambiguous about the orders of Field Marshal Kesselring, who, as the Allies' Salerno landing became bogged down, began to change his mind about abandoning Rome. He told his troops that the Italians were to be disarmed and if necessary attacked, adding that, 'There is no need to show any pity towards these traitors. Heil Hitler!'[17]

Some Italians fought bravely. South of Rome at the Magliana Bridge, beneath the half-constructed buildings of Mussolini's E-42 exhibition area, Germans holding a white flag advanced on a position held by the First Regiment of Sardinian Grenadiers. The Italian commander went to meet them, only to be cut down by machine-gun fire. His soldiers reacted furiously and a battle began that lasted through the night, with the Italians several times losing and retaking their position. The Germans also struggled north of Rome near Monterotondo, where a force of their paratroopers became pinned down by Italian soldiers and local hunters, so badly that by the evening of 9 September, having lost 300 men killed or wounded, the Germans were forced to seek a truce.

Elsewhere, though, the Germans met little resistance. They soon grasped the orders that Italians had been given and advanced on their positions with white flags, then trained their guns on the Italians, disarming them and killing any who resisted. Many Italians, having long ago lost all belief in their government and the war, threw away their weapons, changed their uniforms for civilian clothes and made themselves scarce. The entire La Piacenza division dissolved without trace. Soldiers were also let down by their commanders. Some abandoned their troops. One officer left to make sure his prize racehorses were safe and when he returned to his battalion, three hours later, found it had vanished. A very few units, which included two battalions of Blackshirts, joined the Germans.

By the morning of 10 September the Germans were advancing towards the centre of Rome. Confusion reigned. Streets were deserted, doors and shutters were closed, and buses and trams stood abandoned in mid-journey. Civilians seized weapons, some of which they found in the streets left by deserting soldiers. Carabinieri, concerned to keep order, tried to stop them. A second diarist of these days, who published an account under the name of Jane Scrivener but was later revealed to have been an American nun in Rome, Mother Mary St Luke, saw a column of German prisoners being marched down a street by their Italian guards and assumed the Italians were winning. At eleven she heard that a deal had been struck and that the Germans had agreed not to enter Rome. By noon shells were landing on the city and Italian guns were firing back. In front of Termini railway station German soldiers fired from the window of the Continentale Hotel and were attacked by grenadiers in armoured cars and tram workers throwing bombs.

By the late morning the Germans were close to Porta San Paolo and Ostiense railway station: the same spot where, five years earlier,

Hitler had been welcomed by the cheering crowds. A mixed bag of volunteers hurried to meet them, including Catholic Communists, Bersaglieri soldiers from their barracks in nearby Trastevere and a crowd led by an actor, Carlo Nichi; many of them were unarmed. By one in the afternoon fighting was intense around the Piazza Adolf Hitler in front of the San Paolo Gate but it was a hopelessly unequal struggle. For all their numbers and passion the defenders had no organization, many soldiers had only a few rounds left and their tanks stood no chance against German Panzers. To make matters worse, news was spreading that the king and his government had fled the city. By the afternoon the Germans had broken through Porta San Paolo and were advancing along the same route Hitler had taken in his motorcade: along the Viale Africa to the Colosseum and then down the Via dell'Impero to the Piazza Venezia.

A final battle took place at Termini. A hundred officers and soldiers from Monterotondo arrived on a sequestered train, a small artillery piece on the engine, to help the Romans. They set up machine guns on the platforms, railwaymen fought at their side and it took five hours for the Germans to overwhelm them. The railwaymen they executed. By six in the evening Mother Mary found all was quiet. On the street below her convent she saw German cars speeding by while little knots of Romans talked anxiously together. When she turned on her radio, the Rome station, which before had played only music, she found now broadcast in German or in Italian spoken with a strong German accent.

Rome was occupied.

In the first few days Rome experienced the twentieth-century equivalent of a sacking, which was fairly mild compared to what the city had endured in the past. As businesses reopened and hungry Romans emerged on the streets seeking food, German soldiers looted shops, mugged people of their valuables, took cars and bicycles at gunpoint, and a few Roman women suffered the horror of rape. Romans comforted themselves with the thought that the Allies would

Left: *Allied propaganda urging Italians to join them against the Germans: 'They're kicked out of Sicily. Let's kick them out of Italy.'*

Below: *Allied propaganda against the Social Italian Republic, which was Fascism raised from the grave, after Mussolini was freed from royal captors at an Apennine ski resort by German parachutists.*

arrive soon. Even the gloomiest expected them within two weeks. It would prove to be a very optimistic prediction.

The first bad news came on the evening of 18 September when Romans were treated to a moment of unwanted nostalgia. On their radios they heard Mussolini's voice, praising Hitler, railing bitterly against the king and urging Italians to support him. He sounded so weak that many doubted it was really Mussolini, but it was. He had been rescued a few days earlier in a daring German raid on the Apennine ski resort where he had been held. His escape was bad news for the Romans. He proclaimed himself leader of a new Social Italian Republic and, though he was little more than a German puppet leader, his return provided a rallying point for true believers, and for those who were so compromised that there was no turning back. Fascism, which had seemed dead, staggered back to life. With the example of the Germans beside them, Italy's desperate new Fascists would prove much worse than the old. In early October they set up their Roman headquarters in Palazzo Wedekind on Piazza Colonna, which they guarded with tanks and machine guns.

As the Germans settled in they became more active. Romans of military age were told to report to the authorities for military service or labour. When hardly any did so the Germans seized some on the street. Roundups had begun. The city already had many in hiding, including a thousand freed British prisoners of war along with large numbers of anti-Fascists, and Italian soldiers and officers, and now the numbers swelled. A popular joke of the moment described a group of tourists who asked their guide where they could find the statue of Moses, only to be told that, 'For some days he has been staying in the home of friends.' People hid in convents, in hospitals, and even in the lunatic asylum, causing de Wyss to comment that Rome had never had so many madmen. Most hid in private homes and it became a commonplace that half of Rome was hiding the other half. Large bounties were offered for the surrender of the British prisoners of war and death was threatened to any who concealed them, yet few if any were given up. One elderly Roman woman who hid several

British prisoners told de Wyss that she understood the risks but then she thought of how the prisoners each had a mother worrying about them, and she knew she had to keep them.

On 6 October it was the turn of the king's tall Cuirassier guards to be taken. There was further revenge against the king when the Villa Ada Savoia – where Vittorio Emanuele had had Mussolini arrested – was looted of furniture, paintings, statues, tapestries and even, as Mother Mary reported, bed linen. 'Everything went, including the nails in the walls.'[18] On 8 October the Germans moved against the Carabinieri: the elite police force whose loyalty had always been to the king and who had played a key role in Mussolini's arrest: 1,500 of them were taken away to Germany, many never to return. Fortunately, word of the arrests spread quickly and another 5,000 escaped capture.

The most terrible roundup, though, was yet to come: of Rome's Jews. A fortunate few had left Italy before the war began, when the Racial Laws were first introduced, but most had nowhere to go and no money to take them there. News that the Germans were advancing on the city led some Jews to go into hiding and a wise few stayed hidden, but as days passed and nothing happened most re-emerged. They could not afford to stay without work and did not want to keep imposing on their Catholic friends. Besides, they were the world's oldest Jewish community, who had survived for more than two thousand years and repeated papal attempts to convert them out of existence.

Warnings came. BBC radio broadcast stories of massacres and camps with gas chambers. Rome's chief rabbi, Israel Zolli, who had been brought up in Eastern Europe and knew about pogroms, urged that the synagogue be closed and that the Jewish community should be told to hide or leave the city. Two Jewish Romans, Renzo Levi and Settimio Sorani, who ran the local branch of an Italian Jewish refugee organization DELASEM, and who knew precisely what was happening to Jews in the concentration camps, urged Jews to go south to Allied-controlled territory. There were also warnings, more surprisingly, from Germans in the city, notably two diplomats, the German ambassador to the Holy See, Baron Ernst von Weizsäcker, and his secretary, Albrecht von Kessel. Neither had any liking for the Nazis – Kessel was strongly outspoken against them and Weizsäcker, who was an old-fashioned aristocrat, despised them – and both were as aware as the two DELASEM officials of the fate of Jews elsewhere in Europe (Weizsäcker had personally seen the minutes of the Wahnsee conference that launched the Final Solution). Kessel asked a Swiss contact, Alfred Fahrener, to have Jewish Romans linked to the Vatican spread the word that the community was in grave danger.

Sadly, few Roman Jews took these warnings seriously. The BBC reports were assumed to be the exaggerations of Allied propaganda and Rabbi Zolli was an outsider and not much liked. Besides, so far the Germans had done nothing aggressive. Most Jewish Romans agreed with their community president, Ugo Foà, who assured them that they were safe enough. They were a relatively small community of about 12,000 people and Foà felt they would be of little interest to the Germans, who would not want to risk trouble with the pope. The important thing, he believed, was that Roman Jews should do nothing to give the Germans cause to act against them. They should keep a low profile and quietly carry on with their lives. The furnishings of the Jewish Temple were removed and hidden but no other precautions were taken.

The first move against Jewish Romans came on Sunday 26 September when the Gestapo chief in the city, SS Major Herbert Kappler, summoned the Jewish community's two leaders, Ugo Foà and Dante Almansi, to his office at the main German embassy, Villa Wolkonsky. He told them that Rome's Jews must hand over a ransom of 50 kilograms of gold within two days or 200 of them would be deported. If they paid up, no Jews would suffer any harm. Though some doubted Kappler's promise, most felt he would keep his word. If this seems naïve, Giacomo Debenedetti, a Jewish Roman writer, had an explanation: 'Convinced by centuries of experience that their fate is to be treated like dogs, Jews have a desperate need for human sympathy; and to solicit it, they offer it. Will they behave this way with the Germans? Yes, unfortunately.'[19] Debenedetti also felt that

Jews, thanks to their religious beliefs, had a deep-rooted acceptance of authority and expectation of justice. Nazi beliefs, by contrast, were simpler. Whatever impression Jews might give, all of them were determined enemies of the German people.

The morning after Kappler made his demand a collection point was set up in a room on the second floor of the synagogue complex. At first, few came and a delegation was sent to the Vatican to seek help. Pius XII offered an interest-free loan but in the event it was not needed, as by early afternoon a long queue had formed below the synagogue. Most were poor Jews from the Ghetto area, whose offerings were tiny but when added together soon formed a considerable amount. Rich donors gave generously, and included Christian Romans. When the gold was handed over Rome's Jews felt relieved, convinced that they were now out of danger. Sadly, they could not have been more wrong. The very day before he first demanded the gold, Kappler had received orders from Berlin that Rome's Jews were to be rounded up and deported. Evidence suggests that Kappler organized the gold demand – which was wholly his idea – because he knew he would not be ready to round the Jews up for several weeks and wanted to distract them so they would not go to ground. His ploy succeeded. The Jews were dismayed by further shocks. German troops seized all of the community's documents and later they seized the books of the community's two libraries, which included priceless ancient volumes that had never been catalogued or studied (and which have never been recovered: they were lost to Allied bombing on their journey north or, as some Jewish Romans believe, remain hidden in Germany). Yet even these shocks caused few to go into hiding.

One man tried to save the community from catastrophe and once again, he was a German. Eitel Friedrich Möllhausen, who was the acting German ambassador not to the Vatican but to the Italian state, learned of the roundup order when it first reached Major Kappler. Möllhausen at once drove to Frascati to persuade Kesselring that Jews should not be rounded up but should be used as forced labour: an arrangement Kesselring had employed for Tunisian Jews. Kesselring, who had no troops to spare for any roundups, willingly agreed. Unfortunately Möllhausen's efforts were in vain. The SS in Berlin, realizing that obstacles were being put in their way by local German officials, circumvented them. An SS force under Captain Theodor Dannecker, who had presided over the roundup of Parisian Jews the previous year, was sent to Rome with a detachment of troops.

The first that Rome's Jews knew of Dannecker's arrival was in the early morning of 16 October, when inhabitants of the Ghetto were woken by the sound of exploding grenades and shots fired at their windows. The attack, which lasted for several hours, was intended to keep them in their homes, and it succeeded. At five thirty, as autumn rain poured down, soldiers sealed off the area and began banging on doors.

It is hard to conceive that anything good could come from what happened that day but one solitary thing did: a forty-page account by Giacomo Debenedetti, entitled, *October 16 1943*. Debenedetti's brief masterpiece recounts the unfolding horror not dispassionately – how could it have? – but with a sense of precise, bitter observation, that included the Germans involved. He portrays them not as purposefully cruel but as hurried, and brutal because brutality helped them complete their task. Thus the SS soldiers were constantly shouting, 'For no good reason, probably only to maintain an air of terror and a sense of authority, so that they wouldn't run into any snags and the whole thing would be done quickly.'[20] They did what they had been told and, with one or two exceptions, nothing more. They followed the lists of names they had been given – most of which came from a register kept up under Mussolini's Racial Laws – and banged on doors. To those who answered they gave cards that told them they had twenty minutes to get ready and listed what they must take. Debenedetti imagines their thinking: 'The good glasses – it'll be better to leave them at home. And suitcases, where are we going to get one for everybody? The children will just have to share.'[21]

Some Germans did less than they had been ordered. One woman, whom Debenedetti refers to as Signora S., was warned of what was happening by the shouts of a neighbour. Her leg in a cast from a recent accident, she stumbled down the stairs. Reaching the street she saw two German guards, whom she approached and offered cigarettes, which they accepted. In local legend the two were soon thought of as Austrians:

> 'Taking away all the Jews,' the older of the two answers the woman. She slaps her hand against her plaster cast.
>
> 'But I have a broken leg – going away with my family – hospital.'
>
> 'Ja, ja,' the Austrian nods and gestures with his hand that she can slip away. But while she waits for her family, Signora S. decides to take advantage of her friendship with the two soldiers and save some neighbours. Now it is she who calls up from the street.
>
> 'Sterina, Sterina.'
>
> 'What's the matter?'
>
> 'Get out. They're taking everyone.'
>
> 'In a minute. I'll dress the baby and be right down.'
>
> Unfortunately dressing the baby was fatal. Signora Sterina, her baby, and her entire family were taken.[22]

Signora S. rescued her own family and then went back, like 'nurses who make their rounds during epidemics with a carefree, almost irritating, disdain for prophylaxis, and nevertheless are precisely the ones who get away with it, as if disease had no power over them'.[23] Through pure bravado she persuaded other Germans that she was not herself Jewish and then saved four children of a neighbour.

But most were not so lucky. Some who might have escaped if they had fled at once made the mistake of locking themselves into their homes. The Germans broke down their doors: 'Behind them, stony and stiff as the most frighteningly surrealistic of family portraits, their residents stood in terrified attention – their eyes as if hypnotized and their hearts in their mouths.' They were led along Via del Portico d'Ottavia towards the Theatre of Marcellus:

Straggling single-file down the middle of the street. SS troopers at the head and tail of each little band are guarding them, keeping them more or less in line, prodding them on with the butts of their machine guns although no one is resisting with anything more than tears, moans, cries for mercy, confused questions ... The children search their parents' eyes for reassurance, comfort the latter can no longer give, and this is even more devastating than having to say, 'there isn't any,' to a child asking for bread.[24]

The Jews initially assumed the Germans would want men for forced labour, so it was the men who tried to escape, which some managed to do, clambering over rooftops. Others were saved because they were smokers and had got up early to queue for cigarettes at the bar on the Tiber Island. Of those who were taken away in trucks that day, women outnumbered men two to one, and three-quarters were children.

News of the roundup spread rapidly and all across Rome Jews went to ground. Many fled to the homes of friends. Kappler's report on the operation to his superiors makes it clear that Romans showed no support for the seizures, while many tried to thwart them, hiding Jewish neighbours and blocking solitary arresters. In one instance soldiers knocking at an apartment door were prevented from entering by a Fascist in full Blackshirt uniform who insisted the place was his own. Some Jews were hidden in hospitals and given fake operations. One hid in a hospital morgue.

Many were concealed by the Church. When the monks at Fatebenefratelli hospital on the Tiber Island saw Jews fleeing from the Ghetto they took them in, as did the nuns at the nearby convent of Our Lady of Sion. Some institutions demanded that Jews convert to Catholicism and others required a recommendation from someone known to them, but most took them without question. Many churchmen showed the greatest kindness and sensitivity towards those they gave sanctuary. Jews were hidden by parish priests in rooms by their churches, they were hidden in seminaries, and Jewish children were given places in Catholic boarding schools for negligible payment. Mother Mary wrote proudly that the pope had saved a great number of Rome's Jews, a claim that would be widely believed after the war.

The truth, though, was rather different. Pius XII knew of the roundup almost immediately. A Roman aristocrat, Princess Enza Pignatelli Aragona Cortes, who knew Pius, heard what was taking place from a friend who lived near the Ghetto. Having no car she borrowed one – from the German embassy – and having seen the dejected crowd waiting beneath the Theatre of Marcellus she went direct to the Vatican where she was quickly able to meet Pius and tell him her story. Taken aback by the news, he made a phone call in her presence, probably to the German ambassador to the Vatican, Weizsäcker. Sadly, that was all he did.

The Jews were unlucky in their pope. As we have seen, for several centuries few popes had shown liking towards Jewish Romans and they showed even less after the Jews became supporters of the unified Italy, yet Pius XII was particularly lacking in sympathy. Born Eugenio Pacelli, of a Roman family closely linked with the Vatican, he made his name as a Church lawyer, quickly rose through Church ranks and at the end of the First World War he was posted to Munich. There he witnessed the excesses of the short-lived Bavarian Soviet Republic, which confirmed Pacelli's belief that Bolshevism – which he saw as a strongly Jewish movement – was the Church's greatest threat, and one that must be opposed at any cost. Pacelli was not particular as to whom he employed in his struggle against Bolshevism. In 1933, six years before he became pope, he negotiated an agreement between the papacy and the new Nazi state, under which he promised that powerful German Catholic organizations would keep out of politics, thus helping to clear the way for Hitler to assume absolute power.

The war did not change his views and as Germany struggled, Pacelli, now Pope Pius, hoped to arrange peace between Hitler and the Western Allies so Germany could have a free hand against Russia. Pius had no wish to do anything that might undermine Germany or set the country against the Vatican. Though it is not easy to prove, evidence suggests that Pius may have held anti-Semitic views, as many in the Vatican did at this time. In 1942, when news of the Holocaust emerged, he refused to speak up about what was happening despite strong pressure from President Roosevelt, who smuggled a special representative, Myron Taylor, to Rome to plead with him to act.

Now the Holocaust had come to Pius. The Jews seized in the Ghetto were temporarily held at the Collegio Militare, which was only a few hundred yards from the Vatican Palace, while some of the truck drivers taking them there, eager to do a little sightseeing, stopped right by St Peter's Square. The British ambassador to the Holy See, D'Arcy Osborne, managed to see Pius within hours of the roundup and urged him to protest, but was told that the papacy had no complaints against the German authorities in Rome, as they had respected Vatican neutrality, while protests to Ambassador Weizsäcker had led to the release of many Jews. This was not true. Vatican officials *had* intervened but only on behalf of a handful of Jews who had converted to Catholicism (and without success). Of the 1,250, captives in the Collegio Militare almost a fifth were released, but only because they had managed to convince the SS commander, Theodor Dannecker, that they should not have been seized in the first place. The pope never once protested at the roundup. The Vatican's only comment came nine days afterwards in the Vatican newspaper, the *Osservatore Romano*, but this did not mention the Jews and merely lamented the suffering of all innocents in the war.

Once again, German diplomats did much more. Greatly disappointed by papal inaction, the two German ambassadors, Weizsäcker and Möllhausen, embarked on an elaborate plot in which they tried to alarm the authorities in Berlin by claiming the pope was about to denounce what had happened (though they knew he would do nothing of the kind). They concocted a letter supposedly written by a German bishop in Rome, Alois Hudal, to the German commander in Rome, General Stahel (who was also in on the conspiracy), that warned of the pope's anger, and which was sent to the Foreign Ministry in Berlin with a telegram from Weizsäcker, who again urged that Jews seized in Rome should be released and used as forced labour. It was a forlorn effort. The letter and telegram languished in the Berlin Foreign Ministry for days before being passed on to the SS. The SS were unlikely to have taken any notice and in the event did not need to. By the time Weizsäcker's telegram finally reached them the seized Roman Jews, who numbered more than a thousand, had reached or were about to reach Auschwitz. Most were gassed at once. Of the thousand only fifteen would survive and return to Rome.

The Ghetto roundup was the cruellest episode of the occupation yet, but it would be far from the last terrible event. By late October Romans' predictions that the Allies would appear in two weeks or less seemed sadly optimistic. Naples had been liberated early in the month, after Neapolitans flung the Germans out in a furious insurrection – at great cost to both the city and themselves – but the Allies were then halted by a formidable German defensive line south of Monte Cassino at the Volturno river. The war had stalled. By November bitter graffiti was appearing on Roman walls: *Russians hurry up! The Allies are waiting for you on the Volturno.*

Little by little, life in Rome grew worse. Buses and trams became rarer and more overcrowded. Taxies vanished altogether. Shops bricked up their windows and doors to avoid being looted, giving streets a sinister look, while those that were not boarded up had little on display: shoe polish, insect powder or a few wooden bottles and plates. Luxury jewellery shops sold cheap tin ornaments. The only lively places were cafés, while even here there was little to eat or drink.

By November, as the weather grew cold, all food was in short supply, as were salt and matches, and gas for cooking came on briefly three times per day. Tea and coffee were almost unobtainable and Mother Mary was reduced to drinking coffee substitute made from barley, and tea made from lime leaves, blackberry leaves or dried orange peel. Though the lira was almost worthless, free enterprise found new opportunities. As food grew scarce the black market boomed and for those who had the money it was possible to send a letter and receive a reply from Naples, across Allied lines. For a larger sum one could send oneself.

Posters announced ever-growing lists of forbidden activities. Sabotage, desertion, failing to fulfil labour obligations and possessing a radio transmitter were all punishable by death, as was harbouring Jews or Allied prisoners of war. By now, they were not the only people trying to make themselves scarce. De Wyss told of a Roman woman who was concealing several Italian army officers and was horrified to see a German parachutist marching into her house. It turned out to be her gardener: a German had held him up at gunpoint and forced him to exchange clothes so he could desert. De Wyss also told of two German officers who asked to stay the night in the home of some elderly Italians. The next morning the Germans had vanished, leaving their attaché cases and their uniforms neatly folded on their beds, along with a note that read, 'Thank you for having helped us stop fighting.' De Wyss spoke German and many soldiers told her that all they wanted was to go home to their families.

Occasionally there was a welcome piece of news. On 28 November the Gestapo and members of the Italian African Police raided the headquarters of Rome's Fascists. The Fascists were widely detested for their corruption and aggression: threatening tram conductors with hand grenades to avoid paying the fare, or throwing them at cinema screens because they disliked the film. One of their chiefs, Pollastrini, went too far when he threatened an opera audience with a machine gun because they failed to stand up when the Giovinezza was played. Some of those present had been German. The raid uncovered torture chambers, three torture victims, quantities of stolen goods and a live cow, presumably to provide fresh milk for the Fascists' cappuccinos. Yet Romans' delight would be short-lived. The Blackshirts were soon replaced by others who would prove less braggartly, more efficient and much more dangerous.

At the beginning of November the Germans requisitioned the best hotels on the Via Veneto for their headquarters. They were clearly expecting to stay for some time. Yet they were about to find life more difficult. Early on in the occupation two rival resistance organizations had formed in Rome, the royalist FMCR and the republican CLN. Neither achieved much in themselves, beyond scheming against one another, but from the CLN there emerged several partisan groups which had already blown up a Fascist barracks, assassinated a number of Blackshirts and scattered roads with four-pronged nails, causing havoc to German convoys. In mid-December one of the partisan groups, the communist *Gruppi di Azione Patriottica* or GAP, decided to target German forces so that they would no longer feel safe in the city. During the second half of December they launched a series of sudden, daring attacks. They killed eight Germans dining in a trattoria in the Prati district and then a further eight getting into a truck. They threw bombs through the windows of one of the Via Veneto hotels used by the Germans, the Flora, with devastating results. They attacked the guardhouse of Regina Coeli prison, and three Germans on the Mazzini Bridge were killed by a bomb hurled by a cyclist, who then escaped, pedalling furiously.

Romans may have been pleased that the Germans now had to look over their shoulder but the attacks made their lives harder too. The city had long been subject to a curfew – it had first been imposed by Badoglio – but now it was greatly extended and began at 7 p.m. Bicycles, which had become the best way of getting round the city, were banned and anyone seen cycling would be shot without warning. Streets quickly became filled with tricycles, which were still permitted and became Rome's new trucks, pulling home-made trailers full of goods.

As the partisans grew more active so did the city's Blackshirts. A new force of them had arrived, led by half-Italian, half-German Pietro Koch, who had been given authority by Mussolini to root out those in hiding and members of Rome's resistance. His *Reparto Speciale di Polizia*, which Romans called the *Banda Koch* (Koch's band) proved very useful to the Germans. Until then they had been reluctant to search Church buildings for fear of making trouble with the pope. Now Koch could raid them – with German assistance – and the

SS could disclaim all responsibility. On the night of 21 December three Church institutions were struck and more than fifty people were discovered and taken.

Church properties no longer seemed safe and many left them. Jews went where they could, moving from place to place. A few hid out for a time in their old homes in the now deserted Ghetto. Since the October roundup they had been left largely in peace but now searches and arrests resumed. The authorities offered rewards of 5,000 lire for a Jewish man and 2,000 to 3,000 for women and children. Some Romans – though not many – took the money. There could even be danger from fellow Jews, and a young Jewish woman, Celeste di Porto, gained infamy by helping the Germans. Nicknamed *La Pantera Nera* (the Black Panther) she would stand on the Tiber Island bridges near the Ghetto and point out Jews she recognized. As thanks for her betrayal the Germans later freed her brother, who was due to be executed, but he was so ashamed of his sister that he turned himself in again and was killed.

Romans had an occupied Christmas. Midnight masses were cancelled because of the curfew. The pope's Christmas speech urged Romans to abstain from violence, while avoiding any mention of the crimes that were taking place all around him. By now the city had a new commander, General Mälzer: a heavy drinker who tried to improve his country's battered image by providing Christmas dinner at the Hotel Regina on Via Veneto Hotels for 150 British prisoners of war. A new year began. On 13 January 1944, Romans were distracted from their hunger by the sight of dogfights over their city. Spectators included Mother Mary:

> One Allied airman met his enemy coming head on: the German plane was cut in two, and the American came down as well. In all five American planes came down, but their crews bailed out safely; on landing they were taken prisoners, of course... To those who had never seen anyone bail out before, the parachutes looked like great white blossoms floating earthward.[25]

And then just a few days later there was miraculous news. Mother Mary wrote on 21 January,

> It seems too good to be true. We haven't many details yet, but we are so delighted that nothing seems to matter beyond the fact that they are so close to us, at last. It is as if a cloud had lifted from the city. People in the streets look happier than they have for a long time.[26]

Allied forces had landed at Anzio just thirty miles from Rome. Once again German diplomats hurriedly prepared to leave and there were chaotic scenes at the railway station, where the German transport officials did not know whether munitions should be unloaded or sent back north. Trucks were confiscated and at night de Wyss heard machine guns rattle, as cars roared through the city and planes flew overhead.

Days passed and nothing happened. There was no pounding of guns. De Wyss could not understand: 'The Allies don't advance,' she wrote. 'Why? Why? The way to Rome lies open.'[27] She was quite right, the way to Rome was open, or at least it had been. The Anzio landing remains a controversial subject. An Allied force of 50,000 troops and 5,000 vehicles landed on a stretch of coast defended by 100 Germans. In Rome the Germans had two police battalions that totalled only 1,500 men. The Allied commander General John Lucas could have swept into the city with ease and seized the Alban Hills, which he had also been ordered to occupy. Instead he stayed in his bridgehead and dug in.

Lucas would be widely reviled for his caution. Yet he may have had a point. The last Allied landing at Salerno had been met with such a furious German counter-attack that it was nearly driven back into the sea. Lucas' landing was to have been combined with a breakthrough by the main army below Monte Cassino, but the attack failed. Fifty thousand troops may seem like a large force but by 1944 standards it was modest. By the time de Wyss was wondering why the Allies were not in Rome, Kesselring had already raced reserves down from

northern Italy and his forces outnumbered those of the bridgehead
army by two to one. If Lucas had advanced on Rome he might have
turned the city into battleground. Instead he turned Anzio into a
graveyard where 11,000 Allied troops would die.

Rather than being Rome's salvation the landing was a disaster for
the city. From the start of the occupation the Germans had declared
Rome to be a demilitarized open city, yet this was disingenuous and
they used the city centre, which was comparatively safe from Allied air
attack, as a vast car park for their guns and tanks. With the war now
just thirty miles away, German military traffic through Rome tripled
and the city centre became packed with military equipment. Since the
devastating raid of 19 July Rome had suffered relatively little bombing.
Now, as the Allies struggled to defend their beachhead they struck
the city almost daily, targeting railway yards, stations and gasworks.
Rome is not usually thought of as a city that greatly suffered from
bombing during the Second World War, and the centre was little
touched, but the outskirts were extensively damaged, and an estimated
7,000 Romans died in air raids. Usually there was little warning as the
Germans, insisting that Rome was an open city, did not sound a siren.
When a raid began trams and buses stopped where they were and
people were ordered into shelters, which Mother Mary described as
'death traps, flimsy and ineffectual', and 'full of a more or less hysterical
crowd'.[28] She preferred to trust her luck in a church.

Bombs fell on the *borgate* districts of Quadraro and Centocelle
where Mussolini had dumped anti-Fascists and the poor. On 17
February the Protestant cemetery was hit and the graves of Keats
and Shelley were torn open; on 14 March a raid on the railway
workers' district of San Lorenzo struck women queuing for water
at a street pump – many died and one was decapitated by the blast;
and on 18 March the university hospital area of Policlinico was hit
together with a tram crammed with passengers. All the attacks were
day raids and so early each morning crowds of Romans made their
way to St Peter's Square and spent the day camped out beneath the
colonnades before going back to discover if their homes were still

standing. Some brought their cows. The Allies' constant bombing and their failure to liberate Rome when it seemed they had had the chance made them increasingly loathed. De Wyss wrote that, 'The bitterness against the Allies is so acute that it is difficult to show one's pro-Allied feelings. Admiration for the Germans grows … One needs a strong character indeed not to lose one's faith in future big Allied successes.'[29]

The Anzio landing was also a disaster for the Roman resistance. In the first few months of the occupation members of the FMCR and the CLN, knowing that lines were tapped, had scrupulously avoided communicating by telephone but when they heard of the Anzio landing, assuming that they were hours from liberation, they rang one another freely with the good news. Kappler's SS squads and Koch's gang enjoyed a spree of arrests. Among many others, Colonel Montezemolo, the leader of the FMCR, was captured and his organization soon became a broken force. Word leaked out of terrible tortures endured by captives at the Gestapo's headquarters, on Via Tasso, where Kappler's second in command, SS Captain Erich Priebke, became an enthusiastic self-taught torturer. The headquarters' floors were said to be littered with pulled teeth.

Yet if the Anzio landing had done little for Rome, Rome did a great deal for the soldiers on the beachhead, as they endured pouring rain, shellfire and First World War style trench warfare. Shortly before the landing took place an American agent, Peter Tomkins, was smuggled into Rome to help organize an insurrection to link with an Allied attack on the city. When it became clear that his role was redundant, Tomkins turned his energies to relaying information on German movements. His source was a remarkable information-gathering network improvised by the Socialist Party activist, Franco Malfatti. Malfatti's network was impressively well connected and included Italian officers and officials who had access to the highest German decision-making, doctors who talked to wounded German soldiers, and many scores of people whose homes or farms lay between Rome and Anzio and who watched German movements. Audaciously, Malfatti set up his office in the back room of a German bookshop directly across the road from the German-sequestered Hotel Excelsior on the Via Veneto. Here was brought information on the Germans' attack plans and the precise location of their tanks, gun emplacements and ammunition dumps. All was given to Peter Tomkins, who had the most important details passed to a hidden radio transmitter which then sent them to Allied command. In the middle of February the Anzio battle reached its height and the beachhead came perilously close to being overrun. That it survived, as both Marshal Kesselring and the US General Donovan readily admitted afterwards, was largely down to intelligence: Malfatti's Socialist Information Service.

None of this was known to any but a few Romans. For most, life was an unheroic business of enduring cold – on 6 March it snowed – and trying to find food and a means of cooking it. Mother Mary's nuns began taking in relatives and friends of the convent's servants and by the end of January they had twenty people hiding out. People on the streets looked frozen and hungry and some young children were barefoot. The distant sound of guns at Anzio seemed to taunt Romans. All that they wanted was peace.

Yet peace was still far away. On the late of afternoon of 23 March M. de Wyss went to visit a photographer who developed her films, and who lived on Via Rasella near Piazza Barberini:

I am still shivering … there was a terrific explosion, then screams and yells. Then wild machine-gun fire made me spin round and run for my life, while out of the corner of my eye I saw the Germans catching people who tried to escape. I doubled like a hunted hare and stopped only in the Piazza di Spagna. A boy of about twelve stood near me, panting. He told me that he had been caught already, but had ducked under the German soldier's arms and slipped away. He didn't know what had happened. He was in the street, playing. Then a terrific explosion threw him on to the pavement. He heard shouts, groans, machine-gun fire and saw people running away and did the same.[30]

Rome's partisans had staged a spectacular. The 23rd of March was the 25th anniversary of Fascism's foundation and they had initially intended to strike at a grand parade and rally by the city's Blackshirts, but the Germans, who worried that such an ostentatious display would be resented by hungry Romans, had insisted the Fascist celebrations be reduced to a meeting in the heavily guarded Fascist headquarters, which was now in the old Ministry of Corporations on Via Veneto. The partisans changed their plans. Unwittingly, the Germans had put themselves in the firing line.

The target was around 150 military police of the 11th company of the SS Polizeiregiment Bozen, who for the past few mornings had marched north across Rome to practise at a firing range, returning to their barracks near the Via Nazionale in the afternoon. As it happened, these soldiers were newly German, as they came from the bilingual northern Italian city of Bozen, or Bolzano, that had been annexed by Hitler from Italy only a few months earlier. Two groups of Roman partisans, the Gappisti and the socialist Matteotti Brigade decided to combine their forces in a grand attack that broke the rules of partisan warfare. Partisan assaults worked best when they were small, simple and sudden, as they had been until this point. This attack, which was to take place on the narrowest street on the Germans' route – Via Rasella near Piazza Barberini – involved no fewer than seventeen people, a bomb hidden in a wheeled litter bin and a further action with mortars and machine guns. Yet the operation could hardly have gone more smoothly. The bomb exploded, leaving a huge crater in the road amid dead and injured soldiers. The surviving Germans, when they were hit by the partisans' mortars, thought they had been attacked from the rooftops above and began firing furiously at windows. All seventeen partisans managed to slip away. With more than half its men killed or wounded the SS company was effectively destroyed.

Yet if the men and women of GAP Central and the Matteotti Brigade had got away scot-free, others would not be so fortunate. The city's commander, General Mälzer, who was on the scene within moments, and had been enjoying a heavy drinking lunch, demanded that all the houses in the vicinity be blown up and that 200 bystanders who had been rounded up – none of whom had had anything to do with the attack – must be shot. The SS chief, Kappler, the acting German ambassador Möllhausen and also Eugene Dollmann – who we last saw by Alaric's supposed tomb in Cosenza, and who was now an SS colonel and Himmler's personal representative in Italy – all tried to calm him down, but before long an even angrier voice joined the fray. News of the incident reached Hitler in his East Prussia command centre, where, unluckily for the Romans, he was enjoying a quiet day and so could devote his full attention to what had happened. Breaking into one of his famous rages he demanded that a whole neighbourhood of the city must be razed to the ground and that for every German who had been killed, thirty or fifty Romans must die.

Kappler managed to reduce the number of Romans to die for each German to ten but this still left him with the problem of who they would be, which grew greater as ever more soldiers died of their wounds – eventually there were thirty-three – raising the total required. After an increasingly desperate search his eventual selection included a few captured partisans, several dozen Jews awaiting deportation (the youngest was only fifteen), two anti-Fascist priests, three dozen Italian army officers (one of whom was the FMCR chief colonel Montezemolo, who had bravely stood up to weeks of torture without betraying his comrades) and ten unlucky bystanders rounded up after the bombing, among them a barman and two salesmen in a handbag shop.

The day after the bombing 335 men and boys were driven to a network of cave-like abandoned diggings on the Via Ardeatina just south of the city. It was a chaotic, slipshod massacre, all the more so because nobody wanted to do it. Kappler initially ordered the survivors of the SS unit that had been attacked to do the killings but their commander, SS Major Dobbick, refused, claiming, rather mysteriously, that his soldiers suffered from Alpine superstitions. When the regular army also refused, the task fell on Kappler and his SS staff, most of whom were not soldiers but office workers who had hardly fired a gun. To help them through the ordeal they were given quantities of cognac and became drunk, shooting increasingly wildly. Even the number of prisoners was wrong. Thirty-three soldiers had died in the attack so according to Kappler's logic, only 330 should have been brought. Five had been taken by mistake, though they would be killed anyway for what they had witnessed.

The first of the victims, who were tied together in pairs and led into the diggings, put up no resistance, but others did. One was beaten to death. Some were shot repeatedly when the first bullets failed to kill them, and several dozen were executed so inexpertly that their heads were severed from their bodies. Some were not killed at first but suffocated under the weight of corpses piled on top of them. Months later, when the diggings were explored, one body was found some distance away from the rest. The man had still been alive when the Germans blew up and sealed the entrance, and had crawled into a corner to die alone. The killing, which would become known as the *Fosse Ardeatina* (the Ardeatina diggings), was the worst atrocity of the war in Italy.

The Germans announced the reprisal, keeping back any details of where it had taken place, claiming that all those killed had been communists or Badoglio supporters. Yet most Romans still felt angrier towards the Allies. When de Wyss questioned people a few days after the killings she found that though they hated the Fascists, most of all they resented the Allies far more than the Germans: 'People say: "The Germans are good and human. Provided you don't irritate them they are very kind." It made me so angry to hear it that I could hardly speak.'[31]

At least the main cause of Romans' anger towards the Allies – their bombing of the city – was largely over. Few raids took place after the Via Rasella attack. Spring finally arrived and the Romans no longer froze, though they were hungrier than ever. Frequently the bread ration failed to materialize and when it did it was hardly nutritious. De Wyss had her tiny daily loaf tested by a chemist friend who told her that, as well as rye, dried chickpeas and maize flour, it contained mulberry leaves and elm tree bark. Mother Mary noticed how starved everyone looked, 'It gives one a heartache to see it. No longer is it complimentary to allude to loss of weight; on the contrary the subject is tactfully avoided.'[32] In early April, she reported that two women who had been brought to the Littorio Hospital in Monteverde suffering from shock after an air raid had died in their hospital beds – of hunger.

The Vatican tried to bring food into the city, using trucks marked with Vatican colours, but some were unwittingly bombed by Allied aircraft, while matters were not helped when German trucks also used Vatican colours, or drove behind Vatican trucks in the hope that they would be protected. By mid-April, newspapers were filled with personal ads offering valuables for sale as people tried to raise money to buy extortionate black market food. Even dog meat was exorbitant, while the city's cats had long vanished. Bread riots broke out among Roman women queuing at bakeries. In one incident ten women who attacked a bakery in the Via Ostiense area, which supplied German troops, were taken to the Tiber and shot. By May, even wealthy Romans were going hungry.

As well as starved, Romans were frightened. Manhunts for forced labour continued. In March one of those hiding out in Mother Mary's convent, Nello, was seized, to the despair of his family. Several times he managed to avoid being deported, by slipping to the back of a queue of those to be sent north, and when he was sent to clear rubble by the Via Ostiense he managed to dart under a train carriage and escape. Others were less fortunate. In mid-April, after three Germans were killed in the Quadraro *borgate*, a huge manhunt was conducted there and 2,000 men and boys were seized, of whom 750 were sent north to Germany. Half never returned. Jews continued to be taken, along with members of the Roman resistance and partisan fighters.

The Koch gang was now as active as Kappler's SS and their base, the Pensione Jaccarino on the Via Romagna, near the main railway station, was infamous. Mother Mary heard that it had,

> ... the same hideous instruments as the one in Via Tasso; pincers for pulling out teeth and fingernails, whips, rods, and means of heating knives red hot. Some of our friends who live near there and hear the screams and groans, particularly at night, say that it is diabolical ... It seems impossible to be writing all this in cold blood, as if they were just a matter of course, but then it is a matter of course; it would be incredible if we were not right up against it. And one is so utterly helpless![33]

Romans were beginning to lose hope. For months the Allied line had hardly moved and people guessed – correctly – that Italy was no longer a priority for the Americans and British, who were now focused on an approaching invasion of France. But then, when it seemed as if nothing would ever change, on 12 May news came of another Allied offensive in the Monte Cassino area. The British commander in Italy, General Alexander, had given himself a large numerical advantage over the Germans by secretly moving troops across from the Adriatic coast, and by giving the false impression that he was planning a new landing north of Rome. His superior numbers told. After several days of fighting, their defensive line was breached and the Germans began to fall back in retreat.

News of the breakthrough soon reached Rome. As Mother Mary wrote, 'Rome is tense. The Romans are in high spirits but they dread what the Germans may do before they go.'[34] They remembered Naples, where insurrection had left the city extensively damaged and many Neapolitans dead. Already the mood in some parts of Rome was growing ugly and Mother Mary reported that no German now dared go alone into Trastevere. If Romans feared an outbreak of street fighting so did the German commander, General Mälzer, who ordered food to be distributed in the city's poorest areas. He had no wish to have Romans rise against him when German troops were trying to escape through the city.

There was no doubt that they would soon be doing precisely that. On 27 May de Wyss saw German trucks loading up: 'They are going away! They are really going away!'[35] That same night a steady stream of German vehicles sped through the city, heading north. Romans queuing by water fountains excitedly told one another that it couldn't be long now. A small minority were anything but pleased. On 26 May the Allies' Anzio radio station had broadcast the names of those who had helped the Blackshirts and Germans. The next day Mother Mary wrote, 'Two of the informers mentioned yesterday by the Anzio wireless are the porter of a house which we know, and his wife. They have specialized in reporting the whereabouts of Jews. This morning they are sitting in their lodge shedding tears; and well they may.'[36] It was Italians who had most to fear. One of the nuns' house guests witnessed an interchange between a German soldier and a Blackshirt that graphically illustrated the Fascists' predicament: '"Me," said Jerry, "I do this" – and he held up his hands; "you," pointing an imaginary gun at the republican's chest, "poum, poum, poum, finish!"'

It was at this moment that something shameful occurred on the Allied side. US General Clark managed to break out from the Anzio beachhead and so, five months late, his force was finally ready to achieve its original purpose and, in a mini-Stalingrad, cut off the German 10th Army as it fled north. Clark, though, was determined to go down in history as the man who captured Rome. His superior, General Alexander, had ordered him to cut off the Germans at the town of Valmontone, but Clark sent only a token force in that direction while his main force turned north. The retreating Germans would escape. Not that the Romans cared. All they wanted was to be rescued.

On the night of 3 June, Mother Mary used her diary to try and calm herself, like 'the small boy who whistled when going down a dark alley', and she told herself, 'I do not think that the Germans will make Rome a battlefield. (But the fighting is very close tonight.)'[37] Happily, her prediction would be right. As it had been so many times in the past, Rome was lucky. Treasures that had survived Alaric, Totila, Robert Guiscard, Charles V's Spanish and Lutherans and the French siege of 1849 survived once again. Mother Mary believed that this was the pope's work and there was no doubting that Pius had urged the Germans to leave his native city untouched, but it is doubtful that he had much influence. Kesselring decided not to make Rome into a battlefield because it made no strategic sense. German troops in the city would be encircled and captured and he had none to waste. Even then Rome did not remain entirely unscathed. On 4 June, as the Germans withdrew from the city, it was rocked by huge explosions. The Macao Barracks in the Castro Pretorio – once home to the emperor's Praetorian Guard – was blown up, along with the Fiat works on Via Manzoni, the telephone exchange and several railway yards. More would have been destroyed had not quick-thinking Romans disabled explosives. Even trees on the main boulevards had been planted with mines, which, fortunately, the Germans had no time to detonate

De Wyss went on to a terrace of her building with a pair of binoculars and saw trucks and scores of officers' cars on the move: 'There is no doubt. They are retreating! My heart beats. Finally they go away!' Afterwards she went into the streets of the city to watch:

There were lorries and wagons so overloaded with soldiers that they all hung around in bunches; carts with soldiers, also soldiers on horseback, peasant vehicles crammed with dead-tired men. Once soldiers passed riding oxen, finally came endless rows of those going on foot. Their faces grey with fatigue, eyes popping out, mouths wide open, they limped, barefoot, dragging their rifles after them ... Near Porta Pinciana a German soldier stops me; 'Is that the right way to Florence?' he asks. I am taken aback. 'To Florence? But that is about three hundred kilometres.' His face is grey. He goes away without waiting for my answer.[38]

Mother Mary watched them go too:

The Germans went on, wild-eyed, unshaven, unkempt, on foot, in stolen cars, in horse-drawn vehicles, even in carts belonging to the street cleaning department. There was no attempt at military formation. Some of them dragged small ambulances with wounded in them. They went, some with revolvers in their hands, some with rifles cocked … Whereas last September they came with machine guns trained on the Romans, it was a different matter now. They were frightened.

As to the Romans, '… unobtrusively and ironically they began to stroll about the streets mainly used for German traffic. They made no remarks, but looked on with Olympian serenity.' The most piteous sight was that of the Italians who had thrown in their lot with the Germans:

> Some Blackshirt soldiers, members of the pitiable Barbarigo and Nettuno Divisions, were desperately waving to occupants of German motor cars, begging for a lift. The latter … passed on, unheeding … Two of them, who tried to climb up on a gun carriage in Piazza del Popolo, were kicked off by German parachute men.[39]

The German soldier who told a Blackshirt, 'You poum, poum, poum, finish,' was prophetic. After the war the Fascist police commander in Rome, Pietro Caruso, would be executed, as would Pietro Koch, and of course Mussolini himself, whose corpse was famously strung up by the feet above a Milan petrol station. The Germans involved got off more lightly. Kesselring and Mälzer were both sentenced to death but their killings were cancelled. Kesselring was jailed for six years and released. Kappler was jailed for twenty-nine years before escaping to Germany, where he died the following year. His assistant in the Rome SS, Erich Priebke, who had proved such an enthusiastic torturer, escaped to Argentina using a Vatican-issued Red Cross passport, only to be unmasked by an American television news reporter almost fifty years later. He was extradited to Italy and jailed in 1997 and released some years later. The SS captain responsible for the Ghetto roundup, Theodor Dannecker, was captured by the Americans and hanged himself in his cell.

The Germans were still withdrawing through the northern outskirts of the city when the Allies began to appear from the south. The first American tanks made their way into the city cautiously, wary of snipers and booby traps. Soon after dusk they reached the Tiber Island, where Romans at first assumed they were German. When they realized their mistake the Americans found themselves overwhelmed by a huge, noisy welcome. The first Mother Mary knew of their arrival was when she was looking out from her convent and, 'Suddenly, from the direction of Porta Pia, came a burst of wild cheering.' She had her own first sighting of the Allies early the next morning: 'Opening a window at about 6 o'clock, I saw one little jeep with four American soldiers in it, making its way slowly and soundlessly along the street. No one else was about. The thing looked so solitary, yet so significant in the cool stillness of the dawn. I had it all to myself for a few seconds.'⁴⁰

Allied troops were soon pouring into the city through the southern and eastern gates: Porta San Sebastiano, Porta Maggiore, Porta San Giovanni and Porta San Paolo, where the Germans had broken into Rome nine months earlier. Mother Mary went to Via Veneto, where she saw Romans applauding every car that passed, every plane that flew overhead and laughing and congratulating one another for having survived. Two lines of American soldiers marched down the street:

> They were dusty, battle-worn and unshaven, but they smiled and waved in response to the greetings of the crowd. They had roses in the muzzles of their rifles, and miniature Italian flags which had been thrown to them; they had roses stuck in the camouflage nets of their helmets, and in their shirts. One has read these things in books and accepted them as fiction, never dreaming of witnessing them as we did today.⁴¹

Mother Mary also described how, as if by magic, bicycles appeared from their hiding places – and not only bicycles:

> The population of Rome seemed double what it had been; men who had been hiding for months – patriots, Italian soldiers; Allied prisoners of war who had escaped from their prison camps, young men of military age and persecuted Jews – were out and about.[42]

They were many. Of Rome's 12,000 Jews, more than 10,000 had survived.

The nightmare was over. To Romans the previous four years felt like a time to forget. As well as hunger and fear they had also experienced humiliation. After Mussolini's boasts that Italy was a powerful, modern nation the country had been led into a war in which it had been unable to defend itself. Romans had been let down by their leaders and had seen their state and their army disintegrate around them.

Yet in some ways the nine months of Nazi occupation, terrible though they were, were the Romans' finest hour. Centuries of cynicism and distrust of authority had borne fruit. In other parts of occupied Europe people assisted the Nazis in their work. The Romans were not all angels and some cooperated with the Nazis, whether for money or short-term advantage, but they were few. Many Roman churchmen and women showed the greatest concern and sensitivity towards Jews. Of ordinary Romans, a Jewish woman, Olga Di Veroli said, 'They opened their house to us, they gave us their bedrooms. There's no way around it: the people of Rome opened their hearts to us. Some did so out of self-interest, but a lot of them did it out of pure generosity. What little they had they shared with us.'[43]

The great majority of Romans thwarted the occupiers. They thwarted them with information, gathered through a vast network of people who saved the Allied beachhead at Anzio. They thwarted them with bureaucracy, issuing fake documents. They thwarted them with inaction and disobedience, and by hiding the people that Nazism demonized, at great risk to their own lives. Most of all they thwarted them with their humanity, by refusing to be carried along by an ideology of fear and hatred.

AFTERWORD

Rome is now a sprawling metropolis of almost three million people. Today's pilgrims arrive on high-speed trains and budget air flights. Romans take the motorway ring road to visit out of town shopping malls. The Colosseum, the Pyramid of Cestius and the Circus Maximus each has its own underground station. The Lateran has a superstore. The offices of Mussolini's Ministry of Africa houses the UN Food and Agricultural Organization. The city's mayor, Virginia Raggi (Rome's first female ruler since Marozia in the tenth century), represents a populist party, the Five Star Movement.

A cosmopolitan city once more, Rome's immigrants come from all over the world: from South America to Eastern Europe, and from the Philippines and Bangladesh and Eritrea. Some arrivals have made the perilous sea journey from Libya, just across the Mediterranean from Sicily. As it has been many times in the past, Rome is a city full of soldiers, who guard government buildings, embassies and piazzas against the latest perceived threat of terrorism. In February 2015, ISIS militants in Libya posted online their intention of descending on Rome.

Yet if Rome has changed greatly since it was liberated in 1944, the city centre has not. Mussolini's unfinished projects – the Via della

Conciliazione, the area around the Tomb Augustus and E-42 (now EUR) – were completed after the war (often by the same architects who began them, and who managed to leap from the sinking ship of Fascism just in time) and the Ara Pacis is enclosed by a new and controversial building by the American architect Richard Meier. Otherwise, though, hardly a brick has changed.

In consequence, though few tourists realize it, the Rome they see is very much Mussolini's Rome. The main roads they find noisy include Mussolini's boulevards that bulldozed their way through old neighbourhoods. If they look closely they will find Fascist insignia everywhere. Occasionally the fasces have been scratched out, leaving telltale outlines, but often even these remain intact and there are Fascist eagles and Anno Fascisti dates by the hundred. The facade of the former GIL youth organization centre in Trastevere still has its Fascist slogan: NECESSARIO VINCERE PIV NECESSARIO COMBATTERE. The Senior Judicial Advisory Office has a helmeted Mussolini above each window and in EUR a frieze still depicts Mussolini sitting proudly on a horse. By Foro Olimpico – formerly the Foro Mussolini – Roma and Lazio football fans make their way to the stadium beneath the 300-ton obelisk that still proclaims MUSSOLINI DUX.

Is this wrong? Perhaps a little. In Germany, Nazi insignia have been carefully removed. True, Mussolini's regime was far less murderous than those of Hitler or Stalin, yet Italian Fascism is often treated lightly precisely because of this comparison. If it had existed in a calmer age its crimes would seem more shocking. A little disturbingly, in view of how badly Mussolini let his country down, some Italians feel nostalgia for the Fascist era, regarding it as a time when life, if not perfect, was easier, better organized and safer. As well as impracticable, it would be wrong for Fascist Rome to be erased, as it should be present in Rome's historical layers, but there is a case for some of the more ostentatious monuments to be pulled down a peg or two. Perhaps they could be surrounded by another, even newer layer of Rome, in the form of a little disrespectful street art.

After two and a half millennia of floods, earthquakes, fires, plagues, sieges, attacks and political urban planning it is remarkable what has survived in Rome. Treasures have been preserved from the era of each sacking we have looked at. In the Capitoline Museum you can still see the foundations of the temple to Jupiter Best and Greatest that dominated the city's skyline when Brennus and his Gauls attacked in 387 BC. In the Villa Giulia Etruscan Museum you can see the beautiful terracotta statue of Apollo that once decorated a temple in Rome's first rival, Veii.

You can still see most of the Aurelian Wall that failed to keep out Alaric and his Visigoths in 410. You can cross the Bridge of Cestius by the Tiber Island that was built in Cicero's time when the Roman Republic was fighting to survive. You can see classical temples, the remnants of the city's great baths – of Caracalla, of Diocletian and Trajan – along with the ruins of Domitian's Palace on the Palatine, Augustus' tomb, and his exquisite Temple to Peace. And of course there is the greatest pagan Roman temple of them all: the Pantheon, which remains little changed from when it was built, almost nineteen centuries ago. Though the first St Peter's is long gone, other churches from this early time still stand, including Santa Costanza, whose mosaics of rural scenes and staring blue faces catch the moment when paganism was melting away before Christianity.

You can see churches that were new when Totila's Ostrogoths broke into the city, such as Santa Maria Maggiore and the exquisite Santa Sabina, which, after sixteen centuries, still has its original carved wooden doors. You can see the Asinarian Gate beside which Isaurians shimmied down a rope to let Totila's army into Rome. A kilometre to the south-west you can walk through the Porta Latina above which Robert Guiscard's soldiers slipped quietly into the city.

Of the Rome that existed in 1527 numerous medieval towers remain, though they can be hard to spot, as many have become merged with later blocks of housing. A few, like that of the Casa di Dante in Trastevere, remain much as they once were: standing on the corner of a medieval town house around a courtyard. Also in Trastevere you can find poky medieval homes with their telltale staircases on the outside. Near the Colosseum you can visit Paschal II's magnificent revenge church, San Clemente, and if you descend into the deep excavations beneath you can see the remains of the church of his hated anti-pope predecessor, Clement III, along with – deeper again – a temple to Mithras and rooms from the town house of a wealthy classical Roman, who was probably also an early Christian. In the Castel Sant'Angelo you can visit the papal apartments where Benvenuto Cellini melted down Pope Clement's golden tiaras. And of course there are Renaissance churches, palaces and, greatest of all, the Sistine Chapel.

Of the Rome that Garibaldi defended in 1849 it is hard to know where to begin as so much has survived. This is the Rome visitors are usually most conscious of with its fountains, its Renaissance and Baroque facades, its great parks, and of course St Peter's and its square, encompassed by Bernini's vast curved colonnades. Less often noticed are the images of the Madonna and clouds of cherubs that look down from almost every street corner, most of which appeared under the ultra-conservative popes of the early nineteenth century. Also overlooked are the sixteenth-century city walls that Garibaldi defended, whose damage during the French bombardment has been carefully repaired.

As we have just seen, almost every inch of Fascist Rome has survived. The Romans have even preserved mementos of the Nazi occupation. Look up at the walls of apartment blocks on Via Rasella and you will see small holes left by the shrapnel from the Gappisti bomb and by bullets fired up by the German soldiers. The city's Gestapo headquarters on Via Tasso – where members of Rome's resistance, Allied prisoners of war and some Jewish Romans were subjected to terrible tortures – has been preserved as a museum.

There are also less visible vestiges of the city's long past, such as the Romans' distinctive way of viewing the world. This is not always praiseworthy. After two thousand years of handouts Romans can be tough, fatalistic, and eager to catch whatever pennies chance sends their way. Some are downright corrupt. In 2014 a huge scandal was uncovered that became known as *Mafia Capitale*, in which city contracts were awarded to shell companies and hundreds of millions of euros of taxpayers' money was stolen.

But the Romans are also very warm. For a city of three million people Rome can be an astonishingly friendly place that feels more like a village than a metropolis, and where everybody seems to know everybody else by their first name. Having been subjected to twenty centuries of imperial, papal, royal and Fascist self-aggrandizement Romans possess, as we have seen, a finely tuned sense of scepticism. Millennia of ups and downs have also given them their particular brand of cynical humour. One of its latest manifestations came in 2015 when ISIS Islamists in Libya announced their intention to descend on the city. Romans replied on Twitter with pictures of traffic jams, warning ISIS of transport strikes, or telling them, *Let us know when you'll get here and how many you'll be so we can put the pasta on.*[1]

Romans love grumbling and frequently complain that Rome is chaotic, that nothing works, and praise other places – almost anywhere will do – where they are certain everything is far better. Yet scratch a little and you will find that Romans are immensely proud of their city. As they should be.

ACKNOWLEDGEMENTS

I WOULD LIKE TO THANK the libraries of Rome and their librarians. I have spent many happy days researching in the Arthur and Janet C. Ross Library of the American Academy, the Library of the British School at Rome, the American Studies Centre, the Biblioteca di storia e contemporanea di Roma and the Deutsches Historiches Institut in Rom.

I would like to thank my agent, Georgia Garrett, and Will Atkinson and James Nightingale at Atlantic for their hard work to make a success of this book, and Margaret Stead for first having had faith in it. I would like to thank Matteo Canale, Tom Govero, Robert Twigger and Andrew Nadeau for their invaluable advice on the text. Most of all I would like to thank my wife Shannon and our children Alexander and Tatiana for putting up with my obsession with this city, which has become our home.

NOTES

Chapter One

1. Livy, *The Early History of Rome*, trans. Aubrey de Sélincourt (1960)
2. Ibid.
3. Ibid.
4. Ibid.
5. Ibid.
6. Ibid.
7. Ibid.

Chapter Two

1. 1. Eugene Dollman, *Un Libero Schiavo* (1968)
2. avid Karmon, *The Ruin of the Eternal City: Antiquity and Preservation in Renaissance Rome* (2011)
3. rom Peter Brown, *The Cult of Saints* (1982)
4. Zozimus, *A New History, Book V*, Green and Chaplin (1814)
5. Ibid.
6. Ibid.
7. Ibid.
8. Ibid.
9. Sozomen, *Ecclesiastical History, Vol. IX*, Nicene and Post-Nicene Fathers, Second Series, Vol. 2, trans. Chester D. Hartranft (1890)
10. Procopius of Caesarea, *History of the Wars, Book III, The Vandalic War*, trans. H.B Dewing (1916)
11. Ibid.
12. Jerome, *Letter CXXVII (To Principia)* Nicene and Post-Nicene Fathers, Second Series, Vol. 6, trans. W.H. Freemantle, G. Lewis and W.G. Martley (1893)
13. Orosius, *A History Against the Pagans, Vol. 7*
14. Ibid.
15. Sozomen, *Ecclesiastical History, Vol. IX*, Nicene and Post-Nicene Fathers, Second Series, Vol. 2, trans. Chester D. Hartranft (1890)
16. Jerome, *Letter CXXVII (To Principia)* Nicene and Post-Nicene Fathers, Second Series, Vol. 6, trans. W.H. Freemantle, G. Lewis and W.G. Martley (1893)
17. Peter Brown, *Augustine of Hippo* (1966)

Chapter Three

1. Procopius of Caesarea, *The Anecdota* or *Secret History*, The Loeb Classic Library No. 290, trans. H.B. Dewing (1935)
2. Ibid.
3. Magnus Aurelius Cassiodorus, Letter, from Bryan Ward-Perkins, *From Classical Antiquity to the Middle Ages, Urban Public Building in Northern and Central Italy, AD 300–850* (Oxford Historical Monographs) (1984)
4. Procopius of Caesarea, *A History of the Wars*, Vol. VI, xviii, Loeb Classic Library, trans. H.B. Dewing (1924)
5. Procopius of Caesarea, *A History of the Wars*, Vol. VI, xxv, Loeb Classic Library, trans. H.B. Dewing (1924)
6. Procopius of Caesarea, *History of the Wars*, Vol. II, xxii, Loeb Classic Library, trans. H.B. Dewing (1916)
7. Ibid.
8. Procopius of Caesarea, *A History of the Wars*, Vol. VII, xvii, Loeb Classic Library, trans. H.B. Dewing (1924)
9. Procopius of Caesarea, *A History of the Wars*, Vol. VII, xix, Loeb Classic Library, trans. H.B. Dewing (1924)
10. Ibid.
11. Procopius of Caesarea, *A History of the Wars*, Vol. VII, xx, Loeb Classic Library, trans. H. B. Dewing (1924)
12. Ibid.
13. Procopius of Caesarea, *A History of the Wars*, Vol. VII, xxii, Loeb Classic Library, trans. H.B. Dewing (1924)
14. Ibid.
15. Ibid.
16. Paul the Deacon, *History of the Langobards*, trans. William Dudley Foulke (1907)

Chapter Four

1. *The Annals of Lambert of Hersfeld*, trans. G.A. Loud, Leeds History in Translation Website, Leeds University (2004)
2. Ibid.
3. William of Malmesbury, from G.A. Loud: *The Age of Robert Guiscard: Southern Italy and the Norman Conquest.*
4. Amatus of Montecassino, from G.A. Loud, *Conquerors and Churchmen in Norman Italy*, in Variorum Collected Studies series, July 1999
5. Geoffrey of Malaterra, *The Deeds of Count Roger of Calabria and Sicily and of His Brother Duke Robert Guiscard*, trans. Kenneth Baxter Woolf, Michigan (2005)
6. Letter 18, of Henry IV, From *Imperial Lives and Letters of the Eleventh Century*, trans. Theodor E. Mommsen and Karl F. Morrison (1962)

7. Geoffrey Malaterra, *The Deeds of Count Roger of Calabria and Sicily and of His Brother Duke Robert Guiscard,* trans. Kenneth Baxter Wolf (2005)
8. Ibid.

9. William of Apulia, *The Deeds of Robert Guiscard*, trans. G.A. Loud (1096–99)
10. Geoffrey Malaterra, *The Deeds of Count Roger of Calabria and Sicily and of His Brother Duke Robert Guiscard,* trans. Kenneth Baxter Wolf (2005)

Chapter Five

1. From Dr Ludwig Pastor, *The History of the Popes from the Close of the Middle Ages* (1923)
2. Luigi Guicciardini, *The Sack of Rome,* trans. James H. McGregor (1993)
3. Ibid.
4. Benvenuto Cellini, *The Autobiography of Benvenuto Cellini,* trans. George Anthony Bull (1956)
5. Luigi Guicciardini, *The Sack of Rome,* trans. James H. McGregor (1993)
6. *I Diarii di Marino Sanuto*, Vol. LXV (1902) p. 167
7. *I Diarii di Marino Sanuto*, Vol. XLI (1902) pp. 129–31
8. Benvenuto Cellini, *The Autobiography of Benvenuto Cellini,* trans. George Anthony Bull (1956)

9. *I Diarii di Marino Sanuto*, Vol. LXV (1902) p165–7
10. *I Diarii di Marino Sanuto*, Vol. XLV (1902) p133
11. Luigi Guicciardini, *The Sack of Rome,* trans. James H. McGregor (1993)
12. Ibid.
13. Ibid.
14. Ibid.
15. Judith Hook, *The Sack of Rome* (1972)
16. *I Diarii di Marino Sanuto*, Vol. XLI (1902) p. 129–31
17. Benvenuto Cellini, *The Autobiography of Benvenuto Cellini,* trans. George Anthony Bull (1956)
18. Ibid.

Chapter Six

1. John Francis Maguire, *Rome: Its Rulers and its Institutions* (1858)
2. Margaret Fuller in *These Sad but Glorious Days: Dispatches from Europe 1846–50*, eds Larry J.

Reynolds and Susan Belasco Smith (1991) dispatch 22 December 1848

3. Margaret Fuller in *These Sad but Glorious Days: Dispatches from Europe 1846–50*, eds Larry J. Reynolds and Susan Belasco Smith (1991) dispatch 20 February 1849

4. Hortense Cornu, quoted from Fenton Bresler, *Napoleon III: A Life* (1999)

5. George Gordon Byron, 6th Baron Byron, letter to Thomas Moore, 25 March 1817

6. From J.A. Hilton, *A Sign of Contradiction: English Travellers and the Fall of Papal Rome* (2010)

7. William Wetmore Story, *Roba di Roma* (1863)

8. John Murray, *Handbook for Travellers in Central Italy*, third edition (1853)

9. William Wetmore Story, *Roba di Roma* (1863)

10. Nathaniel Hawthorne, *Notebooks*, 1858

11. Ruskin quotes from '"It was dirty but it was Rome", Dirt, Digression and the Picturesque', in Richard Wrigley, *Regarding Romantic Rome* (2007)

12. William Wetmore Story, *Roba di Roma* (1863)

13. Mrs Hamilton Gray, *Tour of the Sepulchres of Etruria*, London 1840

14. Charles Dickens, *Pictures from Italy* (1846)

15. Sir George Head, *Rome: A Tour of Many Days* (1849)

16. Ibid.

17. Lady Morgan, *Italy* (1821)

18. Nathaniel, from eds Paolo Ludovici and Biancamaria Pisapia, *Americans in Rome 1764–1870* (1984)

19. Sir George Head, *Rome: A Tour of Many Days* (1849).

20. Odo Russell in Noel Blakiston, *The Roman Question: Extracts from the Despatches of Odo Russell from Rome 1858–70* (1962)

21. From Fiorello Bartoccini, *Roma nell'Ottocento: Il tramonto della "Città Santa": nascita di una Capitale* (1985)

22. John Murray, *Handbook for Travellers in Central Italy*, third edition (1853)

23. William Wetmore Story, *Roba di Roma* (1863)

24. Ibid.

25. From Susan Vandiver Nicassio, *Imperial City: Rome under Napoleon* (2005)

26. From Mary Gibson, *Prostitution and the Italian State 1860–1915*

27. From Margherita Pelaja, *Scandali: Sessualità e violenza nella Roma dell'Ottocento*

28. Ibid.

29. Sir George Head, *Rome: A Tour of Many Days* (1849)

30. William Wetmore Story, *Roba di Roma* (1863)

31. Ibid.

32. Charles Dickens, *Pictures from Italy* (1846)

33. William Wetmore Story, *Roba di Roma* (1863)

34. Ibid.

35. Ibid.

36. Ibid.

37. Ibid.

38. Charles Dickens, *Pictures from Italy* (1846)

39. William Wetmore Story, *Roba di Roma* (1863)

40. Lady Morgan, *Italy* (1821)
41. William Wetmore Story: *Roba di Roma* (1863)
42. Sir George Head: *Rome: A Tour of Many Days* (1849)
43. Ibid.
44. Ibid.
45. Ibid.
46. William Wetmore Story, notes, in Henry James, *William Wetmore Story and his friends* (1903)
47. *The Times*, 9 May 1849
48. Margaret Fuller: *These Sad but Glorious Days: Dispatches from Europe 1846–50*, eds Larry J. Reynolds and Susan Belasco Smith (1991) dispatch 21 June 1849
49. From George Macaulay Trevelyan, *Garibaldi's Defence of the Roman Republic* (1907)
50. Margaret Fuller: *These Sad but Glorious Days: Dispatches from Europe 1846–50*, Ed Larry J Reynolds & Susan Belasco Smith, (1991) dispatch 10 July 1849
51. Ibid.
52. William Wetmore Story, *Roba di Roma* (1863)
53. Margaret Fuller: *These Sad but Glorious Days: Dispatches from Europe 1846–50*, eds Larry J. Reynolds and Susan Belasco Smith (1991) dispatch 15 November 1849
54. Odo Russell in Noel Blakiston, *The Roman Question: Extracts from the Despatches of Odo Russell from Rome 1858–70* (1962) dispatch 12 July 1860
55. From Derek Beales, *Garibaldi in England: The Politics of Italian Enthusiasm* in eds. John A. Davis and Paul Ginsborg, *Society and Politics in the Age of the Risorgimento: Essays in Honour of Denis Mack Smith* (1991)

Chapter Seven

1. M. de Wyss, *Rome Under the Terror* (1945)
2. Denis Mack Smith, *Italy and its Monarchy* (1992)
3. M. de Wyss, *Rome Under the Terror* (1945)
4. From Borden W. Painter, Jr, *Mussolini's Rome: Rebuilding the Eternal City* (2005)
5. Roland G. Andrew, *Through Fascist Italy, An English Hiker's Pilgrimage* (1935)
6. From Emilio Gentile, *In Italia ai Tempi di Mussolini: Viaggio in compagnia di osservatori stranieri* (2014).
7. From Perry Willson, *Women in Twentieth Century Italy* (2009)
8. From Emilio Gentile, *In Italia ai Tempi di Mussolini: Viaggio in compagnia di osservatori stranieri* (2014)
9. Ibid.
10. From Paul Corner, *The Fascist Party and Popular Opinion in Mussolini's Italy* (2012)
11. Ibid.
12. Claudio Fracassi, *La Battaglia di Rome* (2014)
13. Ibid.
14. Ibid.
15. Ibid.

16. Ibid.

17. Robert Katz, *Fatal Silence: The Pope, the Resistance and the German Occupation of Rome* (2003)

18. Jane Scrivener / Mother Mary St Luke, *Inside Rome with the Germans* (1945)

19. Giacomo Debenedetti, *October 16, 1943*, trans. Estelle Gilson (2001)

20. Ibid.

21. Ibid.

22. Ibid.

23. Ibid.

24. Ibid.

25. Jane Scrivener / Mother Mary St Luke, *Inside Rome with the Germans* (1945)

26. Ibid.

27. M. de Wyss, *Rome Under the Terror* (1945)

28. Jane Scrivener / Mother Mary St Luke, *Inside Rome with the Germans* (1945)

29. M. de Wyss, *Rome Under the Terror* (1945)

30. Ibid.

31. Ibid.

32. Jane Scrivener / Mother Mary St Luke, *Inside Rome with the Germans* (1945)

33. Ibid.

34. Ibid.

35. M. de Wyss, *Rome Under the Terror* (1945)

36. Jane Scrivener / Mother Mary St Luke, *Inside Rome with the Germans* (1945)

37. Ibid.

38. M. de Wyss, *Rome Under the Terror* (1945)

39. Jane Scrivener / Mother Mary St Luke, *Inside Rome with the Germans* (1945)

40. Ibid.

41. Ibid.

42. Ibid.

43. Olga Di Veroli interviewed by Alexander Stille, from Alexander Stille, *Benevolence and Betrayal: Five Italian Jewish Families under Fascism* (1991)

Afterword

1. *La Repubblica*, 21 February 2015

SOURCES AND BIBLIOGRAPHY

Chapter One

I

The best evidence concerning Gallic warriors in Italy – and their nakedness – comes from a terracotta frieze found at Civitalba in Marche that dates from almost a century after the battle on the Allia, and which matches a written description of Gallic warriors at the battle of Telamon, fought some seventy years later. A full account of what is known about Italy's Celtic peoples and their struggles with Rome is offered by J. H. C. Williams in *Beyond the Rubicon: Romans and Gauls in Republican Italy* (2001). Williams strongly favours July 387 BC as the date for the battle on the Allia (which could theoretically have taken place in July 386 instead). *I Celti in Italia* by Maria Teresa Grassi (Milan 2009) describes finds discovered in Celtic Senone graves. Barry Cunliffe's *The Ancient Celts* (1991) remains a classic on the subject and Peter Berresford Ellis, *A Brief History of the Druids* (2002) though more controversial, offers insights into early Celtic society.

It is Ellis who points out that the name Brennus probably meant king. For the close connection between early Latin and Celtic languages see Nicholas Ostler, *Empires of the Word: A Language History of the World* (2006).

II

T. J. Cornell, *The Beginnings of Rome: Italy and Rome from the Bronze Age to the Punic Wars (c.1000–264 BC)* (1995) provides an encyclopaedic account of Rome's origins, topography, defences, society and politics, dealing clearly with the complex arguments that surround every issue, and many details in this chapter are drawn from Cornell's account. Gary Forsythe, *A Critical History of Early Rome, from Prehistory to the First Punic War* (2006) offers a useful addition to Cornell's work. Mary Beard, *S.P.Q.R. A History of Ancient Rome* (2015) adds fascinating further insights into Rome's early years.

On Romans' early beliefs see Mary Beard, John North and Simon Price,

Religions of Rome, Volume I, a History (1998). The comparison between Olynthos and classical Italian cities is drawn from Andrew Wallace-Hadrill's *Houses and Society in Pompeii and Herculaneum* (1994). On Romans' early diet see Fabio Parasecoli, *Al Dente: A History of Food in Italy* (2014). For Rome's games and the procession from the Capitoline see Filippo Coarelli, *Rome and Environs: An Archaeological Guide,* trans. James L. Clauss and Daniel P. Harmon (2014) and H. H. Scullard, *Festivals and Ceremonies of the Roman Republic,* (1981). For early Veii see H. H. Scullard's *The Etruscan Cities and Rome* (1967).

III

The notion that later Romans wove misleading stories from misunderstood inscriptions on the temple of Juno Moneta is proposed by Gary Forsythe. J. H. C. Williams details evidence that the Romans paid off the Gauls and that all of the city, including the Capitoline, may have fallen to them. Williams also offers an intriguing parallel with the Greek city of Delphi, which was attacked a century after Rome, in 279 BC, by Gauls, also led by a king, Brennus, and about which stories of a heroic holdout also grew up, despite evidence that the Gauls were victorious and paid off. Williams suggests Livy's stories may have been inspired by this Greek heroic invention.

Chapter Two

I

On Himmler's visit to Cosenza see Peter Longerich, *Heinrich Himmler* (2013); Eugene Dollmann, *Un Schiavo Libero* (1968) and Eugene Dollmann, *Roma Nazista* (2002). Dollmann was a keen storyteller and had every reason to distance himself from Himmler, who employed Dollmann as his personal Italian informant for some years, so his tale of the French diviner is questionable but there is no doubt that Himmler came to Cosenza that morning to see Alaric's supposed grave. A year and a half later he pressured the Italian police chief, Bocchini, to send an expedition to Cosenza to search for it.

On the origins of the Goths, their struggles with the Roman Empire, the evolution of the Visigoths, Alaric's progress to Rome and the likely composition of the horde that followed him, see Peter Heather, *The Goths* (1996); *Goths and Romans 332–489* (1991) and also his magnificent portrait of this era, *The Fall of the Roman Empire, A New History* (2005). In the latter Heather suggests Stilicho made his seemingly strange decision to go to war with the Eastern Roman Empire because he could see trouble coming on the Rhine frontier and wanted to augment his troops by taking a key recruiting area in the Balkans that had passed to the Eastern Empire. On the need for Germanic leaders to keep their followers supplied with plunder see also E. A. Thompson, *The Visigoths in the Time of Ulfila* (1966).

On causes of the Empire's late fourth-century crisis and the Western Empire's eventual fall, Heather emphasizes the advances made by Germanic peoples as they became more numerous and their states larger and more sophisticated. An analysis focusing on Roman weaknesses can be found in Adrian Goldsworthy: *How Rome Fell: Death of a Superpower* (2009). Goldsworthy emphasizes the role of the Empire's constant civil wars and also notes some doubtful military innovations that appeared in the fourth century, notably the tendency to house troops away from the front line in cities, where they may have become distracted by comforts.

II

On early fifth-century Rome's topography the classic account remains Richard Krautheimer, *Rome, Profile of a City, 312–1308* (1980). An excellent accompaniment that focuses more closely on archaeological discoveries can be found in Bryan Ward-Perkins, *From Classical Antiquity to the Middle Ages, Urban Public Building in Northern and Central Italy, AD 300–850 (Oxford Historical Monographs)* (1984). A detailed and more up-to-date study from an archaeological viewpoint is offered by Neil Christie, *From Constantine to Charlemagne, an Archaeological History of Italy AD 300–800* (2006).

On ordinary life in Rome during its imperial glory days the best single account is still Jérôme Carcopino's *Daily Life in Ancient Rome, the People and the City at the Height of the Empire*, trans. Henry T. Rowell (1975). More recent portraits of classical Rome at its height include Alberto Angela, *A Day in the Life of Ancient Rome* (2011). For all aspects of Rome in the fifth century, including its walls, its architecture, amenities, society, government and ornamental republican political posts, see Bertrand Lançon, *Rome in Late Antiquity, Everyday Life and Urban Change, AD 312–609*, trans. Antonia Newell (2000). On different marbles, see Amanda Claridge, *Rome, an Oxford Archaeological Guide* (1998). The itinerary of Rome's amenities is from Lançon.

For the domestic side of imperial government see Andrew Wallace-Hadrill, 'The Imperial Court' in *The Cambridge Ancient History, X, The Augustine Empire, 43 BC–69 AD* (1996). For the House of Romulus see Claridge. For the demise of Roman theatre and the macabre ending of the Laureolus drama of the late first century AD, see Carcopino. For the frailties of the Colosseum, see David Karmon, *The Ruin of the Eternal City: Antiquity and Preservation in Renaissance Rome* (2011). For its entertainments see Angela, who offers a vivid account of what took place in the arena. For Valentian I's witch trials of senators (AD 369–371) see Lançon. For new imperial architectural styles that used vaulted concrete see William L. MacDonald, *The Architecture of the Roman Empire, Volume 1, an Introduction* (1965). On the likelihood that something went badly wrong with the columns of the Pantheon's portico, see Claridge. On how art and inscriptions grew cruder during the Third Century Crisis, and also on pagan beliefs and their demise, see Robin Lane Fox, *Pagans and Christians in the Mediterranean World, From the 2nd Century* AD *to the Conversion of Constantine* (1986). On aristocratic Romans' views on sex see Angela. On the early Church's distaste for sex of almost any kind, see Lane Fox.

For the demise of paganism see *Religions of Rome, Volume I, a History*, by Mary Beard, John North and Simon Price (1998) and John R. Curran's *Pagan City and Christian Capital, Rome in the Fourth Century* (2000), which succeeds in breathing life into this elusive era. On possessed Christians found outside cathedrals (in France rather than Rome, though one imagines they would have been outside Roman churches, too) see Peter Brown, 'Sorcery, Demons and the Rise of Christianity: from later Antiquity into the Middle Ages' in Peter Brown, *Religion and Society in the Age of Augustine* (1972). For the displacement of guardian angels by martyr saints, and also for security measures used to restrain over-zealous pilgrims from reaching saints' remains, see Peter Brown, *The Cult of the Saints, its Rise and Function in Latin Christianity* (1981). For the rediscovery and invention of new martyr saints for Rome by Bishop Damasus, and Peter's role as gatekeeper to heaven, see Alan Thacker, 'Rome of the Martyrs: Saints, Cults and Relics, Fourth to Seventh Centuries' in *Roma Felix – Formation and Reflections of Mediaeval Rome*, ed. Éamonn Ó Carragáin and Carol Neuman de Vegvar (2008). For the likelihood that St Peter never came to Rome, and for

Pope Pius XII's excavations beneath the altar of St Peter's, see R. J. B. Bosworth, *Whispering Cities: Modern Rome and its Histories* (2011). On violence between rival candidates to be bishop of Rome see Curran.

On Rome's aqueducts and baths, see Krautheimer. On Rome's food convoys and distribution, see Lançon. For early fifth-century Rome's super-rich see Lançon and Curran. For imperial Roman food, dinner parties and haute cuisine, including recipes, see Patrick Faas, *Around the Roman Table*, trans. Shaun Whiteside (1994). On Roman apartments see Carcopino. On the unhealthiness of Rome see Vivian Nutton, 'Medical Thoughts on Urban pollution' in Valerie M. Hope and Eireann Marshall (eds), *Death and Diseases in the Ancient City* (2009) and also Neville Morley, 'The Salubriousness of the Roman City' in Helen King (ed.), *Health in Antiquity* (2005). On malaria see Robert Sallares, *Malaria and Rome, a History of Malaria in the Ancient City* (2002). On doctors and medicine, see Ralph Jackson, *Doctors and Disease in the Roman Empire* (1988). For slaves see Keith Bradley, *Slavery and Society at Rome* (1994). On the relative lack of women visible on the streets, and the greater legal independence of women in the Empire's heyday, see Carcopino.

The battles over the statue of Victory and account of conflicts between Christian ascetics and their less zealous Christian relatives, and Jerome's loathing of the latter, are both drawn from Curran. Also from Curran comes the intriguing notion that Valerius Pinianus and Melania the

Younger's efforts to divest themselves of their wealth was a factor in the fall of Stilicho, and so helped bring about Alaric's attack on Rome. Likewise from Curran comes the willingness of moderate Roman Christians, and even Christian emperors, to tolerate a pagan nostalgia in their lives.

III

On Alaric's sieges of Rome, Ravenna and then Rome again, see Peter Heather, *The Fall of the Roman Empire* and Pierre Courcelle, *Histoire Littéraire des Grandes Invasions Germaniques* (1948). On how the Visigoths entered Rome and what they did there, an excellent analysis of the primary sources is to be found in Ralph W. Mathisen, 'Roma a Gothis Alarico duce capta est, Ancient Accounts of the Sack of Rome in 410 CE' in Johannes Lipps, Carlos Machado and Philipp von Rummel (eds), *The Sack of Rome in 410 AD, The Event, its Context and its Impact* (2013). On archaeological evidence of destruction in Rome, see Antonella Camaro, Alessandro Delfino, Ilaria de Luca and Roberto Menghini, 'Nuovi dati archeologici per la storia

del Foro di Cesare tra la fine del IV e la meta del V secolo' in Johannes Lipps, Carlos Machado and Philipp von Rummel, *The Sack of Rome in 410 AD, The Event, its Context and its Impact* (2013). On archaeological evidence concerning damage to homes and an overall assessment see, in the same volume, Riccardo Santangeli Valenziani, 'Dall'evento al dato archeologico. Il sacco del 410 attraverso la documentazione archeologica'.

On the later adventures of the Visigoths see Peter Heather, *The Goths*. On Augustine of Hippo's response to the sack of Rome, see Michele Renee Salzman, 'Memory and Meaning. Pagans and 410' in Johannes Lipps, Carlos Machado and Philipp von Rummel (eds), *The Sack of Rome in 410 AD, The Event, its Context and its Impact* (2103); also see Peter Brown, *Augustine of Hippo* (1966) and Peter Heather, *The Fall of the Roman Empire*. On the revival of Rome after the 410 sack see Elio Lo Cascio, 'La popolazione di Roma prima e dopo il 410' in Johannes Lipps, Carlos Machado and Philipp von Rummel (eds), *The Sack of Rome in 410 AD, The Event, its Context and its Impact* (2013).

Chapter Three

I

On Queen Amalasuntha see Kate Cooper, 'The Heroine and the Historian: Procopius of Caesaria and the Troubled Reign of Queen Amalasuntha' in Jonathan J. Arnold, M. Shane Bjornlie and Kristina Sessa (eds), *A Companion*

to Ostrogothic Italy (2016) and also, in the same volume, Gerda Heydemann, 'The Ostrogothic Kingdom: Ideologies and Transitions'.

On the rise of the Ostrogoths and the composition of their fighting forces in Italy see Peter Heather, 'The Goths' (1996) and 'Gens and Regnum among the Ostrogoths' in H-W. Goetz, J. Jarnut and W. Pohl (eds), *Regna and Gentes: The Relationship between Late Antique and Early Mediaeval Peoples and Kingdoms in the Transformation of the Roman World.*

II

As this chapter deals with events that follow relatively soon after those of the last, there is some overlap in sources. For all aspects of the city's infrastructure, buildings, society and population see Richard Krautheimer, *Rome, Profile of a City, 312–1308* (1980); Bertrand Lançon, *Rome in Late Antiquity, Everyday Life and Urban Change, AD 312–609*, trans. Antonia Newell (2000); Bryan Ward-Perkins, *From Classical Antiquity to the Middle Ages, Urban Public Building in Northern and Central Italy, AD 300–850 (Oxford Historical Monographs)* (1984); Neil Christie, *From Constantine to Charlemagne, an Archaeological History of Italy AD 300–800* (2006) and also Peter Llewellyn, *Rome in the Dark Ages* (1971).

On the Vandal attack on Rome, see Andy Merrills and Richard Miles, *The Vandals.* On the struggle by imperial authorities to preserve Rome's heritage see Christie. On Theodoric's reign and his attempts to shore up Rome's infrastructure and traditions, see Jonathan J. Arnold, *Theodoric and the Roman Imperial Restoration* (2014). On

the schism between papal candidates Symmachus and Laurentius see Jeffrey Richards, *The Popes and the Papacy in the Early Middle Ages 476–752* (1979). Also see Richards for Theodoric's religious disputes with Byzantium, and Justinian's replacement of Pope Silverius with Pope Vigilius. For imperial–papal disputes see also Llewellyn.

III

On the tactics of Belisarius, Witigis and Totila, see E. A. Thompson: *Romans and Barbarians: The Decline of the Western Empire* (1982). On clippings, the logothete and other instances of Byzantine rapacity see Llewellyn. On bubonic plague, see Lester K. Little (ed.), *Plague and the End of Antiquity, the Pandemic of 541–750* (2008). On Justianian's falling out with Pope Vigilius over the Three Chapters see Richards. On the demise of the Ostrogoths see Peter Heather, *The Goths.* For the demise of bathing, see Ward-Perkins and Christie. See both and also Krautheimer for the demise of Roman institutions and the preservation of classical buildings as churches. On the demise of the Senate and of Rome's old aristocracy, see T. S. Brown, *Gentlemen and Officers: Imperial Administration and Aristocratic Power in Byzantine Italy, AD 554–800.*

Chapter Four

I

H. E. J. Cowdrey, *Pope Gregory VII 1073–1085* (1998) offers a detailed if uncritical account of his reign. A full account of his nemesis can be found in I. S. Robinson's *Henry IV of Germany, 1056–1106* (1999). For the rise of Robert Guiscard and the Normans in southern Italy see G. A. Loud, *The Age of Robert Guiscard: Southern Italy and the Norman Conquest* (2000); G. A. Loud, 'Conquerors and Churchmen in Norman Italy' in *Variorum Collected Studies series, July 1999,* and also Kenneth Baxter Woolf's *Making History: The Normans and their Historians in the Eleventh Century* (1995). The fullest original narrative is that of Geoffrey of Malaterra, *The Deeds of Count Roger,* trans. Kenneth Baxter Woolf (2005).

II

Richard Krautheimer, *Rome, Profile of a City, 312–1308* (1980) once again is a classic on this period. For a more up-to-date account that covers every facet of Rome's topography, population, politics, society, economy and rituals, and from which many details in this chapter are drawn, see Chris Wickham, *Medieval Rome: Stability and Crisis of a City, 900–1150* (2015). It is Wickham who compares the Church reformers with early Russian revolutionaries. For archaeological evidence concerning Rome's eighth-century revival see Neil Christie, *From Constantine to Charlemagne, an Archaeological History of Italy* AD *300–800* (2006). Details on the Major Litany procession are from Joseph Dyer, 'Roman Processions of the Major Litany (litanae maiores) from the Sixth to the Twelfth Centuries' in *Roma Felix – Formation and Reflections of Medieval Rome,* ed. Éamonn Ó Carragáin and Carol Neuman de Vegvar (2008).

Debra Birch, *Pilgrimage to Rome in the Middle Ages – Continuity and Change* (2000) offers a detailed and lively account of the subject. For some of medieval Romans' imaginative tales concerning the city's ruins see the twelfth-century description of the city, *Mirabilia Urbis Roma* (The Marvels of Rome) which, among many claims, reports that Noah landed his ark on the Gianicolo Hill to re-found the human race. The likely cause of the collapse of half of the Colosseum's outer wall is from David Karmon's *The Ruin of the Eternal City: Antiquity and Preservation in Renaissance Rome* (2011). For Rome in the centuries prior to the Norman sack see both Krautheimer and Peter Llewellyn's *Rome in the Dark Ages* (1971).

The question of which aqueducts functioned when is discussed in Bryan Ward-Perkins' *From Classical Antiquity to the Middle Ages, Urban Public Building in Northern and Central Italy,* AD *300–850 (Oxford Historical Monographs)* (1984) and by Katherine Wentworth Rinne in *The Waters of Rome: Aqueducts, Fountains and the Birth of the Baroque City* (2010). For Romans' material possessions see Patricia Skinner, 'Material Life' in David Abulafia (ed.), *Italy in the Central Middle Ages 1000–1300* (2004). For changes in cuisine and ingredients see Fabio Parasecoli, *Al Dente: a History of Food in Italy* (2014). For health and medicine see Patricia Skinner, *Health and Medicine in early Mediaeval Southern Italy* (1996) and also Robert Sallares, *Malaria and Rome: A History of Malaria in Ancient Italy* (2002). Rome's Jewish community and the observations of Benjamin Tudela are examined by Marie-Thérèse Champagne and Ra'anan S. Boustan, 'Walking in the Shadows of the Past: The Jewish Experience of Rome in the Twelfth century' in Louis I. Hamilton (ed.), *Rome Re-Imagined: Twelfth-century Jews, Christians and Muslims Encounter the Eternal City* (2011). For women's lives in this period see Patricia Skinner, *Women in Mediaeval Italy 500–1200* (2001). Anxious (Genoese) fathers worried about inheritance are examined by Steven Epstein in David Abulafia (ed.), *The Family in Italy in the Central Middle Ages 1000–1300* (2004).

III

For eleventh-century warfare see: J. F. Verbruggen, *The Art of Warfare in Western Europe during the Middle Ages* (1997) and Philippe Contamine, *War in the Middle Ages,* trans. Michael Jones (1984). The most detailed chronology of the complex events of 1081–84 remains that of Ferdinand Gregovius: *A History of Mediaeval Rome, Vol. 4, Part 1,* trans. Annie Hamilton (1905). For an analysis of Guiscard's sack of Rome see Louis I. Hamilton's acute and highly enjoyable 'Memory, Symbol and Arson: Was Rome sacked in 1084?' in *Speculum* XXVIII, April 2003, which my account closely follows. For details on the 1300 Jubilee and Rome's decline during the Avignon years see Richard Krautheimer, *Rome, Profile of a City, 312–1308* (1980). On how Romans' desire to preserve their classical past helped inspire their drive for a civic government independent of the popes see David Karmon, *The Ruins of the Eternal City: Antiquity and Preservation in Renaissance Rome* (2011).

Chapter Five

I

For the conclave of 1523 see Herbert M. Vaughan, *The Medici Popes* (1908) and Dr Ludwig Pastor, *A History of the Popes, Volume IX, Adrian VI and Clement VII,* trans. Ralph Francis Kerr *(*1923). The best account of the events leading up to the 1527 sack, the sack itself and its aftermath,

on which this chapter has drawn many details, is Judith Hook's *The Sack of Rome* (1972). André Chastell, *The Sack of Rome, 1527* (1983) examines the event from a cultural and artistic angle. Eric Russell Chamberlin, *The Sack of Rome* (1979) offers a highly entertaining if less reliable narrative. On Clement VII and Michelangelo see William E. Wallace,

'Clement VII and Michelangelo: An Anatomy of Patronage', and for Clement's musical talents see Richard Sherr, 'Clement VII and the Golden Age of the Papal Choir', both in Kenneth Gouwens and Sheryl E. Reiss (eds), *The Pontificate of Clement VII: History, Politics, Culture* (2005). On Leo X's jailing of five cardinals see Kate Howe, 'The Political Crime of Conspiracy in Fifteenth and Sixteenth Century Rome' in Trevor Dean and K. J. P. Howe (eds), *Crime, Society and the Law in Renaissance Italy* (1994). On the causes of the duke of Urbino's feud with the Medici and for his role in these events see Cecil H. Clough, 'Clement VII and Francesco Maria della Rovere, Duke of Urbino' in Kenneth Gouwens and Sheryl E. Reiss (eds), *The Pontificate of Clement VII: History, Politics, Culture* (2005). On Renaissance warfare in Italy see F. L. Taylor *The Art of War in Italy 1494–1529* (1921). On the character and rise of Charles V see William Maltby, *The Reign of Charles V* (2002).

II

For a full and lively account of all aspects of Renaissance Rome, including its topography, buildings and population, its government, artists, popes and prostitutes see Peter Partner, *Renaissance Rome: A Portrait of a Society* (1979) from which many details in this chapter are drawn. For further details, including an account of papal ceremonial and the humanist rediscovery of the city's classical past see Charles L. Stinger, *The Renaissance in Rome* (1998). For the role of individual families see Anthony Majanlahti, *The Families Who Made*

Rome, a History and a Guide (2006). On Rome's Jewish community see Attilio Milano, *Il Ghetto di Roma* (1988). On Rome's topography, medieval fortress towers, churches, bell towers, houses and the conservatism of Rome's church decoration see Richard Krautheimer, *Rome, Profile of a City, 312–1308* (1980). On Renaissance palaces see Elizabeth S. Cohen and Thomas V. Cohen, *Daily Life in Renaissance Italy* (2001).

On the 1450 pilgrim disaster, the bridge and road buildings that ensued, and also Renaissance city churches see Loren Partridge, *The Renaissance in Rome* (1996) and also David Karmon, *The Ruins of the Eternal City: Antiquity and Preservation in Renaissance Rome* (2011). On the Sistine Chapel see Loren Partridge, *Michelangelo: The Sistine Chapel Ceiling, Rome* (1996). On the origins of the papacy's office selling and other financial irregularities see Elisabeth G. Gleason, *Gasparo Contarini: Venice, Rome and Reform* (1993). On Lucrezia Borgia see Katherine McIver, *Wives, Widows, Mistresses and Nuns in early Modern Italy: Making the Invisible Visible through Art and Patronage* (2012). On Pasquino feeling insulted by being called a cardinal, and the note left on the door of Adrian VI's doctor's door, see Partner.

On Romans' use of Tiber water and Clement VII's fondness of it, see Katherine Wentworth Rinne, *The Waters of Rome: Aqueducts, Fountains and the Birth of the Baroque City* (2010). On medicine and the French Disease see Roger French and Jon Arrizabalaga, 'Coping with the French Disease: University Practitioners' Strategies and Tactics in the Transition from the Fifteenth to the Sixteenth Centuries' in Roger Kenneth French, Jon Arrizabalaga and Andrew Cunningham (eds), *Medicine from the Black Death to the French Disease* (1998).

On all aspects of everyday Renaissance Italian life from crime to cleanliness to courtesans with circular beds, see Elizabeth S. Cohen and Thomas V. Cohen, *Daily Life in Renaissance Italy* (2001) from which many details in this chapter have been drawn. For a fascinating glimpse of Renaissance Rome underworld life as seen through contemporary transcripts of investigative interrogations, see Thomas V. Cohen and Elizabeth S. Cohen, *Words and Deeds in Renaissance Rome* (1993). On Renaissance Rome's jails see Giuseppe Adinolfi, *Storia di Regina Coeli e delle carcere di Roma* (1998).

On Rome's plague of stone-throwing boys and also the tradition of Roman youths trying to impress girls by bull-baiting see Robert C. Davis, 'The Geography of Gender in the Renaissance' in Judith C. Brown and Robert C. Davis (eds), *Gender and Society in Renaissance Italy* (1998). On women's inheritance and dowries see Samuel K. Cohn, Jr, *Women in the Streets: Essays on Sex and Power in Renaissance Italy* (1996); Christiane Klapisch-Zuber, *Women, Family and Ritual in Renaissance Italy* (1985) and Trevor Dean and K. P. J. Lowe (eds), *Marriage in Italy 1300–1650* (1998).

On Roman food and cuisine and Bartolomeo Scappi's feast see Katherine A. McIver, *Cooking and Eating in Renaissance Italy: From Kitchen to Table* (2014); Fabio Parasecoli, *Al Dente: A History of Food in Italy* (2014); Alberto Capatti and Massimo Montanari, *Italian Cuisine: A Cultural History*, trans. Aine O'Healy (2003) and also Elizabeth S. Cohen and Thomas V. Cohen. On humanists in Rome see John F. Amico, *Renaissance Humanism in Papal Rome* (1983). All details on the humanist Pierio Valeriano are drawn from Julia Haig Gaisser's fascinating article, 'Seeking Patronage under the Medici Popes: A Tale of Two Humanists' in Kenneth Gouwens and Sheryl E. Reiss (eds), *The Pontificate of Clement VII: History, Politics, Culture* (2005). On the fate of Rome's classical remains see David Karmon, *The Ruins of the Eternal City: Antiquity and Preservation in Renaissance Rome* (2011).

III

As indicated, primary sources on the sack of Rome quoted include *I Diarii di Marino Sanuto* (1902) (my translations) also Benvenuto Cellini, *The Autobiography of Benvenuto Cellini*, trans. George Anthony Bull (1956) and Luigi Guicciardini, *The Sack of Rome*, trans. James Harvey McGregor (1993). Details gleaned from legal documents before, during and at the end of the sacking are all drawn from Anna Esposito and Vaquero Piniero's fascinating article, 'Rome during the Sack: Chronicles and Testimonies from an Occupied City' in Kenneth Gouwens and Sheryl E. Reiss (eds), *The Pontificate of Clement VI: History, Politics, Culture I* (2005). On England's missions to gain

Clement VII's agreement to Henry VIII's divorce, including the strange proposal that Henry should take two wives, and also Francesco Gonzaga's description of Rome after the sack, see Catherine Fletcher, *Our Man in Rome: Henry VIII and his Italian Ambassador* (2012). On Clement VII's bounce back from disaster, see Barbara McClung Hallman, 'The "Disastrous" Pontificate of Clement VII: Disastrous for Giulio de' Medici?' in Kenneth Gouwens and Sheryl E. Reiss (eds), *The Pontificate of Clement VII: History, Politics, Culture* (2005). On the 1530 and 1557 floods see Katherine Wentworth Rinne (above). On preparations for Charles V's 1535 visit see David Karmon, *The Ruins of the Eternal City: Antiquity and Preservation in Renaissance Rome* (2011). On the sinister career of Cardinal Carafa/Pope Paul IV see Partner.

Chapter Six

I

For Pius IX's flight from Rome see Owen Chadwick, *A History of the Popes 1830–1914* (1998) and John Francis Maguire, *Rome: Its Rulers and its Institutions* (1858). On France's Revolutionary and Napoleonic occupations of Rome see R. J. B. Bosworth, *Whispering Cities* (2011); Susan Vandiver Nicassio, *Imperial City: Rome, Romans and Napoleon, 1796–1815* (2005) and Frank J. Coppa, *The Modern Papacy since 1789* (1998). On the Trastevere uprising of 1798 see Massimo Cattaneo, 'Trastevere: Myths, Stereotypes and Reality of a Roman Rione between the eighteenth and nineteenth centuries' in Richard Wrigley (ed.), *Regarding Romantic Rome* (2007). On the reactionary popes of the earlier nineteenth century see Bosworth, Chadwick and Coppa. On the role of the arts in the Risorgimento, see Lucy Riall, *Garibaldi: Invention of a Hero* (2007). On Pius IX's election and early, radical period and his falling out with the Romans see Chadwick and Bosworth. On Mazzini see Denis Mack Smith, *Mazzini* (2008). On Garibaldi's early years and Mazzini's role in his rise to fame see Riall, who offers a fascinating study of the role of publicity in the Risorgimento. On Louis Napoleon see Fenton Bresler, *Napoleon III: A Life* (1999).

II

On Rome's Renaissance walls, see Peter Partner, *Renaissance Rome 1500–59, A Portrait of a Society* (1976). On the repair to Rome's drains see Katherine Wentworth Rinne, 'Urban Ablutions: cleansing Counter-Reformation Rome' in Mark Bradley and Kenneth Stow (eds), *Rome, Pollution and Propriety: Dirt, Disease and Hygiene in the Eternal City from Antiquity to Modernity* (2012). On Rome's repaired aqueducts and new fountains see Katherine Wentworth Rinne, *The Waters of Rome: Aqueducts, Fountains and the Birth of the Baroque City* (2010). On the transformation of Rome by Alexander VII and Bernini see Richard Krautheimer, *The Rome of Alexander VII, 1655–1667* (1985).

On interruptions to the Grand Tour see Edward Chanery, *The Evolution of the Grand Tour: Anglo-Italian Cultural Relations since the Renaissance* (1998). For the earl of Shrewsbury's money-saving stay and eminent writers and artists who stayed in Rome see J. A. Hilton, *A Sign of Contradiction: English Travellers and the Fall of Papal Rome* (2010) and also Paolo Ludovici and Biancamaria Pisapia (eds), *Americans in Rome 1764–1870* (1984). On how visiting writers were struck by Rome's filth, their different opinions as to which city was filthiest, and also Napoleonic French efforts to clear antiquities of accretions see Richard Wrigley, "'It was dirty but it was Rome'": Dirt, Digression and the Picturesque' in Richard Wrigley, *Regarding Romantic Rome* (2007). On grand plans to remake Rome in preparation for Napoleon's visit see Nicassio. On the destruction of antiquities to remake Rome see David Karmon, *The Ruin of the Eternal City: Antiquity and Preservation in Renaissance Rome* (2011). On the new fascination with the Etruscans see Lisa C. Pieraccini, 'The English, Etruscans and "Etouria": The Grand Tour of Etruria' in *Etruscan Studies* Vol. 12 (2009). On Rome's fast days, clocks, time and its infuriating post office see Sir George Head, *Rome: A Tour of Many Days* (1849).

On Rome's population see Fiorella Bartoccini, *Roma nell'Ottocento: Il tramonto della 'Città Santa': nascita di una Capitale* (1985). For the decline of Rome's aristocracy see Giacomina Nenci, *Aristocrazia romana tra '800: I*

Rospigliosi (2004). On new intimacy in Italian aristocratic families see Marzio Barbagli, 'Marriage and Family in Nineteenth Century Italy' in John A. Davis and Paul Ginsborg (eds), *Society and Politics in the Age of the Risorgimento: Essays in Honour of Denis Mack Smith* (1991). On nineteenth-century Roman food see Fabio Parasecoli, *Al Dente: A History of Food in Italy* (2014) and Alberto Capatti and Massimo Montanari, *Italian Cuisine: A Cultural History*, trans. Aine O'Healy (2003). On the rising number of illegitimate births and the worsening survival rates of infants in foundling hospitals see Marzio Barbagli, 'Marriage and Family in Nineteenth Century Italy' in John A. Davis and Paul Ginsborg (eds), *Society and Politics in the Age of the Risorgimento: Essays in Honour of Denis Mack Smith* (1991). And also Maria Sophia Quine, *Italy's Social Revolution: Charity and Welfare from Liberalism to Fascism* (2002). On the make-up of Rome's population see Bartoccini.

On knife fights see Silvio Negro, *Seconda Roma* (1943). On life under Leo XII see Bosworth. On the *cicisbei*, see Maurice Andrieux, *Daily Life in Papal Rome in the Eighteenth Century*, trans. Mary Fitton (1969). On the little that is known of prostitution in the last decades of papal Rome see Mary Gibson, *Prostitution and the Italian State 1860–1915* (1999). On the Church's moral policing of Rome, see Margherita Pelaja, *Scandali: Sessualità e violenza nella Roma dell'Ottocento* (2001). On the involvement of local Roman communities in moral policing see Domenico Rizzo, 'Marriage on Trial: Adultery in Nineteenth Century

Rome' in Perry Willson, *Gender, Family and Sexuality in Italy 1860–1945* (2004) and Domenico Rizzo, 'L'Impossibile privato, Fama e pubblico scandalo in età liberal', in *Quaderni Storici* No. 112, April 2003. On Odo Russell's struggles with wayward female English grand tourists see Noel Blakiston, *The Roman Question: Extracts from the Despatches of Odo Russell from Rome 1858–70* (1962). On the leniency of papal justice see Margherita Pelaja (above). On Rome's jails and attempts to comfort the condemned before executions see Giuseppe Adinolfi, *Storia di Regina Coeli e delle carceri romane* (1998). On the San Michele institution see Elena Andreozzi, *Il pauperismo a Roma e l'ospizio Apostolico San Michele* in *San Michele a Ripa: Storia e Restauro*, Istituto della Enciclopedia Italiana Fondata da G. Treccani (1983).

On Rome's Ghetto see Attilio Milano, *Il Ghetto di Roma* (1964). On the possibility that the Ghetto was cleaner than visitors realized, see Kenneth Stow, 'Was the Ghetto Cleaner ...' in Mark Bradley and Kenneth Stow (eds), *Rome, Pollution and Propriety: Dirt, Disease and Hygiene in the Eternal City from Antiquity to Modernity* (2012). On Roman Jewish dialect see Crescenzo del Monte, 'Glossario del dialetto giudaico-romanesco' in the same author's *Sonetti Postumi Giudaico-Romaneschi e Romaneschi* (1955). On grand tourists' mistaken ideas as to the cause of malaria, see Richard Wrigley, 'Pathological Topographies and Cultural Itineraries: Mapping "mal'aria" in eighteenth and nineteenth century Rome' in Richard Wrigley and George Revill (eds), *Pathologies of Travel* (2000).

On the Ghetto and malaria see Robert Sallares, *Malaria and Rome: A History of Malaria in Ancient Italy* (2002). On the papal procession on the feast of Corpus Domini see William Wetmore Story, *Roba di Roma* (1863).

III

One of the fullest accounts of the Roman Republic's struggle to survive remains George Macaulay Trevelyan, *Garibaldi's Defence of the Roman Republic* (1907), from which my account draws many details. For a more critical examination of Garibaldi's role see Riall. For an account, admittedly partisan against Pius IX, of events after the fall of Rome, see Luigi Carlo Farini, *The Roman State, Volume 4, Book VII*, trans. W. E. Gladstone (1851). Farini details the attack by the papal police and French troops on the Ghetto. Also see Bolton King, *A History of Italian Unity, being a Political History of Italy from 1814 to 1854, Volume I* (1899). See also Denis Mack Smith, *Mazzini*; Margaret Fuller, *These Sad but Glorious Days: Dispatches from Europe 1846–50*, ed. Larry J. Reynolds and Susan Belasco Smith (1991); Robert N. Hudspeth (ed.), *Letters of Margaret Fuller Vol. IV* (1984) and Friedrich Althaus (ed.), *The Roman Journals of Ferdinand Gregorovius 1852–74*, trans. Mrs Gustavus W. Hamilton (1907). The figure of 20,000 people fleeing Rome is from Chadwick. The attempt to burn down the Quirinal Palace on the day Pius returned is from Mary Francis Cusack, *The Life and Times of Pope Pius IX* (1878). On Rome's gasworks on Circo Massimo see Maguire and Bosworth.

On the assassination attempts against Louis Napoleon see Bresler. On Garibaldi's visit to England see Derek Beales, 'Garibaldi in England: The Politics of Italian Enthusiasm' in John A. Davis and Paul Ginsborg (eds), *Society and Politics in the Age of the Risorgimento: Essays in Honour of Denis Mack Smith* (1991). For the chants of *'Viva Verdi'* see Story. For Romans' boycotts and Pius sending his executioner to scare his parishioners see *The Roman Journals of Ferdinand Gregorovius* (above), 8 March 1860. On papal repression see Odo Russell in Blakiston. On the doctrine of papal infallibility see Chadwick and Bosworth. On Pius' last months as ruler of Rome, on the capture of the city by Italian forces and the journey of Pius' corpse to San Lorenzo see Bosworth and David L. Kertzer, *Prisoner of the Vatican: The Popes, the Kings, and Garibaldi's Rebels in the Struggle to Rule Modern Italy* (2004).

Chapter Seven

I

For Mussolini's arrest by the king see Anthony Majanlahti and Amadeo Osti Guerazzi, *Roma occupata 1943–44, Itinerari, storia, immagini* (2010) and Nello Ajello, La caduta, 'Il commando a Badoglio è fatta' a Villa Savoia il Re si libera del duce, 25 July 2013.

The account of the Fascist Grand Council Meeting is from M. de Wyss, *Rome Under the Terror* (1945). De Wyss is an elusive source and a little should be said about what is known – or rather not known – about her. We lack even her first name. Her publisher, Robert Hale Ltd, London, says only that she is '… a lady who was in Rome continuously during the last stages [of the war] and who had reliable sources of extraordinary information'. The detail and accuracy of her account and the rapidity with which the book appeared – a year after Rome's occupation ended – suggest it is reliable, though her name is probably a pseudonym (she evidently did not want her identity known). From the text it is clear she had already experienced Nazi occupation in another location prior to her living in Rome. The speed and thoroughness of her investigations, her at times eccentric English and her regular complimentary references to the Swiss diplomatic authorities all suggest she was a Swiss journalist covering the war in Italy.

For the life of Vittorio Emanuele III see Denis Mack Smith, *Italy and its Monarchy* (1992). For the US bombing raid on 19 September 1943 and Roman celebrations after Mussolini's fall see Robert Katz, *Fatal Silence: The Pope, the Resistance and the German Occupation of Rome* (2003) and de Wyss. On the career of Badoglio see Giovanni de Luna, *Badoglio: Un militare al potere* (1974). On Rome's lack of preparedness for air attacks see R. J. B. Bosworth, *Whispering Cities: Modern Rome and its Histories* (2011).

II

For all aspects of Liberal Rome, including its building booms, its new facilities and its many constructions to promote itself and challenge the popes, see Bosworth, *Whispering Cities*. For further details on Liberal Rome including ineffectual development plans and also destruction that was avoided see Spiro Kostof, *The Third Rome, 1870–1950, Traffic and Glory* (1973). For Lanciani's work in Rome, and especially for Liberals' remaking of Rome for propaganda purposes see Bosworth. For the presence of non-Catholic churches inside Rome's walls see Kostof and Bosworth. The dissident intellectual who described the Vittoriano as a *'Vespasiano di Lusso'*, was Giovanni Papini (see Bosworth). Also see Bosworth for Jewish politicians and generals and for Garibaldi's proposal of a Tiber canal.

For Mussolini's life see R. J. B. Bosworth, *Mussolini* (2002) and Denis Mack Smith, *Mussolini* (1981). On Romans' initial indifference towards Fascism see Bosworth, *Whispering Cities*. On all aspects of Fascist demolitions and rebuilding of Rome see Borden W. Painter, Jr, *Mussolini's Rome: Rebuilding the Eternal City* (2005); Spiro Kostof; Bosworth, *Whispering Cities* and also Joshua Arthurs, *Excavating Modernity: The Roman Past in Fascist Italy* (2012). For Mussolini's loathing of foreign tourists' love of the picturesque see Arthurs. For the cost of Mussolini's demolitions in terms of homes lost see Painter. For André Gide's observations see Emilio Gentile, *In Italia ai Tempi*

di Mussolini: Viaggio in compagnia di osservatori stranieri (2014). For Cardinal Pallotta's criticisms of the idea of a broad road leading to St Peter's see Richard Krautheimer, *The Rome of Alexander VII, 1655–1667* (1985). On Rome's Fascist constructions see Painter.

On the GIL Fascist youth movement see Edward R. Tannenbaum, *The Fascist Experience: Italian Society and Culture 1922–45* (1972). On Foro Mussolini see Painter and Bosworth, *Whispering Cities*. On the Mostra della Rivoluzione Fascista see Bosworth, Painter and Roland G. Andrew, *Through Fascist Italy, An English Hiker's Pilgrimage* (1935). On Fascism's early hostility towards tourism see Gentile. On Mussolini's omnipresence on posters, in photographs and on postcards see Gentile and Bosworth, *Whispering Cities*. Also see Bosworth for the Anni Fascisti, the Fascist calendar and competition with the Church. On the surviving remnants of the Ghetto degli Inglesi, the illegality of fancy dress and travel possibilities to Rome see Karl Baedeker, *Rome and Central Italy, Handbook for Travellers, sixteenth revised edition* (1930).

On Italians' increasing longevity see Massimo Livi-Bacci, *A History of Italian Fertility During the Last Two Centuries* (1977). On the dopolavoro after-work leisure organization, Italy's media under Fascism and intellectual life see Tannenbaum. On how Fascist corporations and Fascist welfare favoured the wealthy and exploited employees see also Jonathan Dunnage, *Twentieth Century Italy: A Social History*

(2002). On how welfare funds were regularly raided by the Fascist state to pay for grand projects see Maria Sophia Quine, *Italy's Social Revolution: Charity and Welfare from Liberalism to Fascism* (2002). On Rome's aristocrat Fascist mayors see Painter. On everyday life in the Case Popolari and Romans' struggle to keep clean see Gian Franco Venè, *Mille lira al mese: vita quotidiana della famiglia nell'Italia Fascista* (1988). On the *borgate* see Quine, Gentile and Painter. On the *barruché* see Bosworth, *Whispering Cities*.

On Fascism's view of women see Perry Willson, *Women in Twentieth Century Italy* (2009) and also Tannenbaum and Quine. Mussolini's claim that work could make women sterile is from Willson. On Fascism's approval of brothels see Dunnage. On Fascist rewards to prolific parents and Mussolini's prohibition of photographs of women with small dogs see Tannenbaum. On the danger of women being out alone and Rome's lack of night-time culture see Gentile. On Fascist violence and control of Italians, internal exile and the fate of the Roman tinsmith Ruggeri Leggi see Michael R. Ebner's fascinating analysis of how the threat of physical violence always underlays Fascism, *Ordinary Violence in Mussolini's Italy* (2011). On the effect on Jewish life of the 1938 Racial Laws see Ebner and also Michele Sarfatti, *The Jews in Mussolini's Italy: From Equality to Persecution* and Susan Zuccotti (2006) *The Italians and the Holocaust: Persecution, Rescue and Survival* (1987). On corruption among Fascist officials,

their accusations of sexual immorality against one another and the diminishing success of Fascist propaganda see Paul Corner's fascinating and revealing study of one of the more reliable sources of information at this time – spies informing the regime of the state of the nation – in *The Fascist Party and Popular Opinion in Mussolini's Italy* (2012). On the failure of Fascism's great projects see Livi-Bacci, Tannenbaum, Corner and Quine. On the fragility of Italy's control of Abyssinia see Richard Pankhurst, *The Ethiopians, A History* (1998). On Fascism's failure to instil anti-Semitism in Italians, Starace's much-loathed innovations, Italians' increasing apathy and the coffee crisis of 1938–39 see Corner. On Fascist propaganda's failure to persuade Italian women see Willson.

On Hitler's 1938 visit to Rome and also Colonel J. Hanley's observations of the crowd in Piazza Venezia on the day war was declared, see Painter. On Italians' lack of enthusiasm for the German alliance and the war see Corner. On the unprepared state of Italy's military in 1940 see R. J. B. Bosworth, *Mussolini's Italy: Life Under the Dictatorship* (2005). On Mussolini's disastrous record as a military tactician see Denis Mack Smith, *Mussolini*. On the Folgore Parachute Division see John Bierman and Colin Smith, *Alamein, War Without Hate* (2002). On Rome's coastline being guarded by two soldiers sharing one pair of boots and the final celebration of Empire Day see de Wyss. On the third and final Mostra della Rivoluzione Fascista see Painter.

III

A clear and highly detailed account of the last hours of the Badoglio regime and the fall of Rome to German forces can be found in Claudio Fracassi, *La Battaglia di Rome* (2014). Details of the two American generals' dinner and their meeting with Badoglio are from Fracassi, as are the meeting of the king's council at the Quirinal Palace, the flight of the king and his ministers, the orders they gave Italian forces and Italian resistance (and non-resistance) to German forces. The story of the Italian officer who deserted his troops to check on his racehorses is from M. de Wyss. Mother Mary, another invaluable diarist of these events, is also rather elusive, if less so than de Wyss. Her account *Inside Rome with the Germans* was published in 1945 under the pseudonym of Jane Scrivener and it was only some decades later that she was revealed to be an American nun in Rome, Mother Mary St Luke, who was living in a convent not far from Via Veneto.

On the fall of Rome and the beginning of the occupation see also Katz, *Fatal Silence*. The joke about tourists and the statue of Moses is from Alexander Stille, *Benevolence and Betrayal: Five Italian Jewish Families under Fascism* (1991). Stille's insightful and humane account of these terrible times includes a chapter on the struggle to survive by members of the Roman Di Veroli family. On the gold ransom demanded of Rome's Jews, the theft of the synagogue libraries and the Ghetto roundup of 16 October, Robert Katz, *Black Sabbath: A Journey Through a Crime Against Humanity* (1969) offers a full, detailed and powerful account. For the likelihood that the gold demand was a ruse to put the Jews off their guard see also Susan Zuccotti, *Under His Very Windows: The Vatican and the Holocaust in Italy* (2002). On life for Jewish Romans before the occupation and warnings ignored, including by German diplomats, see Stille and also Katz. Debenedetti wrote *October 16, 1943* shortly after the liberation but quotes in the text are from the translation by Estelle Gilson (2001). On Kappler's report detailing how Romans tried to thwart the roundup see Katz, *Fatal Silence*. On details of which Catholic institutions took in Jews and what conditions – if any – they required see Zuccotti. On the rise of Pius XII and his response to Nazism and the Holocaust see John Cornwell, *Hitler's Pope, The Secret History of Pius XII* (1999). On the intervention by Princess Enza Pignatelli Aragona Cortes see Katz, *Fatal Silence* and Stille. On Pius' lack of response to the Ghetto roundup see Zuccotti, Cornwell, Katz *Fatal Silence* and Katz *Black Sabbath*. On the efforts by German diplomats to save Jewish Romans see Katz (both titles).

The graffiti urging the Russians to hurry up is from M. de Wyss, as are the accounts of deserting Germans. Details of Rome's declining transport and bricked-up shops are from both de Wyss and Mother Mary. The raid on Rome's Fascist HQ is from de Wyss. On the background to Roman resistance to the Germans and attacks on Germans in December 1944 see Katz,

Fatal Silence. Also see Katz and de Wyss and Mother Mary for new curfews and other restrictions and also raids on Church establishments by Koch's gang. On Celeste di Porto see Stille.

On the Anzio landing, the bombing raids that followed, the arrests of Rome's resistance and also on Peter Tomkins and Malfatti's information-gathering network see Katz, *Fatal Silence*. On Allied bombing of Rome see also de Wyss and Mother Mary. On the Via Rasella bomb and the ensuing Fosse Ardeatina massacre see Robert Katz, *Fatal Silence*, whose account my narrative follows. On German trucks painted with Vatican colours and keeping close to Vatican food trucks see Mother Mary. On General Clark's dash for Rome see Katz, *Fatal Silence*. On German demolitions in the city see Mother Mary.

INDEX

A NOTE ABOUT
THE AUTHOR

Matthew Kneale was born in London in 1960, the son and grandson of writers. He studied Modern History at Magdalen College, Oxford. Fascinated with diverse cultures, he travelled to more than eighty countries and tried his hand at learning a number of foreign languages, including Japanese, Ethiopian Amharic, Romanian and Albanian. He has written five novels, including *English Passengers*, which was shortlisted for the Booker Prize and won the Whitbread Book of the Year, and one previous work of non-fiction, *An Atheist's History of Belief*. For the last fifteen years he has lived in Rome with his wife and two children.